Respectfully yet relentlessly pressi
ners in New Testament, this thorou

advances a reading both distinctive and yet more traditional than many of today's dominant paradigms. Horton also exposes some of our blind spots, properly challenging mischaracterizations of the Reformers. In contrast to some New Testament scholars driven too much by modern philosophic premises, Horton is often more faithful to ancient interpretations relevant to the biblical cultures. As a New Testament scholar, I profited repeatedly from his historical context for various theological approaches in modern New Testament scholarship.

Craig Keener, F. M. and Ada Thompson Professor of
Biblical Studies, Asbury Theological Seminary

This is a superb theological study that creatively retrieves the doctrine of justification from the patristic era to the Reformation. Horton seeks to revitalize the contemporary ecumenical discussion regarding justification by showing not only the enduring merits of the Reformation's exegetical, theological, and pastoral legacy, but also its hermeneutical and theological superiority to alternative views, namely, Roman Catholic, Radical Orthodoxy, the new perspective on Paul, and new Finnish interpretations. Some of his interpretations are questionable, for example, "the triumph of Nominalism occurred with the Counter-Reformation (Council of Trent) rather than with the Reformation." Still, I came away from reading this engaging book marked by a careful and generous listening to others, both reenergized with a passion for understanding the long-running doctrinal conversation about God, grace, and justification and challenged to engage critically the author's vision.

Eduardo J. Echeverria, professor of philosophy and systematic
theology, Sacred Heart Major, Archdiocesan Seminary of Detroit

This is a serious and important work coming from a leading Reformed theologian. It concerns a pivotal doctrine that was at the heart of the Reformation and that continues to provoke differences between Protestants and Catholics. Both Protestant and Catholic readers—not only scholars but also theologically interested laity—will profit by wrestling with this learned historical study.

Gerald R. McDermott, Anglican Chair of
Divinity, Beeson Divinity School

It is not often one finds a book ranging across the three "CDs"—the Damascus Document, Augustine's *City of God*, and Barth's *Church Dogmatics*! This is a volume bristling with theological insight and intellectual energy. Add to that Horton's learning and clarity, and you have that rare thing—a gripping and intelligent treatment of justification.

> **Simon Gathercole,** reader in New Testament, University of Cambridge, fellow and director of studies in theology, Fitzwilliam College

Doctrine, as the Reformers never tired of saying, flows from and leads back to Scripture. Michael Horton has demonstrated this thesis with *Justification*, a project that is at once a rich and rigorous exegetical investigation of the doctrine of justification and at the same time a model of theologically engaged scriptural interpretation. As all theology must, this book drinks from the well of Scripture as it walks the path of reading and doctrine towards the horizon of praise and proclamation. The result, both exegetically informed and theologically significant, is good news "for your bones and mine" (Luther): God justifies the ungodly in Christ, an unconditioned gift given in the word of promise that creates faith.

> **J. A. Linebaugh,** lecturer in New Testament, Cambridge University, fellow, Jesus College

This work is very impressive and a major contribution to the clarification of the significant issues. Horton anchors his presentation of the Protestant Reformers' teaching on the justification of the sinner in an extensive, carefully wrought exploration of the biblical roots, and he anchors conceptualizations of the relationship between sinners and their Creator within a covenantal framework that takes seriously both the sacramental nature of how God operates and the re-creative power of the gospel delivered by Christ. He challenges false interpretation of the Reformers' understanding of justification with thorough, perceptive assessments of patristic and medieval doctrines of justification, providing an alternative that capitalizes on the sixteenth-century insights to address the twenty-first-century person in the midst of the turmoil of our times.

> **Robert Kolb,** professor emeritus of systematic theology, Concordia Seminary, Saint Louis

NEW STUDIES IN DOGMATICS

JUSTIFICATION

VOLUME 1

NEW STUDIES IN DOGMATICS

JUSTIFICATION

VOLUME 1

MICHAEL HORTON

MICHAEL ALLEN AND SCOTT R. SWAIN,
GENERAL EDITORS

ZONDERVAN

Justification, Volume 1
Copyright © 2018 by Michael Horton

This title is also available as a Zondervan ebook.

Requests for information should be addressed to:
Zondervan, *3900 Sparks Dr. SE, Grand Rapids, Michigan 49546*

ISBN 978-0-310-49160-6

Cover design: Micah Kandros Design
Interior design: Kait Lamphere

Printed in the United States of America

19 20 21 22 23 24 25 26 27 28 /LSCC/ 15 14 13 12 11 10 9 8 7 6 5 4 3 2

CONTENTS

SERIES PREFACE

New Studies in Dogmatics follows in the tradition of G. C. Berkouwer's classic series, Studies in Dogmatics, in seeking to offer concise, focused treatments of major topics in dogmatic theology that fill the gap between introductory theology textbooks and advanced theological monographs. Dogmatic theology, as understood by editors and contributors to the series, is a conceptual representation of scriptural teaching about God and all things in relation to God. The source of dogmatics is Holy Scripture; its scope is the summing up of all things in Jesus Christ; its setting is the communion of the saints; and its end is the conversion, consolation, and instruction of creaturely wayfarers in the knowledge and love of the triune God until that knowledge and love is consummated in the beatific vision.

The series wagers that the way forward in constructive theology lies in a program of renewal through retrieval. This wager follows upon the judgment that much modern theology exhibits "a stubborn tendency to grow not higher but to the side," to borrow Alexander Solzhenitsyn's words from another context. Though modern theology continues to grow in a number of areas of technical expertise and interdisciplinary facility (especially in both the exegetical and historical domains), this growth too often displays a sideways drift rather than an upward progression in relation to theology's subject matter, scope, and source, and in fulfilling theology's end. We believe the path toward theological renewal in such a situation lies in drawing more deeply upon the resources of Holy Scripture in conversation with the church's most trusted teachers (ancient, medieval, and modern) who have sought to fathom Christ's unsearchable riches. In keeping with this belief, authors from a broad evangelical constituency will seek in this series to retrieve the riches of Scripture and tradition for constructive dogmatics. The purpose of retrieval is neither simple repetition of past theologians nor repristination of an earlier phase in church history; Christianity, at any rate, has no golden age east of Eden and short of the kingdom of God. Properly understood, retrieval is an inclusive and enlarging venture, a matter of tapping into a vital root and, in some cases, of relearning a lost grammar of theological discourse, all for the sake of equipping the church in its contemporary vocation to think and speak faithfully and fruitfully about God and God's works.

While the specific emphases of individual volumes will vary, each volume will display (1) awareness of the "state of the question" pertaining to the doctrine under discussion; (2) attention to the patterns of biblical reasoning (exegetical, biblical-theological, etc.) from which the doctrine emerges; (3) engagement with relevant ecclesiastical statements of the doctrine (creedal, conciliar, confessional), as well as with leading theologians of the church; and (4) appreciation of the doctrine's location within the larger system of theology, as well as of its contribution to Christian piety and practice.

Our prayer is that by drawing upon the best resources of the past and with an awareness of both perennial and proximate challenges to Christian thought and practice in the present, New Studies in Dogmatics will contribute to a flourishing theological culture in the church today. Soli Deo Gloria.

MICHAEL ALLEN AND SCOTT R. SWAIN

AUTHOR'S PREFACE

As the first part of a two-volume project, the present work explores the doctrine of justification from the patristic era through the Reformation. The second volume will take up the topic from biblical-theological, exegetical, and systematic-theological vantage points, engaging significantly with contemporary debates in biblical (especially Pauline) scholarship. So while this volume is more descriptive, the second will be more constructive.

This volume is an exercise in historical theology—and that, of a quite limited scope. The Reformation happened for a myriad of reasons, of course. The one that I focus on here is quite narrow, hardly sufficient to explain such a massive convulsion. Without this reason, however, the Reformation remains inexplicable at a fundamental level.

I offer the disclaimer at the outset that this study is much more narrowly focused on the history of ideas, in particular the doctrine of justification. In an era far different than our own, political, economic, and other cultural factors cannot be neatly disaggregated from strictly theological ones. It is anachronistic to assume that doctrinal matters were epiphenomenal in premodern Christendom, and it would be too cynical to say that such matters were a ruse for the *real* (i.e., sociopsychological, economic, political) reasons for influential movements and new paradigms. Though this is admittedly a very narrow slice of things, the developments and debates under investigation were themselves culture-shaping. Many people did really care about God, heaven and hell, and salvation.

I try in chapter 1 to provide a map for contemporary discussions of justification, identify my principal interlocutors in both volumes, and explain why I think that ours is an especially good time to explore the doctrine of justification.

Considering a wider frame in patristic sources than the word "justification" and its cognates, chapter 2 surveys the remarkable consensus on the "great exchange" as a significant and encompassing motif for the application of redemption. From there, I compare Origen's and Chrysostom's Romans commentaries at the relevant points, inserting Augustine into the discussion via his later writings. Chapter 3 offers a representative litany of statements from the ancient church on justification more particularly.

In chapter 4 I turn to the seminal developments in the medieval period, focusing especially on the role of sacramental penance, the heading under which justification was usually treated (albeit briefly). Here we explore Thomas Aquinas's formative interpretation of justification, which, significantly, he moved back under the main topic of grace. From there, chapter 5 examines the momentous changes in the doctrine with John Duns Scotus and William of Ockham. From there we trace the Reformers' (especially Luther's) road from penance to Christ (ch. 6) and their interpretation of the "great exchange" (ch. 7).

With this background, we launch into the main treatment of justification by the magisterial Reformers (ch. 8) and the new direction of Christian existence from the word (i.e., gospel) to faith, which produces good works (ch. 9). Chapter 10 engages the hermeneutical and theological significance of the Reformation's understanding of the law and the gospel and the resultant covenantal scheme that became formative in Reformed theology. Chapter 11 argues, controversially, that the triumph of nominalism is more accurately attributed to the Council of Trent than to the Reformers. And we conclude by exploring the role of justification in the Christian life in chapter 12.

ACKNOWLEDGMENTS

There are too many friends and colleagues to thank everyone for their input on these two volumes, especially the second. I mention only the following: my Westminster Seminary California colleagues David VanDrunen, Zach Keele, and Joshua Van Ee. There are many other scholars whose ears I have bent to rehearse the arguments in both volumes, especially Mike Allen and Jono Linebaugh. In addition, Tom Wright has been a generous conversation partner, critic, and friend over many years and in various opportunities that we have had to wrestle together over these issues that we both take so seriously. Despite substantial disagreements on this subject, he has helpfully challenged my exegesis at certain points. Another colleague Silverio Gonzalez gave great feedback on some chapters, and for that I'm grateful. These scholars have offered sources that enhanced my arguments and critiques that at least reduced the number of obvious errors, for which I alone am responsible.

I am also indebted to my White Horse Inn colleagues: three decades of collaboration and (more importantly) friendship with fellow Reformed minister Dr. Kim Riddlebarger, Dr. Rod Rosenbladt and his Lutheran cohorts, and Baptist pastor Ken Jones. Our producer, Shane Rosenthal, gave invaluable input and resources. I am also thankful to Mark Green and my assistant, Leslie Wilson, who carved out writing hours amid a busy schedule with great dedication. Thanks also are due to series editors Michael Allen and Scott Swain and to Katya Covrett and Matthew Estel at Zondervan Academic for their expertise and friendship.

Gratitude should also be expressed to my brother, Larry, who first introduced me to this amazing doctrine. As always, I am grateful to my church family and to my wife, Lisa, and children for sharing with me and allowing me to share with them in the joy of being "found in him, not having a righteousness of my own that comes from the law, but that which comes through faith in Christ, the righteousness from God that depends on faith" (Phil 3:9).

ABBREVIATIONS

AB   Anchor Bible Commentary

ANF   *The Ante-Nicene Fathers.* Edited by Alexander Roberts
         and James Donaldson. 1885–87. 10 vols. Repr.,
         Edinburgh: T&T Clark, 1989.

BDAG   *A Greek-English Lexicon of the New Testament and Other
         Early Christian Literature.* 3rd ed. Edited by Walter Bauer,
         Frederick William Danker, William F. Arndt, and Wilbur
         Gingrich. Chicago: University of Chicago Press, 2000.

CCC   *The Catechism of the Catholic Church.* New York: USCCB,
         1995.

CD   *Church Dogmatics.* By Karl Barth. Edited by T. F. Torrance
         and G. W. Bromiley. Edinburgh: T&T Clark, 1957–77.

CO   *Ioannis Calvini opera quae supersunt omnia.* Edited by
         Guilielmus Baum, Eduard Cunitz, and Eduard Reuss.
         10 vols. Brunsvigae: Schwetschke, 1871.

DS   *Enchiridion symbolorum definitionum et declarationum de rebus
         fidei et morum.* Edited by Heinrich Denzinger and Adolf
         Schönmetzer. Barcinone: Herder, 1973.

Haer. *Against Heresies.* By Irenaeus.

Inst. *Institutes of the Christian Religion.* By John Calvin. Edited
         by John T. McNeill. Translated by Ford Lewis Battles.
         Philadelphia: Westminster, 1960.

JBL   *Journal of Biblical Literature*

JSNT   *Journal for the Study of the New Testament*

LW   *Luther's Works.* Edited by Jaroslav Pelikan and Helmut
         T. Lehmann. Philadelphia and St. Louis: Fortress and
         Concordia, 1955–.

17

NICNT	New International Commentary on the New Testament
NPNF[1]	*The Nicene and Post-Nicene Fathers*, Series 1. Edited by Philip Schaff. 1886–89. 14 vols. Repr., Peabody, MA: Hendrickson, 1994.
NPNF[2]	*The Nicene and Post-Nicene Fathers*, Series 2. Edited by Philip Schaff and Henry Wace. 1896–1900. 14 vols. Repr., Peabody, MA: Hendrickson, 1994.
NSBT	New Studies in Biblical Theology
PG	Patrologia Graeca. Edited by J.-P. Migne. 162 vols. Paris, 1857–86.
PL	Patrologia Latina. Edited by J.-P. Migne. 217 vols. Paris, 1844–64.
ST	*Summa Theologica*. By Thomas Aquinas. Translated by the Fathers of the English Dominican Province. Westminster, MD: Christian Classics, 1981.
TDNT	*Theological Dictionary of the New Testament*. Edited by Gerhard Kittel. Translated and edited by Geoffrey W. Bromiley. 10 vols. Grand Rapids: Eerdmans, 1964–76.
WA	*D. Martin Luthers Werke: kritische Gesammtausgabe*. 120 vols. Weimar, 1883–2009.
WBC	Word Biblical Commentary
WUNT	Wissenschaftliche Untersuchungen zum Neuen Testament

CHAPTER 1

THE RIGHT TIME TO (RE)CONSIDER JUSTIFICATION

In response to the Black Death of 1348–50, the Church of England called for weeks of special prayers and fasting. However, in the 1980s, the church called for more government funding for medical research.[1] Drawing on this example, sociologist Steve Bruce explains, "Individualism, egalitarianism, liberal democracy, and science and technology all contribute to a general sense of self-importance, of freedom from fate." Consequently, "In the world of the mainstream churches and in the cultic milieu of alternative spirituality people are now generally unwilling to subordinate themselves to an external authority."[2]

It is an exaggeration to call the Middle Ages an age of faith, particularly when the Fourth Lateran Council in 1215 felt obliged to require all Christians to attend church once a year. Yet to whatever extent it was filled with hypocrites and hucksters, in terms of a public horizon of meaning, there was a sense of belonging to a history that will be brought to its denouement by the return of Christ to raise the dead, judge the world, and deliver his elect. Even the maps were drawn to make one look up, with the earth's landmasses and oceans congealing around the majestic God enthroned in Jerusalem at the center.[3] For them, living in this present age is but a preparation for everlasting life

---

1. Steve Bruce, *Secularization: In Defence of an Unfashionable Theory* (Oxford: Oxford University Press, 2011), 44.
2. Bruce, *Secularization*, 45.
3. Charles Taylor, *A Secular Age* (Cambridge, MA: Harvard University Press, 2007), 164, 178.

or death. In that world, the question "How can a sinner be accepted by a holy God?" at least made sense on all sides.

But we occupy an age in which the shared horizon of meaning stops at the ceiling. We do not look up as if living in this world is but an intimation of something greater. Following Feuerbach, Friedrich Nietzsche announced that the upper world, with its hierarchy descending from God to the angels and the intelligent souls, had been wiped from the horizon of the modern consciousness. Proclaiming himself more the herald than the author, Nietzsche advocated an "inverted Platonism," and Sigmund Freud demythologized the religious impulse as little more than a powerful neurosis.

Transcendence moved indoors. No longer inhabiting the highest place in the cosmos, the enchanted world came to occupy the deepest places of the self. There may be "transcendence" *within* this world. A baseball game or a ballet performance may bristle with intimations of the sacred. Cresting the summit of a glistening granite peak may fill one with an overwhelming sense of the sublime. Joining a march may exhilarate one's soul by participating in something larger than oneself, the arc of history that bends toward justice. But these quasi-mystical moments occur within time, nature, history, and the self, rather than from eternity breaking into time. Is there a desire that cannot be satisfied with a smartphone?

Whatever important differences among themselves, the Protestant Reformers and their critics inhabited a world in which ferocious debates over guilt and grace made sense. They were quite literally life-and-death matters. Unlike the subconscious terrors of the Dadaists, the frightful visions of Hieronymus Bosch depicted real places of torment. The reliefs of *The Last Judgment*, with the sword protruding from Christ's mouth, reminded worshipers as they entered that they stood on precarious ground, ready to be consumed by God's wrath apart from the ministrations of the ecclesiastical hierarchy.

Surely in an age like ours, many imagine that our best hope in reaching secular neighbors is to persuade them that God somehow still fits somewhere in the immanent frame.[4] There may be no heaven above us or hell below us, but God can help us have our best life now. The once-familiar warning that "it is appointed for man to die once, and after that

---

4. I borrow this phrase from Taylor, *A Secular Age*, 539–93.

comes judgment" (Heb 9:27) may no longer have much purchase, but we may still be able to find divine empowerment for our life projects. Wherever God is and whatever God does, it is inside of us: inner peace, happiness, satisfaction, and comfort. And it is never threatening. How can the struggle to find a gracious God be relevant in an age when people are not gripped by a sense of God's reality and presence, his holiness and majesty, which provoke the question in the first place?

I have no idea how many times I have heard or read contemporary theologians and pastors assert with solemn finality that Luther's question "How can I find a gracious God?" is just not ours today. In addition, many New Testament scholars today argue that it was not the apostle Paul's question either. Indeed, they argue, the broad swath of New Testament (especially Pauline) interpretation since the patristic era has failed to recognize that the principal question is not how individuals are "saved" but how to tell who belongs to the covenant community. In other words, it is more about ecclesiology than soteriology. Or, as other contemporary scholars suggest, the gospel is about liberation from the powers of darkness, especially oppressive political and economic systems, rather than about personal salvation. This is a way of moving God outdoors, as it were, but as the justifier of those on the right side of justice. Is there any justification for *the ungodly*? For a host of reasons, we have found the question itself quite beside the point.

Consequently, we can move on as if the question of justification, much less the arcane debates surrounding it, matters little to the average person today. Or can we? Is the move toward pure immanence actually motivated by a secret terror? Are we trying to secure ourselves against the indictments of our conscience, the nagging feeling that we cannot quite put our finger on? In other words, is not the effort to "suppress the truth in unrighteousness"—even to the point of idolatry or, for that matter, atheism—at bottom an effort to evade an objective and therefore condemning evaluating our life? The God who beholds "men's depths and dregs," had even "crept into my dirtiest corners," said Nietzsche's ugliest man. "On such a witness I would have revenge—or not live myself. The God who beheld everything, *and also man:* that God had to die! Man cannot *endure* it that such a witness should live."[5]

---

5. Friedrich Nietzsche, "Thus Spake Zarathustra," in *The Philosophy of Nietzsche*, trans. Thomas Common (New York: Random House, n.d.), 207.

But the price of this evasion is steep, even if only in existential terms. "Man is nothing else but that which he makes of himself," Sartre asserted, and bears "the entire responsibility for his existence squarely upon his own shoulders."[6] That is an astonishing doctrine. Is it any wonder that we would rather be accountable for this burden to ourselves rather than to an external authority who has the power—and the right—to judge us? Is not such secularized Pelagianism (as if the heresy itself is not already secularized enough) the incubator of so many of our anxieties?

Robert Jay Lifton, a psychiatrist and pioneer in brain research, observes that the source of many neuroses in society today is a nagging sense of guilt without knowing its source.[7] The anxiety is "a vague but persistent kind of self-condemnation related to the symbolic disharmonies I have described, a sense of having no outlet for his loyalties and no symbolic structure for his achievements."[8] I interpret this theologically as suggesting that there is no external law to measure oneself by or external gospel through which one becomes re-scripted "in Christ." "Rather than being a feeling of evil or sinfulness," he says, "it takes the form of a nagging sense of unworthiness all the more troublesome for its lack of clear origin."[9]

But when has the question, "How can I be saved?" ever been a common question of the average person? Regardless of whether this was an urgent question of Jews of the Second Temple period (and it was, as I demonstrate in the second volume), evidently the preaching of Jesus and the apostles provoked the question as they exposed human guilt, corruption, and death and pointed to Golgotha and the empty tomb as its solution. Jesus upbraided the religious specialists for refusing him because they "trusted in themselves that they were righteous" and, consequently, missed the main point of their Scripture. Evidently, the apostle Paul did not find a ready audience for his message either, reporting that most Jews found it "a stumbling block" and most Greeks found it simply "foolishness." Many of Pelagius's auditors found it more relevant to discuss self-improvement rather than obsess with Augustine over

---

6. Walter Kaufman, *Existentialism from Dostoevsky to Sartre* (New York: Penguin Random House, 1975), 291.

7. Robert J. Lifton, *The Protean Self: Human Resilience in an Age of Fragmentation* (Chicago: University of Chicago Press, 1999), 101.

8. Robert J. Lifton, "The Protean Self," in *The Truth About the Truth: De-confusing and Re-constructing the Postmodern World*, ed. Walter Truett Anderson (New York: Putnam, 1995), 133.

9. Lifton, "The Protean Self," 133.

salvation. In a letter to Cardinal Sadoleto, John Calvin offered a rebuke that nevertheless exuded genuine sympathy, even friendship. Those like Sadoleto, who cannot understand why so many people wrestle with the question of justification, are basically inexperienced in life, Calvin surmises.[10] They have never had a serious crisis of conscience. Their spiritual development seems frozen on the verge of adolescence. In short, the burden has always been on the gospel to make itself relevant as people passed by shaking their heads or just ignoring it.

So I remain unmoved by dismissals of the Reformation's formulation of justification and its broader quest as little more than the product of an early modern obsession with the self. "Tortured subjectivity" is what you get when "God is dead," while you nevertheless feel a sense of guilt and despair that vaguely comes from somewhere other than your inner self or the people around you. Say whatever you like about the Protestant Reformers, but they were not obsessed with introspection. On the contrary, they were gripped by the experience of meeting a stranger, an other, to whom they were accountable. Luther didn't fear an inner judgment but a real one on the great stage of history, with banners flying and a fight to the death. Whoever this God was, he was not manipulable by the subjective wants or wish-projections of mortals. One would never invent this sort of religion as therapy for self-improvement, self-empowerment, and tranquility of mind. And regardless, Luther would not have recognized such a religion, much less sympathize with it. If there are lingering doubts about that, I hope that this book lays them to rest.

I write this book with the conviction that it is always relevant to proclaim the justification of the ungodly, although we have a long way to go to explore what that means. God has not changed. Nor can God's work in Christ be undone. Humanity still faces the same plight—a conscience that knows deep down we were meant for something that we cannot define, much less find our way to. It is always the right time to tell the story that God is always telling us. Its controversial status already points to the fact that, true or false, we are dealing with reality and not with our projection of God.

---

10. Such typical statements of the Reformers challenge the critique that their teaching was "extrinsicist," having nothing to do with the affections and inner life. In defense of this point, see Simeon Zahl, "On the Affective Salience of Doctrines," *Modern Theology* 31, no. 3 (July 2015): 428–44.

This is the first of a two-volume project. In the present volume I offer at least one version of the story as to how and why the Reformation happened, focusing entirely on the historical development. Luther did not rise Phoenix-like from the ashes of Christendom but from a very specific development and debate within it. Of course, there are myriad reasons for why the Reformation happened and not all of them doctrinal or even intellectual. But in an era when historians generally consider religion, much less theology, to be epiphenomenal to the real reasons (economic, political, social, etc.), we have to exercise some historical sympathy to comprehend an age in which doctrine could roil a whole civilization. My scope will be on that long-running doctrinal conversation about God, grace, and justification.

The second volume focuses entirely on the biblical-theological and exegetical issues in the light of contemporary debates about justification.

In both books, I do not pretend to be a dispassionate scholar but engage the academic debates in order to understand and articulate the heart of the gospel. I do so from a particular ecclesial location as a Reformed minister and theology professor, yet with a commitment to gleaning insights from other traditions and insights from contemporary biblical scholarship. Although my conclusions are consistent with the confession that I make with my brothers and sisters in a particular communion, my goal is not simply to repristinate but to engage.

JUSTIFICATION AND A DIVIDED CHURCH

According to the current position of the Roman Catholic Church, "Justification is not only the remission of sins, but also the sanctification and renewal of the interior man."[11] Justification is therefore regarded as a process of becoming actually and intrinsically righteous. The first justification occurs at baptism, which eradicates both the guilt and corruption of original sin.[12] Due entirely to God's grace, this initial justification infuses the habit (or principle) of grace into the recipient. By cooperating with this inherent grace, one merits an increase of grace and, one hopes, final justification.[13] So while initial justification is by grace alone, final justification and perseverance depend also on the

---

11. *CCC*, 492, quoting the Council of Trent (1574), DS 1528.
12. *CCC*, 482.
13. *CCC*, 483.

believer's works, which God graciously accepts as meritorious.[14] Since the believer's progress in holiness cannot adequately cancel the guilt of sin, he or she must be refined in purgatory before being welcomed into heaven.[15]

In Scripture, especially in Paul, Luther discovered that the righteousness God *is*, by which he condemns us, is the same righteousness God *gives*, freely, as a gift, through faith in Jesus Christ (Rom 3:19–31). This "marvelous exchange" of Christ's righteousness for the sinner's guilt was beautifully articulated by some medieval theologians, such as Bernard of Clairvaux (1090–1153). However, understanding justification as an exclusively forensic (legal) declaration, based on the imputation of Christ's righteousness through faith alone, was the chief insight of the Reformation. In this way, the broader consensual understanding of the "great exchange" attained its most refined and satisfying formulation.

But if that is even close to being the case, why did it take so many centuries before this ostensibly clear message was rediscovered? And should we really believe that a perturbed monk discovered the revolutionary heart of the gospel that the greatest minds of Christendom had missed? In any case, why does it matter to us now?

At its core, the paradigm shift that Luther experienced—and many others at the same time, some even before—was that justification is not a process of becoming righteous but a declaration that one is righteous before God solely on the basis of Christ and solely through faith. This righteousness is a gift to which no human can contribute. Human beings, even as regenerate, are in no moral condition to cooperate sufficiently with grace to attain final justification. Even faith is a gift of God's grace. In short, all of our justifying righteousness is found in Christ, not in us. The Reformers did not thereby exclude the process of becoming holy. Rather, they argued that through union with Christ we receive both justification and sanctification, and these distinct acts must never be confused or separated.

Considerable progress has been made, especially since Vatican II, in understanding each other's positions. The *Joint Declaration on the Doctrine of Justification* (1999), which included representatives of the Vatican and the Lutheran World Federation, achieved a consensus sufficient

---

14. *CCC*, 486–87.
15. *CCC*, 268.

to announce that the condemnations from the sixteenth century no longer apply to the partner in dialogue.[16] Yet the *Joint Declaration* did not achieve the results for which many hoped. As Eberhard Jüngel judges, "The understanding that allegedly has been reached rests on ground which proves at places quite slippery."[17] On the Lutheran side, the confessional doctrine of justification was surrendered at crucial points, particularly the conflation of faith and love and therefore justification and sanctification.[18] On the Roman Catholic side, soon after the statement was released, the Vatican issued disclaimers and even corrections of the *Declaration*, noting that it does not have any binding status.[19]

None of this means that the ecumenical project has reached an impasse. On the contrary, genuine dialogue begins with an honest recognition of remaining differences. On one hand, mainline Protestantism mourns over the wounds that Calvin said "must cause us to cry a river of tears." On the other hand, despite significant attempts on both sides to deal honestly with the severe doctrinal divide, conclusions thus far have carried us no further toward a common confession, and mainline Protestantism, as well as a Roman Catholic academy also infected by the obsession with modernity, has little to offer in regard to the future. The only hope is "that word above all earthly pow'rs," which can be heard again because Christ is risen and the Holy Spirit spreads his gracious presence among all who confess Christ's name.

---

16. Lutheran World Federation and the Roman Catholic Church, *Joint Declaration on the Doctrine of Justification* (Grand Rapids: Eerdmans, 2000), 10–11.

17. Eberhard Jüngel, *Justification: The Heart of the Christian Faith*, trans. Jeffrey F. Cayzer (London: Bloomsbury, 2014), xxxix. The chief critic of the *Joint Declaration* when it appeared, Jüngel (who has also been long engaged in ecumenical discussions) wrote this entire book as a way of clarifying the Lutheran doctrine.

18. *Joint Declaration*, 18, with the section titled "Justification as Forgiveness of Sins *and Making Righteous*" (my emphasis). In the act of justification, faith is defined as love (32). The document acknowledges (22) that it is still the Roman Catholic position that while concupiscence remains in believers, it is not properly called sin (hence, the denial of "simultaneously justified and sinful"). Further, "When Catholics affirm the 'meritorious' character of good works, they wish to say that, according to the biblical witness, a reward in heaven is promised to these works" (25). Whatever is said further to qualify this, nothing of traditional Tridentine theology has been changed. Thus, "The teaching of the Lutheran churches presented in this *Declaration* does not fall under the condemnations of the Council of Trent" (26) only because they are not the teachings that Trent condemned. In other words, the LWF essentially adopted the Roman Catholic position on these traditional differences. This is not to say that there are no impressive points of agreement in which to rejoice, but the *Declaration* takes the classic Roman Catholic side on the points that have been church-dividing.

19. See "Response of the Catholic Church to the Joint Declaration of the Catholic Church and the Lutheran World Federation on the Doctrine of Justification," http://www.vatican.va/roman_curia/pontifical_councils/chrstuni/documents/rc_pc_chrstuni_doc_01081998_off-answer-catholic_en.html.

JUSTIFICATION AND MODERN THEOLOGY

It is also the right time to reconsider this doctrine because of the interest that has been provoked in contemporary scholarship from diverse fields. Not since the Reformation has there been so much controversy in the academy surrounding the doctrine of justification.

To place the current debates over justification in proper context, it is worth reminding ourselves that for centuries now, at least in mainline Protestant theology, the doctrine (in its pristine confessional form) has largely been assimilated to other concerns, rejected on a priori ethical and philosophical grounds, or simply ignored. Following a basically Socinian line of thinking, Immanuel Kant and other Enlightenment figures dismissed the assumptions undergirding the doctrine as well as justification itself.[20] Paul Ricoeur was not exaggerating when he called Kant's anthropology "Pelagian."[21] In deference to a thoroughly ethical system, Albrecht Ritschl expunged from Christianity everything that presupposed any notion of objective guilt and divine wrath or justice needing to be satisfied. Thus, much of modern theology has followed Kant in concluding, like Dorothee Sölle, that the notion of Christ's righteousness being imputed to sinners qua sinners "destroys the ethical core of personality, namely, responsibility."[22]

Across the Roman Catholic-Protestant divide, modernity and the myriad trends that have come and gone under its thrall have perhaps separated conservatives and progressives within each communion more than between them. The Reformation debate seems to pale in the face of the outright Pelagian anthropological assumptions of the modern age, aptly summarized as "moralistic, therapeutic deism."[23] Within a therapeutic outlook, even when the old terms are used, they acquire new meanings. Sin becomes dysfunction, and redemption is code for

---

20. Named after its leader, Faustus Socinus, Socinianism arose as a radical Protestant movement in the late sixteenth and seventeenth centuries that rejected the doctrines of the Trinity, the divinity of Christ, substitutionary atonement and justification. Regardless of direct influences, Immanuel Kant reflects the convictions and even the arguments of this rationalistic movement. There were many influences on the Enlightenment (and Kant in particular), but pietism and rationalism were a common background of its leading figures.

21. Paul Ricoeur, *Figuring the Sacred: Religion, Narrative, and Imagination* (Minneapolis: Fortress, 1995), 81.

22. Dorothee Sölle, *Christ the Representative: An Essay in Theology after the 'Death of God'* (London: SCM, 1967), 78–79.

23. Christian Smith and Melinda Lundquist Denton, *Soul Searching: The Religious and Spiritual Lives of American Teenagers* (New York: Oxford University Press, 2009), 118–71.

recovery. Peace with God—and with each other through that primary relationship—is not denied; it is just absent. Justification, if it figures in at all, becomes a way of talking about inner peace of mind, self-acceptance, social justice, and liberation from norms that have not been elected by the autonomous self. Obviously, accommodation has proved fatal. In my view at least, recovering the clear message that the Reformers proclaimed over against medieval distortions can alone bring a fresh discovery of the gospel in our day when Protestantism itself has surrendered to modern Pelagianism and Gnosticism.

Even within conservative Protestantism, the consensus over the doctrine of justification has been exaggerated. There have been remarkable revivals of the doctrine periodically, including the recent upsurge in the United States of a "New Calvinism." At the same time, there is a resurgence of Anabaptist and pietist approaches that challenge what they perceive as the more dominant influence of the magisterial Reformation.[24] As an offshoot of mainline Protestantism, evangelicalism has always been a confluence of various theological streams, some of them quite inimical to the Reformation heritage.

Although the classic evangelical view does enjoy considerable privilege, the doctrine is frequently taken for granted or sidelined in favor of more ostensibly relevant interests. Again, this is not a recent phenomenon. A "Plan of Union" for American Protestantism, based on an "evangelical creed," was put forward in 1920. Princeton theologian B. B. Warfield observed that the new confession being proposed "contains nothing which is not believed by Evangelicals," and yet ". . . nothing which is not believed . . . by the adherents of the Church of Rome, for example." He noted, "There is nothing about justification by faith in this creed." But then again, he observed, there is nothing in the statement about the Trinity, the deity of Christ and the Holy Spirit, the atonement, or sin and grace.[25] "Is this the kind of creed which twentieth-century Presbyterianism will find sufficient as a basis for

---

24. Stanley Grenz challenged the older evangelical preoccupation with "Christ alone" as the material principle and "Scripture alone" as the formal principle of the Christian faith. See Grenz, *Revisioning Evangelical Theology* (Downers Grove, IL: InterVarsity, 1993), 62. Brian McLaren makes the same point in *A Generous Orthodoxy* (Grand Rapids: Zondervan, 2004), 221. For both writers, as for the generation of evangelicals that preceded them, the heart of Christianity is our imitation of Christ's example, which—for McLaren (on the above-cited page)—does not even require one to become a Christian but only to be better Buddhist, Muslim, or Jewish followers of Jesus.

25. B. B. Warfield, "In Behalf of Evangelical Religion," in *Selected Shorter Writings of Benjamin B. Warfield*, vol. 1, ed. John E. Meeter (Nutley, NJ: Presbyterian and Reformed, 1970), 386.

co-operation in evangelistic activities? Then it can get along in its evangelistic activities without the gospel. For it is precisely the gospel that this creed neglects altogether." "Fellowship is a good word," Warfield concludes, "and a great duty. But our fellowship, according to Paul, must be in 'the furtherance of the gospel.'"[26]

In Warfield's day, evangelical union meant the uniting of what then constituted the majority of mainline Protestantism in America, yet even the National Association of Evangelicals is united today by a statement of faith that affirms nothing that is distinctively evangelical. Although there are two points on the necessity of the Holy Spirit's work in regeneration and sanctification (affirmed also by Roman Catholic and Orthodox traditions), no mention is made of justification.[27]

Even where there is rather widespread affirmation of the doctrine in theory, much of popular preaching and piety in American evangelicalism is oriented toward therapeutic moralism and culture wars. As Arminian theologian Roger E. Olson notes, the default setting is "not Arminianism but semi-Pelagianism or outright Pelagianism."[28] In fact, after his US tour, Dietrich Bonhoeffer described America as "Protestantism without the Reformation."[29]

RENEWED INTEREST IN JUSTIFICATION

So the very fact that justification—even in its raw Lutheran and Reformed confessional form—has become a focus of so much scholarly activity and popular interest (pro and con) both within evangelicalism and beyond is both bewildering and an encouraging sign of the doctrine's enduring vitality.

Especially since the 1943 encyclical of Pius XII *Divino Afflante Spiritu* and the subsequent Second Vatican Council, biblical scholarship has led to some surprising convergences. As we will see in volume 2, even leading Catholic exegetes today affirm that justification is a forensic term

---

26. Warfield, "In Behalf of Evangelical Religion," 387.
27. "Statement of Faith," National Association of Evangelicals, https://www.nae.net/statement-of-faith/.
28. Roger Olson, *Arminian Theology* (Downers Grove, IL: InterVarsity, 2005), 28, including n20.
29. Dietrich Bonhoeffer, "Protestantism without the Reformation," in *No Rusty Swords: Letters, lectures and Notes, 1928–1936*, ed. Edwin H. Robertson, trans. Edwin H. Robertson and John Bowden (London: Collins, 1965), 82–118.

that means "to declare righteousness" rather than "to make righteous" (as the Latin Vulgate translation rendered it).[30]

Quite frequently, however, criticisms of the Reformation doctrine from the quarters of biblical scholarship trade in caricature, lacking adequate familiarity with the primary sources; in many cases, "Luther" is an unacknowledged pseudonym for Ritschl, Harnack, and Bultmann. The old history of religions "Hebrew versus Hellenistic" rubric retains its lure despite decades of refutation.[31] Accordig to this theory, everything that we do not like (e.g., an interest in individual salvation, *ordo salutis*, forensic concepts, etc.) reflects a Hellenizing trend.[32]

Paul used to be cast as the great corruptor of Jesus's teaching, but the blame seems to have moved to the Reformers. According to others, Luther and Calvin are salvaged, but their successors (the Protestant "scholastics") become the villains who distorted the original Reformers' teaching. It is intriguing that traditional Reformation interpretations of justification are considered at all today after centuries of opprobrium. In fact, the last few decades have shown a remarkable scholarly interest in Reformed and Lutheran scholasticism, which has evinced an equally remarkable catholicity of spirit and engagement with the whole history of exegesis and theology.[33] In recent years some critics have reconsidered their own sharp objections and have even encouraged greater appreciation for the Reformation's insights and exegesis. When the debate is based on careful exegesis, defenders of the Reformation perspective are on their home ground and have nothing to fear by having traditional assumptions tested.

---

30. E.g., Joseph Fitzmyer, *Romans*, Anchor Yale Commentaries 33 (New York: Doubleday, 1993), esp. 116–19; and Brendan Byrne, *Romans*, Sacra Pagina (Collegeville, MN: Liturgical, 1996), 57.

31. See for example Adolf von Harnack, *History of Dogma*, vol. 1 (Boston: Little, Brown, 1902), 48–60.

32. The decisive criticism is often associated with the work of James Barr, "The Old Testament and the New Crisis of Biblical Authority," *Interpretation* 25 (1971): 24–40; cf. Barr, *The Semantics of Biblical Language* (Oxford: Oxford University Press, 1961). Also of major significance is Martin Hengel, *Judentum und Hellenismus: Studien zu ihrer Begegnung unter besonderer Berücksichtigung Palästinas bis zur Mitte des 2 Jh.s v.Chr.* (Tübingen: Mohr, 1973); English trans., *Judaism and Hellenism: Studies in Their Encounter in Palestine During the Early Hellenistic Period*, 2 vols. (London: SCM, 1974). Cf. Troels Engberg-Pedersen, ed., *Paul Beyond the Judaism/Hellenism Divide* (Louisville: Westminster John Knox, 2001). For a survey of its relation to debates within evangelical theology, see Michael Horton, "Hebrew or Hellenistic," *Journal of the Evangelical Theological Society* 45, no. 2 (June 2002): 317–41.

33. For example, on the Reformed side the way has been led by Richard Muller, Irena Backus, Willem Van Asselt, Eef Dekker, Susan Schreiner, R. S. Clark, and Carl Trueman; on the Lutheran side, Robert Preus, Robert Kolb, Timothy Wengert, and others.

It may be helpful at the outset to identify some (though by no means all) of the major programs challenging the Reformation's view of justification since I will be interacting with these important critiques throughout this work. I will provide a more thorough summary of the positions among biblical scholars in volume 2.

The New Perspective on Paul

In the wake of E. P. Sanders's *Paul and Palestinian Judaism* (1977), a "new perspective on Paul" emerged that challenged traditional categories related to justification. Here I merely summarize the most noteworthy points of agreement in this paradigm-shifting trend.

First, the Judaism known in the days of Jesus and Paul was not a form of legalistic works-righteousness. Rather, Sanders argued, it is a form of "covenantal nomism," a matter of "getting in" by grace and "staying in" by keeping the law and, upon transgression, finding forgiveness through repentance. In Sanders's view, this system is permeated with grace. Interestingly, though, Sanders concludes that Paul rejected this covenantal nomism in favor of a "participationist eschatology," where union with Christ replaces Torah.[34]

Second, Paul's sharp dichotomy between works/faith arises in a specific debate over gentile inclusion. Thus the question about justification is not "How can I be saved?" but "How do we know who belongs?" "Works" refers merely to the boundary markers (e.g., circumcision and dietary regulations) that exclude gentiles, not to self-effort in obtaining salvation. Paul insists that faith alone is the badge of membership. It is therefore not a question of soteriology (how one is saved) but of ecclesiology (identifying membership).[35]

There are significant differences among scholars identified with the new perspective. N. T. Wright, for example, emphasizes the narrative of Abraham as a new Adam, with the promise by God of a worldwide family. Another essential element is that Israel's continuing exile serves as the backdrop to the Messiah's mission. For Wright, justification is not about how people are saved (which he often identifies with a quasi-gnostic separation of the soul from the body) but about the end of

---

34. E. P. Sanders, *Paul and Palestinian Judaism* (Philadelphia: Fortress, 1977), 447–521.

35. N. T. Wright, *What Saint Paul Really Said: Was Paul of Tarsus the Real Founder of Christianity?* (Grand Rapids: Eerdmans, 1997), 119. For a more moderate version of the thesis, see Michael F. Bird, *The Saving Righteousness of God: Studies on Paul, Justification, and the New Perspective* (Eugene, OR: Wipf and Stock, 2007).

exile and the gathering of gentiles into Abraham's worldwide family as forgiven and empowered participants in God's plan to make things right in the world under the Messiah's lordship.

As we will see, the Reformers encounter many of the central theses of the new perspective in their day: that salvation is about ecclesiology rather than soteriology; that "covenantal nomism" provides an adequate paradigm for a grace-affirming type of religion; that Paul's phrase "works of the law" refers to ceremonial boundary markers excluding gentiles rather than to the Torah as a whole. Nevertheless, recent scholarship also poses fresh challenges as well as crucial insights. Nearly all my engagement with the new perspective occurs in volume 2.

Radical Orthodoxy

Of more interest in this volume is a movement that began in the 1990s through the leadership of John Milbank together with Catherine Pickstock, Graham Ward, and other Anglo-Catholic thinkers of breathtaking imagination. Although the movement he founded is not characterized by scriptural exegesis, John Milbank has hailed the new perspective as an ally of Radical Orthodoxy.[36] An ally for—and against—what exactly?

For Radical Orthodoxy, the story begins in Alexandria, the hub in the second and third centuries for the intersection of pagan Neoplatonism (Plotinus and Porphyry), Christianity (Clement and Origen), and Gnosticism (Basilides and Valentinus). Origen and Plotinus were both students of Ammonius Saccas, the founder of Neoplatonism. Radical Orthodoxy is especially enthusiastic about the theurgic Neoplatonism of Iamblichus and Proclus, mediated to Christianity especially through Pseudo-Dionysius, who until the fourteenth century was considered the convert named in Acts 17 when Paul addressed the Athenian philosophers. (There are more citations of Dionysius in Thomas Aquinas's *Summa theologiae* than any other sources besides the Bible.)

The main point of convergence in metaphysics that Radical Orthodoxy seeks to revive is the image of the cosmos as a chain of being with no missing links between heaven and earth. All material reality participates in the rungs above it so that the ladder of being is completely

---

36. John Milbank, "Paul Against Biopolitics," in *Paul's New Moment: Continental Philosophy and the Future of Christian Theology*, ed. John Milbank, Slavoj Žižek, and Creston Davis (Grand Rapids: Brazos, 2010), 55–56, including n69.

filled. There is no space for autonomous elements that might colonize a realm of the "secular."

The narrative with which Radical Orthodoxy is most concerned is that of a decline from the Dionysian vision of the early Middle Ages particularly through the paradigm-shifting ideas of John Duns Scotus, radicalized by William of Ockham, and carried into modernity by the Protestant Reformation. Known as nominalism, this decadent program of late medieval theology set the West (not only in theology but in every other aspect of culture) on the trajectory toward secularism.

First, as the story goes, by positing a natural end for human nature distinct from a supernatural end, Thomists like Cajetan (unlike Aquinas himself) opened up space for "the secular"—a realm that is ungraced by God's presence, order, and the final end of the beatific vision.

Second, nominalism introduced the heresy of a univocity of being. Where earlier theology, going back all the way to the patristic era, insisted that creation participates analogically in God (and is therefore wholly dependent), univocity rendered God a being among other beings. Now human existence and agency were no longer viewed as suspended in God; rather, existence was seen as something that God and human beings share identically. God and humans were now regarded as separate and autonomous agents, competing for their share of the ontic pie. God and humans were now "efficient causes" alongside each other, provoking debates about whose activity in salvation counts most: God's or ours.

Consequently, a realm was invented, drained of its symbolic participation in God, identified as "the natural." This secular space spread until it colonized even the supernatural realm—leading to our secular age.[37]

This metaphysical "extrinsicism" was the shared horizon of both Reformation and Counter-Reformation movements, Milbank charges.[38] If nominalists made justification sound like a Pelagian attempt of human beings to merit salvation by doing what lies within them, the Reformers' extrinsic and forensic verdict was just as ill conceived. By recovering the pre-Scotist analogical metaphysics, we avoid unnecessary and erroneous debates that force a false choice between God and humans as causes

---

37. The major statement of this thesis is John Milbank's *Theology and Social Theory: Beyond Secular Reason* (Oxford: Blackwell, 1990).

38. John Milbank, Catherine Pickstock, and Graham Ward, eds., *Radical Orthodoxy: A New Theology* (London and New York: Routledge, 1999).

of salvation. In every meritorious work of human beings, God is the efficient cause. Just as with our existence itself, our union with God is attained through participation in and therefore cooperation with grace.

Especially in recent years, Milbank has followed Bruno Blumenfeld's interpretation of Paul, with the apostle arguing in Romans 1 and 2 that "all people everywhere should have been able (and by implication have sometimes been able) to acknowledge the true God and that all people everywhere are saved according to their obedience to the unwritten justice of God—in other words, according to ethical works (!) in the broadest sense."[39] According to Milbank, Paul suggests "that it is indeed by faith that one is essentially able to be just, that is to say, ethical under the governance of the law of nature."[40] "And *dikaiosynē* always meant 'justice' or a 'binding together in justice' in the contemporary Greek or Judeo-Greek context and never 'imputed salvation,'" and the "Hebrew equivalents . . . never implied anything imputational."[41] Indeed, following Douglas Harink, Milbank stresses that "'justification' in Paul is the divine action of really making just, not of imputing justice."[42]

If the new perspective presents an exegetical challenge to the Reformation view of justification, Radical Orthodoxy contends that the doctrine is the offspring of a broader metaphysics that dissolved the sacred tapestry of Christian Neoplatonism in the acids of nominalism.

This interpretation of the Reformation in general and its doctrine of justification in particular as a carrier of nominalist univocity and extrinsicism into modernity informs several important projects, including Charles Taylor's *A Secular Age* (2007) and Brad Gregory's *The Unintended Reformation* (2012).[43] It has also made a considerable impact on some evangelical and Reformed scholars. Hans Boersma contends, "The Reformation teaching of justification by faith alone (*sola fide*) exemplified a great deal of continuity with the nominalist tradition.

---

39. John Milbank, "Paul against Biopolitics," 55. Reference is made throughout this essay (and here) to Bruno Blumenfeld, *The Political Paul: Justice, Democracy, and Kingship in a Hellenistic Framework* (London: Continuum, 2001).

40. Milbank, "Paul against Biopolitics," 56.

41. Milbank, "Paul against Biopolitics," 56.

42. Milbank, "Paul against Biopolitics," 55n69, drawing liberally from Douglas Harink, *Paul among the Postliberals: Pauline Theology beyond Christendom and Modernity* (Grand Rapids: Brazos, 2003).

43. Taylor acknowledges his debt to John Milbank's narration of the Scotus story at various points throughout *A Secular Age* (Cambridge, MA: Belknap, 2007); so too Brad Gregory, *The Unintended Reformation* (Cambridge, MA: Harvard University Press, 2012), with the influences of the Radical Orthodoxy narrative evident throughout.

This continuity centered on the imputation of Christ's righteousness."[44] I will examine this claim especially in chapter 11.

Inspired by John Howard Yoder's vision of the church as an alternative *polis*, Stanley Hauerwas and Douglas Harink represent a convergence of Anabaptist, New Perspective, apocalyptic, Radical Orthodoxy, and postliberal (especially "Yale School") emphases.[45] As Milbank asserts, "Harink also correctly stresses that 'justification' in Paul is the divine action of really making just, not of imputing justice; that 'the faith of Christ' is primarily such and not 'faith in Christ'; and that *ekklēsia* is a political project."[46] Closely affiliated with this school is the "apocalyptic" trajectory in New Testament (especially Paul) studies led by J. Louis Martyn and, above all, Douglas Campbell.

New Finnish Interpretation of Luther

According to the above proposals, the Reformation interpretation of justification is the foil for alternative perspectives. In short, the Reformers were wrong. In contrast, Tuomo Mannermaa and his colleagues at the University of Helsinki argue that Luther's view was actually closer to an Eastern Orthodox conception of *theosis* or deification.[47]

Emerging in Lutheran-Orthodox dialogues during the last two decades of the twentieth century, this thesis argues that Luther's theology of justification is based on the indwelling presence of Christ in the believer as the form of faith. Thus, justification is not a mere declaration based on the imputation of Christ's righteousness through faith, as we find in Melanchthon and the Book of Concord, as well as in Calvin and the Reformed tradition. Rather, for Luther, through faith Christ deifies the soul, communicating (indeed, *being*) the essential righteousness of God indwelling believers. The moniker for this position seems to have originated in the English-speaking world with the book edited by Carl E. Braaten and Robert W. Jenson, *Union with Christ: The New Finnish*

---

44. Hans Boersma, *Heavenly Participation: The Weaving of a Sacramental Tapestry* (Grand Rapids: Eerdmans, 2011), 92; cf. *Nouvelle Théologie and Sacramental Ontology* (New York: Oxford University Press, 2013).

45. See especially Douglas Harink, *Paul Among the Postliberals: Pauline Theology Beyond Christendom and Modernity* (Grand Rapids: Brazos, 2003).

46. Milbank, "Paul against Biopolitics" 55–56n69.

47. One prominent example is the "evangelical catholic" circle associated with Robert Jenson and Carl Braaten and the new Finnish interpretation of Luther led by Tuomom Mannermaa and others. Tuomo Mannermaa, *Christ Present in Faith: Luther's Doctrine of Justification*, ed. Kirsi Stjerna (Minneapolis: Fortress, 2005). I interact with these views in *Covenant and Salvation: Union with Christ* (Louisville: Westminster John Knox, 2007), 127–260.

Interpretation of Luther (Eerdmans, 1998). Trained under Mannermaa, Lutheran-Pentecostal theologian Veli-Matti Kärkkäinen has also applied this new interpretation of Luther to his own constructive project.[48]

Critics have challenged the thesis at many points, especially by noting its striking similarities to that of Andreas Osiander, a colleague of Luther's who was excluded for his idiosyncratic view of justification.[49] Furthermore, the Finnish scholars place most of the burden for their interpretation on Luther's pre-1520 works, which do not reflect his mature teaching.[50]

Closely related is what we could call a new interpretation of Calvin, associated especially with T. F. Torrance and James B. Torrance. Like Mannermaa on the Lutheran side, Thomas Torrance was a pioneer in the mainline Reformed-Orthodox conversations and displayed a pronounced antipathy toward Augustine and the "Latin heresy" that he believed to pervade Western theology.[51] Like the Helsinki circle's take on Luther and Lutheranism, these scholars pit Calvin against the Calvinists. While Calvin (anticipating Karl Barth) emphasized the unconditional character of God's grace, they argue, his followers (especially the architects of "federal theology") reduced Reformed teaching to a contractual, conditional, and individualistic system. The covenant of works/covenant of grace scheme of Reformed scholasticism is essentially the same as Luther's law/gospel antithesis. Among other problems, this places the law before grace, as if there could be any relationship between God and human beings that was not based on grace.[52]

---

48. Veli-Matti Kärkkäinen, *One with God: Salvation as Deification and Justification*, Unitas Books (Collegeville, MN: Liturgical, 2004); Kärkkäinen, "Justification as Forgiveness of Sins and Making Righteous: The Ecumenical Promise of a New Interpretation of Luther," *One in Christ* 37, no. 2 (April, 2002): 32–45; Kärkkäinen, "The Ecumenical Potential of Theosis: Emerging Convergences between Eastern Orthodox, Protestant, and Pentecostal Soteriologies," *Sobornost/ Eastern Churches Review* 23, no. 2 (2002): 45–77; Kärkkäinen, "The Holy Spirit and Justification: The Ecumenical Significance of Luther's Doctrine of Justification," *Pneuma: The Journal of the Society for Pentecostal Studies* 24, no. 1 (2002): 26–39; "Salvation as Justification and Deification: The Ecumenical Potential of a New Perspective on Luther" in *Theology between West and East: Honoring the Radical Legacy of Professor Dr. Jan M. Lochman*, ed. Frank Macchia and Paul Chung (Eugene, OR: Cascade, 2002), 59–76.

49. Robert Kolb and Charles P. Arand, *The Genius of Luther's Theology: A Wittenberg Way of Thinking for the Contemporary Church* (Grand Rapids: Baker Academic, 2008), 48.

50. Carl R. Trueman, "Is the Finnish Line a New Beginning? A Critical Assessment of the Reading of Luther Offered by the Helsinki Circle," *Westminster Theological Journal* 65 (2003): 231–44. This issue is devoted to the new Finnish view, with critiques by Trueman, Mark Seifrid, and Paul Metzger, and a response by Robert Jenson, 245–50.

51. T. F. Torrance, "Karl Barth and the Latin Heresy" in *Karl Barth: Biblical and Ecumenical Theologian* (Edinburgh: T&T Clark, 1990).

52. The bibliography continues to grow, but here are the most seminal essays for and against the "Calvin vs. the Calvinists" thesis. Pro: James B. Torrance, "The Concept of Federal Theology,"

Although these highly revisionist interpretations of the Reformers have been either ignored or refuted by specialists, they continue to enjoy wide circulation mainly through scholars in other fields (such as philosophy, religion, and biblical studies). Douglas Campbell's interpretation of Paul, we will see, is formulated in opposition to the Reformers and "Justification theory," with pervasive and acknowledged dependence on the highly controversial theses of Thomas F. Torrance and James B. Torrance.

Like E. P. Sanders's Paul and Mannermaa's Luther, Torrance's Calvin is focused on union with Christ rather than justification. Albert Schweitzer argued in 1931 that justification was a "subsidiary crater" within a larger doctrine of union with Christ.[53] Affirming Schweitzer on this point, N. T. Wright observes, "If what mattered was being 'in Christ', rather than the logic-chopping debates about justification, then one was free to live out the life of Christ in new and different ways."[54] Many biblical scholars and theologians agree, including Richard Hays, Douglas Campbell, and Michael J. Gorman.[55] Michael Allen rightly judges, "In each case, the doctrine [of justification] is being juxtaposed with some notion of participation or deification, as if these are at odds."[56]

CONCLUSION

Individualism, Extrinsicism, Forensicism, Legalism. These and other unsavory epithets have become standard ways of dismissing the Reformation (at least Lutheran and Reformed orthodoxy) with one broad

in *Calvinus Sacrae Scripturae Professor*, ed. William H. Neuser (Grand Rapids: Eerdmans, 1994); Torrance, "Covenant or Contract," *Scottish Journal of Theology* 23, no. 1 (February 1970): esp. 53; cf. Basil Hall, "Calvin against the Calvinists," in *John Calvin*, ed. G. E. Duffield, Courtenay Studies in Reformation Theology (Appleford: Sutton Courtenay, 1966). Con: Richard A. Muller, *After Calvin: Studies in the Development of a Theological Tradition* (New York: Oxford University Press, 2004); cf. Carl Trueman and R. S. Clark, eds., *Protestant Scholasticism: Essays in Reassessment* (Carlisle: Paternoster, 1998); Paul Helm, *Calvin and the Calvinists* (Edinburgh: Banner of Truth Trust, 1982); Willem J. van Asselt and Eef Dekker, eds., *Reformation and Scholasticism: An Ecumenical Enterprise* (Grand Rapids: Baker Academic, 2001).

53. Albert Schweitzer, *The Mysticism of Paul the Apostle* (Baltimore: Johns Hopkins University Press, 1998), 138–40, 223–25.

54. Wright, *What Saint Paul Really Said*, 14.

55. Richard Hays, "Participation in Christ as the Key to Pauline Soteriology," in *the Faith of Jesus Christ: The Narrative Substructure of Galatians 3:1–4:11*, 2nd ed. (Grand Rapids: Eerdmans, 2002), xxix–xxxiii; Douglas Campbell, *Deliverance of God: An Apocalyptic Reading of Justification in Paul* (Grand Rapids: Eerdmans, 2010); Michael Gorman, *Inhabiting the Cruciform God: Kenosis, Justification, and Theosis in Paul's Narrative Soteriology* (Grand Rapids: Eerdmans, 2009).

56. Michael Allen, *Justification and the Gospel: Understanding the Contexts and Controversies* (Grand Rapids: Baker Academic, 2013), 37.

sweep. These challenges to a traditional Reformation understanding of justification come from diverse quarters and specializations. Yet there are important lines of convergence.

Most notably, they all trade on a decline narrative: the idea of a falling away from a relatively golden age or great thinker. Of course, in any such narrative there must be heroes and villains. My narrative is more complicated, as we will see. There is no golden age. Even the apostolic era was rife with schism, immorality and heresy, as the Epistles (and Revelation 2–3) attest.

I hope at least to challenge binaries and false choices both in historical descriptions of the Reformation's views and in exegetical and doctrinal conclusions. One test of a good theory is its resilience, despite anomalies, to wholesale abandonment. The fact that justification is one of the most hotly debated and controversial doctrines in biblical and theological scholarship today is a sign of the significance of the doctrine, however interpreted, in Scripture and tradition. The doctrine of justification is alive and well, even if traditional views of what it means are being challenged from all sides. Even those challenges become exciting opportunities to reconsider what we mean by the justification of the ungodly.

If I am not mistaken, some of the most extreme reactions and counterreactions have subsided or have moderated in recent years. Taking advantage of those calmer waters, I endeavor in these volumes to engage more constructively than polemically, assimilating important insights from critics as well as defending the enduring merits of the Reformation's exegetical, theological, and pastoral legacy.

CHAPTER 2

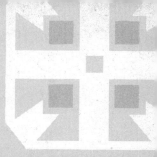

"O SWEET EXCHANGE!"

A Broader Lens for Discovering the Patristic Consensus

One of the earliest and most widely attested motifs in patristic literature with respect to justification is the "great exchange" between Christ and the believer. The phrase itself seems to originate with the anonymous late first- or early second-century *Epistle to Diognetus*: "In whom was it possible for us, the lawless and ungodly, to be justified, except in the Son of God alone? *O sweet exchange*, O the incomprehensible work of God, O the unexpected blessings, that the sinfulness of many should be hidden in one righteous person, while the righteousness of one should justify many sinners!"[1]

This chapter and the next progress in three concentric circles from general to specific matters: the great exchange, patristic interpretation of the main arguments in Paul's Letter to the Romans relative to our topic, and finally, common patterns in patristic statements about justification itself.

Beginning with the great exchange is helpful for several reasons. First, it provides a wider berth for integrating a broad range of images in the canonical Scriptures, for example:

- The domestic image of being washed and clothed in clean garments (e.g., Ezek 16:10–14; Zech 3; Matt 22:11–14; Rom 13:12–14; 1 Cor 15:51–54; 2 Cor 5:1–4; Gal 3:26–27; Eph 4:20–24; 6:10; Col 3:9–10, 12).

---

1. *The Epistle to Diognetus* 9:4–5, in *The Apostolic Fathers in English*, trans. and ed. Michael W. Holmes (Grand Rapids: Baker, 2006), 298.

- Economic language of crediting (Num 21:4–9; John 3:14–15). In fact, Romans 4 uses a mixture of crediting (Rom 4:3–12, 22) and inheriting (Rom 4:13–21).
- Both Old and New Testaments combine horticultural metaphors such as grafting (Ps 80:8–10; Isa 5:1–2; 2:21; 15:6; Mark 12:1–12; John 15; Rom 12:4–5; 1 Cor 6:15–16).
- Architectural images of building with Christ as the integrating feature (2 Sam 7:11; 1 Cor 3:9; Eph 4:11–16; Tim 3:15; 1 Pet 2:5).
- Marriage is a prominent term for the union of Yahweh with his people throughout Scripture, as are familial images more generally, especially adoption (Ezek 16:1–53; Hos 1:2; 11:1–12; 1 Cor 6:15–17; Eph 5:23–32; Rev 19:7, 9; 21:9).

Besides marital there are martial images of deliverance, victory, ransom and a truce established between enemies. In addition, there are cultic images of sacrifices, both of thanksgiving and of guilt (substituting the animal for the sinner's life).

We find pictures of feasting (between erstwhile enemies, no less), redemption from the slave market, the many judicial-political images of reckoning, declaring, judging, naming, and so forth. The public ratification-rites of circumcision and Passover, baptism and Eucharist, are treasure chests of the great exchange, laden with a rich variety of these images. Simon Gathercole observes, "There has perhaps been too much separation of images such as justification, forgiveness, and reconciliation when such a separation does not really seem to work with Paul; for him, one image often suggests another (Rom. 3:24–26; 5:8–9; 2 Cor. 5:17–21)."[2] Actually, the more that we recognize the distinct note struck by each element, the more likely we are to hear the symphony that clearly has justification as a recurring theme underlying and weaving in and out of the others. Instead of a central dogma, I suggest with John Murray that union with Christ is an umbrella motif covering all the elements in the application of redemption.[3] Union with Christ is simply another way of referring to the great exchange.

Second, the great exchange helps us to take our starting point not

---

2. Simon Gathercole, "The Doctrine of Justification in Paul and Beyond," in *Justification in Perspective; Historical Developments and Contemporary Challenges*, ed. Bruce L. McCormack (Grand Rapids: Baker Academic, 2006), 224–25.

3. John Murray, *Redemption Accomplished and Applied* (Grand Rapids: Eerdmans, 2015), 171–72.

from church-dividing differences over justification itself but from the consensus of teaching in the ancient church. The expanding cracks in that consensus during the Middle Ages and especially in the sixteenth century will occupy most of this volume. However, it is helpful, I think, to begin with a wider lens. In doing so, I hope to demonstrate that even in the patristic era the clearest articulations of the great exchange went hand-in-hand with clear affirmations of justification through faith alone apart from works. There have been ingenious ways of reconciling contradictory dogmatic formulations between Roman Catholic and Protestant traditions.[4] In my view, these fail either to persuade or to foster genuine agreement and therefore reconciliation. Yet the much older tradition of trading proof texts from Scripture and the ancient Christian writers has not quite proved terribly fruitful. The various schools of Pauline scholarship in the last century have only contributed more reductionisms and false choices to the history of justification interpretation. Taking a step back and exploring an uncontested formula may provide a better ecumenical starting point.

Third, taking the great exchange as our point of departure helps to identify justification as it is embedded in its own rich environment of election, redemption, adoption, the new creation, and glorification. It helps us to discern the unique role of justification, with its own varied scriptural images, in this great exchange.

Lutheran theologian Eberhard Jüngel argues that justification is the central dogma from which all others are deduced.[5] Even Catholic theologian Michael Schmaus declares, "All that Paul has to say about grace is summed up in the phrase 'justification of sinners.'"[6] If sound theology

---

4. One theory that I have in mind is developed in George Lindbeck's *The Nature of Doctrine* (Louisville: Westminster John Knox, 1984), which combines Wittgenstein's analysis of grammatical rules and Clifford Geerz's cultural-linguistic account of incommensurable systems.

5. Eberhard Jüngel, *Justification: The Heart of the Christian Faith*, trans. Jeffrey F. Cayzer (London: Bloomsbury, 2014), 15–49, though it is the main argument of the entire book. On p. 25 he critiques Martin Kähler's statement in that justification is "not a so-called principle from which one can logically deduce the whole of Christian knowledge without any specific preceding information." Instead, Kähler says, it is "a focal point of departure from which the connecting lines to all others actually flow" (*Die Wissenschaft der christlichen Lehre von dem evangelischen Grundartikel aus im Abrisse dargestellt*, 3rd ed. [1905; repr., Waltrop Spenner, 1994], 67). Jüngel's laudable defense of the doctrine's importance reflects a distinctly modern (nineteenth-century) method of seeking a central dogma from which all other doctrines can be deduced. It is clear enough that Luther himself came to his understanding of justification by searching for the God who is revealed in Scripture and in the process discovered the gift of righteousness *from* God that answers the righteousness *of* God by which he judges.

6. Michael Schmaus, *Dogma*, vol. 6, *Justification and Last Things* (London: Sheed and Ward, 1977), 46.

were produced by extrapolating the whole system from a central dogma, then justification might be a good candidate. Surely it is true that the God we know in Christ is none other than the one who justifies the wicked, that justification lies at the heart of what it means to be human *coram deo*, that the church is the community of sinful believers gathering to confess their sins and to receive absolution, and that justification is the eschatological verdict rendered here and now. However, elevating even justification to the role of a central dogma comes at a steep cost—to it and to the whole system of Christian teaching. First, in a trail of such modern projects, it reduces theology to anthropology, thereby abstracting justification from its grounding in the being of the triune God.[7] To be sure, we must not wait until everything else is set into place before talking about justification, since this eschatological act of God in Christ forces us to question our assumptions and well-reasoned conclusions. As Scripture interprets Scripture, so all doctrines must interpret the others, and justification is no exception—which is also why justification itself cannot be made the "hermeneutical category" by which all other doctrines are judged.[8] Second, the central dogma approach abstracts justification from the rich network of Christ's work and gifts that give to justification itself its basis, shape, and effect. Hence, the importance of focusing on the "great exchange," as the Reformers themselves did, as the broader horizon. Third, instead of establishing its significance, reducing all articles to justification leads eventually to the assimilation of sanctification to justification, which is really no different than the reverse assimilation. Analogous to God in a pantheistic framework, if justification is everything, then it is nothing—at least nothing distinct from everything else.

The central-dogma approach has led to various projects that have deduced their entire systems from the feeling of absolute dependence (Schleiermacher), God's moral kingdom (Ritschl), election (Barth),

---

7. John Webster, "*Rector et iudex super omnia genera doctrinarum?* The Place of the Doctrine of Justification," *What Is Justification About? Reformed Contributions to an Ecumenical Theme*, eds., Michael Weinrich and John P. Burgess (Grand Rapids: Eerdmans, 2009), 35. John Webster is surely correct when he says that "the ruler and judge over all other Christian doctrines is the doctrine of the Holy Trinity." "The doctrine of the Trinity is not one doctrine among others; it is both foundational and pervasive. To expound any Christian doctrine is to expound with varying degrees the directness the Trinity if the Trinity; to expound the doctrine of the Trinity in its full scope is to expound the entirety of Christian dogmatics."

8. Eberhard Jüngel, *Justification: The Heart of the Christian Faith*, trans. Jeffrey F. Cayzer (London: Bloomsbury, 2014), 47.

deliverance (Käsemann), sanctification (Roman Catholic and Anabaptist/Holiness traditions), and glorification (Orthodoxy).[9] Having exhausted the available loci as candidates for a "theology of . . ." with such marvelous erudition, it is hoped that we can now leave behind central dogmas and return to the premodern skill of thinking from the Trinity and attributes of God to God's works in creation, providence, and salvation (wherein justification attains its appropriately crucial position); the new creation and ecclesiology; and the final resurrection, judgment, and "life everlasting."

The Reformers did call justification "the article by which the church stands or falls," and this was no hyperbole in the heat of battle.[10] Nevertheless, it is anachronistic to assume that they had in mind a central-dogma theory that would only appear four centuries later. Far from deducing all articles from justification, Luther considered justification the precise articulation of what we mean when we say that "God was in Christ reconciling the world to himself" (2 Cor 5:19) through Christ's life, death, and resurrection. This is evident from the Smalcald Articles (pt. 2, art. 1) on "The Chief Article." Elsewhere he can define the gospel without even using the term: "The Word of God is the Gospel of God concerning his Son who was made flesh, suffered, rose from the dead, and was glorified through the Spirit who sanctifies."[11] Yet apart from justification, none of this matters for us.

---

9. By deducing I mean treating one idea as the fundamental principle from which all the other doctrines in a given system may be extrapolated. The other ideas don't have to be defended on their own terms but follow logically from the main idea.

10. Of the article of justification Luther famously declared, "The church stands, if this article stands, and the church falls, if it falls" (WA 40.3:352). Bucer called it the "chief article of religion" (quoted in Frank A. James III, introduction to *Predestination and Justification: Two Theological Loci*, trans. and ed. Frank A. James III, Peter Martyr Library 8 (Kirksville, MO: Sixteenth Century Essays & Studies, 2003), xxxiii. According to Calvin, it is "the primary article of the Christian religion," "the main hinge on which religion turns," "the principal article of the whole doctrine of salvation and the foundation of all religion" (*Inst.* 3.2.1; 3.11.1).

"For unless you first of all grasp what your relationship to God is, and the nature of his judgment concerning you, you have neither a foundation on which to establish your salvation nor one on which to build piety toward God," Calvin warns (*Inst.* 3.11.1). All the other abuses—pilgrimages, merits, satisfactions, penances, purgatory, tyranny, superstitions and idolatry—flow from this corruption of the faith at its source. According to Peter Martyr Vermigli, "This doctrine is the head, fountain, and mainstay of all religion. Therefore, we should be most sure and certain of this above all" (Vermigli, *Locus on Justification*, in *Predestination and Justification*, 96–97). When Luther speaks of the doctrine as the judge of other doctrines, he is suggesting that doctrines of free will, merit, etc. must surrender to this article. It would be anachronistic to impute a nineteenth-century historical method of "central dogma theory" to the Reformer.

11. Luther, "The Freedom of a Christian," in *LW* 34:346.

THE GREAT EXCHANGE: WIDENING THE SEMANTIC FIELD

Even in pre-Christian Judaism there are intimations of certain aspects of the great exchange. "Surely justification is of God," according to the Qumran community (1QS 11:9–15).

> If I stumble, God's loving-kindness forever shall save me. If through sin of the flesh I fall, my justification will be by the righteousness of God which endures for all time. . . . Through his love he has brought me near, by his loving-kindness shall he provide my justification . . . and through His exceeding goodness shall he atone for all my sins. By his righteousness shall he cleanse me of human defilement.[12]

Righteousness is a divinely-given status here, identified as "justification," with the consequence of cleansing from defilement (sanctification). To be sure, this is far from a *doctrine* of justification, and there are numerous contrary formulas to this one in the Qumran community alone. Nevertheless, it evinces a conviction that the great exchange conveys so richly.

Turning to the earliest Christian writings, we come first to the Odes of Solomon, a mostly complete copy of which was discovered in 1909. Note the bridal imagery and wide range of images in this collection of Jewish Christian hymns from sometime in the first or second century:

> I love the Beloved [and] have been *united to him*. . . . The Lord *renewed me with his garment* and *possessed me* by his Light. And from above he *gave me immortal rest*, and I became like the land which blossoms and rejoices in its fruits. . . . I have *put on incorruption* through his name, and *stripped off corruption by his grace. Death has been destroyed* before my face, and *Sheol has been vanquished*. . . . [E]*ternal life* has arisen in the Lord's land, and it has become known to his faithful ones, and been given without limit *to all that trust in him*. . . . I was *justified by my Lord*, for my salvation is incorruptible. . . . *My chains*

12. Michael Wise, Martin Abegg, Jr., and Edward Cook, trans., *A New Translation of the Dead Sea Scrolls* (New York: HarperOne, 2005), 143. I am grateful to Shane Rosenthal for this and the following reference.

were cut off by his hands . . . and I walked in him and was saved. . . .
Glory to you, our Head, O Lord Messiah. . . . I became mighty in
your truth and holy in your righteousness. . . . *He justified me by his
grace, for I believed in the Lord's Messiah.*[13]

The inclusion of such varied aspects of redemption in union with the
Beloved is striking.

I referred to *The Epistle to Diognetus* as the first mention of the precise
phrase "sweet exchange." The passage is worth quoting at length:

So then, having already planned everything in his mind together
with his Son . . . he took upon himself our sins; he himself gave
up his own Son as a ransom for us, the holy one for the lawless, the
guiltless for the guilty, the just for the unjust, the incorruptible for
the corruptible, the immortal for the mortal. For what else but his
righteousness could have covered our sins? In whom was it possible
for us, the lawless and ungodly, to be justified, except in the Son
of God alone? O sweet exchange, O the incomprehensible work of
God, O the unexpected blessings, that the sinfulness of many should
be hidden in one righteous person, while the righteousness of one
should justify many sinners! Having demonstrated, therefore, in the
former time the powerlessness of our nature to obtain life, and having now revealed the Savior's power to save even the powerless, he
willed that for both these reasons we should believe in his goodness
and regard him as nurse, father, teacher, counselor, healer, mind,
light, honor, glory, strength, and life, and not be anxious about food
and clothing.[14]

Ignatius (martyred c. 107) says that he is "not therefore justified"
by the sufferings he has encountered but by Christ.[15] Polycarp, another
early second-century martyr, writes in his Epistle to the Philippians,
"Let us then continually persevere in our hope, and the earnest of our
righteousness, which is Jesus Christ, 'who bore our sins in his own body
on the tree'" and "endured all things for us, that we might live in Him."[16]

---

13. James H. Charlesworth, "Odes of Solomon," in *The Old Testament Pseudepigrapha*, ed.
J. H. Charlesworth, (Garden City, NY: Doubleday, 1985), 2:735–61.

14. *The Epistle to Diognetus* 9:1–6.

15. *The Epistle of Ignatius to the Romans* 5 (*ANF* 1:75).

16. *The Epistle of Polycarp* 8 (*ANF* 1:35).

Irenaeus's classic text *Against Heresies* (c. 175) returns frequently to the great exchange with expansive breadth. In fact, Irenaeus's entire soteriology can be characterized as a discourse on this motif, as Christ recapitulates (literally reheadships) the history of Adam, undoing his transgression and becoming the head of his new humanity.[17] Everything that Christ accomplished in his humiliation and glorification recapitulates what was lost under the first covenant with Adam (which Irenaeus even calls a "legal covenant"). What is lost is not only recovered but is exceeded in the "evangelical covenant." After all, Jesus not only undoes Adam's sin but wins the prize of immortality and everlasting glory that Adam fell short of attaining as covenant head. "For the law," Irenaeus says, "merely made sin to stand out in relief, but did not destroy it." What we required, being human, was God himself to assume a human nature to save us.[18]

Jesus showed himself to be the Word of God not only in his incarnate life, says Irenaeus, "but also by means of His passion." Adding the "two trees" to the exchange imagery, he writes,

> For doing away with that disobedience of man which had taken place at the beginning by the occasion of a tree, "He became obedient unto death, even the death of the cross"; rectifying that disobedience which had occurred by reason of a tree, through that obedience which was [wrought out] upon the tree [of the cross]. . . . In the second Adam, however, we are reconciled, being made obedient even unto death. For we were debtors to none other but to Him whose commandment we had transgressed at the beginning. . . . For this cause, too, did Christ die, that the Gospel covenant being manifested and known to the whole world, might in the first place set free His slaves; and then afterwards, as I have already shown, might constitute them heirs of His property, when the Spirit possesses them by inheritance.[19]

Once more, the untroubled jumbling of distinct but related aspects of salvation is remarkable especially against the backdrop of contemporary tendencies toward false dichotomies. While each aspect retains its

---

17. *Haer.* 3.18.7 (*ANF* 1:448).
18. *Haer.* 3.18.2–7 (*ANF* 1:445–48).
19. *Haer.* 5.16.3 and 5.9.3 (*ANF* 1:544, 535).

distinct character, there is no choice between incarnation and Christus Victor images over against a cross-centered emphasis on vicarious sacrifice (a typical contrast in modern characterizations of the East versus the West). Nor do these writers set forensic, covenantal, salvation-historical, and personal aspects over against transformative, relational, and apocalyptic-cosmic ones.

Since "We neither please God with good deeds nor atone for our sins," counsels Cyprian (third century), "let us of our inmost heart and of our entire mind ask for God's mercy."[20] He adds, "Believe and live," for "the approach to God's mercy is open, and the access is easy to those who seek and apprehend the truth."

> This grace Christ bestows; this gift of his mercy he confers upon us, by overcoming death in the trophy of the cross, by redeeming the believer with the price of His blood, by reconciling man to God the Father, by quickening our mortal nature with a heavenly regeneration. If it be possible, let us all follow him; let us be registered in his sacrament and sign. He opens to us the way of life; he brings us back to paradise; he leads us on to the kingdom of heaven. [We are] made by him the children of God [therefore] we shall ever live with Him rejoicing.[21]

Even Origen of Alexandria (184–253) argues that "since [Paul] want[s] to show that God gives the inheritance of the promises not as something due but through grace, he says that the inheritance from God is granted to those who believe, not as a debt of a wage but as the gift of faith."[22] Not even faith merits grace, since "even the very faith by which we seem to believe in God is confirmed in us as a gift of grace."[23] Death is the penalty for sin. "But because Christ, erasing this IOU with his own blood, affixed it to his own cross, we ought to be crucified according to the old man, who was subject to sin, so that 'the body of sin may be destroyed and we might no longer be enslaved to sin.'"[24] "King Sin" gives its wages—death. "But it was not worthy of God to

---

20. Cyprian, *The Epistles of Cyprian* 7.2 (*ANF* 1:286).
21. Cyprian, *The Epistles of Cyprian* 7.2 (*ANF* 1:286).
22. Origen, *Commentary on the Epistle to the Romans*, vol. 1, *Books 1–5*, trans. Thomas P. Scheck (Washington, DC: Catholic University of America Press, 2001), 258–59.
23. Origen, *Commentary on the Epistle to the Romans, Books 1–5*, 259.
24. Origen, *Commentary on the Epistle to the Romans, Books 1–5*, 364.

give his soldiers wages as something owed, but as a gift and a grace, which is 'eternal life in Christ Jesus our Lord.'"[25] Origen joins marital to martial metaphors, especially in his *Commentary on the Song of Songs*. "The *myrrh* signifies his death He underwent, alike as Priest for the People and as Bridegroom for the Bride. . . . 'The fragrance of Thine ointments'—that is, the spiritual and mystical meaning—'is above all spices' of moral and natural philosophy."[26]

A half-century later, patriarch of Constantinople John Chrysostom observed,

> For it was not as much as we must have to do away the sin only, that we received of His grace, but even far more. For we were at once freed from punishment and put off all iniquity and were also born again from above (John 3:3) and [we] rose again with the old man buried, and were redeemed, justified, led up to adoption, sanctified, made brothers of the Only-begotten, and joint heirs and of the one Body with Him, and counted for His Flesh, and even as a Body with the Head, so were we united unto Him![27]

Chrysostom even distinguishes justification and sanctification here. Elsewhere he rhapsodizes on the great exchange: a grace that "has allowed Him that did no wrong to be punished for those who had done wrong. . . . Him that was righteousness itself, 'He made sin,' that is allowed Him to be condemned as a sinner, as one cursed to die" so that we might be not just "'righteous,' but 'righteousness,' indeed 'the righteousness of God.'"[28]

> For this is the righteousness of God, when we are justified not by works, in which case it would be necessary that not even a spot should be found, but by grace, in which case all sin is done away. And this, at the time that it does not allow us to be lifted up (for it is entirely the free gift of God), teaches us also the greatness of what

---

25. Origen, *Commentary on the Epistle to the Romans, Books 6–10*, 17.

26. Origen, *The Song of Songs, Commentary and Homilies*, ed. R. P. Lawson, Ancient Christian Writers 26 (New York: Paulist, 1957), 72–73.

27. Chrysostom, *The Epistle to the Romans*, in NPNF[1] 11:403.

28. Chrysostom, *Homilies on 2 Corinthians* 11.5, as cited in Nick Needham, "Justification in the Early Church Fathers," in *Justification in Perspective*, ed. Bruce McCormack (Grand Rapids: Baker Academic, 2006), 35.

is given. For what came before was a righteousness of the law and of works, but his is the righteousness of God.[29]

Athanasius's *On the Incarnation of the Word* (318) is replete with references to the great exchange. The familiar distinction between Greek (deification-centered) and Latin (sacrifice-centered) theologies is yet another modern construct in the search for a central dogma.[30] Athanasius says, for example, "The Word became flesh in order *both* to offer this sacrifice *and* that we, participating in His Spirit, might be deified."[31]

Augustine also made ample use of the exchange motif. He observes in the *Confessions* (c. 398),

> But the true Mediator . . . Christ Jesus appeared between mortal sinners and the immortal Just One . . . because the reward of righteousness is life and peace, [that] He might, by righteousness . . . cancel the death of justified sinners, which He willed to have in common with them. Hence He was pointed out to holy men of old; to the intent that they, through faith in His Passion to come, even as we through faith in that which is past, might be saved.[32]

In the following section, the bishop of Hippo jumbles together metaphors: "Victor and Victim," "Priest and Sacrifice," who provides "medicine" to heal "my infirmities," and who was made flesh so that we might not "despair of ourselves."[33] Soon thereafter Christ is "my ransom."[34] Only in union with Christ can the fruit of good works blossom. As he writes elsewhere, "A wheel does not run nicely in order that it may be round, but because it is round."[35]

---

29. Chrysostom, *Homilies on 2 Corinthians* 11.5.

30. Gustav Aulén's *Christus Victor* (1930; repr., New York: Macmillan, 1958) encouraged this typology, but it belongs to a more general approach in nineteenth- and early twentieth-century historiography. In this approach, one identifies a central idea from which an entire system is ostensibly deduced. Inevitably the method is susceptible to distortion particularly by abstracting ideas from their historical development and contexts and also by its tendency to exaggerate contrasts between systems based on their different governing idea. There are clear signs of this tendency in much of biblical scholarship as well, not least in Douglas Campbell's *The Deliverance of God*.

31. Athanasius, *De decritus* 14, emphasis added, quoted in J. N. D. Kelly, *Early Christian Doctrines*, rev. ed. (Peabody, MA: Prince, 2004), 277n2.

32. Augustine, *Confessions* 10.43.68 (*NPNF*[1] 1:162).

33. Augustine, *Confessions* 10.43.69 (*NPNF*[1] 1:162).

34. Augustine, *Confessions* 10.43.70 (*NPNF*[1] 1:162).

35. Augustine, "To Simplician," 1.2.3, in *Augustine: Earlier Writings*, ed. J. H. S. Burleigh (Louisville: Westminster John Knox, 1953), 388.

PATRISTIC ITINERARIES

Irenaeus of Lyons and Origen of Alexandria represent two distinct trajectories that weave in and out of each other in church history.[36] Though Origen opposed the Gnostics, he was profoundly shaped by the Alexandrian milieu that gave rise to Philo's Middle Platonism, Neoplatonism, and Gnosticism. This broader worldview presupposed an exit-return cosmology, with spiritual beings cascading down the ladder from the One to the lowest rungs of earthly matter.

In Origen's conception, a precreation rebellion of angelic and human souls accounts for their different levels of existence in this world—"and when they reach the neighborhood of the earth they are enclosed in grosser bodies, and last of all are tied to human flesh."[37] As they fell by their free will, they can ascend the ladder by the same and merit union with God. The purpose of this life is moral and intellectual education. Christ is chiefly a source of enlightenment who by his example leads us on our contemplative and ethical ascent from the lower world to reunion with the One, shedding our human carapace.[38] Eventually, all souls, even Lucifer, will reach the One again, although another fall is always possible. Just as this world was preceded by many, it will be succeeded by many as well. In every case, the journey follows a circular pattern, and "the end is like the beginning."[39]

A disciple of Polycarp, who is believed to have been a disciple of the apostle John, Irenaeus is remembered for his antignostic treatise *Against Heresies*. So it is not surprising that he counters their fatal dichotomies between Yahweh and Christ, Old and New Testaments, matter and spirit, and lower and upper worlds. Over against Origen's exit-return cosmology, Irenaeus follows the promise-fulfillment pattern that he finds from Genesis to the Apocalypse. Thus, the end can never be like

---

36. I documented their approaches on key points relative to our topic in Michael Horton, "Atonement and Ascension," in *Locating Atonement: Explorations in Constructive Dogmatics*, ed. Oliver Crisp and Fred Sanders (Grand Rapids: Zondervan Academic, 2015), 226–50.

37. Origen, *On First Principles*, trans. G. W. Butterworth (Gloucester, MA: Peter Smith, 1973), 1.4.1 (41).

38. For example, we might compare Origen (*On First Principles* 2.10.3.) and Irenaeus (*Haer.* 5.9.4–5.10.2) on their interpretation of 1 Corinthians 15:50, where Paul declares that "flesh and blood cannot enter the kingdom of God, nor does the perishable inherit the imperishable." Both reject gnostic interpretation, but Irenaeus emphasizes that Paul is not contrasting physical body and immaterial soul but ungodly and godly. In the resurrection the Spirit will *restore* our flesh and blood and in fact bestow immortal glory (5.13.1–3). Origen, however, invokes trichotomy and is ambiguous about the nature of the resurrected body (2.11.2; 3.6.2).

39. Origen, *On First Principles*, 1.6.2 (53).

the beginning, since the glory of our inheritance in Christ as our head is far more glorious than anything that we possessed in Adam.

These radical differences were certain to produce varying approaches to justification. In the closing years of the fourth century, Anastasius bishop of Rome wrote a letter to the bishop of Jerusalem praising the condemnation of Origen's teachings by a synod in Egypt.[40] Nevertheless, Origen remained a respected figure by many, and through Evagrius of Pontus and other disciples, Origenism became a major impetus for monasticism, and through that movement it continued to exercise an enormous influence on Eastern and Western theologies.[41] Einar Molland observes,

> In all the works of Origen there is hardly a passage where he conceives of the relation of the Law and Gospel in the Pauline terms of *nomos* and *charis*, the role of the Law being to convince mankind of sin and bring all men under the judgment of God, whereas redemption comes by Grace through the Gospel. . . . Origen thus conceives of the difference and contradiction of the Law and the Gospel in quite other terms than those of judgement and grace, viz., in the terms of imperfect and perfect religion.[42]

Irenaeus of Lyons discussed justification in the wider context of the doctrine mentioned above: *anakephalaiosis* (recapitulation; literally "reheadshiping"). As we have inherited death, condemnation, and corruption in Adam, we have inherited life, justification, and freedom

---

40. Scheck explains, "The pope virtually anathematized Rufinus (Origen's translator) and claimed that Origen's object was to disintegrate the Christian faith. . . . A century and a half later in 543, the Emperor Justinian (527–65) issued an edict denouncing Origen by name. A list of his doctrines was formally condemned at the Fifth Ecumenical Council in 553. . . . Among the condemned doctrines were his Christological subordinationism; his eschatological speculation, which included the conjecture that all rational beings including Satan and the demons may eventually be restored to grace; the doctrine of pre-existence of souls; his theory about previous worlds and future world cycles; his speculation that the final state of salvation may be disembodied; and his purgatorial understanding of hell. . . . In spite of posthumous anathematizations against him, his condemnation never really 'took.'" Scheck, introduction to *Commentary on the Epistle to the Romans, Books 1–5*, by Origen, trans. Thomas P. Scheck (Washington, DC: Catholic University of America Press, 2001), 6–7.

Especially in recent years the status of this council has been questioned, although it has been regarded traditionally as an ecumenical council particularly in the East. One scholar who questions the status on historical grounds is Richard Price, *The Acts of the Council of Constantinople of 553—2 Vol Set: With Related Texts on the Three Chapters Controversy* (Liverpool: Liverpool University Press, 2009), 270–86.

41. See Joseph W. Trigg, *Origen*, Early Church Fathers (London: Routledge, 1998), 63–66.

42. Scheck, introduction to *Commentary on the Epistle to the Romans, Books 1–5*, by Origen, 22, quoted 23, from Einar Molland *The Conception of the Gospel in the Alexandrian Theology* (Oslo: J. Dybwad, 1938), 121.

in Christ. As Michael Schmaus observes, justification was associated with sonship by Origen's predecessor, Clement of Alexandria, while the fourth-century Cappadocian fathers (Gregory of Nazianzus, Gregory of Nyssa, and Basil of Caesarea) introduced the motif of "deification." "In the translation of Platonic ideas to the realm of Christian teaching on salvation, the scriptural texts concerning the only-begotten Son of God (Jn. 1:14), the firstborn among many brothers (Rom. 8:29; Col. 1:15), and the indwelling of the Spirit became the foundation of the deification theory."[43] For Origen, justification is being "made just through the indwelling Christ, who is justice."[44]

Origen undeniably launched a tradition in exegesis at odds in important respects with other streams in the patristic era. "Thus, because Origen conceives justification to be an effective sanctification in which sin is expelled and grace is established in the believer's soul, it cannot be attributed to faith alone. . . . On the other hand, there are striking statements in Origen's *Commentary* where Origen insists that justification is by faith alone."[45] Throughout, he strongly desires to discourage indifference toward good works. "For the gift of forgiveness is not a license to sin, since forgiveness applies to *past sins, not future ones*."[46] For him, the Pauline phrase "works of the law" refers to boundary markers.[47] Origen also launched the first arguments in favor of purgatory and levels of being based on merit—views rejected in the Christian East and West until the High Middle Ages, as we will see.

We may identify the Irenaean trajectory as a theology of *redemption*, focused on Christ's descent in the flesh and ascent in the flesh carrying us in his train by the work of the Holy Spirit to share in his exalted humanity. And we may identify the Origenist trajectory as a theology of *ascent*, away from this world and its bodily history, through therapeutic contemplation and moral rigor.

Intersecting like two rivers, Origenist and Irenaean thought flows in and out of each other in both Eastern and Western theologies. As we

---

43. Michael Schmaus, *Dogma*, vol. 6, *Justification and Last Things* (London: Sheed and Ward, 1977), 46–47.

44. Scheck, introduction to *Commentary on the Epistle to the Romans, Books 1–5*, by Origen, 26.

45. Scheck, introduction to *Commentary on the Epistle to the Romans, Books 1–5*, by Origen, 37, 39.

46. Scheck, introduction to *Commentary on the Epistle to the Romans, Books 1–5*, by Origen, 41, emphasis added.

47. Scheck, introduction to *Commentary on the Epistle to the Romans, Books 1–5*, by Origen, 41–42.

will see later, Luther and Calvin identify explicitly with Irenaeus over Origen. The Reformers had no difficulty affirming glorification (even designating it "deification") but with eschatological participation in Christ as the grounds and justification as the legal basis. While they appealed to Irenaeus frequently, the Protestant Reformers were sharply critical of Origen, as we will see.[48]

Other differences emerged in later centuries, two of which are worth mentioning here. The first is the Byzantine (Greek) distinction between essence and energies.[49] According to this position, there can be no such thing as "created grace" (a category that emerged through Thomas Aquinas). Grace is never *something* (a creaturely substance) but always the activity of *someone* (the triune God, especially the Holy Spirit).[50] Second, and related to the first point, the East lacks the notion of a created habit ("supernatural grace" or *donum superadditum*) added to Adam's nature to keep him from falling. The Latin view of the fall is actually weak, according to the East (which is ironic given the usual Western judgment that the East is "soft" on sin, especially in its rejection of the doctrine of original sin). What has been lost, after all, but the supernatural gift added to nature? Speaking for the Greek view, Vladimir Lossky says that the fall is not only a removal of an original sanctifying justice but a corruption of *human nature* as such. "The deprivation of Grace is not the cause," Lossky says, "but rather the consequence of the decadence of

48. Scheck observes, "In the *Commentary* Origen uses the expression, or an approximation of the expression, 'justification by faith alone,' on numerous occasions, both approvingly and disapprovingly. These passages were hotly disputed during the age of the Reformation. The magisterial Protestants (Luther, Melanchthon, Calvin, Beza) cited the texts in which Origen repudiated the 'formula' of 'justification by faith alone' to show that Origen was no true Christian but a Pelagian or even a pagan" (Scheck, introduction to *Commentary on the Epistle to the Romans, Books 1–5*, by Origen, 33).

49. Origen, *Commentary on the Epistle to the Romans, Books 6–10*, 138. Origen wrote, "We even need to realize that it is one thing for there potentially to be existence in a subject, it is another thing for it to be in actuality or effectual achievement, what the Greeks call *dunamis* and *energeia*." However, this distinction appears to be owing more to Aristotelian than Platonic/ Neoplatonic influences. See David Bradshaw, *Aristotle East and West: Metaphysics and the Division of Christendom* (Cambridge: Cambridge University Press, 2007). As Roman Catholic theologian Michael Schmaus summarizes the Western view, "When [God] broke through his own transcendence to create a reality distinct from himself, this was an act of grace, insofar as it was an act of love and mercy" (Schmaus, *Dogma*, 6:xiv). "The medieval theologians coined the term 'supernatural' grace," Schmaus adds. "It will be recalled that the word 'supernatural' became current, although in a different sense, in the circle of Neoplatonic theologians around the year 500. In the modern sense, 'supernatural' does not simply express the transcendence of God; it goes beyond that to say that the life to which God has ultimately destined man cannot evolve out of the resources of man's own nature but can only be received as a gift from God. Supernatural grace means the call man has received from God to share in his own tripersonal life" (x–xi).

50. Vladimir Lossky, *The Mystical Theology of the Eastern Church* (Crestwood, NY: St. Vladimir's Seminary Press, 1976), 88–89, 132.

our nature."[51] Greek soteriology sees salvation as the healing of human nature through Christ's incarnation, life, death, resurrection, and ascension, which brings immortality and sharing in Christ's glory.

Despite their differences, both East and West are indebted to the system of Pseudo-Dionysius, a Syrian monk of the late fifth or early sixth centuries, who until the fifteenth century was thought to have been the philosopher converted by Paul's speech in Athens (Acts 17:34). Subsequently, though by no means due exclusively to his influence, medieval/Byzantine writers considered justification a process of renewal and deification. The focus became the salvation of the interior individual (the soul or intellect) by earnest effort enabled by God's supply of grace. To the extent that the Dionysian paradigm reigned, salvation was generally viewed in terms of the Neoplatonic-Origenist ascent of the soul through purgation and contemplation toward union with God. Outside the monastery, the average layperson could ascend this ladder through the ministrations of the ecclesiastical hierarchy. Hence, the importance of the system of penance that will emerge in the Carolingian era. Irenaeus's biblical theology, focused on recapitulation, remained faintly legible beneath the elaborate Dionysian overwriting.

READING ROMANS: ORIGEN TO AUGUSTINE

Moving from the wider circle of the great exchange, the remainder of this chapter heads toward the target—justification—by way of one more concentric circle: patristic engagement with Paul's Letter to the Romans. After all, the long debate over justification can be described in general terms as a debate over this famous epistle, a debate that I will join in volume 2, but will here attend to the earliest commentators.

Origen (c. 184–253)

Earlier Christian writers peppered and sanctioned their teaching with appeals to Romans, but the honor goes to Origen for the first extant commentary on the entire epistle, composed around 246. In contrast with his more speculative theological treatise *On First Principles* (*Peri Archo̅n*), the Romans commentary displays Origen's exegetical skill, with rare knowledge of Hebrew as well as the Greek Septuagint. Many of

---

51. Lossky, *Mystical Theology*, 132. This formulation reflects some convergence with the doctrine of original sin, despite the rejection of this doctrine by the Christian East.

his earlier speculations (especially the schematic significance of his tripartite anthropology) remain evident, but they are in the background.

He acknowledges in the preface that Paul "makes use of expressions which sometimes are confused and insufficiently explicit," which heretics employ to teach that "the cause of each person's actions is not to be attributed to one's own purpose but to different kinds of natures." "And, from a handful of words from this letter they attempt to subvert the meaning of the whole of Scripture, which teaches that God has given man freedom of will."[52] The heretics he has in mind are the Gnostics and pagans who deny human freedom due to the "natures" produced by the stars.[53] For Marcion and his ilk, there is no continuity between the God of Israel and the God we meet in Jesus Christ; Origen's more polemical remarks must be seen in that light as he emphasizes continuity between the law (as Old Testament) and the gospel or "new law" (as New Testament) and personal responsibility and freedom over against astral fatalism.[54]

After arraigning the gentiles' idolatry, immorality, and superstition (well-known to Origen in his Alexandrian context), Paul turns to the Jews who boast in "the works of the law." Like the gentiles, who "by covenant" are also under the natural law, Jews have failed to keep it in its written form as the Torah. However, the Neoplatonist anthropology shapes Origen's understanding of "flesh" and "spirit," with "the works

---

52. Origen, *Commentary on the Epistle to the Romans, Books 1–5*, 53.

53. For example, the Gnostics apparently appealed to Paul's opening statement about being set apart for the gospel from his mother's womb "because goodness was inherent in his nature; just as, in contrast, it says in the Psalms of those who are evil in nature, 'For they have been set apart as sinners from the womb'" (Origen, *Commentary on the Epistle to the Romans, Books 1–5*, 64). Thus, according to the Gnostics, sin is not a universal condition into which all of humanity, created naturally good, has fallen, but is something essential to some natures as good is to others. Later, in considering Romans 6:16, he observes, "Therefore we ought always to remember these things and not bring forth worthless complaints as an excuse for sin: 'I sinned because the devil made me do it!' or, 'under the compulsion of nature!' or, 'my fated condition!' or, '[I sinned due to] the course of the stars!' Rather, listen to the frank opinion of Paul in which he says, 'To whom you present yourselves for obedience as slaves, you are the slaves of the one whom you obey, either of sin or of righteousness'" (Origen, *Commentary on the Epistle to the Romans, Books 6–10*, 7). Philo's most emphatic defenses of human responsibility are similarly provoked by pagan dualism.

54. Ironically, Scheck properly cautions against interpreting Origen in the light of Augustine-Pelagius, much less the Reformation debate, while nevertheless treating the magisterial Reformers as heirs of the Marcionites and Gnostics (Scheck, introduction to *Commentary on the Epistle to the Romans*, 23). But it's quite clear that the heretics were saying something quite different from the Reformers. Anyone who is open at least to the historical sources, as I note in the following chapter, will recognize that, if anything, the Reformers (especially Calvin) are critical of the *medieval* position for espousing a kind of Manichean attribution of sin to nature as such, and they emphasize, over against Anabaptism, the continuity of Old and New Testaments. In both cases, Calvin and his colleagues are especially exemplary of both these points.

of the law" falling on the former side of the ledger. "For as long as a person *lives in the body*, he cannot be justified or declared righteous, but [only] when he *departs from the body* and leaves the struggle of this life."[55] Those who merely follow the Mosaic commands are merely "worthless servants," but the one who "has fulfilled the commands *and adds to them this as well, that he preserves the state of virginity*, he is no longer a worthless servant but will be called a good and faithful one."[56] It seems extreme for Paul to say that "no one does good," Origen says. "It does not seem to me that the Apostle Paul wanted to make such an incredible assertion." Rather he means that "no one has brought it to perfection and entire completion."[57] "'By works of the law, therefore, shall no flesh be justified in his sight,' should be understood, in my opinion, that nothing that is flesh and that lives according to the flesh can be justified by the law of God."[58]

Thus, in Romans 3:20, Paul is merely opposing the inferior natural law to Torah. He is *not* saying, as do the heretics, that "these are justified . . . not by works but by the grace of God, through the redemption accomplished for them by Jesus Christ himself."[59] Rather, the apostle is saying merely that the law of Moses "surpasses and rises above" the law of nature.[60] The natural law revealed God as Creator.

> But because all had come under sin, doubtless they were likewise estranged from the glory of God because they were able neither to receive it in any respect whatsoever nor to merit it. . . . Therefore the righteousness of God through faith in Jesus Christ reaches to all who believe, whether they are Jews or Greeks. It justifies those who have been cleansed from their past crimes and makes them capable of receiving the glory of God; and it supplies this glory not for the sake of their merits nor for the sake of works, but freely to those who believe. . . . He gave himself as the redemption price.[61]

---

55. Origen, *Commentary on the Epistle to the Romans, Books 1–5*, 194–95, emphasis added.

56. Origen, *Commentary on the Epistle to the Romans, Books 1–5*, 196.

57. Origen, *Commentary on the Epistle to the Romans, Books 1–5*, 197.

58. Origen, *Commentary on the Epistle to the Romans, Books 1–5*, 206–7.

59. Origen, *Commentary on the Epistle to the Romans, Books 1–5*, 209.

60. Origen, *Commentary on the Epistle to the Romans, Books 1–5*, 210–11. Paul's first mention of *nomos* (law) is anarthrous, but the second has a definite article. Natural law (general revelation) does not reveal that Christ is the Son of God, for example. "This righteousness of God, therefore, which is Christ, is indeed disclosed apart from the natural law, but not apart from the law of Moses or the prophets. . . . It is therefore apart from this law that the righteousness of God, which is Christ, has been disclosed, attested by the law of Moses and the prophets" (Origen, *Commentary on the Epistle to the Romans, Books 1–5*, 213–14).

61. Origen, *Commentary on the Epistle to the Romans, Books 1–5*, 215.

Being "cleansed from their *past* crimes" recurs throughout the commentary. When Origen affirms justification by grace (even by the gift of Christ's merits), it is always with respect to sins before conversion. With the slate wiped clean, believers can now pursue holiness, attaining the merit needed for final glory.

When Paul speaks of "propitiation in his blood," Origen repeats his claim that "he forgives them their *past* sins." "For God is just, and the one who is just could not justify the unjust; for that reason he wanted there to be the mediation of a propitiator so that those who were not able to be justified through their own works might be justified through faith in him."[62] He turns to Exodus and Leviticus to determine the meaning of a "propitiatory," both in relation to the ark of the covenant and the sacrifices.[63] Jesus is "the propitiatory and priest and sacrifice which is offered for the people. . . . And this propitiation comes to every believer by way of faith."[64]

Hence, Paul's appeal to Abraham: "Now if Abraham believed and was justified by faith, doubtless it will be logical that even now whoever believes in God through faith in Jesus Christ would be justified with the believer Abraham. . . . He is saying that the justification of faith alone suffices, so that the one who only believes is justified, even if he has not accomplished a single work."[65] Then it is reasonable to ask, "'Who has been justified by faith alone without works of the law?'" He mentions the thief on the cross and the woman who anointed Jesus's feet in Luke 7:37–39.[66] However, one should be warned that "the remission is not given for future crimes, *but only past ones.* Now then let us return to our theme. A human being is justified through faith; the works of the law contribute nothing to his being justified."[67]

Note that even Origen, despite his own primary theological convictions, recognizes that Paul clearly teaches justification through faith alone, apart from works. Despite heavy-handed qualifications (such as "remission for past crimes, not future ones"), he cannot draw another conclusion from the text. In fact, he draws connections to other passages. In Jesus's parable from Luke 18:11–13, the publican embraced

---

62. Origen, *Commentary on the Epistle to the Romans, Books 1–5,* 216–17, emphasis added.
63. Origen, *Commentary on the Epistle to the Romans, Books 1–5,* 217–23.
64. Origen, *Commentary on the Epistle to the Romans, Books 1–5,* 223.
65. Origen, *Commentary on the Epistle to the Romans, Books 1–5,* 225–26.
66. Origen, *Commentary on the Epistle to the Romans, Books 1–5,* 226–27.
67. Origen, *Commentary on the Epistle to the Romans, Books 1–5,* 228, emphasis added.

"the humility of the cross of Christ," while the Pharisee boasted in his works. As for us, "Who will legitimately boast about his own chastity when he reads what is written, 'anyone who has looked at a woman to lust after her has already committed adultery with her in his heart?'"[68]

What is the "law of works" that Paul opposes to the "law of faith"? Is it the law of Moses and the natural law? Letter versus Spirit? Whatever we conclude, says Origen, boasting must be excluded because Jews and Greeks alike are justified "in consideration of faith alone."[69] The law is not set aside by faith but fulfilled in Christ's advent.[70] Along with his concern to refute a Marcionite antithesis between Old and New Testaments is a frank acknowledgement of Paul's emphasis on the antithesis between faith and works on the point of justification. "Through this entire passage, then, the Apostle clearly makes known that there are two kinds of justification, one of which he designates as by works and the other by faith."[71]

At the same time, Origen qualifies his conclusion out of a dominating concern to avoid antinomianism. If works and faith cannot coexist in justification, neither can *sin* and faith. "Therefore the proof of true faith is that sin is not being committed."[72] The close attention to Paul *and* the quick qualification follow again when Origen comes to 4:13: "In faith there is the gift of the one who justifies; in works, however, there is the righteousness of the one who repays."[73] Nevertheless, "Faith cannot be reckoned as righteousness to one who believes in part, but only to him who believes completely and perfectly."[74] This justification by faith is "the beginning of being justified by God," Origen says, and such faith will "bring forth the fruit of works." "The root of righteousness, therefore, does not grow out of the works, but rather the fruit of works grows out of the root of righteousness, that root, of course, of righteousness which God also credits even apart from works."[75] Thus we have the beginnings of an exegetical tradition for both Tridentine and Reformation readings: justification as a process *and* works being the fruit rather than completion of justifying faith. "For he

---

68. Origen, *Commentary on the Epistle to the Romans, Books 1–5*, 228.
69. Origen, *Commentary on the Epistle to the Romans, Books 1–5*, 229–30.
70. Origen, *Commentary on the Epistle to the Romans, Books 1–5*, 236.
71. Origen, *Commentary on the Epistle to the Romans, Books 1–5*, 238.
72. Origen, *Commentary on the Epistle to the Romans, Books 1–5*, 239.
73. Origen, *Commentary on the Epistle to the Romans, Books 1–5*, 243.
74. Origen, *Commentary on the Epistle to the Romans, Books 1–5*, 244.
75. Origen, *Commentary on the Epistle to the Romans, Books 1–5*, 245.

is not speaking of righteous men when he says that faith is reckoned to them as righteousness. . . . Surely [Paul] is saying instead that faith is reckoned as righteousness for the one who did not have righteousness before he had this faith."[76]

Even if one could not be accused of having transgressed natural law, justification would not be given apart from faith. "For it is faith which is reckoned as righteousness," Origen observes.[77] After all, we are spiritually dead. "The coming of Christ found us in this condition, but he gave us life by his grace, as the same Apostle also says elsewhere, 'And when we were dead in our transgressions and sins, he raised us up together with him.'"[78] Interestingly, Origen does not seem to regard faith as needing to be perfected by love in order to justify. Faith is "the first beginnings and the very foundations of salvation; hope is certainly the progress and increase of the building; however love is the perfection and culmination of the entire work"—not of faith itself (as Aquinas will argue) but of salvation as a whole.[79]

Origen hardly ignores the story of Israel, wrapped around the Abrahamic promise. Because justification from past sins is by grace through faith alone, Abraham "becomes therefore a father of both peoples. Through faith he is a father of those who are uncircumcised; through the flesh, of those who are circumcised."[80] Paul even contrasts works and faith in terms of a wage versus "the inheritance of the promises not as something due but through grace" that is granted through "the gift of faith."[81] Not even faith merits grace, since the apostle says that "even the very faith by which we seem to believe in God is confirmed in us as a gift of grace."[82] The inheritance "is firm because it is not from the law but through grace."[83]

Yet the Neoplatonic dichotomy (inner/spiritual vs. outer/material) vies for control over his otherwise natural reading of the text.

> On this account, it seems to me, he says that the things which come through grace are even more firm than the things which come from

---

76. Origen, *Commentary on the Epistle to the Romans, Books 1–5*, 247.
77. Origen, *Commentary on the Epistle to the Romans, Books 1–5*, 262.
78. Origen, *Commentary on the Epistle to the Romans, Books 1–5*, 264.
79. Origen, *Commentary on the Epistle to the Romans, Books 1–5*, 268.
80. Origen, *Commentary on the Epistle to the Romans, Books 1–5*, 248.
81. Origen, *Commentary on the Epistle to the Romans, Books 1–5*, 258–59.
82. Origen, *Commentary on the Epistle to the Romans, Books 1–5*, 259.
83. Origen, *Commentary on the Epistle to the Romans, Books 1–5*, 260.

the law: because the latter are outside of us, whereas the former are within us; the latter consist of fragile material and thus can easily be rubbed off; the former things, however, are inscribed by the Spirit of God and, having been impressed in the depths of the soul, preserve their firmness forever.[84]

Origen seems to switch to the inner-outer dichotomy whenever he especially wants to avoid the Marcionite antithesis of Old and New Testaments. "No room is left for the interpretation that there is one God of the law, but that the Father of the Lord Jesus Christ is another."[85] As he moves further toward chapter 7, this correlation of old and new covenants with external observances (especially circumcision, dietary laws and Sabbaths) versus internal piety (purity of mind) dominates.

Although *at the moment of justification* the justified are ungodly, Origen gives no place to *simul iustus et peccator.* "For it is not possible that righteousness can be reckoned to a person who has any unrighteousness dwelling in him, even if he believes in him who raised the Lord Jesus from the dead."[86] Properly speaking, says Origen (commenting on Rom 5:9), it is not faith that justifies but the blood of Christ.[87] Enemies are reconciled, but in varying degrees, with the most worthy as "God's ultimate friends because of the merits of their virtues."[88] Salvation is never a one-size-fits-all proposition. Just as the differing ranks in this world are based on merits in the spiritual realm before creation, so too the ladder for final beatitude is based on merits.

Pelagius could appeal reasonably to some statements, but Origen does not reject "original sin" outright: "We have already said above that by means of Adam's transgression a certain access, as it were, was given by which sin, or the death of sin, or condemnation, spread to all men." Condemnation *is* death and vice versa.[89] On one occasion he can say, "So then Adam offered sinners a model through his disobedience; but Christ, in contrast, gave the righteous a model by his obedience."[90] Yet later he states, "For all of us human beings who have been conceived from the seed of a man coming together with a woman, must of necessity employ

---

84. Origen, *Commentary on the Epistle to the Romans, Books 1–5*, 261.
85. Origen, *Commentary on the Epistle to the Romans, Books 1–5*, 274–75.
86. Origen, *Commentary on the Epistle to the Romans, Books 1–5*, 275.
87. Origen, *Commentary on the Epistle to the Romans, Books 1–5*, 298.
88. Origen, *Commentary on the Epistle to the Romans, Books 1–5*, 299–300.
89. Origen, *Commentary on the Epistle to the Romans, Books 1–5*, 340.
90. Origen, *Commentary on the Epistle to the Romans, Books 1–5*, 344.

that utterance in which David says, 'in iniquities I have been conceived and in sins did my mother conceive me.'" Only Christ is excepted, for "he possessed in no respect whatsoever the contamination of sin, which is passed down to those who are conceived by the operation of lust."[91]

Origen continues to emphasize that justification through faith is merely the beginning. The final judgment constitutes the real moment of justification according to meritorious virtues. In Romans 5:17, Paul does not say that "life reigns" but "*will* reign" (βασιλεύσουσιν). When? After all, those who are saved finally are those who not only hear the word but obey it.

> For although it is promised that a person may eventually come out of prison, nevertheless it is ordained that no one can come out from there unless each one pays back even the last penny [Mt 5:26]. But if not even the penalty of one penny, which is that of the smallest sin, is remitted until it is atoned for in prison by means of punishments, how is it possible for someone to be set free by the hope of being exempted from punishment, or how will he regard the gift of grace as a license to sin?[92]

Here we see a hint of Origen's idea of purgation after death, taught explicitly in *On First Principles*, as a necessary remedy to remaining vices. The concept of salvation as a moral and spiritual pedagogy, with God's judgments as merely remedial rather than retributive, is spread throughout that work.[93] There is a "twofold resurrection": "the first in which we rise with Christ from earthly things in mind, purpose, and faith as we ponder heavenly things and seek after what is future; the second in which will be a general resurrection in the flesh of all."[94]

---

91. Origen, *Commentary on the Epistle to the Romans, Books 6–10*, 49.

92. Origen, *Commentary on the Epistle to the Romans, Books 1–5*, 335.

93. See Joseph A. Trigg, *Origen*, Early Church Fathers (New York: Routledge, 1998), 29. Though it only attained dogmatic status centuries later (and only in the West), the hypothesis of purgatory seems to have been enunciated first by Origen, based on his idea of a universal restoration of all souls (including Lucifer), yet through an arduous process of education and suffering. The translator, Thomas P. Scheck, observes, "Origen's unique eschatological views are seen here: A future restoration is promised, but it is conditional and not necessarily abiding" (*Commentary on the Epistle to the Romans, Books 1–5*, 335n262).

94. Origen, *Commentary on the Epistle to the Romans, Books 1–5*, 368, 374–78. See 374n573. The second "resurrection" is less obvious in Origen's thinking, especially compared with *On First Principles*, where it seems that the bodily resurrection on the last day is quite explicitly rejected (along with the resurrection of Christ's physical body). Yet here he seems to rebut his arguments from *On First Principles* (3.3.5) with respect the possibility of a future fall.

Origen asserts repeatedly that death is the penalty for guilt, which all inherit from Adam. This challenges a common contrast between Greek and Latin soteriologies: the former treats salvation as the answer to death, and the latter as an answer to guilt and condemnation. Like Paul, even Origen regards death as the *penalty* for sin; once the guilt and condemnation are abolished, so too is death. Further, Origen argues that Christ's legal satisfaction of justice for sin's guilt is the basis for liberation from sin's tyranny.[95] Indeed, he says, "All the Scriptures testify to the fact that Christ became a sacrifice for the sake of sin and was offered for the cleansing of sins," citing various passages concerning his sin-bearing for us.[96]

Origen turns next to Romans 7. For Paul, the "body of sin" refers to the vices of the old self.[97] "What then shall we say? That the law is sin?" (Rom 7:7). The law he has in mind is not Torah but natural law inscribed on the conscience of all, says Origen.[98] Paul's statement, "I was once alive without the law," is a personal testimony to natural law, corresponding to the period of one's life prior to the age of accountability.[99] "For that law [of Moses] is a spiritual law and a life-giving Spirit for those who understand it spiritually. But the one who understands it in a fleshly way recalls it as a law of the letter and a letter that kills."[100]

So in Romans 7 Paul is assuming the *persona* of a gentile under natural law, struggling but always succumbing to vice.[101] The person he has in mind is a neophyte, describing "the weakness in those who receive the beginnings of conversion."[102] This weak believer has undertaken "the initial phases of a conversion" in desiring the good, "but he could not yet come to the accomplishment of the good."[103] This could not be Paul himself, but the apostle adopts this persona to encourage new believers not to give up.[104]

> This is why it must not be imagined that all at once, when a person expresses the will, he immediately becomes transferred into Christ Jesus from the slavery of the law of sin, so that he would possess

---

95. Origen, *Commentary on the Epistle to the Romans, Books 1–5*, 364.
96. Origen, *Commentary on the Epistle to the Romans, Books 6–10*, 49–50.
97. Origen, *Commentary on the Epistle to the Romans, Books 1–5*, 365.
98. Origen, *Commentary on the Epistle to the Romans, Books 6–10*, 30.
99. Origen, *Commentary on the Epistle to the Romans, Books 6–10*, 31–33.
100. Origen, *Commentary on the Epistle to the Romans, Books 6–10*, 37.
101. Origen, *Commentary on the Epistle to the Romans, Books 6–10*, 38.
102. Origen, *Commentary on the Epistle to the Romans, Books 6–10*, 39.
103. Origen, *Commentary on the Epistle to the Romans, Books 6–10*, 42.
104. Origen, *Commentary on the Epistle to the Romans, Books 6–10*, 43.

nothing in him any longer that could serve as grounds for sin's condemnation. For in each person righteousness searches for its own portions and it tests to see if one has been reformed and corrected so that it can find no unjust work in the man, on the basis of which condemnation would follow.[105]

It becomes increasingly clear that for Origen being united to Christ is a goal rather than the beginning and source of the Christian life. Through the Spirit, we may now fulfill the law; it was this new obedience that Christ made possible "through the sacrifice of his flesh." The law was weak, but with the Spirit it can now be fulfilled and this virtue averts condemnation and merits greater benefits.[106] We have "spirits of slavery" in childhood "until we come to the age when we merit receiving the Spirit of adoption of sons and become now a son and lord of everything."[107] "Someone becomes an heir of God when he merits receiving the things that belong to God."[108] Unlike Irenaeus, Origen does not interpret this historically, in terms of old versus new covenants, but anthropologically and literally as referring to an individual's passing from childhood to the age of accountability.

Interestingly, not even "the resurrection of the body" in Romans 8:11 can be interpreted straightforwardly in terms of the prophetic and early Jewish expectation. It may refer to bodily resurrection, says Origen, but "I think [it] points to the body of the Church as a whole."[109] The creation was "subjected to vanity," and the body was the source of "vanity" in contrast with the "noble and rational" soul that the body imprisoned. "Wisdom was also saying this through Solomon, 'The corruptible body weighs down the soul, and this earthly tent burdens the very thoughtful mind' [Wisdom 9:15]." This is why Paul "prefers to be away from the body and to be present with the Lord. . . . This is [what it means] to be freed from the slavery of corruption unto the freedom of the glory of the sons of God."[110]

---

105. Origen, *Commentary on the Epistle to the Romans, Books 6–10*, 45.
106. Origen, *Commentary on the Epistle to the Romans, Books 6–10*, 49–50.
107. Origen, *Commentary on the Epistle to the Romans, Books 6–10*, 63.
108. Origen, *Commentary on the Epistle to the Romans, Books 6–10*, 64.
109. Origen, *Commentary on the Epistle to the Romans, Books 6–10*, 77–78. This seems to be the view of Radical Orthodoxy. See John Milbank, in *Radical Orthodoxy: A New Theology*, ed. John Milbank, Catherine Pickstock, and Graham Ward (London: Routledge, 1999), 179–81; cf. Graham Ward, *Cities of God* (New York and London: Routledge, 2000), 154–67.
110. Origen, *Commentary on the Epistle to the Romans, Books 6–10*, 70–71.

Upon reaching Romans 8:29–39, Origen takes a defensive posture, more concerned to tell us what Paul is *not* saying even though he acknowledges that it seems to be saying that salvation, grounded in predestination, is by God's grace alone. Already in treating Romans 1:1 he says that he says that Paul was set apart from his mother's womb by "the merits which entitled him to be set apart for this purpose," which God foreknew.[111] However, Origen is more ambiguous on 8:29–39. He recognizes that this knowing is intimate, personal familiarity with someone, as many examples from Scripture show. God does not foreknow ("know" in this intimate sense, as loved ones before time) those whom he has not chosen, even though of course, as omniscient, he knows *about* them.[112] He even assaults the position that he argued at the beginning of his commentary when he says, "And behold, into what an absurd interpretation they would fall who understand in this case the foreknowledge of God, as if only someone who knows before what will come to pass afterwards."[113] "But if 'to foreknow' is taken in the sense we have stated above, i.e., 'to receive in affection and to unite with oneself,' it will be true that just as he has not predestined everyone, so he has not foreknown everyone."[114]

To complicate matters, Origen returns to his earlier position that God "placed his own love and affection" on some "because he knew what sort of persons they were."[115] All are called outwardly, but only some are called inwardly.[116] However, "called according to his purpose" does not imply causality, for God "knows that a pious mind and the longing for salvation is in them." Origen even acknowledges that this seems to contradict what he has said earlier. In any case, he asserts that not even foreknowledge is "the cause of our salvation or destruction." "Nor will justification depend solely upon the calling; nor has being glorified been completely removed from our power."[117] In short, "The cause of each person's salvation is not placed in the foreknowledge of

---

111. Origen, *Commentary on the Epistle to the Romans, Books 1–5*, 65–66. He says that Paul "gave the reasons for his own election as found in himself, and in the One who 'knows all things before they take place' [Dan 13:42 LXX]" (Origen, *Commentary on the Epistle to the Romans, Books 1–5*, 64).

112. Origen, *Commentary on the Epistle to the Romans, Books 6–10*, 85–86.

113. Origen, *Commentary on the Epistle to the Romans, Books 6–10*, 87.

114. Origen, *Commentary on the Epistle to the Romans, Books 6–10*, 91.

115. Origen, *Commentary on the Epistle to the Romans, Books 6–10*, 88–89.

116. Origen, *Commentary on the Epistle to the Romans, Books 6–10*, 89–90.

117. Origen, *Commentary on the Epistle to the Romans, Books 6–10*, 90.

God but in one's own purpose and actions."[118] Whatever he has said to the contrary earlier, this is his final position. We have encountered several contradictions so far, some of them even acknowledged. In part this is due to the fact that, on one hand, he wants to do justice to Paul's argument and that, on the other, he is alert to the dangers of Marcionite interpretations and gnostic and pagan fatalism.

Continuing his treatment of election in Romans 9, Origen introduces the remarkable theory that the entire argument is not Paul's own but adopts the *persona* of a heretical objector. Paul himself believes that it *would* imply "injustice on God's part" if salvation were "not of the one who wills or runs but of God who shows mercy."[119] To be sure, "It depends on God, *once all obstacles have been removed*, for the work to reach completion. . . . God grants the success and completion to the work, [so] it is assuredly pious and religious, while God and man do what is in themselves, to attribute the chief part of the work to God rather than to man."[120] Whether we will be good or evil "depends on our will"; God's part is to reward or punish those acts.[121] God saw the purity of Jacob's heart and the impurity of Esau's and chose Jacob "because of the purity and simplicity of his soul."[122] In *On First Principles*, in fact, Origen had argued, "Jacob was worthily loved by God according to pre-existing merits."[123] God "has prepared these vessels for glory not through some arbitrary or fortuitous grace, but because they have purged themselves from the aforementioned defilements."[124]

In contrast with the merely "saved," he conjectures, "Those who are saved through 'the election of grace' are shown to have more perfect souls." They have added "works of virtue" to "the gift of grace."[125] When Paul adds, "But if grace, it is no longer on the basis of works," Origen again pushes back: "works" means the ceremonies separating Jews from gentiles (circumcision and food laws), not works in general. "These, then, and works of this nature are the ones on the basis of which he says no one can be saved."[126]

---

118. Origen, *Commentary on the Epistle to the Romans, Books 6–10*, 91.
119. Origen, *Commentary on the Epistle to the Romans, Books 6–10*, 113.
120. Origen, *Commentary on the Epistle to the Romans, Books 6–10*, 116, emphasis added.
121. Origen, *Commentary on the Epistle to the Romans, Books 6–10*, 118.
122. Origen, *Commentary on the Epistle to the Romans, Books 6–10*, 121.
123. Origen, *On First Principles*, 2.9.7, 135.
124. Origen, *Commentary on the Epistle to the Romans, Books 6–10*, 122.
125. Origen, *Commentary on the Epistle to the Romans, Books 6–10*, 158.
126. Origen, *Commentary on the Epistle to the Romans, Books 6–10*, 159.

Origen adds that many of those who are called are not chosen.[127] Even a statement of evangelical assurance ("Who will lay any charge against God's elect?") is turned by Origen into a warning. This is a pattern throughout his commentary. An advocate only helps if "your past sins, which were wiped out through baptism, should not be imputed to you. But if after these things you should again transgress and do not wash these things away with any tears of repentance, you will be offering material to your accuser to bring an indictment against you."[128]

It is precisely such comments that weakened the efficacy of baptism and required further sacramental purgation for sins committed after baptism. From this position, Origen launches into his theory of "penal purifications, when the fire of Gehenna purifies with torments the one whom neither apostolic doctrine nor the evangelical word have purified, according to what is written: 'And I will purify you with fire leading to purity' [Is 1:25]. But for how long a time and how many ages this purging, which is applied by means of penal fire, exacts torments from sinners only he is able to know to whom 'the Father gave all judgment.'"[129]

Chrysostom (c. 347–407)

The next large-scale Romans "commentary" (actually a series of homilies) to appear was that of John Chrysostom, the great patriarch of Constantinople celebrated especially for his preaching. In fact, along with Augustine, he was John Calvin's favorite patristic exegete. Reading Chrysostom, it soon becomes apparent that we are in an entirely different atmosphere than Origen's commentary.

As early as his comments on Romans 1:17, Chrysostom says that justification is a "righteousness not thine own, but that of God. . . . For you do not achieve it by toilings and labors, but you receive it by a gift from above, contributing one thing only from your own store, 'believing.'"[130] "From faith to faith" he interprets in a redemptive-historical manner:

---

127. Origen, *Commentary on the Epistle to the Romans, Books 6–10*, 95–96.
128. Origen, *Commentary on the Epistle to the Romans, Books 6–10*, 96. It is interesting to note here one of the few places where Origen's earlier speculations appear in the commentary, at page 103: Paul's mention of "nothing in all creation" being able to "separate you from the love of God in Christ," *could* mean "a creation besides the one we see," says Origen (perhaps thinking of the "other worlds" before this one), but could also be merely adding to the list of things that exist now that cannot separate us.
129. Origen, *Commentary on the Epistle to the Romans, Books 6–10*, 185.
130. Chrysostom, *The Epistle to the Romans*, in *NPNF*[1] 11:349 (hom. 2).

And first with a short sentence he lays open a vast sea of histories to one who has a capacity for seeing them . . . showing [from the OT] that both the just and the sinners were justified in that way even then, wherefore also he made mention both of the harlot and of Abraham. For since what God gives transcends reasoning entirely but reason teaches that we need faith.[131]

He interprets the apostle's argument in 2:13–16 as a challenge to hypocrisy: "For if it is by the Law you claim to be saved, in this respect, he says, the Gentile will stand before you, when seen to be a doer of what is written in the Law."[132] "For the conscience and reason doth suffice in the Law's stead," since "God made man" in the beginning with a knowledge of virtue and vice and able to choose between them, and "Providence" cared for everyone even before the giving of the law.[133]

On Romans 3:9–21, Chrysostom comments,

He had accused the Gentiles, he had accused the Jews; it came next in order to mention the righteousness which is by faith. For if the law of nature availed not and the written Law was of no advantage, but both weighed down those that used them not aright, and made it plain that they were worthy of greater punishment, then after this the salvation which is by grace was necessary.[134]

The apostle's argument attempts to lay all low that "they might with much earnestness run unto Him who offered them the remission of their sins, and accept grace through faith." Boasting in the law "puts you to the greater shame: it solemnly parades forth your sins before you. . . . Here he utters a great thing, and such as needed much proof. For if they that lived in the Law not only did not escape punishment, but were even the more weighed down thereby, how without the Law is it possible not only to escape vengeance but even to be justified?"[135] Yet in order that they might not despair, he adds (vv. 24–25), "being justified by his grace." Everything thus far has led to this point. Even the types

---

131. Chrysostom, *The Epistle to the Romans*, in *NPNF*[1] 11:349.
132. Chrysostom, *The Epistle to the Romans*, in *NPNF*[1] 11:364.
133. Chrysostom, *The Epistle to the Romans*, in *NPNF*[1] 11:365.
134. Chrysostom, *The Epistle to the Romans*, in *NPNF*[1] 11:375 (hom. 7).
135. Chrysostom, *The Epistle to the Romans*, in *NPNF*[1] 11:376.

and shadows of the Law proclaimed this gospel, especially through the sacrifices, says Chrysostom.[136]

The "declaring of His righteousness" is not only a manifestation of the righteousness that belongs to God, "but that He doth also make them that are filled with putrefying sores of sin *suddenly righteous*. . . . Doubt not then: for it is *not of works, but of faith*; and shun not the righteousness of God, for it is a blessing in two ways: because it is easy and also open to all men."[137] He adds that Paul returns in 3:27 yet again to the contrast between the law and the gospel. "For since all were convicted, He therefore saves by grace." The apostle has carefully and patiently built up his argument to this conclusion, "that it was possible to be saved by the Law and by our own labors and well-doings, . . . so that after they were by every argument clearly convinced of inability to help themselves, He then saved them by His grace."[138]

In contrast with Origen's reduction of Paul's "works of the law" to boundary markers, Chrysostom understands law/works as encompassing all human efforts to attain salvation apart from grace, "our own labors and well-doings" as he says above.

> But what is the "law of faith"? It is being saved by grace. Here he shows God's power, in that He has not only saved, but has even justified and led them to boasting, and this too without needing works, but looking for faith only. . . . Do you see how great faith's preeminence is? How it has removed us from the former things, not even allowing us to boast of them?[139]

Paul is no longer speaking of Jews and gentiles, but of everyone.[140] "For when a man is once a believer, he is straightaway justified." He adds, "Since after this grace whereby we are justified there is need also of a life suited to it."[141] Notice the logical priority: justification by grace through faith, apart from works, with works as the fruit.

Chrysostom connects Paul's argument thus far with chapter 4:

---

136. Chrysostom, *The Epistle to the Romans*, in *NPNF*¹ 11:377.
137. Chrysostom, *The Epistle to the Romans*, in *NPNF*¹ 11:378, emphasis added.
138. Chrysostom, *The Epistle to the Romans*, in *NPNF*¹ 11:378.
139. Chrysostom, *The Epistle to the Romans*, in *NPNF*¹ 11:379.
140. Chrysostom, *The Epistle to the Romans*, in *NPNF*¹ 11:379.
141. Chrysostom, *The Epistle to the Romans*, in *NPNF*¹ 11:380.

He had said that the world had become guilty before God and that all had sinned, and that boasting was excluded, and that it was impossible to be saved otherwise than by faith. He is now intent upon showing that this salvation, so far from being a matter of shame, was even the cause of a bright glory and a greater than that through works. . . . For a person [Abraham] who had no works, to be justified by faith was nothing unlikely. But for a person richly adorned with good deeds *not* to be made just from them but from faith, this is the thing to cause wonder, and to set the power of faith in a strong light.[142]

Here the apostle "pitches the battle for faith against works. . . . For there are two 'gloryings,' one of works and one of faith. . . . For he that glories in his works has his own labors to put forward, but he that finds his honor in having faith in God has a much greater ground for glorying to show in that it is God that he glorifies and magnifies."[143]

Unlike Origen, Chrysostom is convinced that the "boasting" that Paul excludes is not merely *Jewish* confidence in its distinctive rites but the confidence that all people since the fall have had in their moral ability—over against God's grace in Christ. Paul's Jewish objectors maintained "that it was not possible to be justified by faith."[144] But the apostle argues that circumcision was an act of faith *following upon* and *signifying* the justification that Abraham already possessed.[145] Interpreting verses 13–15, he says, ironically,

Circumcision then does but proclaim that there is no need of circumcision. For he that clings to the Law, as if of saving force, does disparagement to faith's power, and so he says, 'faith is made void,' that is, there is no need of salvation by grace. . . . Now if it worketh wrath, and renders them liable for transgressions, it is plain that it makes them so to a curse also, not worthy of inheriting, but of being punished and rejected. . . . Punishment then being removed, and righteousness succeeding from faith, there is no obstacle to our becoming heirs of the promise.

---

142. Chrysostom, *The Epistle to the Romans*, in *NPNF*[1] 11:385.
143. Chrysostom, *The Epistle to the Romans*, in *NPNF*[1] 11:386.
144. Chrysostom, *The Epistle to the Romans*, in *NPNF*[1] 11:473.
145. Chrysostom, *The Epistle to the Romans*, in *NPNF*[1] 11:388.

In this way, both Jews and gentiles are saved by grace.[146] The soteriological argument (justification through faith alone) entails the ecclesiological conclusion (for Jew and gentile alike).

As he verges into Romans 5, Chrysostom even distinguishes between justification and sanctification.[147] While Origen interprets these same verses as implying warnings against future lapses, Chrysostom interprets them as assurances of God's persevering grace. "If then He hath brought us near to Himself when we were far off, much more will He keep us now that we are near. . . . But we brought faith only as our contribution. And so he says, 'by faith unto this grace.'"[148] Chrysostom emphasizes this point that "grace alone through faith alone" is the basis not only for the beginning but for the continuation of salvation. "For it was not only that we might have simple remission of sins that we were reconciled; but that we might receive also countless benefits. . . . For this is the nature of God's grace. It has no end, it knows no bound, but evermore is on the advancement to greater things, which in human things is not the case."[149] This is why we can glory even in our tribulations because God is using them to work out his saving purposes toward us.[150] "For there is no one else that will save us, except He who so loved us when we were sinners, as even to give Himself up for us. Do you see what a ground this topic affords for hope?" That God is *willing* can hardly be in dispute, since he gave up his Son. But he is also *able* to save, "from the very fact of His having justified men who were sinners. What is there then to prevent us anymore from obtaining the things to come? Nothing!"[151] The unabashed emphasis on assuring believers of the surpassing greatness of God's grace in Christ contrasts with Origen's repeated interjections and disclaimers.

Turning to the Adam-Christ contrast in Romans 5:13 ("For sin indeed was in the world before the law was given, but sin is not counted where there is no law"), Chrysostom claims that Paul is not referring to the transgression of Torah, "the transgression, that is, of the Law, but that of Adam's disobedience which marred all things. Now what is the proof of this?" He argues,

---

146. Chrysostom, *The Epistle to the Romans*, in *NPNF*[1] 11:389.
147. Chrysostom, *The Epistle to the Romans*, in *NPNF*[1] 11:395.
148. Chrysostom, *The Epistle to the Romans*, in *NPNF*[1] 11:396.
149. Chrysostom, *The Epistle to the Romans*, in *NPNF*[1] 11:396.
150. Chrysostom, *The Epistle to the Romans*, in *NPNF*[1] 11:396–97.
151. Chrysostom, *The Epistle to the Romans*, in *NPNF*[1] 11:398–99.

The fact that even before the Law all died: for 'death reigned,' he says, 'from Adam to Moses, even over them that had not sinned.' How did it reign? 'After the similitude of Adam's transgression, who is the figure of Him that was to come.' Now this is why Adam is a type of Christ. How a type? Why in that as the former became to those who were sprung from him, although they had never eaten of the tree, the cause of that death which by his eating was introduced; thus also did Christ become to those sprung from Him, even though they had not wrought righteousness, the Provider of that righteousness which through His Cross He graciously bestowed on us all.[152]

Chrysostom clearly understands Paul as teaching that Adam's transgression is the basis of our condemnation and death. In fact, he argues from the more difficult (original sin) to the more obvious (justification): "For that one man should be punished on account of another does not seem to be much in accordance with reason. But for one to be saved on account of another is at once more suitable and more reasonable. If then the former took place, much more may the latter."[153] Our enemy Death has surely been defeated by Christ, but Chrysostom recognizes that death is an effect of a deeper cause:

What armed death against the world? The one man's eating from the tree only. If then death attained so great power from one offence, when it is found that certain received a grace and righteousness out of all proportion to that sin, how shall they still be liable to death? And for this cause, he does not here say 'grace,' but 'superabundance of grace.' For it was not as much as we must have to do away the sin only, that we received of His grace, but even far more. For we were at once freed from punishment and put off all iniquity and were also born again from above (John 3:3) and rose again with the old man buried, and were redeemed, justified, led up to adoption, sanctified, made brothers of the Only-begotten, and joint heirs and of the one Body with Him, and counted for His Flesh, and even as a Body with the Head, so were we united unto Him![154]

152. Chrysostom, *The Epistle to the Romans*, in *NPNF*[1] 11:402.
153. Chrysostom, *The Epistle to the Romans*, in *NPNF*[1] 11:402.
154. Chrysostom, *The Epistle to the Romans*, in *NPNF*[1] 11:403.

So far is this great Greek father from contrasting Christ's victory over death with his securing forgiveness and liberation from the condemnation of original sin that he even makes the latter the basis for the former.[155] We also notice again the clear distinction between justification and sanctification as twin benefits of union with Christ.

Chrysostom also has a clear concept of humanity inheriting Adam's guilt and corruption without speculating about the method of transmission (viz., the lust of sexual intercourse). "Now that by Adam's death we all became mortals he had shown clearly and at large," along with the basis for this mortality: namely, "that the punishment too was brought in by one upon all." He proves "that the world was condemned from Adam. . . . And how did sin abound? The Law gave countless commands. Now since they transgressed them all, transgression became more abundant. Do you see what a great difference there is between grace and the Law? For the one became an addition to the condemnation, but the other, a further abundance of gifts."[156]

The evangelical emphasis continues into Chrysostom's treatment of Romans 6 (hom. 11). Once more in contrast with Origen, he understands baptism not merely as a first grace that makes it possible for us then to merit further grace, and eventually glory, by one's virtues.

> For this is *not* the only thing Baptism has the power to do—to obliterate our former transgressions; for it *also* secures against subsequent ones. . . . For as His Body, by being buried in the earth, brought forth as the fruit of it the salvation of the world; thus ours also, being buried in baptism, bore as fruit righteousness, sanctification, adoption, countless blessings. And it will bear also hereafter the gift of the resurrection.[157]

As we will see, it was just such passages that Calvin and other Reformers would quote against the medieval doctrine of penance, which assumes with Origen that baptism does not suffice for the whole Christian life.

---

155. My unspoken target of criticism here is Gustav Aulén's *Christus Victor* (1930), which was massively influential in advancing a sweeping contrast between the Christian East and West in terms (respectively) of belief in Christ's death as primarily victory as opposed to sacrifice and substitution.

156. Chrysostom, *The Epistle to the Romans*, in NPNF[1] 11:403–4.

157. Chrysostom, *The Epistle to the Romans*, in NPNF[1] 11:408, emphasis added.

The problem is not the law per se, as Paul argues in Romans 8, but our moral inability to keep it because of sin.[158] Rather than make final justification conditional on works, Chrysostom teaches, "For the righteousness of the Law, that one should not become liable to its curse, *Christ has accomplished for you.*"[159] Throughout these sermons Chrysostom is stirred by Paul's emphasis on the "superabundance of grace."

> He does not say, 'Who shall lay anything to the charge of God's' servants? or of 'God's faithful ones?' but 'of God's elect.' . . . *He does not say, it is God who forgave our sins, but what is much greater, 'It is God that justifies.'* For when the Judge's sentence *declares us just,* and a Judge such as that too, what signifies the accuser? . . . for He has *both elected and justified us,* and the wondrous thing is that it was also *by the death of His Son* that He did so. Who then is to condemn us, since God crowns us, and Christ was put to death for us, and not only was put to death, but also after this intercedes for us?[160]

If he "'spared not His own Son' for you, and elected you, and justified you, why be afraid anymore?"[161] Here Chrysostom explicitly defines justification as a judicial verdict, beyond mere forgiveness, with Christ's death as the ground, sustained by his mediatorial intercession.

In fact, in Chrysostom's sermons, the shadow of Paul's argument in Romans 5 is cast across the rest of the epistle through Romans 9. "For when he was discussing how by Christ being justified all the rest enjoyed that righteousness, he brought in Adam's case, saying, 'For if by one man's offence death reigned, much more they which receive abundance of grace shall reign in life.'"[162] Chrysostom argues that election is based on foreknowledge: God knew from eternity that Esau would reject Christ and Jacob would believe.[163] Nevertheless, unlike Origen, he is happy to see such foreknowledge in causal terms. Paul by such

---

158. Chrysostom, *The Epistle to the Romans*, in *NPNF*[1] 11:432 (hom. 13): "Again, he seems indeed to be disparaging the Law. But if any one attends strictly, he even highly praises it, by showing that it harmonizes with Christ and gives preference to the same things. For he does not speak of the badness of the Law, but of 'what it could not do;' and so again, 'in that it was weak,' not 'in that it was mischievous or designing.'"

159. Chrysostom, *The Epistle to the Romans*, in *NPNF*[1] 11:433, emphasis added.

160. Chrysostom, *The Epistle to the Romans*, in *NPNF*[1] 11:454–55, emphasis added.

161. Chrysostom, *The Epistle to the Romans*, in *NPNF*[1] 11:455.

162. Chrysostom, *The Epistle to the Romans*, in *NPNF*[1] 11:464.

163. Chrysostom, *The Epistle to the Romans*, in *NPNF*[1] 11:464–69.

strong language "shows that all is not one's own, for that it requires grace from above."[164]

Other Patristic Commentaries

It would seem odd to skip over Augustine, but his Romans commentary (c. 394) is unfinished, and the *Propositions from the Epistle to the Romans* is more complete but hardly an exegetical work.[165] Neither reflects his mature theology. Distracted from this project, he returned to it shortly afterward only to feel overwhelmed by it. Yet even in this early stage he held that faith is opposed to works in justification, but faith alone (our part in salvation) *merits* all grace, including regeneration.[166] Only two years later (in *ad Simplicianum*) he would shudder in horror at these comments.[167] In contrast with his anti-Pelagian works, *Unfinished Commentary on the Epistle to the Romans* is driven by an anti-Manichean polemic. As with Origen, the focus on Manicheanism no doubt provoked him to emphasize moral freedom and responsibility. More illustrious of Augustine's mature interpretation of Romans would be *De spiritu et littera*, the *Enchiridion*, and the anti-Pelagian works to which I refer below.

Pelagius wrote his commentary on Romans in Rome between 406 and 409. Significantly, Pelagius (like Origen and *unlike* Chrysostom and Augustine) interpreted "works of the law" exclusively as circumcision, ceremonies, and dietary laws.[168] In this way, Paul could be seen as excluding some but not all works from any justifying role. Despite multiple condemnations, Pelagius's *Romans* was read, digested, and quoted in many medieval commentaries.

---

164. Chrysostom, *The Epistle to the Romans*, in *NPNF*[1] 11:469.

165. Augustine, *Augustine on Romans from the Epistle to the Romans and Unfinished Commentary on the Epistle to the Romans*, trans. and ed. Paula Fredriksen Landes (Atlanta: SBL, 1982). See esp. Landes's introduction.

166. Augustine, *Propositions from the Epistle to the Romans*, in *Augustine on Romans: Propositions from the Epistle to the Romans; Unfinished Commentary on the Epistle to the Romans*, trans. Paula Fredriksen Landes (Chico, CA: Scholars' Press, 1982). Pages 29 and 35 will serve as examples: "Nor did God predestine anyone except him whom he knew would believe and who would follow the call" (29). "But that mercy was given to the preceding merit of faith, and that hardening [of Pharaoh] to preceding impiety" (35).

167. Landes, introduction to *Augustine on Romans*, x–xii.

168. Charles P. Carlson Jr., *Justification in Earlier Medieval Theology* (The Hague: Martinus Nijhoff, 1975), 24.

CHAPTER 3

JUSTIFICATION IN THE ANCIENT CHURCH

Having broadly surveyed patristic comments on the great exchange and more narrowly examined two major interpretations of Romans, we turn to remarks specifically on the topic of justification. Syllabi of quotations have limited value, given the occasional nature of much patristic theologizing and the variance of views expressed even by the same author—indeed, often in the same text. Nevertheless, such catalogues demonstrate at least that key components of what would become the Reformation interpretation were widely circulated in the ancient church.

ANTE-NICENE WRITERS

In his late first-century letter to the Corinthians, Clement of Rome argues that the great heroes of the old covenant "were highly honored, and made great, not for their own sake, or for their own works, or for the righteousness which they wrought, but through the operation of His will." "And we, too, being called by His will in Christ Jesus," he adds, "are *not justified by ourselves*, nor by our own wisdom, or understanding, or godliness, or works which we have wrought in holiness of heart; *but by that faith* through which, from the beginning, Almighty God has justified all men; to whom be glory for ever and ever. Amen."[1]

Similarly, the Epistle of Barnabas (late first to early second century) teaches, "Having received the forgiveness of sins, and placed our trust in the name of the Lord, we have become new creatures, formed again

---

1. Clement of Rome, *To the Corinthians* 32:1–4 (*ANF* 1:13). All emphases in these quotations are added.

from the beginning. . . . How? His word of faith; His calling of promise."[2] In his famous epistle, Polycarp (reputedly a disciple of the apostle John) refers to works as the fruit rather than basis of God's saving grace: "The diadems of those who are truly chosen of God and our Lord . . . *by grace ye are saved, not of works*, but by the will of God through Jesus Christ."[3] Ignatius of Antioch confesses, "My authentic archives are His cross and death and resurrection, and the faith which bears on these things, by which I desire, through your prayers, to be justified. He who disbelieves the Gospel disbelieves everything along with it."[4]

Likewise, Irenaeus advises, "We should not, either by trusting to works of righteousness, or when adorned with super-eminent gifts of ministration, by any means be lifted up with pride, nor should we tempt God, but should feel humility in all things."[5] Abraham was circumcised "after that justification by faith," showing that "circumcision and the law of works occupied the intervening period," although in both old and new covenants justification is by grace, for "Christ is the treasure which was hid in the field . . . since He was pointed out by means of types and parables."[6] "For 'all men come short of the glory of God,' and are *not justified of themselves*, but by *the advent of the Lord*—they who earnestly *direct their eyes toward His light*."[7] Far from focusing on the incarnation to the exclusion of Christ's vicarious sacrifice, Irenaeus repeatedly invokes the latter as well as the former: "Truly the death of the Lord became the means of healing and remission of sins."[8] "Abraham himself," along with the other patriarchs, "were justified . . . without the law of Moses" but only "through faith in God's promise."[9]

"Every mystery which is enacted by our Lord Jesus Christ asks only for faith," according to Marius Victorinus.

> The mystery was enacted at that time for our sake and aimed at our resurrection and liberation, should we have faith in the mystery of Christ and in Christ. For the patriarchs prefigured and foretold that

---

2. *The Epistle of Barnabas* 16 (*ANF* 1:147).

3. *Epistle of Polycarp*, in *The Apostolic Fathers*, ed., Jack N. Sparks, trans. William R. Schoedel (Nashville: Thomas Nelson, 1978), 127.

4. Ignatius of Antioch, *Epistle to the Philadelphians* 8 (*ANF* 1:84).

5. *Haer.* 5.22.2 (*ANF* 1:550).

6. *Haer.* 4.25.1–26.1 (*ANF* 1:495–96).

7. *Haer.* 4.27.2 (*ANF* 1:499).

8. *Haer.* 4.27.2 (*ANF* 1:499).

9. *Haer.* 4.16.2 (*ANF* 1:481).

man would be *justified from faith*. Therefore, just as it was *reckoned as righteousness* to Abraham that he had faith, so we too, if we have *faith in Christ* and every mystery of his, will be sons of Abraham. *Our whole life will be accounted as righteous.*[10]

Christ is our righteousness, says the fourth-century Cappadocian theologian Basil. "This is perfect and pure boasting in God, when one is not proud on account of his own righteousness but knows that he is indeed unworthy of the true righteousness and is (or has been) *justified solely by faith in Christ.*"[11]

Ambrose (c. 339–97) acknowledged,

Thus I do not have the wherewithal to enable me to glory in my own works, I do not have the wherewithal to boast of myself, and so I will glory in Christ. I will not glory because I have been redeemed. I will not glory because I am free of sins, but because sins have been forgiven me. I will not glory because I am profitable or because anyone is profitable to me, but because Christ is an advocate in my behalf with the Father, because the blood of Christ has been poured out in my behalf.[12]

He adds, "Therefore let no one boast of his works, because no one can be justified by his works; but *he who is just receives it as a gift*, because he is *justified by the washing of regeneration*. It is *faith*, therefore, which delivers us *by the blood of Christ*, because blessed is he whose sins are forgiven, and to whom pardon is granted."[13]

Even those whose works appear outwardly pious are nevertheless ungodly because their works are "performed without faith," says Augustine.

But when someone believes in him who justifies the impious, that faith is reckoned as justice to the believer, as David too declares

---

10. Marius Victorinus, *Epistle to the Galatians* 1.3.7, in *Ancient Christian Commentary on Scripture*, New Testament 8, *Galatians, Ephesians, Philippians*, ed. Mark J. Edwards (Downers Grove, IL: InterVarsity, 1998), 39.

11. Quoted in Martin Chemnitz, *Examination of the Council of Trent* (St. Louis: Concordia, 2007), 505.

12. Ambrose, *Jacob and the Happy Life* 1.6.21, in *Seven Exegetical Works*, Fathers of the Church (Washington, DC: Catholic University of America Press, 1972), 133.

13. Ambrose, *Letter 73: Ambrose to Irenaeus* 11, quoted in George Finch, *A Sketch of the Romish Controversy* (London: Norman, 1831), 220.

that person blessed whom God has *accepted* and *endowed* with righteousness, *independently of any righteous actions* (Rom 4:5–6). What righteousness is this? *The righteousness of faith, preceded by no good works, but with good works as its consequence.*[14]

Consistent with his comments on Romans, Chrysostom writes elsewhere, "The calling is from the Father, but the cause of it is the Son. He it is who hath brought about reconciliation and bestowed it as a gift, for we were not saved by works in righteousness."[15] He goes so far as to say that "those who relinquish the Law are not only not cursed, but blessed, and they who keep it, not only not blessed, but cursed. *For the Law requires not only faith but works also, but grace saves and justifies by faith* (Eph. ii:8.). . . . You see how he proves that they are under the curse who cleave to the Law, because it is impossible to fulfill it."[16] The Law accomplished two things, he argues: "It has schooled its followers in a certain degree of virtue and has pressed on them the knowledge of their own sins. And this especially made them more zealous to seek the Son, for those who disbelieved, disbelieved from having no sense of their sins."[17]

But now that faith has come, some wish to use the law as a cosavior with Christ. In this way, says Chrysostom, "It is the destruction of our salvation." "If a candle which gave light by night kept us when it became day, from the sun, it would not only not benefit, it would injure us; and so doth the Law, if it stands between us and the greater benefits. . . . Wonderful! see how mighty is the power of Faith, and how he unfolds as he proceeds!" Not only in the beginning but throughout, salvation is "*by Faith, not by the Law.*"[18] "And by riches here [2 Cor 8:9] he means the knowledge of godliness, the cleansing away of sins, justification, sanctification, the countless good things which He bestowed upon us and purposes to bestow."[19] In a homily on Galatians, Chrysostom teaches, "If faith in Him, [Paul] says, avails not for our justification,

14. Augustine, *Expositions of the Psalms 1–32*, ed. John E. Rotelle, OSA, trans. Maria Boulding, OSB, Works of Saint Augustine 3.15 (Hyde Park, NY: New City, 2000), exp. 2 of Ps 31 (370), emphasis added.

15. Chrysostom, *Commentary on Galatians* 1:6 (NPNF[1] 13:7).

16. Chrysostom, *Commentary on Galatians* 3:8 (NPNF[1] 13:26).

17. Chrysostom, *Commentary on Galatians* 3:22 (NPNF[1] 13:29).

18. Chrysostom, *Homilies on 1 Corinthians* 6.1 (NPNF[1] 12:29).

19. Chrysostom, *Homilies on 2 Corinthians* 17.1, quoted in Nick Needham, "Justification in the Early Church Fathers," in *Justification in Perspective: Historical Developments and Contemporary Challenges*, ed. Bruce L. McCormack (Grand Rapids: Baker Academic, 2006), 28n9.

but it is necessary again to embrace the law, and if, having forsaken the law for Christ's sake, we are not justified but condemned for such abandonment, then we shall find Him, for whose sake we forsook the law and went over to faith, the author of our condemnation."[20] According to Chrysostom, justification is a "royal pardon."[21]

Recognizing Paul's distinction between law and gospel, Chrysostom says that Ephesians 2:11–12 "makes a wide distinction between command and ordinance." The latter "means faith" rather than "precept," believing in the word of Christ rather than ascending to the heavens. "Instead of a certain manner of life, He brought in faith. For that He might not save us to no purpose, He both Himself underwent the penalty, and also required of men the faith that is by doctrines."[22] As we have seen above in his Romans homilies, Chrysostom repeatedly affirms that justification is by grace alone through faith alone in Christ alone, apart from works. To be sure, faith produces good works, but the former alone is the instrument of justification. This faith is received by a passive act and is itself a gift of grace:

> Now in what case, tell me, does faith save without itself doing anything at all? Faith's workings themselves are a gift of God, lest anyone should boast. What then is Paul saying? Not that God has forbidden works but that he has forbidden us to be justified by works. No one, Paul says, is justified by works, precisely in order that the grace and benevolence of God may become apparent.[23]

Significantly, Chrysostom's does not think of justification as a process: "For when a human being is *once a believer*, he is *immediately justified*."[24]

POST-NICENE WRITERS

Theodore of Mopsuestia (c. 350–428) argues, "On the one hand, they [the Jews] have disregarded the justification from God promised to us; on the other hand, having supposed that by their own works and

---

20. Chrysostom, *Homilies on Galatians* 2:17, cited in Needham, "Justification in the Church Fathers," 29n17.

21. Chrysostom, *The Epistle to the Romans* 3:27 (NPNF[1] 11:379).

22. Chrysostom, *Homilies on Ephesians* 2:11, 12, hom. 5 (NPNF[1] 13:72).

23. Chrysostom, *Homily on Ephesians* 4.2.9, in *Ancient Christian Commentary on Scripture*, NT 8:134.

24. Chrysostom, *The Epistle to the Romans* 1:17 and 3:30.

by following the law in their conduct, they would be able to save them-selves, they made no effort to believe in Christ and to receive the jus-tification thenceforth promised to us by grace."[25] Similarly, Theodoret of Cyrrhus (c. 393–460) writes, "And the only begotten Word of God himself, having clothed himself with Adam's nature, and having kept it uninitiated from all sin, offered it on our behalf and, having paid the debt of that nature, he discharged the common debt of all men."[26] On Romans 10:3, Theodoret contrasts "their own righteousness" with "'the righteousness of God . . . which comes *by grace through faith.*"[27]

Jerome himself says that "God justifies by faith alone" (*Deus ex sola fide justificat*).[28] On this basis, he goes so far as to say, "He who with all his spirit has placed his faith in Christ, even if he die in sin, shall by his faith live forever."[29] Since "the law condemned sinners . . . and was in no way merciful," wrote Cyril, the fifth-century patriarch of Alexandria, did we not require "a merciful high priest," "one who would abrogate the curse, check the legal process, and free the sinners with forgiving grace and commands based on gentleness?" God will not remember our sins. "For we are *justified by faith, not by works of the law,* as Scripture says (Gal. 2:16). By faith in whom, then, are we justified? Is it not in him who suffered death according to the flesh for our sake? Is it not in one Lord Jesus Christ?"[30] He adds, "For truly the compassion from beside the Father is Christ, as he takes away the sins, dismisses the charges and *justifies by faith,* and recovers the lost and makes [them] stronger than death. For what is good and he does not give? . . . For *by him and in him* we have known the Father, and *we have become rich in the justification by faith.*"[31]

Commenting on Matthew 20:7 in the fourth century, Hilary of Poitiers observes, "*Wages cannot be considered as a gift,* because they are due to work, but God has given fresh grace to all men by *the justification*

25. Theodore of Mopsuestia, *In Epistolas B. Pauli Commentarii,* in PG 66:845, quoted and trans. by Lee Charles Irons, *The Righteousness of God: A Lexical Examination of the Covenant-Faithfulness Interpretation* (Tübingen: Mohr Siebeck, 2015), 12.

26. Theodoret of Cyrrhus, PG 82.60, quoted and trans. Irons, *The Righteousness of God,* 13.

27. Theodoret of Cyrrhus, PG 82.164, quoted and trans. Irons, *The Righteousness of God,* 13.

28. Jerome, *In Epistolam Ad Romanos,* 10.3 (PL 30:692D).

29. Jacques Le Goff, *The Birth of Purgatory,* trans. Arthur Goldhammer (Chicago: University of Chicago Press, 1984), 61.

30. Cyril of Alexandria, *Against Nestorius,* in *Cyril of Alexandria,* trans. Russell Norman, Early Church Fathers (London: Rutledge, 2000), 165.

31. Cyril of Alexandria, *Commentary on Hosea,* in *Ancient Christian Commentary on Scripture,* New Testament 14, *The Twelve Prophets,* ed. Alberto Ferreiro (Downers Grove, IL: InterVarsity, 2003), 29.

of faith."[32] The medieval idea (as refined by Aquinas) that our merits can be called "wages" and "a gift" remains a contradiction at this point.[33]

We have seen above that even Origen concluded "faith *alone*" from Romans 3 and 4, although this referred only to *past* sins. However, Clement, Basil, Chrysostom, and Jerome were quite happy to ascribe justification—past, present, and future—to grace alone in Christ alone through faith alone, even employing the phrase *sola fide*. The highly influential fourth-century writer dubbed Ambrosiaster, because he was thought erroneously to have been Ambrose bishop of Milan, commented on 1 Corinthians 1:4, "God has decreed that a person who believes in Christ can be saved without works. *By faith alone he receives the forgiveness of sins.*"[34] In fact, for the justified, "faith alone is the way by which he is made perfect."[35] On Romans 3:24, he comments, "They are justified freely because they have not done anything nor given anything in return, but *by faith alone* they have been made holy by the gift of God."[36] Indeed, "No one is justified before God except by faith."[37] Like Abraham, "The *ungodly is justified before God by faith alone.*"[38] Didymus the Blind (4th cent.) wonders how "some say" that "works are more honorable than faith," as the soul is more honorable than the body.

> I have looked into this matter in some detail and shall try to explain my position on this. It is undoubtedly true that the spirit is nobler than the body, but this does not mean that works can be put before faith, because a person is saved by grace, *not by works but by faith.* There should be no doubt but that faith saves and then lives by doing its own works, so that *the works which are added to salvation by faith* are not those of the law but a different kind of thing altogether.[39]

---

32. Cited in George Finch, *A Sketch of the Romish Controversy* (London: G. Norman, 1831), 230.

33. Aquinas says that "wage" and "reward" are synonymous with "merit" in *ST* I-II, Q. 114, A. 10 (2:1160).

34. Ambrosiaster, in *Ancient Christian Commentary on Scripture*, New Testament 7, *1–2 Corinthians*, ed. Gerald Bray (Downers Grove, IL: InterVarsity, 1999), 6.

35. Ambrosiaster, in *Ancient Christian Commentary on Scripture*, New Testament 6, *Romans*, ed. Gerald Bray (Downers Grove, IL: InterVarsity, 1999), 65, emphasis added.

36. Ambrosiaster, in *Ancient Christian Commentary on Scripture*, NT 6:101, emphasis added.

37. Ambrosiaster, in *Ancient Christian Commentary on Scripture*, NT 6:103.

38. Ambrosiaster, in *Ancient Christian Commentary on Scripture*, NT 6:112, emphasis added.

39. Didymus the Blind, in *Ancient Christian Commentary on Scripture*, New Testament 11, *James, 1–2 Peter, 1–3 John, Jude*, ed. Gerald Bray (Downers Grove, IL: InterVarsity, 2000), 34, from *Commentary on James* 2:26, emphasis added. See PG 39:1732.

According to Fulgentius, a sixth-century bishop,

> The blessed Paul argues that we are saved by faith, which he declares to be not from us but a gift from God. Thus there cannot possibly be true salvation where there is no true faith, and, since this faith is divinely enabled, it is without doubt bestowed by his free generosity. Where there is true belief through true faith, true salvation certainly accompanies it. Anyone who departs from true faith will not possess the grace of true salvation.[40]

The *sola* in *sola fide* therefore had a distinguished pedigree long before Luther.

In a recent essay Nick Needham has provided a helpful collection of patristic quotations on justification. First, the common usage is forensic. "It would seem a minor strand of patristic teaching that sees justification as meaning moral transformation, what Protestant theology calls 'regeneration' or 'sanctification.'"[41] In fact, the church fathers often distinguish between justification and sanctification. Needham cites the fourth-century writer Marius Victorinus: "We know that a man is not justified by the works of the law but through faith and the faith of Jesus Christ. . . . It is faith alone that gives justification and sanctification."[42]

Further, Needham observes, the context is usually judicial. "For example, the fathers frequently set 'justify' and 'condemn' antithetically against each other, as equal and opposite verdicts or judgments."[43] For example, Methodius prays, "Set me free from the yoke of condemnation, and place me under the yoke of justification."[44] Athanasius writes to the bishops in Egypt, "Whom God has condemned, who shall justify?"[45] Gregory of Nazianzus declares, "How much more does

---

40. Fulgentius, *On the Incarnation* 1, in *Ancient Christian Commentary on Scripture*, New Testament 8, *Galatians, Ephesians, Philippians*, ed. Mark J. Edwards (Downers Grove, IL: InterVarsity, 1998), 133–34.

41. Needham, "Justification in the Early Church Fathers," 28.

42. Marius Victorinus, *Commentary on Galatians* 2:15–16, in *Justification by Faith*, ed. H. George Anderson, T. Austin Murphy, and Joseph A. Burgess (Minneapolis: Augsburg, 1985), 114, cited in Needham, "Justification in the Early Church Fathers," 28n9.

43. Needham, "Justification in the Early Church Fathers," 29.

44. Methodius, *Oration on Simeon and Anna* 8, cited in Needham, "Justification in the Early Church Fathers," 29.

45. Athanasius, *To the Bishops of Egypt* 19, cited in Needham, "Justification in the Early Church Fathers," 29.

the passion of Christ justify us?"[46] "But the flesh of Christ condemned sin," says Ambrose, "which He felt not at His birth, and crucified by His death, so that in our flesh there might be justification through grace, in which before there had been pollution by guilt."[47] Christ "justifies" and "defends," rather than "accuses and condemns," according to Hilary of Poitiers, and Ambrose writes, "In Adam I fell, in Adam I was cast out of Paradise, in Adam I died. How shall the Lord call me back, unless He finds me in Adam, so that as I was liable to guilt and owing to death in him, so now in Christ I am justified?"[48]

Second, justification in the patristic sources is also a crediting or reckoning of righteousness to the sinner.[49] Needham claims, "The only individual father of note who appears to stand out strongly and quite consistently as an exception to this pattern is Clement of Alexandria. . . . When Clement says 'justify,' he mostly seems to mean 'sanctify.'"[50]

Third, the church fathers speak of faith—even faith *alone*—as the instrument of justification, although they do not employ formally the later medieval categories like *instrumentum*. "For faith towards God justifies a person," according to Irenaeus.[51] These sources are replete with the phrase "justified through faith alone."[52] We may add a fourth

---

46. Gregory of Nazianzus, *Orations* 38.4, cited in Needham, "Justification in the Early Church Fathers," 29.

47. Ambrose, *On Repentance* 1.3.13, cited in Needham, "Justification in the Early Church Fathers," 29n17.

48. Ambrose, *On the Decease of His Brother Satyrus* 2.6 (PL 16:1374), cited in Needham, "Justification in the Early Church Fathers," 30.

49. "For the goodness and the lovingkindness of God, and His boundless riches," Justin Martyr explains, "hold righteous and sinless the person who, as Ezekiel tells, repents of sins; and reckons sinful, unrighteous, and impious the person who falls away from piety and righteousness to unrighteousness and ungodliness" (quoted in Needham, "Justification in the Early Church Fathers," 32). Ambrosiaster argues, "How then can the Jews imagine that through the works of the law they are justified with Abraham's justification, when they see that Abraham was *justified not from the works of the law, but by faith alone*? Therefore there is no need of the law, since an impious person is *justified with God through faith alone*" (Ambrosiaster, *Commentary on Paul's Epistles*, on Rom 4:5 [PL 17:86], cited in Needham, "Justification in the Early Church Fathers," 33). Tertullian says that God will "*impute righteousness to those who believe in him . . . and declare the Gentiles to be his children through faith*" (Tertullian, *Against Marcion* 5.3, cited in Needham, "Justification in the Early Church Fathers," 33). See Irenaeus 4.16.2. Jerome, too, says that we find our justification in Christ, "*not our righteousness*, nor *in ourselves*" (Jerome, *Expositio In Primam Epistolam Ad Corinthiios* [PL 30:820], cited in Needham, "Justification in the Early Church Fathers," 35n29).

50. Needham, "Justification in the Early Church Fathers," 37.

51. *Haer.* 4.5.5 (*ANF* 1:467).

52. As noted above, Chrysostom asserts, "For you do not achieve it by toilings and labors, but you receive it by a gift from above, contributing one thing only from your own store, believing" (*Epistle to the Romans* on 1:17). "Do not doubt, then: for it is *not by works, but by faith*," he says (*Epistle to the Romans* on 3:25). According to Ambrosiaster, "They are justified freely because, neither working anything nor returning payment, they are *justified by faith alone as a gift of God*" (Ambrosiaster, *Commentary on Paul's Epistles*, on Rom 3:24 [PL 17:83], cited in Nick Needham,

general observation: these writings set mercy in opposition to the believer's merits.[53]

Of course, we cannot read later refinements into these sources. Furthermore, opposing quotations could be cited. Yet these samples demonstrate the important point that the major components of the Reformation's teaching on justification are near at hand: a judicial verdict that an ungodly person is declared just only on the basis of Christ's righteousness, received through faith alone, which is itself the gift of God, with works as the fruit. Some of these components will continue to be heard especially through the Augustinian tradition. But for the most part, no major figure in the Middle Ages will articulate as clearly the doctrine that we have discovered in the ancient writers.

AUGUSTINE

It is certainly the case that Pelagius borrowed heavily from Origen and his Latin translator, Rufinus, sided with Pelagius over Augustine.[54] Further, the views of Origen and Pelagius are comparable on many points. Nevertheless, we should beware of anachronism. Origen's nemesis was not Augustine but gnostic and pagan fatalism (much like Augustine himself in his earlier writings).[55] It is reasonable that the most vehement defenses of human responsibility, including merit and the conditionality of salvation, would be an overreaction provoked by gnostic theory of "natures" (that is, souls being created either good or evil and therefore unaccountable for their lot).

Soon after Augustine became a bishop, he wrote a letter that reveals a decisive turning point. "In responding to Simplician's request for clarification of Romans 9:1–29, as Augustine himself put it in his

---

"Justification in the Early Church Fathers," 40). Chrysostom is very clear that justification is through faith alone: "For the law requires not only faith, but also works; but *grace saves and justifies by faith*" (Chrysostom, *Homilies on Galatians,* on 3:12, cited in Needham, "Justification in the Early Church Fathers," 48). We are justified "by faith alone," says Jerome (*Epistle to the Galatians* (PL 30:848), cited in Needham, "Justification in the Early Church Fathers, 48). Basil exhorts that instead of boasting "on account of his own righteousness," the believer "has known himself to be wanting in true righteousness and to be *justified by faith alone in Christ . . .* for we live altogether in the *grace and free gift of God*" (*Homilies on Humility* 22 [PG 31:529–32], cited in Needham, "Justification in the Early Church Fathers, 49).

53. Ambrose, *Psalm 118* 42 (PL 15:1574), cited in Needham, "Justification in the Early Church Fathers," 50.

54. Scheck, introduction *Commentary on the Epistle to the Romans, Books 1–5,* by Origen, 16, 29.

55. Scheck, introduction to *Commentary on the Epistle to the Romans, Books 1–5,* by Origen, 30.

Reconsiderations thirty years later, 'I tried hard to maintain the free choice of the human will, but the grace of God prevailed.'"[56]

Already in *City of God* Augustine included Origen in his sights alongside Pelagius, especially with respect to the Alexandrian's notion of *apokatastasis* (final restoration of all souls).[57] "For as by the sin of one man we have fallen into a misery so deplorable," he wrote, "so by the righteousness of one Man, who also is God, shall we come to a blessedness inconceivably exalted."[58] Further, "Whoever therefore desires to escape eternal punishment, let him not only be baptized, but also justified in Christ, and so let him in truth pass from the devil to Christ. And let him not fancy that there are any purgatorial pains except before that final and dreadful judgment."[59] With Rome under the power of the Vandals and Hippo under siege, Augustine penned *Retractiones* (426 or 427) four years before he died—although he had considered the project fourteen years earlier. The contest with Pelagius refined Augustine's (and the church's) views on grace, and the bishop of Hippo's anti-Pelagian works reflect his mature teaching, which has powerfully influenced the course of church history. Though at first enamored of Origen, Jerome became his most strident Latin critic.

From the mature Augustine's anti-Pelagian writings, we can piece together the chief points relative to justification. First, the distinction between law and gospel in Augustine's *On the Spirit and the Letter* (412) was especially influential for the Reformation. In it, Augustine argued that no one is saved because of free will but because of the liberation of the will by grace through the gift of the Spirit to the elect.[60] Yet Pelagians insist that grace lies in God's gift of the law.

> But they give no heed to what they read: "By the law there shall no flesh be justified in the sight of God." This may indeed be possible before men, but not before Him who looks into our very heart and inmost will, where He sees that, although the man who fears the law keeps a certain precept, he would nevertheless rather do another thing if he were permitted. . . . [Paul] immediately adds what law

---

56. David F. Wright, "Justification in Augustine," in *Justification in Perspective*, ed. Bruce L. McCormack (Grand Rapids: Baker Academic, 2006), 56.

57. Augustine, *The City of God* 21.17 (*NPNF*[1] 2:466).

58. Augustine, *The City of God* 21.15 (*NPNF*[1] 2:464).

59. Augustine, *The City of God* 21.20 (*NPNF*[1] 2:466).

60. Augustine, *A Treatise on the Spirit and the Letter* 7 (*NPNF*[1] 5:85).

he meant, and says, "For by the law is the knowledge of sin." . . .
His words are, "*The righteousness of God* is manifested:" he does not
say, the righteousness of man, or the righteousness of his own will,
but the "righteousness *of God*"—not that whereby He is Himself
righteous, but that with which He endows man when He justifies
the ungodly.[61]

Thus, it is "by the faith where with one believes in Christ" that one is
justified as a gift "bestowed upon us." "It is not therefore by the law,
nor is it by their own will, that they are justified; but they are justified
freely by His grace—not that it is wrought without our will, but our will
is by the law shown to be weak, that grace may heal its infirmity; and
that our healed will may fulfill the law, not by compact under the law,
nor yet in the absence of law."[62]

The "law of faith" is set in opposition to "the law of works," the
former excluding all boasting. "Hastily, indeed, one might say that the
law of works lay in Judaism, and the law of faith in Christianity; foras-
much as circumcision and the other works prescribed by the law are just
those which the Christian system no longer retains."[63] However, this
Origenist interpretation is inadequate. The "works of the law" includes
the moral commands, set over against a gift of faith and righteousness.

What the law of works enjoins by menace, that the law of faith
secures by faith. The one says, 'Thou shalt not covet'; the other says,
'When I perceived that nobody could be continent, except God
gave it to him; and that this was the very point of wisdom, to know
whose gift she was; I approached unto the Lord and I besought Him'
[Wisdom 8:21] . . . Accordingly, by the law of works, God says to
us, Do what I command thee; but by the law of faith we say to God,
Give me what Thou commandest.[64]

Second, the gratuity of justification is lodged in the unconditionality
of election. "[God] does not indeed extend His mercy to them because
they know Him, but that they may know Him; nor is it because they

---

61. Augustine, *A Treatise on the Spirit and the Letter* 14–15 (*NPNF*[1] 5:88–89).
62. Augustine, *A Treatise on the Spirit and the Letter* 15 (*NPNF*[1] 5:89).
63. Augustine, *A Treatise on the Spirit and the Letter* 21 (*NPNF*[1] 5:91).
64. Augustine, *A Treatise on the Spirit and the Letter* 22 (*NPNF*[1] 5:92).

are upright in heart, but that they may become so, that He extends to them His righteousness, whereby He justifies the ungodly."[65] "'But why,' says one, 'is not the grace of God given according to men's merits?' I answer, Because God is merciful." That he does not give this mercy to all is due to the glory of his freedom, since "if He should deliver no one therefrom, He would not be unrighteous."[66]

Third, the Reformers drew upon Augustine's repeated affirmation that justification is a gift, not the result of merits. While the early Augustine had seen salvation in terms of Platonic ascent through contemplation, Peter Brown points out that the controlling idea of early Augustine (before 396) was the ascent to perfection through contemplation, while the Augustine of the anti-Pelagian controversy emphasized that works follow grace.[67] David F. Wright observes that for Augustine justification results from God *bestowing* righteousness as a free gift, by the Spirit rather than by the works of the law.[68] Works follow justification: "For no one acts justly [*justitiam . . . operatur*] unless he has been justified."[69] He opposes grace and merits in justification.[70] Even faith is a gift.[71] Even the beginner in faith is a possessor of righteousness. "As the sermon proceeds, Augustine more than once reiterates that 'you already are among the predestined, the called, the justified.'"[72] (Assurance like this would be condemned at the Council of Trent as wicked presumption.) Grace cannot be preceded by any merits whatsoever, Augustine insists, because the ungodly deserve punishment and not grace, and in any case, they can not will or do anything good apart from grace. Augustine is convinced that this is simply the teaching of the whole church.[73]

Elsewhere he explains that "the righteousness of God" is to be understood not only in an active sense (the justice that condemns) but in a passive sense as well. "God's justice not only that by which he is

---

65. Augustine, *A Treatise on the Spirit and the Letter* 8 (NPNF[1] 5:87).

66. Augustine, *A Treatise on the Spirit and the Letter* 16 (NPNF[1] 5:531).

67. Peter Brown, *Augustine of Hippo: A Biography* (Berkeley: University of California Press, 2013), 96, 145.

68. Wright, "Justification in Augustine," 56–57.

69. Augustine, *Expositions of the Psalms* 110:3 (PL 37:1464), quoted in Wright, "Justification in Augustine," 59.

70. Augustine, *Eighty-Three Various Questions* 76.1 (PL 40:88), quoted in Wright, "Justification in Augustine," 63.

71. Wright, "Justification in Augustine," 65.

72. Augustine, *Sermon* 158.4.4 (PL 38:364), quoted in Wright, "Justification in Augustine," 71.

73. Jarizinho Lopes Pereira, *Augustine of Hippo and Martin Luther on Original Sin and Justification of the Sinner* (Göttingen: Vandenhoek & Ruprecht, 2013), 141, 236.

himself just but also that which he gives to man when he *justifies the godless* (Rom 4.5). This is the justice the apostle sets before us when he says of some people, *Not knowing the justice of God and wishing to establish their own, they did not submit to the justice of God* (Rom 10.3)."[74] For Augustine, salvation is by grace alone and received through faith alone. "[One's] justification," he says, "is obtained by faith." In contrast with Origen, who restricted justification by faith alone to the beginning of faith, Augustine says it is found "in Jesus Christ" alone—"both in so far as it is *begun* within us in reality and in so far as its *perfection* is waited for in hope."[75] Augustine's teaching is summarized best in his quotation from Cyprian: "We must boast in nothing, since nothing is our own."[76]

At the same time, however, Augustine is also the progenitor of the medieval view of justification as a process of renewal (i.e., sanctification). Augustine clearly interprets justification as *making righteous*. The ungodly become righteous (*fiat iustus*). David Wright notes,

> Augustine in fact teaches something close to a declarative justification by faith, perhaps even faith alone, but does so as part of the more comprehensive righteous-making that embraces what most evangelicalism has called sanctification and that hence necessitates a faith effectively operative through love and hope. The key to understanding this is to fasten on justification as both event and process, as both beginning and growth.[77]

Augustine asks, "For what else does the phrase 'being justified' signify than 'being made righteous,'—by Him, of course, who justifies the ungodly man, that he may become a godly one instead? . . . Or else the term, 'They shall be justified' is used in the sense of, They shall be deemed or reckoned as just, just as it is predicated of a certain man in the Gospel, 'But he, willing to justify himself,'—meaning that he wished to be thought and accounted just."[78]

As Friedrich Loofs argued in 1906, justification in Augustine refers to the remission of sins (especially of original sin, through baptism)

---

74. Augustine, *On the Trinity* 14.15.
75. Augustine, *A Treatise on the Spirit and the Letter* 51, 105.
76. Cyprian, *Testimonies to Quirinus* 3.4 (*ANF* 5:528), quoted by Augustine in *On the Predestination of the Saints* 7 (*NPNF*[1] 5:500).
77. Wright, "Justification in Augustine," 70.
78. Augustine, *A Treatise on the Spirit and the Letter* 45 (*NPNF*[1] 5:102).

and the renewal of the inner person, especially the liberation of the will for the good.[79] Jerome's recently translated Greek New Testament (known as the Vulgate) rendered *dikaioō* (to *declare* righteous) as *iustificare* (to *make* righteous). Alister E. McGrath has argued that Augustine was dependent on Jerome's translation.[80] Regardless, the original forensic meaning is not entirely lost on Augustine. In various places, he speaks of justification as a purely gracious declaration that is based on Christ's merits and received through faith rather than by works.[81] Yet Wright justifiably concludes, "I know of no evidence that Augustine ever questioned the accuracy of *justifico* and its cognates as mistranslations of the original Greek (and Hebrew). Hence *justifico* as 'make just/righteous' seemed an obvious explanation of the compound verb, and the rest is history."[82]

Furthermore, it was Augustine who formulated the standard interpretation of justifying faith as requiring love.[83] Importantly, he does not believe, as medieval theology will teach, that faith needs to be *supplemented* or *formed* by love.[84] Humble trust includes hope and love.[85] Nevertheless, his inclusion of love as part of the essence of faith in the event of justification differs rather sharply from the absolute contrast drawn by his predecessors between faith and every pious virtue.

So, ironically, while many Greek fathers who did not affirm unconditional election nevertheless saw justification as a declaration that immediately gifts the believer with the status of perfect righteousness, Augustine bequeaths both an emphatic *sola gratia* monergism (grounded in unconditional election) *and* the idea of justification as a sanctifying process. Yet there are moments when Augustine speaks of justification as neither God's inherent righteousness nor an inherent righteousness in the believer but a "clothing" or "endowment" with Christ's righteousness "when he justifies the ungodly . . . by the faith wherewith one believes in Christ; for just as there is not meant the faith with which Christ Himself believes, so also there is not meant the righteousness

---

79. Friedrich Loofs, *Leitfaden zum Studium der Dogmengeschichte*, 4th rev. ed. (Halle: Niemeyer, 1906), 309–14.

80. Alister E. McGrath, *Iustitia Dei: The History of the Christian Doctrine of Justification*, 3rd ed. (Cambridge: Cambridge University Press, 2005), 1:12–16.

81. See, e.g., Augustine, *A Treatise on the Spirit and the Letter* 45 (*NPNF*[1] 5:102).

82. Wright, "Justification in Augustine," 72.

83. See John Burnaby, *Amor Dei* (London: Hodder and Stoughton, 1938), esp. 77–78, for an excellent treatment of Augustine's view of faith as inherently an act of loving friendship.

84. Burnaby, *Amor Dei*, 79–80.

85. Burnaby, *Amor Dei*, 78.

whereby God Himself is righteous. Both no doubt are ours, but yet they are called God's and Christ's, because it is by their bounty that these gifts are *bestowed* on us."[86] So, "We conclude that a man is not justified by the precepts of a holy life," he concludes, "but by faith in Jesus Christ—in a word, not by the law of works, but by the law of faith; not by the letter, but by the Spirit; *not by the merit of deeds, but by free grace*."[87]

The church's confrontation with Pelagianism forged a considerable consensus (at least in the West) on the doctrine of original sin and the absolute necessity for grace prior to all human decision and effort. Not only Pelagianism but semi-Pelagianism was condemned by successive bishops of Rome and the Council of Orange (529). Even the prayer for God's grace is preceded by God's grace. Anyone who believes that "the very desire for faith, by which we believe in Him who justifies the ungodly, . . . belongs to us by nature and not by a gift of grace" proves "that he is opposed to the teaching of the Apostles, for the blessed Paul says, 'For by grace you have been saved through faith; and this is not your own doing, it is the gift of God.'"[88]

Prosper of Aquitaine (c. 390–455) was a correspondent and indefatigable defender of Augustine. As secretary to Leo I, the bishop of Rome, he wrote several anti-Pelagian works targeting especially the Origenist monk John Cassian, whose views appear to be semi-Pelagian.[89] Prosper persuaded Leo's successor Celestine to oppose by pastoral means the spread of the heresy in Gaul.[90] In fact, Prosper was widely influential in securing a generally Augustinian consensus in the early medieval period.

A new controversy erupted in the Carolingian era with the monk Gottschalk of Orbais, whose views have been largely communicated by his opponents, especially Hincmar the archbishop of Reims. With ample citations from Augustine as well as Prosper, Gregory the Great, and Isidore of Seville, Gottschalk emphasized total depravity, unconditional election, Christ's death for the elect alone, irresistible grace, and

---

86. Augustine, on Rom 3:21, in *A Treatise on the Spirit and the Letter* 15 (*NPNF*[1] 5:89; PL 44.209).

87. Augustine, *A Treatise on the Spirit and the Letter* 22 (*NPNF*[1] 5:93).

88. Council of Orange (529) in *Creeds of the Churches*, ed. John Leith, 3rd ed. (Louisville: John Knox, 1982), canons 3 and 5 (37–44).

89. B. B. Warfield, "Introductory Essay on Augustin and the Pelagian Controversy," in *NPNF*[1] 5:xxi.

90. For a study of Prosper's teaching, see Alexander Hwang, *Intrepid Lover of Perfect Grace: The Life and Thought of Prosper of Aquitaine* (Washington, DC: Catholic University of America Press, 2009). The standard study of Cassian remains Owen Chadwick, *John Cassian* (Cambridge: Cambridge University Press, 1950).

the perseverance of the saints.[91] Even Pope Nicholas III expressed his concurrence with Gottschalk's views on these points.[92]

Nevertheless, as strongly and clearly as *salvation* was understood as by grace alone, in Christ alone, through faith rather than works, *justification* was understood in the Augustinian tradition as synonymous with the entire process of salvation. Hence, the distinct role of justification in the *ordo salutis*—namely, the imputation of Christ's righteousness rather than impartation of inherent righteousness—though not denied, does not seem even to have occurred to these formative theologians of the early medieval era.

---

91. See Gottschalk of Orbais, *Gottschalk and a Medieval Predestination Controversy*, ed. and trans. Victor Genke and Francis X. Gumerlock, Medieval Philosophical Texts in Translation (Marquette: University of Marquette Press, 2010).

92. Victor Genke, introduction to *Gottschalk and a Medieval Predestination Controversy*, by Gottschalk of Orbais, xx–xxi.

CHAPTER 4

JUSTIFICATION, PENANCE, AND THE METAPHYSICS OF GRACE

Lombard and Aquinas

"I hated this word, 'the justice of God,' which by the use and usage of all the doctors I was taught to understand philosophically in terms of the so-called formal or active justice with which God is just and punishes the sinners and unrighteous."[1] Was Luther either ignorant or malicious in this description of medieval theology, as argued in 1905 by Heinrich S. Denifle, OP?[2] This chapter begins to answer that question.

Such investigations are never undertaken in a vacuum but are provoked by contemporary interpretations that one wishes to engage both positively and critically. One of those interpretations that motivates my exploration here is what I call the Scotus Story, as told especially by John Milbank and others associated with the Radical Orthodoxy movement (summarized briefly in chapter 1). Though argued with expansive imagination and erudition, this thesis is not new. It continues the legacy of the *nouvelle théologie* (represented especially by Henri de Lubac and Hans Urs von Balthasar), the English Tractarian movement

---

1. Martin Luther, "Preface to the Complete Edition of Luther's Latin Writings," in *LW* 34:336–37.

2. H. S. Denifle, *Luther and Luthertum* (Mainz: Kirchheim, 1905); followed by Denifle, *Quellenbelege: Die endländischen Schriftausleger bis Luther über Justitia Dei (Rom. 1, 17) und Justificatio* (Mainz: Kirchheim, 1905); followed by Denifle, *Ergänzungen zu Luther und Lutherturn* I (Mainz: Kirchheim, 1905).

before that (especially in the work of Cardinal Newman), the thought of Heinrich S. Denifle and Joseph Lortz before that, all the way back to the archpolemicist of the Counter-Reformation, Johann Cochlaeus.

According to the Scotus Story, the brilliant synthesis of Christian Neoplatonism accomplished by Thomas Aquinas began to unravel with John Duns Scotus (1266–1308). At its core, the Scotist and nominalist apostasy was the concept that being is univocal. No longer identified as the source of our being, agency, and knowledge, God is reckoned a being alongside other beings. Thus, agency was now seen in a competitive relationship—who does more, God or humans—rather than the analogical perspective in which every human act toward the good is simultaneously the result of God's gracious operation.

Of course, a strong view of participation could sometimes collapse into pantheism or at least panentheism as it did with John Scotus Eriugena, Meister Eckhart, and Nicholas of Cusa (figures to be followed, according to Milbank and his working group).[3] However, with Scotus, God and the world begin to drift apart. The autonomous self, with a reserved space for the "secular," at first quite small, grew into a capacious realm that eventually swallowed the "sacred" whole. From Scotus the trail leads to another Franciscan, William of Ockham, and this new philosophy (known as nominalism) was mediated to the modern world by the Reformation, particularly Martin Luther himself.

I sympathize with pieces of this narrative, particularly the role of the late medieval Franciscans in exchanging Thomas's participatory, analogical, and therefore non-competitive account of divine and human agency. But to what extent did this nominalist project contribute to and shape the Reformation? It is not my intention to focus on the Scotus Story, but it will become apparent that I am glancing at it periodically as I seek to answer that question.

LOCATING JUSTIFICATION: THE EMERGENCE OF THE SACRAMENT OF PENANCE

Unknown to Scripture, the idea of human beings meriting God's saving gifts seems to have originated with Tertullian (160–220). Especially after embracing Montanism, Tertullian applied his legal training to the

---

3. These figures, undoubtedly pantheistic or at least panentheistic, represent the type of Christian Neoplatonism that Milbank encourages throughout his prolific *oeuvre*.

quest for a system based on rigorous asceticism. Describing this aspect in close detail, Pierre de Labiolle observes, "The God whom he cherishes is the inflexible and jealous Judge who has established *timor* [caution] as the solid base of man's salvation, who scatters temptations in this world in order to prove His faithful ones, and who holds His vengeance ever ready."[4] While merit was given considerable space in Tertullian, Origen, and Pelagius, a full-blown doctrine of merit awaited the Middle Ages. Surely this concept clashes with the "great exchange," which did not disappear. So what accounts for the demand for a major locus on merit in the medieval period?

One important factor was the emergence of the sacrament of penance. Until Aquinas, justification is largely absent from medieval systems, often only appearing in discussions of penance.[5] It is therefore not surprising that the struggle with penance came before the doctrine of justification in Luther's biography.[6]

PENANCE AND JUSTIFICATION

In the patristic era, penance was a specific exercise of church discipline toward public and heinous sins. The apostles had been given the keys to bind and loose. Concerning a profligate fornicator in the church, Paul even told the Corinthians "to deliver this man to Satan for the destruction of the flesh, so that his spirit may be saved in the day of the Lord" (1 Cor 5:5). Excommunications were to be rare and always directed ultimately to correction and winning back a brother or sister, but the unrepentant were excluded from Holy Communion and therefore salvation if they did not repent.[7]

Later, as Oscar Daniel Watkins chronicles, church discipline became more rigorous, though still limited in scope to public and heinous sins. Tertullian had stimulated this development by encouraging a long and arduous display of repentance through fasting, weeping, prayers, and

---

4. Pierre de Labiolle, *History and Literature of Christianity from Tertullian to Boethius*, trans. Herbert Wilson (London: Routledge, Kegan Paul, 1924), 55–105. Tertullian's enthusiasm drove him into the arms of the Montanist sect, which largely eclipsed his authority among orthodox contemporaries. Yet, like Origen, his influence—for better and for worse—persisted.

5. Charles P. Carlson, Jr., *Justification in Earlier Medieval Theology* (The Hague: Martinus Nijhoff, 1975), 8. Cf. A. M. Landgraf, *Einführung in die Geschichte der theologischen Literatur der Frühscholastik unter dem Gesichtspunkte der Schulenbildung* (Regensburg: Gregorius, 1948), 28–29. Carlson surveys Pauline commentaries from Origen to Nicholas of Lyra.

6. Carlson, *Justification in Earlier Medieval Theology*, 8–9.

7. Cyrille Vogel, *Le pécheur et la pénitence dans l'Église ancienne* (Paris: Cerf, 1982), 36.

other expressions of sorrow before receiving back straying members. Heresy, apostasy, blasphemy, murder, adultery, and fornication were the usual provocations of such measures, as he argued in *De Paenitentia*.[8] Cyrille Vogel has collected a list of sins that would typically qualify for varying degrees of serious discipline.[9] But Tertullian was on the radical end of the spectrum in his day, as Hippolytus's criticism of the bishop of Rome suggests.[10] In any case, there was no formal rite or process; discipline varied from place to place and was left to the judgment of the local bishop. Private confession was not obligatory and, when done, was treated as pastoral counseling rather than as a sacramental rite.[11]

But in the isolated Celtic territories of Britain an independent development of *tariff penance* emerged.[12] In this system, monasteries rather than the secular clergy often exercised discipline over the local community, and penance (with private confession) was increasingly urged even for venial sins. With the migration of many Anglo-Irish monks to the Continent in the ninth century, the practice became influential in the Frankish church. Paulinus II of Aquileia (726–802) argued that "the Christian should confess and do 'true penance' before taking the Eucharist, and that even lesser sins should be confessed."[13] The practice simply evolved and then was in search of a theological explanation. By the time of Alcuin of York in the late eighth century, justification

---

8. Oscar Daniel Watkins, *A History of Penance: Being a Study of the Authorities* (London: Longmans, Green, 1920), 71. Not surprisingly, Tertullian was on the extreme of patristic rigorism, despite his own break with catholic orthodoxy and unity by joining the Montanist sect.

9. Vogel, *Le pécheur et la pénitence*, 14–15. This list includes murder, adultery, fornication (including homosexuality), theft, vanity, sorcery, drunkenness, and perjury among other offenses.

10. Vogel, *Le pécheur et la penitence*, 19–26.

11. In *Justification in Earlier Medieval Theology*, Carlson observes, "The private system was unknown in the ancient Church" (79). "The system of penance as developed by the time of St. Augustine was a recognized and systematized church rite, but differed in a number of important respects from the modern private system." Basically, it was a "drastic disciplinary measure," often leading to excommunication. "And, in the West until the sixth century, all patristic authorities emphatically maintained that penance could be undertaken only once during one's lifetime. . . . The rite was not obligatory," was not a sacrament, and was imposed only for mortal sins. "For venial sins, the Fathers were unanimous in holding that, as in Augustine, 'the daily prayer of the believer makes satisfaction for those daily sins of a momentary and trivial kind which are necessary incidents of this life'" (80, from Augustine, *Enchiridion* 71). Procedures varied from place to place. "The sources do show that confessions were occasionally received but only informally as a pastoral, rather than sacramental, function. The ancient system of penance declined in the late Western Roman Empire both because of its inherent rigor and impracticality and due to a widespread moral relaxation attendant upon the political decadence of the Western Empire" (80). The Celtic practice seemed more amenable to the times (80–81).

12. Bernhard Poschmann, *Penance and the Anointing of the Sick*, trans. Francis Courtenay, Herder History of Dogma (New York: Herder & Herder, 1964), 124–25.

13. Carlson, *Justification in Earlier Medieval Theology*, 82.

became identified with penance and Peter Damian first listed it as a sacrament in the eleventh century.[14]

Gratian's textbook of canon law written in 1150 still knew nothing of a universal norm for penance, much less its status as a sacrament to be applied even in the case of venial sins. But around the same time Peter Lombard affirmed the necessity of oral confession (or at least the intention) and he included penance in his *Sentences* where the first enumeration of the seven sacraments appears.[15] For the first time, the Anglo-Irish practice was now proposed for the faith of the universal church.[16]

There is still no doctrine of justification per se at this point. Lombard speaks of "the doctrine of the *processus justificationis*," but it is a catch-all term rather than a specific topic in its own right.[17] Lombard draws on Gratian's newly minted code and may have had him in mind when he argues repeatedly against "the views of others" who contend that penance ought not to be frequent (and for venial sins), much less a sacrament.[18] It is true, he acknowledges, that Origen, Chrysostom, Augustine, and Ambrose regarded penance as something to be observed only once in a person's lifetime and only for "the graver, more horrendous, and pubic crimes."[19] However, they did not *forbid* regular penance.[20] Even Chrysostom's recognition of the penitent being restored even after multiple falls refers only to the lapsed, not to venial sins, says Lombard.[21] As the Reformers would point out, such arguments from silence betray the "sacrament of penance" as essentially Lombard's invention.

Given its significance for the rest of the story, I will summarize his treatment of justification and penance briefly. Christ merited his own immortality and impassibility, as well as the salvation of the elect,

---

14. Carlson, *Justification in Earlier Medieval Theology*, 83–84, 88. Cf. Pierre Pourrat, *Theology of the Sacraments* (St. Louis: Herder, 1910), 266 and 264n18.

15. Carlson, *Justification in Earlier Medieval Theology*, 104.

16. I should say Latin church, since to this day the Orthodox practice differs significantly from what it regards as the "legalistic" approach of the Roman Catholic Church. See Lewis J. Patsavos, *Spiritual Dimensions of the Holy Canons* (Brookline, MA: Holy Cross Orthodox Press, 2007), 41; Timothy (Kallistos) Ware, *The Orthodox Church* (New York: Penguin, 1993), 290–91.

17. Carlson, *Justification in Earlier Medieval Theology*, 114.

18. Peter Lombard, *The Sentences*, 4 vols., trans. Giulio Silano (Toronto: Pontifical Institute of Mediaeval Studies, 2010), 4:77–82.

19. Lombard, *Sentences*, 4:74–75.

20. Lombard, *Sentences*, 4:75–78. Of course, even if Lombard is correct, one wonders about the state of those (basically Christians generally) who did not enjoy this sacrament, much less the numerous stipulations that Lombard regards as essential to it.

21. Lombard, *Sentences*, 4:77. This is an unusual argument, since on all accounts apostasy (the sin of the lapsed) was mortal—hardly easier to ameliorate than venial sins.

by his life (beginning even at his conception) and death.[22] After describing Christ's suffering, Lombard adds rather shockingly that "the punishment by which the Church binds the penitent would suffice without the aid of Christ's pain, which he suffered for our sake."[23] Penance was therefore unhinged from Christology, separated as a therapy for renewing repentance and faith, and thus fell under the autonomous province of ecclesiastical power. "Christ's pain" is somehow a sine qua non, but the role of Christ's passion seems quite subordinate to the church's administration of the keys.

What is more, at Lombard's hands, the new sacrament threatens to eclipse baptism. While baptism is a sacrament only, says Lombard, "penance is called both a sacrament and a virtue of the mind," which he identifies as "an outward" and "an inner penance," respectively, "and each of these is a cause of justification and salvation."[24] The Vulgate's mistranslation of the imperative "Repent" (μετανοεῖτε) as "Do penance" is evident throughout the section.[25] He draws from Jerome the image of penance as "the second plank after shipwreck," which Aquinas adopts as well (in *ST* III, Q. 84, A. 6). This definition contrasts with Augustine and Chrysostom, who emphasized that baptism suffices for the whole of the Christian life, even for the lapsed who return to their baptism; the fathers never mention penance as a sacrament that picks up where baptism left off.[26] However, Origen's sharp distinction between sins committed before baptism (which are wiped away) and postbaptismal offenses (which are not) seems to be an assumption in Lombard's arguments.

"It is called penance," Lombard says, "from 'punishing' and by it each one punishes the illicit things which he has done. The virtue of penance has its beginning in fear."[27] But fear and sorrow are insufficient. "Many shed tears ceaselessly, and do not cease from sin."[28] Furthermore,

---

22. Lombard, *Sentences,* 3:72–74.

23. Lombard, *Sentences,* 3:81.

24. Lombard, *Sentences,* 4:69–70.

25. On this mistranslation point, see Alister E. McGrath, *Iustitia Dei: The History of the Christian Doctrine of Justification,* 3rd ed. (Cambridge: Cambridge University Press, 2005), 99–100. Only with Erasmus's new edition of his *Novum instrumentum omne* in 1516 will the exact translation, "change your mind," be made.

26. See for example Augustine's extended comments on the problem of the unpardonable sin in the *Unfinished Commentary on Romans,* in *Augustine on Romans: Propositions from the Epistle to the Romans and Unfinished Commentary on the Epistle to the Romans,* trans. Paul Fredriksen Landes, SBL Texts and Translations (Chico, CA: Scholars' Press, 1982), 83–89.

27. Lombard, *Sentences,* 4:70.

28. Lombard, *Sentences,* 4:71.

when one falls into the same sin again, the original act of penance "is destroyed," he says, "as are also other goods which had been done earlier, so that they do not receive the reward which they merited when they were done, and which they would have had, if the sin had not followed."[29] Lombard offers a questionable exegesis of the (probably noncanonical) story of the woman caught in adultery. "For the Lord says: *Go, and will to sin no more*. He did not say, 'do not sin,' but 'do not let even the will to sin arise in you.'"[30] Otherwise, "Nothing is left of mercy, because the remitted sins are again repeated."[31]

"In the performance of penance," he adds "three things are to be considered, namely, compunction of heart, confession of mouth, satisfaction in deed."[32] Even among venial sins there are greater and lesser ones, for which Lombard provides his own calculus for making satisfaction.[33] Sin is not remitted ordinarily without confession to a priest, though in extraneous cases (viz., deathbed situations where a priest is not available).[34] Inward penance is insufficient; there must at least be the intention to confess to a priest.[35] If one has time and does not confess to a priest, the sins are not remitted; confession to God alone or to a layperson does not suffice.[36] In fact, one must find not just any confessor but a priest who is sufficiently upright himself.[37] A widespread rebellion against the so-called "wicked priests" in the late medieval period would base itself on precisely this requirement.

A century after Lombard, Bonaventure understands penance as "man's part" in justification.[38] The elements of penance simply *are* now the elements of justification. Already with Bonaventure we meet the *facere quod in se est* (God will not deny grace to "those who do what lies within them"), though, as we will see, it will be radicalized by Scotus and the later Franciscans.

---

29. Lombard, *Sentences*, 4:72–73.

30. Lombard, *Sentences*, 4:73–74.

31. Lombard, *Sentences*, 4:74.

32. Lombard, *Sentences*, 4:88.

33. E.g., for smaller infractions "the Lord's Prayer suffices, together with some fasting and alms-giving, so long as some little contrition precedes and confession is added, if possible"; for the more serious (but still venial) transgressions, "these same things are to be done in satisfaction, but much more vehemently and strictly" (Lombard, *Sentences*, 4:93).

34. Lombard, *Sentences*, 4:94.

35. Lombard, *Sentences*, 4:97.

36. Lombard, *Sentences*, 4:99, 101.

37. Lombard, *Sentences*, 4:102–3.

38. Carlson, *Justification in Earlier Medieval Theology*, 116, from Bonaventure, *Commentary on the Sentences* 4, 14.1.2.3.

METAPHYSICS, MERIT, AND GRACE IN THOMAS AQUINAS'S DOCTRINE OF JUSTIFICATION

More than any other figure, the Irish monk and scholar John Scotus Eriugena (c. 815–877) was responsible for the Carolingian resurgence of Neoplatonism, especially as the translator of and commentator on Pseudo-Dionysius. His thoroughly speculative treatise against Gottschalk on predestination first aroused suspicions of Origenism, confirmed by his defense of universal salvation (*apocatastasis*), for which, in addition to pantheism, he was condemned by two provincial councils. Thus, the Anglo-Irish immigration played a significant part in reviving Origen's thought *and* importing the native penitential practices that assumed a new sacramental resource was needed for postbaptismal sins. Yet Augustine remained the touchstone of Western orthodoxy. Augustine's *caritas* was developed by the scholastics into an elaborate system of infused grace with many distinctions, most significantly between operative and cooperating grace.

Inheriting the consensus that Lombard summarized, Thomas Aquinas was nevertheless the first medieval theologian to relocate justification from a minor subtopic under penance to the heart of his discussion of grace, in the famous question 113 of the *Summa theologiae* I-II.

We have seen that for some church fathers like Origen the initial act of faith merits remission of *past* sins, while others (such as Chrysostom and Augustine) go so far as to treat faith in Christ as remitting all sins. Typically, medieval scholastics followed Augustine in regarding the first justification in baptism as regeneration but followed Origen (indirectly via Lombard) in reckoning that penance was necessary for present and future sins. *Remissio* (forgiveness) now became the *terminus ad quem* (goal) of the process of justification rather than its *terminus a quo* (source). This is a significant turning point in the medieval understanding of the doctrine.

A further important moment came with William of Auxerre (d. 1231). The first scholastic to make significant use of Aristotle, he developed the fourfold scheme of justification that Dominican and Franciscan schools would later take for granted: (1) infusion of grace (*infusio gratiae*), (2) movement of free will (*motus liberi arbitrii*), (3) contrition (*contritio*), and (4) remission of sins (*peccatorum remissio*).[39] Justification is now con-

---

39. McGrath, *Iustitia Dei*, 44.

sidered a physical *motus* (movement) from corruption to righteousness, according to Thomas Aquinas's master, Albertus Magnus.[40]

So two very important moves have been made with respect to justification: with Lombard, the inadequacy of baptism, which now must be supplemented by penance, and with Aquinas, the interpretation of justification in the categories of Aristotelian physics—that is, as a motion (*motus*) from injustice to rectitude. This movement itself was concerned primarily with an infused grace that could restore the proper order of the higher soul over the lower. In addition, remission became seen as the goal rather than the basis of this movement.

At the same time, Aquinas insists that God is the Prime Mover, so that his effectual grace is necessary to move the will to its rest (termination) in God's forgiveness.[41] One is forgiven because one is no longer ungodly but inherently just. However, it is crucial for Aquinas that divine and human agency not be seen in a competitive relationship. In Thomas's participatory metaphysics, God is always the efficient cause of good. Far from threatening human cooperation, God's effectual grace ensures it. God justifies by renewing, exciting, and moving the will to the good, but this is simultaneously the free movement of the person's will. Thus there is no calculus in his thinking where God does some things and human beings do other things. Before we turn to that discussion, however, it will be helpful to explore briefly Thomas Aquinas's *Commentary on Romans*.

The Romans Commentary

Like the early Augustine, the early Thomas was susceptible to semi-Pelagian interpretation, while the Thomas of the Romans commentary and *Summa theologiae* was "Augustinian." Based on his Paris lectures (second sojourn), the commentary was one of his latest works, completed while he was working on (and never finishing) his *Summa theologiae*.[42] In fact, the Romans commentary was completed shortly after the *Prima secundae* (I-II), which included the treatment of grace; therefore, they

---

40. McGrath, *Iustitia Dei*, 44.

41. McGrath, *Iustitia Dei*, 44–45.

42. According to Gilles Emery, "It appears that St. Thomas himself rapidly corrected the text of the first chapters of his commentary. Perhaps this commentary dates from the last years of Aquinas's teaching, in Paris (1271–72) or in Naples (1272–73)" (Gilles Emery, OP, "The Holy Spirit in Aquinas's Commentary on Romans" in *Reading Romans with St. Thomas Aquinas*, ed. Matthew Levering and Michael Dauphinais [Washington, DC: Catholic University of America Press, 2012], 128).

ought to be read together. As Thomas states in the first lecture, Romans ranks first among Paul's epistles. While the others treat the effects of grace in relation to various goods (e.g., in relation to the church in Ephesians or the sacraments in 1 Corinthians, etc.), Romans explores grace "as it is in itself."[43] This warrants moving justification to "grace itself" in the *Summa*, giving justification a systematic prominence that it had not yet enjoyed in medieval theology.

Thomas often thinks in "threes." The gospel "announces the news of man's union with God," a "threefold union": the grace of union, of adoption, and of attainment (or glorification).[44] The process of justification is the glue that holds these together, initiating the pilgrimage in baptism through operative grace (apart from works), meriting an increase of justification through cooperative grace (with works), to the end of attaining final justification of works by grace-enabled merits. Thomas lists three things that make a work good. First, its inherent justice. "The second element that makes a work good is intellectual discernment, whose absence is declared when he says, *there is none who understands.* . . .The third element is a right intention, whose absence is described when he says, *there is none who seeks after God.*"[45] And merit requires three conditions: (1) patience, (2) that the work is good (directed to its proper end) and conforms to natural and revealed law, and (3) "a right intention," namely, "not seeking something temporal, but eternal."[46] However, justification has *four* stages, which had been identified by William of Auxerre: (1) infusion of grace (ordinarily in baptism), (2) movement of free will, (3) contrition (genuine sorrow toward God), and (4) remission of sin.[47]

At Romans 1:4, Aquinas already sets forth a participatory metaphysics: a Neoplatonism adjusted radically to the absolute Creator-creature distinction along with the incarnation. The gospel announces not merely a participation in existence from God but a participation by adoption into his family secured from all eternity by God's predestination.[48]

---

43. Saint Thomas Aquinas, *Commentary on the Letter of Saint Paul to the Romans*, ed. J. Mortensen and E. Alarcón, trans. F. R. Larcher, OP (Lander, WY: Aquinas Institute, 2012), 1.1 (5).

44. Aquinas, *Commentary on Romans*, 1.2 (9).

45. Aquinas, *Commentary on Romans*, 3.2 (95).

46. Aquinas, *Commentary on Romans*, 2.2 (68).

47. Carlson, *Justification in Earlier Medieval Theology*, 119–20.

48. Aquinas, *Commentary on Romans*, 1.3 (13): "Now it is obvious that anything which exists of itself is the measure and rule of things which exist in virtue of something else and through participation. Hence, the predestination of Christ, who was predestined to be the Son of God by nature, is the measure and rule of our life and therefore of our predestination, because we are

"Therefore, just as the man Christ was not predestined to be the natural Son of God because of any antecedent merits, but solely from grace, so we are predestined to be adopted sons of God solely from grace and not from our own merits."[49] As in the *Summa,* the doctrine of predestination looms large over the *Commentary,* grounding the entire process of salvation in God's gratuitous mercy. "For God's love is not called forth by any goodness in a creature, as human love is; rather, he causes the creature's goodness, because to love is to will goodness to the beloved. But God's love is the cause of things: *whatever the Lord desires, he makes* (Ps 135:6)."[50] We are predestined *unto* merits, not *because of* them.

Faith involves "willed assent, with certitude, to that which is not seen."[51] But this is not yet justifying until faith is "perfected by the habit of charity." "Consequently, faith formed by charity is a virtue; but not unformed faith. . . . Consequently, the phrase *lives by faith* must be understood of formed faith."[52] Only when faith is inherently virtuous (moving from assent to love) does it become worthy of justification.

It is intriguing that Aquinas acknowledges an apparent contradiction between 2:17 ("The doers of the law will be justified") and 3:20 ("By the works of the law therefore no human being will be justified"). Not surprisingly, Aquinas says, "The answer is that justification can be taken in three ways": (1) by reputation (i.e., regarded as just); (2) "by doing what is just: *this man went down to his home justified* (Luke 18:14), because the publican performed a work of justice by confessing his sin. In this way is verified the statement that *the doers of the law will be justified,* i.e., by performing the justice of the law"; (3) "in regard to the cause of justice, so that a person is said to be justified when he newly receives justice: *being justified therefore by faith, let us have peace with God* (Rom 5:1)." But justification "cannot be accomplished either by the ceremonial works, which confer no justifying grace, *or by the moral works,* from which the habit of justice is not acquired; rather, we do such works in virtue of an an infused habit of justice."[53] As counterintuitive as it may seem from a Protestant perspective, *within the medieval paradigm* emphasis on infused righteousness is motivated by a concern to avoid any semi-Pelagian

---

predestined to adoptive sonship, which is a participation and image of natural sonship: 'those whom he foreknew he also predestined to be conformed to the image of his Son' (Rom 8:29)."

49. Aquinas, *Commentary on Romans,* 1.3 (13).
50. Aquinas, *Commentary on Romans,* 1.3, (13–14).
51. Aquinas, *Commentary on Romans,* 1.6 (37).
52. Aquinas, *Commentary on Romans,* 1.6 (38), emphasis added.
53. Aquinas, *Commentary on Romans,* 2.3 (74).

(much less Pelagian) notion of attaining righteousness apart from grace. As we will see, to the extent that later theologians make moves in the semi-Pelagian direction, they downplay or eliminate the necessity of this inherent grace.[54] It is therefore inappropriate to identify the concept of justification by infused rather than imputed righteousness as semi-Pelagian. Yet it is striking that according to Thomas the publican in Jesus's parable (Luke 18:14) "went home justified" because he had in fact fulfilled the law through confession (an aspect of penance), yet the justification of the sinner (the *first* justification) cannot be due to works (ceremonial or moral) but only to the habit of grace infused into the soul.

Paul's litany from the Psalter demonstrates that "there is no one righteous," whether Jew or gentile. Aquinas thinks that this means that "no one is just within himself and of himself, but of himself everyone is a sinner and it is owing to God that he is righteous." Furthermore, everyone "has some sin."[55] The law reveals this sin. "Law" can refer to the Old Testament, the Pentateuch, the Decalogue, the ceremonies, or to specific precepts. Here, however, Paul "takes 'law' in a general way," and in Romans 3:20 Paul includes the moral law as elucidating the natural law.[56] After all, he says, "the Apostle" could hardly be saying that the *ceremonial* precepts reveal the knowledge of sin.

> Consequently, the Apostle intends to say that by no works of the law, even those commanded by the moral precepts, is man justified in the sense that justice would be caused in him by works, because as he states below: *and if by grace, it is not now by works* (Rom 11:6). Then when he says, *for by the law,* he proves his statement, namely, that the works of the law do not justify. . . . Consequently, the law is not enough to make one just; another remedy is needed *to suppress concupiscence.*[57]

Aquinas does not reject the view that we cannot be declared righteous before God by the law; the idea would not have occurred to him since justification means something else entirely to him after centuries

54. As I point out in chapter 8, for precisely the same reason the Canons of Dort, a Reformed symbol, condemns the Remonstrant (Arminian) denial of infused habits being prior to any human motion toward God.
55. Aquinas, *Commentary on Romans*, 3.2 (95).
56. Aquinas, *Commentary on Romans*, 5.6. (156).
57. Aquinas, *Commentary on Romans*, 3.2 (99), emphasis added.

of thought reflected in the Vulgate's translation of the verb "to justify" as "to make righteous." Rather, the law is insufficient "to suppress concupiscence"—that is, to tamp down the embers of sinful desire. The law cannot make anyone perfect inasmuch as it is outward, and infuses no new habit for keeping the precept. The law cannot bring about genuine renewal of the mind and heart.

This reminds us that for Aquinas, as for the broader medieval tradition, the principal crisis addressed by grace is *nature* itself. Actual sins arise when the higher soul (oriented to God and spiritual things) allows itself to be pulled down by the lower soul toward the body and its passions. God had given Adam a gracious gift "which was lacking to human nature" as created, so that his soul could keep his body and its passions subordinate. "Thus, therefore, after man's mind was turned from God through sin, he lost the strength to control the lower powers as well as the body and external things," and "became subject to death."[58] The idea of a *donum superadditum*—a gift of grace added to nature in order to enable Adam to yield to his higher soul—is essential to his anthropology. This is how Aquinas interprets Paul's contrast between Spirit and flesh as well, in quite literal terms as the war between the intellect and the body.

This dualism stands in sharp contrast with Chrysostom and, as Bernhard Blankenhorn, OP, points out, is more pronounced than in Augustine.[59] As with Augustine, Aquinas places weight on Wisdom 9:15: "The corruptible body weighs down the soul." But Augustine tends to follow Paul more closely in treating "flesh" as metaphorical for the whole self under the reign of sin and death. Thomas by contrast tends to interpret "flesh" literally as the bodily nature.[60] There are other more Augustinian anthropological moments, especially in the *Summa*, according to Blankenhorn. "Yet it is striking how little place is granted to the inherent weakness of the will in the *Romans Commentary*, whose composition followed shortly after that of the *Prima secundae*."[61]

---

58. Aquinas, *Commentary on Romans*, 5.3 (141).

59. Bernhard Blankenhorn, OP, "Aquinas on Paul's Flesh/Spirit Anthropology in Romans" in *Reading Romans with St. Thomas Aquinas*, ed. Matthew Levering and Michael Dauphinais (Washington, DC: Catholic University of America Press, 2012), 4–30. Blankenhorn adds that the cosmological spheres of Paul's *sarx* and *pneuma* become interiorized in a Platonizing direction. "Augustine thus opens the path to what Krister Stendahl calls 'the introspective conscience of the West'" (11).

60. Blankenhorn, "Aquinas on Paul's Flesh/Spirit Anthropology," 12.

61. Blankenhorn, "Aquinas on Paul's Flesh/Spirit Anthropology," 19–20.

Consequently, although he has at first (*unlike* Origen) interpreted "works of the law" to include the moral commands as well as the ceremonies, he also (*like* Origen) identifies such works with external observances over against the inner work of the Spirit. In fact, observing the contrast between Origen and Augustine (and I would add Chrysostom), Robert Louis Wilken points out that even when Origen cites Titus 3:5 (twice in the Romans commentary), in both cases "works" refers merely to the ceremonies that distinguish Jews from gentiles.[62] Unlike the ceremonies of the old law, which are merely signs pointing to a future reality, "The Sacraments of the new law bring about what they signify."[63]

In any case, it is difficult to imagine how one could interpret "works of the law" as excluding *all works* without sacrificing the idea of justification as a process of becoming holy and thereby meriting (*de condigno*, in fact) final beatitude. It does not occur to Aquinas that Paul is opposing Christ's alien righteousness to ours.

Yet, especially given Protestant criticisms since Luther, it is noteworthy that Thomas demurs explicitly from Aristotle's *Ethics* at this point. It is generally true in human affairs that one becomes good by following good laws. But this is not how it works in justification, Aquinas observes, since "the justice which obtains glory before God is ordained to the divine good, namely future glory, which exceeds human ability."[64] Thomas repeats his anti-Pelagian point that infused grace—causing inherent justice—must come before all merits. Faith does not "exist from ourselves," as if "we merit God's justice, as the Pelagians assert." Rather, "Faith, as the first part of justice, is given to us by God," he says, citing Ephesians 2:8. "But this faith, out of which justice exists, is not the unformed faith about which James says, *faith without works is dead* (Jas 2:26), but it is faith formed by charity." Justification, he repeats, includes "a cleansing that does not occur without charity."[65]

---

62. Robert Louis Wilken, "Origen, Augustine, and Thomas: Interpreters of the Letter to the Romans," in *Reading Romans with St. Thomas Aquinas*, ed. Matthew Levering and Michael Dauphinais (Washington, DC: Catholic University of America Press, 2012), 300. Wilken adds, "Note how differently Augustine puts things: 'Above all else, one should understand that this letter addresses questions of the works of the law and of grace.' Like Origen, Augustine sets up a dialectic between works of the law and works of grace, but for him the term 'law' signifies something more general and is not linked specifically to the Mosaic Law, that is, to [ritual] observance" (299). Nevertheless, Wilkens concludes, "Although Thomas had read Origen, it is Augustine he follows" (297).

63. Aquinas, *Commentary on Romans*, 6.1 (161).

64. Aquinas, *Commentary on Romans*, 4.1 (110).

65. Aquinas, *Commentary on Romans*, 3.3 (101).

Faith only justifies inasmuch as it is already a love ("charity") that bears the fruit of good works. Abraham's believing in God "was reckoned to him as justice" (*reputatum ad iustitiam quod credidit*).[66] It was "not in some outward work but in the inward faith of the heart" that he was justified.[67] Interestingly, despite its loss of the Greek verb's declarative meaning in the rendering of *dikaioō*, the Vulgate did translate *elogisthē*— "was reckoned" (4:3)—with the forensic term *credidit*. When Abraham believed, "It was reputed to him unto justice": *reputatum est illi ad iusti-tiam*.[68] Nevertheless, apparently not even this suggested any notion of imputation as far as Thomas is concerned. Justification is "complete cleansing," he says later in the *Commentary*.[69]

Aquinas does engage Paul's contrast between reward and debt but instead interprets the apostle in a way that contradicts his point entirely. To be good, Thomas explains, a work must not only be intrinsically good (following God's command) but must be "performed under God's impulse in accord with the intention of God who predestines. And in this respect the aforesaid reward is due them by debt, because, as it is stated below: *for whosoever are led by the Spirit of God, they are the sons of God . . . and if sons, heirs also* (Rom 8:14, 17)." Through this faith, "without outward works," one "is called just and receives the reward of justice, just as if he had done the works of justice," and it is "not that he merits justice through faith, but *because the believing itself is the first act of the justice God works in him*."[70] Thus, faith justifies *neither* because it is an empty hand receiving Christ and his righteousness *nor* because it is a natural virtue or act of free will; instead, faith justifies because it is an inherent virtue caused by the infusion of grace. In rewarding faith, then, God is merely crowning his own gift.

When Paul speaks of David as an example of a forgiven sinner, Thomas again digresses from the simplicity of the argument to his own distinctions of various classes of sins: original, actual mortal, and actual venial.[71] The blessed one to whom the Lord does not impute sin can

---

66. Aquinas, *Commentary on Romans*, 4.1 (111).
67. Aquinas, *Commentary on Romans*, 4.1 (111).
68. Aquinas, *Commentary on Romans*, 4.2 (127).
69. Aquinas, *Commentary on Romans*, 5.5 (149).
70. Aquinas, *Commentary on Romans*, 4.1 (112), emphasis added.
71. "Such original sin is said to be forgiven, because the state of guilt passes with the coming of grace, but the effect remains in the form of *fomes* or concupiscence, which is not entirely taken away in this life, but is remitted or mitigated" (Aquinas, *Commentary on Romans*, 4.1 [113]).

refer only to venial sins.[72] Yet even if one accepts this distinction, (a) Paul is not engaging in casuistry but making a particular argument that Thomas misses, and (b) given the facts of David's case (adultery and murder), the sins for which he was pardoned were hardly venial. Paul's point about Abraham being justified before circumcision suggests to Thomas merely the weakness of the Old Testament rites: "That *ex opere operato* circumcision did not have effective power either to remove guilt or to produce justice. It was merely a sign of justice, as the Apostle says here. But through faith in Christ, of which circumcision was a sign, it removed original sin and conferred the help of grace to act righteously." Again, baptism accomplishes this thoroughly for us today, not as a sign but as the reality itself.[73]

What does Paul mean when he says that "the law brings wrath"? The law certainly makes one liable to God's vengeance, Thomas acknowledges, and "the law" here "refers even to moral precepts, not because they command something which makes its observers deserving of God's wrath, but *because the law commands and does not confer the grace to fulfill*, according to 2 Corinthians: *the letter kills, but the Spirit gives life* (2 Cor 3:6), namely, because *the Spirit also helpeth our infirmity* (Rom 8:26)."[74] He underscores the point: "*through faith*, through which we obtain grace, not because faith precedes grace, since it is rather through grace that there is faith: *by grace you have been saved through faith* (Eph 2:8)," but then immediately adds, "i.e., *because the first effect of grace in us is faith*."[75]

Thus, faith justifies not because it embraces Christ's alien righteousness as one's own (again, that would not have occurred to Thomas) but because it is the beginning of sanctification. This is a foundational point for understanding the difference between Roman Catholic and Reformation views of justification. We are a long way from the patristic comments that I quoted in chapter 2; it is assumed now that justification is a process of becoming holy through infused grace and that grace-inspired merits are means to that end. "From this aspect," namely Paul's appeal to faith in exclusion of works, "Christ's death was meritorious and satisfied for our sins."[76] However, Christ's merits merely provide the ground for the believer's meritorious cooperation with infused grace.

---

72. Aquinas, *Commentary on Romans*, 4.1 (114).
73. Aquinas, *Commentary on Romans*, 4.2 (119).
74. Aquinas, *Commentary on Romans*, 4.2 (121), emphasis added.
75. Aquinas, *Commentary on Romans*, 5.1 (130), emphasis added.
76. Aquinas, *Commentary on Romans*, 5.2 (136).

Brian Davies notes that for Thomas (as for Augustine) original sin is "guilt which follows from the fact that the will of Adam runs through his successors."

> In political thinking, he says, people belonging to a state are considered to be members of one body, and all of them together are deemed to be one person. In the same way, he adds, Adam's descendants can be regarded as one body with Adam as their head or soul. On this basis they are implicated in Adam's sin as the limbs of human beings are involved in the will by virtue of which they act voluntarily.[77]

Over against "the Pelagian heretics," Thomas says (on Rom 5:12–21) that according to the Apostle "sin entered this world through Adam not only by imitation but also by propagation, i.e., by a vitiated origin of the flesh in accordance with Ephesians: *we were by nature children of wrath* (Eph 2:3) and the Psalm: *behold, I was brought forth in iniquity* (Ps 51:5)."[78] Actual sins arise from original sin as a condition inherent in all fallen human beings.[79]

"Then," in Romans 8, "[Paul] considers what is involved on God's part who, first of all, predestined believers from all eternity; second, calls them in time; third, sanctifies them."[80] It is worth noting that Thomas can simply replace Paul's term, justification, with sanctification. However, this sanctification is grounded entirely in gracious election. God not only foreknows who will act well but determines whom he will save. "Hence, to claim that some merit on our part is presupposed, the foreknowledge of which is the reason for predestination, is nothing less than to claim that grace is given because of our merits, and that the source of our good works is from us and their consummation from God."[81] This passage underscores the crucial point that complicates the question of merit in Thomas's thinking. He has faced frankly the weighty objections to the whole idea of merit. In Thomas's view, only because God has predestined both the end and the means is merit

---

77. Brian Davies, *The Thought of Thomas Aquinas* (Oxford: Oxford University Press, 1992), 256, based on *ST* I-II, Q. 81, A. 1.

78. Aquinas, *Commentary on Romans*, 5.3 (138).

79. Aquinas, *Commentary on Romans*, 5.3 (104).

80. Aquinas, *Commentary on Romans*, 8.6 (233).

81. Aquinas, *Commentary on Romans*, 8.6 (234).

consistent with grace. Therefore—and this will become important for the later debates up to and including the Reformation—if one were to base election on foreknowledge, the idea of merit would indeed be Pelagian.[82] This point is made more systematically (and emphatically) in the *Summa*.

Furthermore, grace is necessary throughout the process of God's execution of predestination. God issues a "twofold call: one is external and is made by the mouth of a preacher," while the "internal call" is "nothing less than an impulse of the mind whereby a man's heart is moved by God to assent to the things of faith or of virtue. . . . This call is necessary because our heart would not turn itself to God, unless God himself drew us to him."[83] "Furthermore, this call is efficacious in the predestined. . . . Hence, second, he mentions justification, when he says, *and whom he called, them he also justified*, by infusing grace: *they are justified by his grace as a gift* (Rom 3:24). Although this justification is frustrated in certain persons, because they do not persevere to the end, in the predestined it is never frustrated." All of the elect will persevere in grace, by grace.[84]

Given this Augustinian emphasis, we are not surprised that Aquinas (unlike Origen and Chrysostom) does not blink when he comes to Romans 9. "Then when he continues: *nor had done any good or evil*, the Pelagian error is refuted. . . . This also corrects Origen's error who supposed that men's souls were created when the angels were, and that they merited different lives depending on the merits they earned for the good or evil they had done there."[85] "The Pelagian heresy" differs from Origen only in maintaining that "one is counted worthy of mercy on account of preexisting works in this life, though not in another, as Origen supposed." Both versions are beyond the pale, according to Thomas. But what if God *foresaw* that his grace would be used well? This

---

82. Given the hostility of many Catholics to unconditional election today, it is ironic that the Protestant reformers should be targeted for views that were not only affirmed but regarded with such importance by Aquinas. Milbank's fulminations against "arbitrary election" (John Milbank, *Beyond Secular Order: The Representation of Being and the Representation of the People* [Oxford: Wiley-Blackwell, 2013], 225) are difficult to reconcile with his fondness for Augustine and Aquinas. More consistent is Catholic theologian Michael Schmaus, who simply says that the church made a wrong turn with Augustine and that the Thomist perspective is a minority view today (Schmaus, *Dogma*, vol. 6, *Justification and Last Things* [London: Sheed and Ward, 1977], 19).

83. Aquinas, *Commentary on Romans*, 8.6 (235). This entire account would be appropriated by Reformed orthodoxy, including the distinction between external and internal call, with the latter as effectual.

84. Aquinas, *Commentary on Romans*, 8.6 (236). Cf. Davies, *The Thought of Thomas Aquinas*, 166.

85. Aquinas, *Commentary on Romans*, 9.2 (253).

is impossible, he says, because "every benefit God bestows on a man for his salvation is an effect of predestination."[86]

Long before Ockham, Thomas insists that God owes no one mercy. "For since all men are born subject to damnation on account of the sin of the first parent, those whom God delivers by his grace he delivers by his mercy alone; and so he is merciful to those whom he delivers, just to those whom he does not deliver, but unjust to none."[87] Salvation therefore depends not on human willing and exertion, but on the grace of the God who moves the will and the whole soul to good.[88] In the case of unbelief, God "is not said to harden [as in the case of Pharaoh] as though by inserting malice, but by not affording grace."[89]

With respect to the execution of this plan in history, Aquinas understands grace chiefly as a created substance infused into the soul at baptism. I noted in the previous chapter that the very notion of "created grace" is considered an oxymoron in Orthodox teaching. God's gracious energies are neither identical to the divine essence (implying pantheism) nor a created substance. The gift is the Holy Spirit, whose indwelling presence sanctifies and deifies. Apparently, this was also the majority view in the West until Aquinas.[90] Augustine, as we have seen, considered baptism effectual for the whole life, while Origen considered the sacrament effectual for past sins only. Lombard's sacrament of penance picked up where baptism, according to Origen, left off. Here, Aquinas follows in this latter development. The first justification (basically, regeneration) in baptism remits not only original but actual sins *up to that point*, while the sacrament of penance picks up where baptism left off, with purgatory as the final perfection of the soul through suffering.

---

86. Aquinas, *Commentary on Romans*, 9.3 (258).
87. Aquinas, *Commentary on Romans*, 9.3 (259).
88. Aquinas, *Commentary on Romans*, 9.3 (260).
89. Aquinas, *Commentary on Romans*, 9.3 (261–62).
90. As Michael Schmaus explains, "Peter Lombard identified sanctifying grace with love; and further, identified this love with the Holy Spirit." Thus, in Lombard's view, "There was no distinction, in his teaching, between created and uncreated grace." This view obviously underscores the personal dimension: in grace God gives *himself* to us. In explicit rejection of this view, Aquinas understood grace as "an intrinsic quality (accident) of the human person, like and objective determination (*habitus*)" (Schmaus, *Dogma*, 6:74). Schmaus judges that this is a more "static-essential" conception. By contrast, "Bonaventure understood it in a Platonic-Neoplatonic mode as light ceaselessly streaming out from God into man, a conception in which the dynamic character receives greater stress. When an accidental character is ascribed to grace, it is the form and not the content that is meant. As to the content, it exceeds all earthly forms" (Schmaus, *Dogma*, 6:74).

Justification and Merit in the Summa

We have seen that Thomas does indeed have a robust doctrine of grace and the gift of righteousness. Even for Thomas, though, this gift of justification is never a declaration; it is never a complete, perfect, and unassailable righteousness that can withstand God's judgment without trembling. Rather, it is a transforming and medicinal gift that makes one righteous, imperfectly in this life, insofar as humans cooperate (albeit, with effectual grace).

Since I have summarized the main terms of Aquinas's doctrine of justification, I will attend only very briefly to his teaching in the *Summa theologiae*. Before doing so, I will summarize the much earlier teaching on justification, represented by *Scriptum super libros sententiarum*, lectures on Lombard's *Sentences* delivered between 1252 and 1256. Here he argues that grace elevates nature to the beatific vision.[91] Grace makes the person and therefore his or her works pleasing. "Through the added dignity of cooperative grace which 'proportions' these works to God, human action is now treated as *meritorious* before God."[92] However, such merits can hardly be considered *condign*. If the merits of the suffering saints and martyrs are not equal to the reward of glory, surely no one else's can be.[93] But Thomas seems to argue too much, undermining the possibility of merit at all. Even if one has done all, the person is simply doing what he or she is supposed to do. Further, "Merit between people and God is impossible because merit means making another into one's debtor, and God is debtor to no one."[94] (Again it is worth bearing in mind that this idea of "a debtor to no one" plays a significant theological role long before Scotus and Ockham enter the picture.)

But there is debt and then there is *debt*. Unlike condign (outright) merit, congruent merit does not require an exact proportional equality between act and reward. Congruent merit is like a military award. Unlike a contractual obligation, a superior could withhold it without an injustice. Drawing on Aristotle's distinction in book 5 of *Ethics*, Thomas says that congruent merit is based on distributive rather than

---

91. Joseph P. Wawrykow, *God's Grace and Human Action: 'Merit' in the Theology of Thomas Aquinas* (South Bend, IN: University of Notre Dame Press, 1995). The first chapter alone ("The Literature on Merit and Related Concepts") is a bibliographical goldmine.

92. Wawrykow, *God's Grace and Human Action*, 66.

93. Wawrykow, *God's Grace and Human Action*, 69.

94. Wawrykow, *God's Grace and Human Action*, 70, referencing Aquinas, *Scriptum super libros sententiarum II* 27.1.3, ob. 4.

commutative justice.[95] In other words, merit is given from the liberality of the one who grants the reward to those whom it is fitting (*decet*) that such a gift be granted.[96]

However, even after acknowledging objections, Aquinas can affirm a *condign* merit that is nevertheless based on *distributive* rather than strict commutative justice.[97] "Merit places God under no obligation or debt," since the reward is liberally and freely given. But it is merit in the fullest sense.[98]

Then there is the question as to whether the first grace of justification can be merited.[99] Although Thomists differ on the answer, Blankenhorn observes that the Thomas of the *Scriptum* maintains the "quasi semi-Pelagian" view that one may prepare oneself for grace by free will. "This notion of self-preparation for grace is so strong that Thomas implies that the supernatural habit, including justification, is *almost* merited: 'If the human being would prepare himself *by doing what is within himself*, without a doubt grace would follow.'"[100]

Thus we meet the infamous "do what you can" (*facere quod in se est*) maxim of Scotus and the nominalists already in the early Aquinas.[101] "Once the sinner disposes himself for grace by doing what is in him, by God's promise God is bound to grant justifying grace and so perfects the soul."[102] If this is accurate, then one might well locate the decisive turning point toward the thesis not only of a hypothetical concept but the actual reality of a pure nature (*natura purus*), autonomous and independent of grace, not in Scotus or Ockham but in early Aquinas.

However, like Augustine's rather sharp transition, Aquinas's view of

---

95. Wawrykow, *God's Grace and Human Action*, 74.

96. Wawrykow, *God's Grace and Human Action*, 72: "ex congruo autem tantum, quando talis aequalitas non invenitur, sed solum secundum liberalitatem dantis munus tribuitur quod dantem decet" (Aquinas, *Scriptum super libros sententiarum IV* 15.1.3, sol. 4).

97. Wawrykow, *God's Grace and Human Action*, 75.

98. Wawrykow, *God's Grace and Human Action*, 76.

99. Aquinas, *Scriptum super libros sententiarum II* 27.1.4.

100. Bernhard Blankenhorn, OP, "Aquinas on Paul's Flesh/Spirit Anthropology in Romans," 33, emphasis added, quoting Thomas Aquinas, *Scriptum super Sententiis* II (Paris: Sumptibus P. Lethielleux, 1929), 26.1.2, ad 2; 27.1.4; and 28.1.3, ad 5. Blankenhorn explains here the *Scriptum*'s argument: "A human being, even if he would never have committed sin or sinned by omission . . . would have sinned in this, that he did not prepare himself for grace.' In other words, if the fallen creature would act virtuously, grace would almost naturally follow, and hence grace seems virtually merited. This *quasi* semi-Pelagian tendency in the young Thomas is amplified in his notion of ungraced works as the material cause of sanctification, with grace being the formal cause. The natural material cause limits the gratuity of grace, so that the formal cause of justification (grace) is virtually necessary once there is a due disposition of the matter."

101. Wawrykow, *God's Grace and Human Action*, 84–85.

102. Wawrykow, *God's Grace and Human Action*, 86.

merit changes significantly from the *Scriptum* to the *Summa*, particularly the Second Part.[103] There, Aquinas draws a sharp distinction between natural and supernatural orders.[104] Although we can fulfill our natural end naturally, we cannot even desire our supernatural end apart from grace.[105] As Aquinas says, "Adam in a perfect nature, could, by his natural power, do the good *natural* to him without the addition of any gratuitous gift."[106] Adam did not have the natural power to merit *supernatural* life but only the ability to pursue his natural good: namely, temporal happiness.

Thomas's discussion of whether humans are ordered naturally to their supernatural end has provoked a considerable debate among Thomists in the past and in Aquinas scholarship today.[107] Wawrykow is justified in concluding that for the mature Thomas the desire for the supernatural good (*bonum supernaturale* and a *bonum superexcedens*) is not natural but is an "infused virtue."[108] Thomas "contrasts the good *connaturale* [natural] to human being and the *bonum supernaturalis iustitiae*."[109] For example, one can fulfill his virtue of being a good father without desiring the vision of God. Grace is infused to elevate nature to the supernatural.[110] This is required for meritorious good works and is given to the pre-destined.[111] Only through this infused virtue may the elect become partakers of divine nature.[112] Grace is needed for supernatural truth but not for natural.[113] Grace not only elevates; it heals the disorder in the soul (where the appetites of the lower soul have out-ranked reason).[114]

---

103. The *Summa* is organized into three basic parts: *Prima Pars* (I), on God. The Second Part (on the return of rational creatures to God) is divided into *Prima Secundae* (I-II), return in general, and *Secunda Secundae* (II-II), return in specifics. And then the *Tertia Pars* (III), which Thomas failed to complete before his death, treats the means of grace (esp. the sacraments). The discussion of merit comes up at the end of I-II.

104. Wawrykow, *God's Grace and Human Action*, 165–66, citing *ST* I-II, Q. 110, A. 3.

105. Wawrykow, *God's Grace and Human Action*, 167.

106. *ST* I-II, Q. 109, A. 3 (2:1126).

107. *ST* I-II, Q. 109, A. 2 (2:1125). The recent controversy was sparked by Henri de Lubac, arguing that the authentic Thomas affirmed the natural desire for the supernatural end (the beatific vision), but that Thomists from Cajetan to Reginald Garrigou-Lagrange corrupted his teaching. For example, see de Lubac's extraordinary work, *The Mystery of the Supernatural*. Milestones in Catholic Thought (New York: Crossroad, 1998). For a helpful survey of the debate and a defense of the view that Wawrykow sets forth here, see Lawrence Feingold, *The Natural Desire to See God According to St. Thomas*, 2nd ed., Faith and Reason: Studies in Catholic Theology and Philosophy (Washington, DC: Catholic University of America Press, 2004). After close study of the sources, I find Feingold's evidence compelling.

108. *ST* I-II, Q. 109, A. 7, ad. 3 (2:1128).

109. Wawrykow, *God's Grace and Human Action*, 166n40.

110. *ST* I-II, Q. 109, A. 9 (2:1130–31).

111. *ST* I-II, Q. 110, A. 1–2 (2:1132).

112. *ST* I-II, Q. 110, A. 3; Q. 62, A. 1.

113. Wawrykow, *God's Grace and Human Action*, 167, from the *ST* I-II, Q. 109, A. 1.

114. Wawrykow, *God's Grace and Human Action*, 170–71.

The *Summa*'s Treatise on Grace (Q. 109), consisting of ten articles, begins with a litany of scriptural passages confirming that human beings cannot know any truth apart from God's grace. Drawing on Aristotle's *Physics,* Thomas argues that God is both the First Mover of all creaturely movement and the First Act from whom all formal perfection is derived.[115] Just as water cannot be heated apart from fire, human beings are powerless with respect to their supernatural end without a superadded form.[116]

The Second Article addresses the question, "Whether Man Can Wish or Do Any Good without Grace?" Thomas answers in the negative, appealing to Romans 9:16 and various passages from Augustine. Even in the natural state before the fall, humans needed "a gratuitous strength superadded to natural strength . . . in order to carry out works of supernatural virtue, which are meritorious"; how much more so "in the state of corrupt nature."[117]

While the *Scriptum* taught that one may avoid all mortal sin—and thus love God above all else—even apart from grace, Thomas is now eager to affirm that a person "before justification is radically incapable of preparing for grace without God's supernatural help. . . . The preparation for grace demands God's unmerited motion in our free decision. This is abundantly clear in I-II, q. 109, a. 6" (also A. 8).[118] At the same time, the deeper conviction of original sin does not seem to affect the mind as much as the will, in comparison with Augustine. Blankenhorn comments, "Aquinas insists on maintaining a kind of firewall between the will and the speculative intellect, though it is not impregnable."[119]

The goal of human existence is to love God above all things, and "in a state of perfect nature" humans could do what was natural to them "without the addition of any gratuitous gift." He is not speaking here of the rectitude of the mind and its ordering to a supernatural end, which required the superadded gift (*donum superadditum*). He is speaking here merely of that natural love which finds in God the source of its natural origin and fulfillment. Indeed, to love God above all is natural "even to inanimate nature according to the love which can belong to a

---

115. *ST* I-II, Q. 109, A. 1 (2:1123).
116. *ST* I-II, Q. 109, A. 1 (2:1124).
117. *ST* I-II, Q. 109, A. 1 (2:1124).
118. Blankenhorn, "Aquinas on Paul's Flesh/Spirit Anthropology in Romans," 33.
119. Blankenhorn, "Aquinas on Paul's Flesh/Spirit Anthropology in Romans," 36.

creature."[120] It is "natural to seek and love things" that are naturally fit to be loved, and what could be more fit to love than God?

> Hence in the state of perfect nature man referred the love of himself and of all other things to the love of God more than himself and above all things. But in the state of corrupt nature man falls short of this in the appetite of his rational will, which, unless it is cured by God's grace, follows its private good, on account of the corruption of nature. And hence we must say that in the state of perfect nature man did not need the gift of grace added to his natural endowments, in order to love God above all things naturally, although he needed God's help to move him to it; but in the state of corrupt nature man needs, even for this, the help of grace to heal his nature.[121]

Over against "the Pelagian heresy," he says, it is essential to affirm that grace is necessary to fulfill the law.[122] Here, too, we must distinguish between the state of nature and the state of corruption; according to the former, obedience was possible, but not according to the latter. However, even in the state of pure nature, it was possible to obey the law as to "the substance of the works" (viz., acts of "justice, fortitude, and other virtues") but not as to "the mode of acting, i.e., their being done out of charity." To fulfill the commands *in the right manner* required grace even before the fall.[123] "Now everlasting life is an end exceeding the proportion of human nature," based on the preceding argument. "Hence man, by his natural endowments, cannot produce meritorious works proportionate to everlasting life; and for this a higher force is needed, viz., the force of grace." He may certainly do works "natural to man, as to toil in the fields, to drink, to eat, or to have friends, and the like, as Augustine says in his third *Reply to the Pelagians*." But only "when the will is prepared by grace" do human beings even will the good. Just as one may recover health through various medicines, human nature can only be elevated to accomplishing its supernatural end by healing grace.[124]

The objection (one assumes that he has Pelagians in mind in *Obj. 2*) is that "man prepares himself for grace by doing what is in him to do,

---

120. *ST* I-II, Q. 109, A. 3 (2:1126).
121. *ST* I-II, Q. 109, A. 1 (2:1125).
122. *ST* I-II, Q. 109, A. 1 (2:1125).
123. *ST* I-II, Q. 109, A. 4 (2:1126).
124. *ST* I-II, Q. 109, A. 5 (2:1127).

since if man does what is in him to do God will not deny him grace, for it is written (Matt. 7.11) that God gives His good Spirit *to them that ask Him*. But what is in our power, is in us to do."[125] We should note that this formula is equivalent to that of Scotus, Ockham, and Biel, as we will see in due course, but it appears here as an imagined *objection* to his view. Aquinas refutes it first by quoting John 6:44 ("No one can come to me unless the Father who sent me draws him"). "Hence it is clear that man cannot prepare himself to receive the light of grace except by the gratuitous help of God moving him inwardly." It is indeed true that the will freely turns to God, but only "when God turns it, according to Jer. 31.18: *Convert me and I shall be converted, for Thou art the Lord, my God;* and Lament. 5.21: '*Convert us, O Lord, to Thee, and we shall be converted.*'"[126] So even our preparations for grace are prepared by grace. "Therefore by himself he cannot be justified, i.e., he cannot return from a state of sin to a state of justice. . . . Man by himself can no wise rise from sin without the help of grace."[127] Aquinas has completely overturned his earlier teaching in the *Scriptus*.

Sin involves "a triple loss": "stain, corruption of natural good, and debt of punishment." "Now it is manifest that none of these three can be restored except by God."[128] But even one who is in a state of grace "needs a further assistance of grace in order to live righteously." It requires "a further infused habit." Since the soul is never completely healed in this life, cooperating grace is always required.[129] "And hence after anyone has been justified by grace, he still needs to beseech God for the aforesaid gift of perseverance, that he may be kept from evil till the end of his life. For to many grace is given to whom perseverance in grace is not given."[130]

Grace then is a medicinal substance. "Grace, as a quality, is said to act upon the soul, not after the manner of an efficient cause, but after the manner of a formal cause, as whiteness makes a thing white, and justice, just." "And because grace is above human nature," he adds, "it cannot be a substance or a substantial form, but is an accidental form of the soul. Now what is substantially in God becomes accidental in the soul

---

125. *ST* I–II, Q. 109, A. 5 (2:1127).
126. *ST* I–II, Q. 109, A. 6 (2:1128).
127. *ST* I–II, Q. 109, A. 7 (2:1128).
128. *ST* I–II, Q. 109, A. 7 (2:1128).
129. *ST* I–II, Q. 109, A. 9 (2:1130–31).
130. *ST* I–II, Q. 109, A. 10 (2:1131).

participating in Divine goodness, as is clear in the case of knowledge." This is "created grace," he says, "inasmuch as men are created with reference to it, i.e., are given a new being out of nothing, i.e., not from merits, according to Eph. 2.10, *created in Jesus Christ in good works*."[131]

The five articles of question 111 break grace down into three divisions. The first two are *sanctifying grace*, by which man is united to God, and *gratuitous* grace, the spiritual gifts or charisms that we use for the benefit of others. It is sanctifying grace that concerns us here. As whiteness makes a thing white (formally and not efficiently), Thomas says,

> Grace is said to make pleasing, not efficiently, but formally, i.e., because thereby a man is justified, and is made worthy to be called pleasing to God. . . . Grace, inasmuch as it is gratuitously given, excludes the notion of a debt. Now debt may be taken in two ways:—first, as arising from merit; and this regards the person whose it is to do meritorious works, according to Rom 4.4. . . . The second debt regards the condition of nature. Thus we say it is due to a man to have reason, and whatever else belongs to human nature. Yet in neither way is debt taken to mean that God is under an obligation to His creature, but rather that the creature ought to be subject to God, that the Divine ordination may be fulfilled in it, which is that a certain nature should have certain conditions or properties, and that by doing certain works it should attain to something further. And hence natural endowments are not a debt in the first sense but in the second. Hence they especially merit the name of grace.[132]

Besides sanctifying and gratuitous grace, there is *operating* and *cooperating* grace. He has stated (Q. 110, A. 2) that "grace may be taken in two ways: first, as a Divine help, whereby God moves the will and to act; secondly, as a habitual gift divinely bestowed on us. Now in both these ways grace is fittingly divided into operating and cooperating." In operating grace, the act is attributed to the first mover. "Hence after the aforementioned words Augustine subjoins: *He operates that we may will; and when we will, He cooperates that we may perfect*." This is the best definition of his distinction.[133]

---

131. *ST* I-II, Q. 110, A. 2 (2:1133).
132. *ST* I-II, Q. 111, A. 1 (2:1136).
133. *ST* I-II, Q. 111, A. 2 (2:1137).

The third division is between *preventative* and *subsequent* grace and includes his classic statement of their five effects:

> Now there are five effects of grace in us: of these, the first is, to heal the soul; the second, to desire the good; the third, to carry into effect the good proposed; the fourth, to persevere in good; the fifth, to reach glory. And hence grace, inasmuch as it causes the first effect in us, is called prevenient with respect to the second, and inasmuch as it causes the second, it is called subsequent with respect to the first effect. And as one effect is posterior to this effect, and prior to that, so may grace be called prevenient and subsequent on account of the same effect viewed relatively to divers others. And this is what Augustine says (*De Natura et Gratia* xxxi): *It is prevenient, inasmuch as it heals, and subsequent, inasmuch as, being healed, we are strengthened; it is prevenient, inasmuch as we are called, and subsequent, inasmuch as we are glorified.*[134]

Even before the fall, grace was required to elevate nature beyond itself, since partaking of the divine nature transcends human nature. This *donum superadditum* (gift added to nature) was lost in the fall. So now humans must prepare themselves for the infusion of *habitual grace*, but even this preparation is *by the help of God*. So we must again distinguish habitual and helping grace. Thomas adds, "A certain preparation of man for grace is simultaneous with the infusion of grace; and this operation is meritorious, not indeed of grace, which is already possessed, but of glory which is not yet possessed. . . . Since a man cannot prepare himself for grace unless God prevent and move him to good, it is of no account whether anyone arrive at perfect preparation instantaneously, or step by step."[135]

Grace does not merely make conversion possible, but as first mover, God graciously brings it about. Faith is a gift of God created in us by the Holy Spirit.[136] It is an "infused virtue."[137] Faith is assent to the propositions of the Nicene-Constantinopolitan Creed, but charity completes faith by moving the whole soul "towards enjoying God for his

---

134. *ST* I-II, Q. 111, A. 3 (2:1138).
135. *ST* I-II, Q. 112, A. 2 (2:1141).
136. See *ST* II-II, Q. 6, A. 1.
137. Davies, *The Thought of Thomas*, 283.

own sake."[138] While remaining a free act of the will, this movement is finally irresistible. "Hence if God intends, while moving, that the one whose heart He moves should attain to grace, he will infallibly attain to it, according to John 6.45: *Every one that hath heard of the Father, and hath learned, cometh to Me.*"[139] Against certain Thomist interpreters, Wawrykow insists that for Thomas, "Grace not only makes such acts 'easier,' it makes people do these acts."[140] "Similarly, grace as habitual endows the individual with new being," transforming them into "a sharer in the divine nature, so that what is 'owed' to and enjoyed by God likewise becomes 'owed' to those who have been endowed with God's 'nature.' . . . As Romans 8:17 says, 'If sons, then also heirs.'"[141]

Question 113 treats the effects of grace in ten articles. With his dependence on Aristotle's *Physics*, Thomas views justification as *movement* from injustice to its opposite, justice. This dependence is crucial for understanding why Aquinas can only think of justification as a process of becoming righteous. "Justification, taken passively implies a movement towards justice, as heating implies a movement towards heat."[142] Justice is "rectitude of order in the interior disposition of man, in so far as what is highest in man is subject to God, and the inferior powers of the soul are subject to the superior, i.e., to the reason; and this disposition the Philosopher calls *justice metaphorically speaking (Ethic.* v, 11)." Adam's justice was original, a movement from privation to form, by the sheer fact of being created *ex nihilo.* But since the fall, "This justice may be brought about in man by a movement from one contrary to the other, and thus justification implies a transmutation from the state of injustice to the aforesaid state of justice. And it is thus we are now speaking of the justification of the ungodly, according to the Apostle (Rom. 4.5): *But to him that worketh not, yet believeth in Him that justifieth the ungodly,* etc."[143] Sin shuts us out of eternal life, but grace makes us worthy of it. "Hence we could not conceive the remission of guilt, without the infusion of grace."[144] "The justification of the ungodly is brought about by God moving man to justice."[145]

---

138. *ST* II-II, Q. 23, A. 2 (3:1263).
139. *ST* I-II, Q. 112, A. 3 (2:1142).
140. Wawrykow, *God's Grace and Human Action,* 194n98.
141. Wawrykow, *God's Grace and Human Action,* 195.
142. *ST* I-II, Q. 113, A. 1 (2:1144).
143. *ST* I-II, Q. 113, A. 1 (2:1145).
144. *ST* I-II, Q. 113, A. 2 (2:1145).
145. *ST* I-II, Q. 113, A. 2 (2:1146).

While it is true that justification is through faith, Thomas insists,

> The movement of faith is not perfect unless it is quickened by charity; hence in the justification of the ungodly, a movement of charity is infused together with the movement of faith. . . . By natural knowledge a man is not turned to God, according as he is the object of beatitude and the cause of justification. Hence such knowledge does not suffice for justification.[146]

Even being sorry for the sins one cannot remember "cooperates in his justification."[147]

Next, in another definitive passage, Thomas asserts,

> There are four things which are accounted to be necessary for the justification of the ungodly, viz., the infusion of grace, the movement of the free-will towards God by faith, the movement of the free-will towards sin, and the remission of sins. The reason for this is that, as stated above (A. 1), the justification of the ungodly is a movement whereby the soul is moved by God from a state of sin to a state of justice, . . . but the consummation of the movement of the attainment of the end of the movement is implied in the remission of sins; for in this is the justification of the ungodly completed.[148]

Thus, justification consists of both "the infusion of grace and the remission of sin."[149] In fact, in that logical order: infusion of grace is the basis for remission. "The entire justification of the ungodly consists as to its origin in the infusion of grace. For it is by grace that free-will is moved and sin is remitted."[150] The four things in justification happen simultaneously, but there is a logical order: "The first is the infusion of grace; the second, the free-will's movement towards God; the third, the free-will's movement towards sin; the fourth, the remission of sin." Thus, crucially, forgiveness is not the beginning but the goal of the

---

146. *ST* I-II, Q. 113, A. 4 (2:1147).
147. *ST* I-II, Q. 113, A. 5 (2:1148).
148. *ST* I-II, Q. 113, A. 6 (2:1149).
149. *ST* I-II, Q. 113, A. 6 (2:1149).
150. *ST* I-II, Q. 113, A. 7 (2:1150).

process of justification. "The reason for this," he goes on to say, is the order of movement (according to Aristotelian physics).[151]

To summarize, there are *two types of grace* (operating and cooperating), *five effects* (healing the soul, movement of the will to the good, good acts, perseverance, and attaining glory), and *four requirements of justification* (infusion of grace, faith, repentance, and forgiveness).

Finally, question 114 devotes ten articles to merit. He begins,

> Now it is clear that between God and man there is the greatest inequality. . . . Hence there can be no justice of absolute equality between man and God, but only a certain proportion, inasmuch as both operate after their own manner. Now the manner and measure of human virtue is in man from God. Hence man's merit with God only exists on the presupposition of the Divine ordination, so that man obtains from God, as a reward of his operation, what God gave him the power of operation for, even as natural things by their proper movements and operations obtain that to which they were ordained by God.[152]

God is thereby made a debtor not to us but to himself, "inasmuch as it is right that His will should be carried out."[153] Adam and Eve could not have merited eternal life without grace before the fall "because man's merit depends on the Divine pre-ordination. . . . God ordained human nature to attain the end of eternal life, not by its own strength, but by the help of grace; and in this way its act can be meritorious of eternal life."[154]

This is perhaps the greatest difference between the *Scriptum* and the *Summa* interpretation of grace.[155] While Thomas had difficulty bringing himself to accept condign merit without falling into semi-Pelagianism, he now has his formulation. Because merit is grounded in God's unconditional election, we are only being rewarded for what he has predestined in eternity and brought about by his grace in time.

Can we then merit eternal life *condignly*—that is, properly speaking,

---

151. *ST* I-II, Q. 113, A. 8 (2:1151).
152. *ST* I-II, Q. 114, A. 1 (2:1154).
153. *ST* I-II, Q. 114, A. 1 (2:1154). See Wawrykow, *God's Grace and Human Action*, 81.
154. *ST* I-II, Q. 114, A. 1 (2:1154).
155. Wawrykow, *God's Grace and Human Action*, 77–79. Wawrykow points out that the material in the *Scriptum* on merit (*Scriptum super libros sententiarum II* 27.1.3) is spread across "three distinct articles" in *ST* (I-II, Q. 114, A. 1; I-II, Q. 114, A. 3).

not just as an accommodation but as a strict reward? If it proceeded from free will alone, it could not be condign "because of the very great inequality."

> But there is congruity, on account of an equality of proportion: for it would seem congruous that, if a man does what he can, God should reward him according to the excellence of his power. If, however, we speak of a meritorious work, inasmuch as it proceeds from the grace of the Holy Ghost moving us to life everlasting, it is meritorious of life everlasting condignly. For thus the value of the Holy Ghost moving us to life everlasting according to John 4.14: *Shall become in him a fount of water springing up into life everlasting.* And the worth of the work depends on the dignity of grace, whereby a man, being made a partaker of the Divine Nature, is adopted as a son of God, to whom the inheritance is due by right of adoption, according to Rom. 8.17: *If sons, heirs also.*[156]

So, ingeniously, he has pressed his critic with the question: "Are you saying that the work of the Holy Spirit is not worthy of eternal life?"

Faith itself is a gift of God. However, "The act of faith is not meritorious unless *faith . . . worketh by charity* (Gal. 5.6)."[157]

> Therefore man is justified by faith, not as though man, by believing, were to merit justification, but that, he believes, whilst he is being justified; inasmuch as a movement of faith is required for the justification of the ungodly, as stated above (Q. 113, A. 4). God gives grace to none but to the worthy, not that they were previously worthy, but that by His grace He makes them worthy, Who alone *can make him clean that is conceived of unclean seed* (Job 14.4).[158]

In short, "Our works are meritorious from two causes," he stipulates. "First, by virtue of the Divine motion; *and thus we merit condignly*; secondly, according as they proceed from free-will in so far as we do them willingly, and thus they have congruous merit, since it is congruous that when a man makes good use of his power, God should by His

---

156. *ST* I–II, Q. 114, A. 3 (2:1155).
157. *ST* I–II, Q. 114, A. 4 (2:1156).
158. *ST* I–II, Q. 114, A. 5 (2:1157).

super-excellent power work still higher things."[159] So, ironically, works are *condignly* meritorious only because they are preordained and moved by grace. "Whatever the motion of grace reaches to, falls under condign merit."[160] Further, only Christ could merit for another condignly; all others merit for others only congruently.[161]

The first grace (infused habit) can be merited only congruently but still by God's helping grace.[162] Concerned to be "a good disciple of Paul," Wawrykow observes, Aquinas "wants justification to be solely 'by grace.'" But this impulse was at odds with the logic of his argument in the *Scriptus*. Seeing this, Aquinas let go of condign merit, opting for the less realistic congruent merit. "Nevertheless, implicit in his analysis of justification as requiring the self-willed deeds of the sinner in preparation for grace is the teaching that these good works of the sinner do merit congruently the first grace."[163] However, the good works of the *regenerate* do merit condignly. "By every meritorious act a man merits the increase of grace, equally with the consummation of grace which is eternal life," says Thomas.[164] Thus, he can treat as synonyms for such merit even terms such as "reward or wage."[165]

From the preceding summary, we see Aristotle's physics as paradigmatic for Aquinas's account of justification. Justification requires first the infusion of grace that moves free will toward God and against sin, leading to forgiveness.[166] Justification is an inner disposition, the reestablishment of a right order of the soul, with the lower powers of the soul (led by the passions) in subjection to reason once more.[167] Davies says, "For him, therefore, to say that God has forgiven us is equivalent to saying that we have changed direction and turned to him."[168] Herbert McCabe notes, "Our sorrow for sin just *is* the forgiveness of God working within us."[169] Justification—at least the first justification—is an unmerited gift, but it is indistinguishable from sanctification.[170]

---

159. *ST* I-II, Q. 114, A. 6 (2:1158).
160. *ST* I-II, Q. 114, A. 8 (2:1159).
161. *ST* I-II, Q. 114, A. 6 (2:1158).
162. Wawrykow, *God's Grace and Human Action*, 89–90.
163. Wawrykow, *God's Grace and Human Action*, 91.
164. *ST* I-II, Q. 114, A. 8 (2:1159).
165. *ST* I-II, Q. 114, A. 10 (2:1160).
166. *ST* I-II, Q. 113, A. 6 (2:1149).
167. Davies, *The Thought of Thomas Aquinas*, 335–36, from I-II, Q. 113, A. 1.
168. Davies, *The Thought of Thomas Aquinas*, 336.
169. Davies, *The Thought of Thomas Aquinas*, 337, quoting Herbert McCabe, *Hope* (London: Catholic Truth Society, 1987), 17.
170. Davies, *The Thought of Thomas Aquinas*, 338.

CONCLUSION

As in the Romans commentary (written close to the same time as I-II of the *Summa*), unconditional election has now secured a *gracious* interpretation of *condign merit*, at least in Thomas's view. Furthermore, he offers a brilliant Augustinian account of the sinner's turning to God as the result of God's gracious movement of the will and, simultaneously, the person's own free act—an account that will be adopted by the Reformers and their heirs (though identified with regeneration rather than justification).

Despite these qualifications, however, Wawrykow judges, "As it stands now, however, the present article's teaching on congruent merit is perhaps open to serious misunderstanding." While affirming condign merit, his actual argument seems to hedge, to the point in places of making condign merit look a lot like merely congruent merit.[171] In terms of scriptural texts, Thomas refers especially to Romans 6:23: "The grace of God is eternal life." "Conditioned as we are by the Reformation critiques of merit, at first reading this particular text in an argument in favor of merit is rather jarring. The entire passage in Romans seems to contrast what people as sinners deserve (that is, death) with what they freely receive from God (eternal life)."[172]

I will add my own misgivings about Thomas's argument. First, it is important to observe that Thomas has a very forensic view of merit but a thoroughly nonforensic view of justification. "Thomas's teaching about merit in the *Summa* is clearly 'juridical,'" notes Wawrykow. "He explains merit to be a quality of an act which one deserves, in justice, a reward from God."[173]

Indeed, medieval theology and ecclesial practice seem hardly interested in anything more than legal bookkeeping. However, when it comes to *justification*, ironically, the judicial aspect is lacking except perhaps as a way of saying that God merely judges the persons and the works to be what they in fact are in themselves. Justification for Thomas Aquinas includes forgiveness *and* renewal. It is both an event (the first justification or regeneration in baptism) and a process (sanctification). In other words, justification is an all-inclusive term for "salvation."

---

171. Wawrykow, *God's Grace and Human Action*, 198.
172. Wawrykow, *God's Grace and Human Action*, 203.
173. Wawrykow, *God's Grace and Human Action*, 203.

We have seen that Thomas recognizes the forensic character of "reckoning" implicitly in his Romans commentary, but it plays no role in his doctrine of justification, which instead follows Aristotle's analysis of motion. Perhaps this is due in part to the Vulgate's rendering of Paul's λογίζομαι (to reckon or impute) and its cognates with suitably legal equivalents, like *repute*, while mistakenly translating the legal term δικαιόω (to justify) with the transformative word *iustificare* (to make righteous). In any case, Aristotle's doctrine of physical motion and his definition of justice in his ethics (viz., distributive and commutative) are more determinative than exegesis in the formulation of his doctrine of justification.

It is not surprising, then, that Aquinas does not offer any account of positive imputation, although there is the nonimputation of sin—that is, not counting it against us as damning despite their intrinsic malice. Not even the *nonimputation* of sin's guilt is "wholly forensic," Bruce D. Marshall observes. "Since it presupposes that love which by nature creates value in what it loves, rather than attribute a value it fails to impart, God's refusal to impute sins must share in the production of love's effect. In this case, the effect is sanctifying grace, the interior transformation that makes us acceptable to God." It both "*frees* us from being worthy of eternal punishment" and "*makes* us worthy of eternal life."[174] The stain (*macula*) on the soul is also removed.[175] The inner transformation by grace makes one acceptable and one's works meritorious, so that the will is able now to cooperate and truly merit an increase of grace and final justification.[176] In short, God forgives us now because, by his grace, we have become forgivable.

Nevertheless, seeking convergences with Luther, Marshall suggests, "Aquinas cannot, in any case, be summoned as chief witness for a transformational theology of justification, in opposition to a dispositional and forensic one." After all, "There must be a purely forensic moment in justification." This moment turns out to be the remission of *past* sins, which God cannot change, since they are done, but which he graciously refuses to charge to our account. "He remembers our sins no more, as Scripture often consoles us by teaching. This too belongs among the

---

174. Bruce D. Marshall, "*Beatus vir*: Aquinas, Romans 4, and the Role of 'Reckoning' in Justification," in *Reading Romans with St. Thomas Aquinas*, ed. Matthew Levering and Michael Dauphinais (Washington, DC: Catholic University of America Press, 2012), 230.

175. Marshall, "*Beatus vir*," 232–33.

176. *ST* I-II, Q. 109, A.2 (2:1125).

blessings of those who share the faith of Abraham, who are blessed because the Lord remits their sin, and does not reckon it against them."[177]

But what about present and future sins? We find ourselves back in Origen's commentary on Romans but now with an elaborate system for the relatively new sacrament of penance. For these postbaptismal transgressions God has graciously made provision. Penance turns out also to be forensic in a way (indeed, very much determined by quid pro quo accounting), but there is no hint of a full justification on the basis of Christ's righteousness, which is imputed to believers. So, interestingly, there is a quasi-forensic moment in nonimputation that is not caused by any inner transformation—where God regards one as having *not* done what he or she clearly *has* done. But no imputation (negative or positive) that is *purely* forensic. And even God's forgiveness is conditioned by, if not identical with, the believer's repentance.

Second, it seems that Aquinas grants too much (of course, not explicitly granting anything, since he was not debating the Reformers) when he argues that merit is gracious because *Christ* has merited our ability to merit his gifts. Just as we receive Adam's original sin "through bodily generation, . . . Christ's merit is communicated to others only through the spiritual regeneration of baptism, by which we are incorporated into Christ."[178] It is clear therefore that Aquinas has a robust conception of the imputation of merits from one person to another and that Christ is among those donors. "Meriting means establishing a right to a reward."[179] And Christ did so merit condignly for himself and for others. Also in *De Veritate*, the final question (29) treats grace and merit, with the same conclusions as above: Christ could merit (A. 6), could merit for others (A. 7), and did so from the first moment of his conception (A. 8).[180]

So why is the imputation of Christ's condign merits insufficient for acquiring the justification of all who are united to him? On the terms of Thomas's project, one cannot reject the Reformation concept of imputation simply on the basis that it assumes a nominalist "extrinsicism."[181] If that were the case, then *any* transfer of merit from one person to

---

177. Marshall, "*Beatus vir*," 237.

178. *ST* III, Q. 19, A. 4, ad. 3, as quoted in Wawrykow, *God's Grace and Human Action*, 103–4.

179. Wawrykow, *God's Grace and Human Action*, 104.

180. Wawrykow, *God's Grace and Human Action*, 137.

181. I have in mind the critique especially of John Milbank and other Radical Orthodoxy scholars, echoed by Hans Boersma, *Heavenly Participation: The Weaving of a Sacramental Tapestry* (Grand Rapids: Eerdmans, 2011), 92; cf. Boersma, *Nouvelle Theologie and Sacramental Ontology* (New York: Oxford University Press, 2013).

another would be proscribed. More to the point in relation to Aquinas: if Christ is at least among those whose merits are imputed to others, then what is lacking that would require not only the additional merits of Mary and the saints but the condign merits of believers themselves?

Third, while Thomas has commendably moved justification out from under the locus of penance, he discusses merit in relation to penance as well. Penance restores one to grace, such that the merits accrued prior to the lapse are still counted.[182] An increase of justification is merited by cooperation. Perseverance is due to predestination, so it is unmerited.[183] Yet the means of such perseverance is the meritorious cooperation of believers. Again, I cannot see how recourse to election as the eternal basis saves the theory from contradiction when the execution of the decree is merited by the elect. Regardless, in the actual experience of Christians—which, after all, pertains to the execution of salvation rather than God's secret predestination—the emphasis falls on the conditionality of salvation by becoming worthy of final bliss. Hence, the denial of assurance of election in the sixth session of the Council of Trent is consistent with Thomas's doctrine at this point. As unconditionally gracious as election is, it remains a divine secret until final justification, which itself is merited condignly by grace. I fail to see how this last sentence is not a contradiction in terms. This leads directly to the next question.

Fourth, given that his theory of justification turns entirely on an inner movement of the soul from injustice to justice, Thomas cannot allow certainty in knowing one's election. We cannot know we have grace by revelation or by certainty, but there is a certain conjectural knowledge that is possible "by signs; and thus anyone may know he has grace, when he is conscious of delighting in God, and of despising worldly things, and inasmuch as a man is not conscious of any mortal sin." So we can know that we have faith, hope, and love for "the gifts of glory," "although we do not know for certain that we have grace to enable us to merit them."[184] Despite Aquinas's dependence on Augustine, his account of justification lacks the bishop's clear opposition between merit and mercy, with justification given through faith alone. Not only Augustine, but as we have seen, the broader patristic consensus

---

182. Wawrykow, *God's Grace and Human Action*, 221.
183. Wawrykow, *God's Grace and Human Action*, 227, from *ST* I-II, Q. 114, A. 8–9.
184. *ST* I-II, Q. 112, A. 5 (2:1144).

attributes justification to grace alone, through faith alone, because of Christ alone.

Regardless of the role of unconditional election and effectual grace in theory, experientially one must wonder whether this is any different than trusting in one's own works for everlasting life. Since we never know our election, and since, for Thomas, Christ is not "the mirror of our election" as he is for Luther and Calvin, average believers are left to find their election in themselves, hoping that their merits qualify them for life. Does this even come close to the repeated assurances found in Scripture?

Obviously, these are questions that one might expect a Protestant to raise concerning Aquinas's doctrine of justification. As the story unfolds, however, the firewall that he has carefully erected against Pelagian interpretations of merit becomes dismantled.

CHAPTER 5

"DO WHAT YOU CAN"
Scotus and the Rise of Nominalism

What was the matter with Luther? Our quest for an answer has taken has through the relevant distinctions in Lombard and Aquinas. Our story picks up with the momentous centuries that followed Aquinas.

The Reformer could have had the entire scholastic tradition in mind when he quipped during his Heidelberg Disputation (1518), "He who wishes to philosophize by using Aristotle without danger to his soul must first become thoroughly foolish in Christ."[1] It would not be surprising if he had Aquinas especially in mind, but the Angelic Doctor was hardly unique in his fondness for the ancient known simply as the Philosopher. Luther's main target was Aristotle's argument in *Ethics* that good laws make good people. As we have seen, Aquinas went out of his way to reject that point in his treatment of justification, so either Luther did not have Aquinas in mind here, or he was mistaken—or, and this is the view to which I incline, he was generalizing, with such examples in mind as the impact of the Philosopher's *Physics* on Aquinas's doctrine of justification. We have seen how Aristotle's physics dominates the *Treatise on Grace* in the *Summa*, especially in defining justification. Quoting Aristotle, Thomas takes for granted that *movement* drives the definition, and he yields entirely to Aristotle in determining the elements involved in the motion from injustice to justice in salvation. If anything, though, Scotus, Ockham, and Biel went further than Aquinas, ignoring his warning against Aristotle's "good laws make good people" argument. So it is more likely that Luther had those three in mind rather

---

1. Martin Luther, "Twelve Philosophical Theses," in *Heidelberg Disputation*, in *LW* 31:41 (thesis 29).

than Aquinas, although the Reformer felt no special calling to defend Aquinas either.

Whatever Luther's problems with the Angelic Doctor and the Philosopher, they were mediated by the late medieval scholastics who had moved a good deal farther from an Augustinian framework. Archbishop of Canterbury Thomas Bradwardine (1290–1349), dubbed *Doctor profundus*, wrote the treatise *Against the New Pelagians* that includes his autobiographical account of discovering in Romans, especially its ninth chapter, a doctrine of grace that he had not been taught in school.[2] If Luther's description of education in his day maliciously caricatures the situation, as Heinrich Denifle asserted, then Bradwardine must have as well. Since the views of nominalist theologians provoked Luther's reaction, it is essential to provide some account of their teaching here.

Even during his lifetime, Aquinas fell victim to a massive backlash against Aristotle occasioned by the heresies, real and imagined, of Aristotelians influenced by the Islamic philosopher Averroës (Ibn Rushd, c. 1126–98).[3] The bishop of Paris and the university regents charged Aristotelian philosophy with encouraging pantheism.[4] Aquinas engaged these thinkers critically (including a treatise against Averroës's doctrine of panpsychism). However, in the sweeping denunciations, even some of Aquinas's theses made it into the condemnations of 1277, though this action was later rescinded.[5] Averroism itself weakened, until revived in the Renaissance especially by Giordano Bruno, but the sudden slamming of the door on Aristotle and the emphasis on divine omnipotence and freedom opened new ones.

---

2. Thomas Bradwardine, "Against the New Pelagians," in *Forerunners of the Reformation: The Shape of Late Medieval Thought*, ed. Heiko Oberman (Minneapolis: Augsburg Fortress, 1981), 43–66.

3. Like the earlier Islamic philosopher Avicenna (Ibn-Sīnā, c. 980–1037), Averroës's Aristotle was read through Neoplatonist spectacles. The works of Proclus had been attributed falsely to Aristotle and Avicenna gave the philosopher a distinctly Neoplatonist interpretation. See Richard H. Popkin, ed., *The Columbia History of Western Philosophy* (New York: MJF Books), 184–85.

4. Among the worrisome theses of Aristotle defended by Averroës were the eternity of the world and an emanationist cosmology that made God and the world codependent, as causes must be affected by their effects. Various other positions called into question, at least implicitly, divine omnipotence, divine omniscience, providence, and the existence of particulars. Though identified as "pantheism" (or even atheism), the system was closer to what is now identified as panentheism.

5. Edward Grant, *A Source Book in Medieval Science* (Cambridge: Harvard University Press, 1974), 47–48. Targeted especially was Siger of Brabant had developed an ingenious "two truths theory" to explain how, in his view, one thing could be true in philosophy but not in theology and vice versa. In view of the narrative of Radical Orthodoxy, it is worth observing at this point that Aquinas's fragile integration of reason and revelation was coming undone not yet at the hands of the nominalists but of Neoplatonist Aristotelians.

Thomas Aquinas's junior by only thirty-five years was the preacher and fellow Dominican Meister Eckhart. His later years were spent under a cloud of suspicion and repeated heresy trials on the charge of pantheism.[6] Taking Neoplatonism to its extreme edges, many of Eckhart's sermons indeed suggest pantheism (or at least panentheism) in the tradition of John Scotus Eriugena (c. 815–77).[7] "Escaped from this prison of creation, 'the soul is unified with the godhead itself in such a way that it has lost its identity in the same way as a drop of wine disappears in the sea.'"[8] It is not the fall, but creation itself, that represents the tragic separation of the soul from its union with divinity. Despite papal condemnation, Eckhart's views continued to attract interest, particularly through Nicholas of Cusa, Johann Tauler, and the anonymous authors of the *Theologia Germanica*, which, ironically, Luther translated into German. To the extent that Neoplatonism dominated, the biblical problem of sin and grace became a metaphysical problem of nature and grace: redemption (from the *nihil* to which the lower world tends) by moral and contemplative ascent.[9]

Through the labors of the Franciscan John Duns Scotus, however, a different path was blazed. The Paris Condemnations of 1277, when

---

6. In 1329, two years after Eckhart's death, the Avignon Pope John XXII condemned the mystical genius in the bull *In agro dominico* for teaching pantheism: the fusion of the soul with God. Michael Schmaus, *Dogma*, vol. 6, *Justification and Last Things* (London: Sheed and Ward, 1977), 75.

7. While in pantheism there is no ontological distinction between God and world, panentheism teaches that God is more than the world but that they are mutually dependent. Thus, the world remains necessary to God's being. The views of Eriugena and Eckhart are probably best characterized as pantheistic; in any case, no distinction existed at this time between pantheism and panentheism. See John Cooper, *Panentheism: The Other God of the Philosophers* (Grand Rapids: Baker Academic, 2006), 13–63.

8. Heiko A. Oberman, *The Harvest of Medieval Theology: Gabriel Biel and Late Medieval Nominalism* (Durham, NC: Labyrinth, 1983), 328–29.

9. Ironically, John Milbank treats as exemplary thinkers many who were condemned on the charge of pantheism and in most cases were in fact guilty as charged (at least of panentheism), a strange position to be defending under the umbrella of Radical Orthodoxy. In another irony, Milbank dismisses Luther as a nominalist despite the strange fact that the German reformer translated one of the textual links between Eckhart and the modern world. Milbank's historical descriptions (especially of anything related to the Reformation) are mostly overconfident blusters without grounding in the sources. Nevertheless, he is exactly right, I think, when he says that "late medieval and Renaissance advocates of the high dignity of the human soul and human capacity, like Eckhart, Cusanus and Mirandola, may lie in far greater continuity with the high Middle Ages and stand far less unambiguously at the threshold of modernity than is usually supposed" (Milbank, *Beyond Secular Order: The Representation of Being and the Representation of the People* [Oxford: Wiley-Blackwell, 2013], 99). In other words, (a third irony) in an effort to overcome univocity, Milbank draws on the radical mysticism that conflates Creator and creation but recognizes (correctly) that the Neoplatonism-soaked Renaissance was in fact part of the medieval tradition. Hence, we should avoid a myopic obsession with a *separation* of the world from God that overlooks the ways in which the *confusion* of God and the world sowed its own seeds of modernity (e.g., Bruno, Hobbes, Spinoza, Hegel, etc.).

Scotus was only twelve, had already set a course away from the medieval synthesis represented by Aquinas and probably played a significant role in Scotus's development.[10] Regardless, the age was ripe for a new paradigm. Aquinas's star was fading and with it the delicate balance of revelation and reason, God and the world, the intellect and the will, nature and grace, divine omnipotence and the reliable regularity of his ordained power.[11] By Aquinas's death, scholasticism was torn between, on the one hand, conflation of Creator and creation (pantheism or at least panentheism) and, on the other, a separation (incipient deism, with greater space given to ungraced nature). Far from merging (the tendency of the Neoplatonist trajectory), God and the world began to drift apart with Scotus. The object of theology (Being) was separated from the object of philosophy (beings).

A third thoroughfare, not quite a highway, was blazed by Thomas Bradwardine and followed by Gregory of Rimini: the *via Augustini moderna*, in opposition to the Pelagian theses of the Ockham, Biel, and other nominalists. Universities often preferred one school, but increasingly accommodations were made for greater variety. For example, just prior to Luther's arrival, the new Wittenberg University was obliged by its statutes to teach according to one of three schools: the *via Thomae*, the *via Scoti*, and the *via Gregorii*.[12] But soon the *via Ockhami* was added to the list. The Augustinian polemics against the thought of Scotus, Ockham, and Biel cautions against lumping the whole group together under the nominalist label, which came into circulation a century after Ockham. This chapter focuses mainly on the Franciscan (Scotist) trajectory.

---

10. David C. Lindberg argues for a direct influence of the Paris Condemnations on Scotus in *Science in the Middle Ages*, Chicago History of Science and Medicine (Chicago: University of Chicago Press, 1978), 107–8.

11. With Scotus and Eckhart, Stephen Wigley notes, Thomas's ontological project is left behind. "In the one instance being is reduced to a dull and prosaic rationalism in which all sense of wonder and awe is lost; in the other, the sense of being lost in God becomes so all-embracing that any distinction between God and the world disappears" (Stephen Wigley, *Balthasar's Trilogy: A Reader's Guide* [London: T&T Clark, 2010], 59). Cf. Hans Urs von Balthasar, *The Glory of the Lord*, vol. 5, *The Realm of Metaphysics in the Modern Age*, ed. Brian McNeil, CRV, and John Riches, trans. Oliver Davies et al. (San Francisco: Ignatius, 1991), 12. It is somewhat ironic that in many contemporary retrievals of Christian Platonism that claim the mantle of "orthodoxy," Thomas is blended nicely with figures with whom he would not have kept honest company. Then the line is neatly drawn from Scotus to Ockham to Luther as the trail toward a secular age. However, even the original proponents of the *Nouvelle théologie* recognize that this is simplistic.

12. Alister E. McGrath, *Luther's Theology of the Cross* (Oxford: Basil Blackwell, 1985), 31.

JOHN DUNS SCOTUS (1265–1308)

Born at Duns, Scotland, near the English border, John entered the Franciscan Order early in life and eventually became a lecturer, then professor, at Oxford and Paris. The best-known Scotus in contemporary thought is a character in a story—the Scotus Story—in which the Subtle Doctor plays the villain's part as the unwitting progenitor of our secular age.[13] If Scotus is the villain, Aquinas is the hero—but not just any Aquinas. Those who tell the Scotus Story labor to extricate Thomas from his epigones, Dominicans from Thomas Cajetan (1469–1534) to Réginald Garrigou-Lagrange (1877–1964).

Over against nearly every major interpreter of Thomas, Henri de Lubac and the *Nouvelle théologie* circle (a pejorative epithet coined by Garrigou-Lagrange) argued with great erudition that according to Thomas human beings possess the natural end (telos) for the beatific vision (though of course, not the capability of attaining it apart from grace).[14] These scholars argue that it was the Dominican Thomist, Tommaso Cajetan (Luther's nemesis, ironically), who launched the erroneous view that Thomas emphasized a natural end and a supernatural end, with only the latter requiring grace. This distinction, they argued, provided the category for a neutral space—a realm of autonomy, nature, and reason separate from participation in God, grace, and revelation. In short, they invented "the secular." In this view, Aquinas appears to be the first and last genuine Thomist and the end of a golden age of Christian Neoplatonism that began with Origen. Milbank has carried forward de Lubac's thesis, broadening and radicalizing it considerably, with Scotus as the progenitor of modernity, leading to Ockham and the Reformation, the Enlightenment and postmodern nihilism.[15] In brief,

---

13. By "Scotus Story," I am referring to a now popular genealogy of secularism that leads from Scotus and Ockham to Luther and Calvin to Adam Smith and Nietzsche. I am borrowing the label "Scotus Story" from the excellent work by Daniel P. Horan, *Postmodernism and Univocity: A Critical Account of Radical Orthodoxy and John Duns Scotus* (Minneapolis: Fortress, 2014), 7.

14. On the historical background, see Jürgen Mettepenningen, *Nouvelle Théologie—New Theology: Inheritor of Modernism, Precursor to Vatican II* (London: T&T Clark, 2010).

15. Consistent with his panentheistic inclinations in ontology, Milbank's epistemology renders revelation merely a higher intensity of the illumination that undergirds reason's knowledge of anything (John Milbank, Catherine Pickstock, and Graham Ward, eds., *Radical Orthodoxy: A New Theology* [London and New York: Routledge, 1998], 24). In Milbank's *Truth in Aquinas* (New York: Routledge, 2000), coauthored with Catherine Pickstock, a radically Neoplatonist Thomas emerges who seems suspiciously like a modern idealist. Thus, in terms of epistemology as well as ontology, Milbank and Pickstock slide toward a merely quantitative rather than qualitative distinction between God and world. See Paul DeHart, "On Being Heard but Not Seen:

this interpretive trajectory overemphasizes Aquinas's continuity and Scotus's discontinuity with the earlier medieval tradition. Both figures continued the earlier debates and contributed their own distinct emphases and formulations.

If we are to understand Scotus, it is important to place him in his own context. Aquinas was not his main target, and indeed in many respects he agreed with Thomas's overall program. Extending the theological tracks that had been laid by Bonaventure, Scotus's differences with Thomas are evidence less of a restless gaping toward modernity than of an intramural Franciscan-Dominican debate.[16]

Almost two generations had passed since the towering labors of Aquinas and Bonaventure, and significant theological projects had emerged in the meantime. Scotus primarily engaged those thinkers, and his chief target was not Aquinas but the Augustinian theologian Henry of Ghent.[17] Like Thomas, Henry had studied under Albertus Magnus, but Henry did not share his master's enthusiasm for his fellow student. As regent master Henry helped to craft the condemnations of the University of Paris in 1277 that included propositions against Aquinas.[18] Ironically, Scotus set out to strengthen Aquinas's overall program in the face of opponents like Henry of Ghent. Even Scotus's views on penance discussed below should be seen in this light.

Crucial questions should be raised about the extent to which Scotus's

---

Milbank and Lash on Aquinas, Analogy and Agnosticism," *Modern Theology* 26, no. 2 (April 2010): 243–77. This tendency to interpret Aquinas as a panentheist is evident also, for example, in Milbank, *Beyond Secular Order*, 26: "For in his *Sentence Commentary* Aquinas remarkably stated, anticipating Eckhart, that the Trinitarian and created outgoings are 'essentially' the same, and only distinguished by 'the addition of a sort of relation to the temporal effect.'" The statement is problematic from an orthodox perspective, but it is taken from the *Scriptum*, which does not represent Thomas's mature views (see *ST* I, Q. 2, A. 3; I, Q. 45, A. 1; and I, Q. 4, A. 2).

16. E.g., the emphasis on the will over the intellect and therefore of theology as a practical rather than theoretical discipline is characteristic Franciscan. Scotus deepened and to some extent went beyond earlier statements of his school on these questions, just as Aquinas shaped his tradition well beyond Dominic—in fact, to the point of drawing condemnations from the University of Paris and the Roman curia.

17. Richard Cross, *Duns Scotus* (Oxford: Oxford University Press, 1999), 4–5. It may be noted that Cross is one of the leading Scotus specialists and, though a critical scholar, is generally sympathetic to his program.

18. For a variety of reasons, Henry was wary of Aquinas's influence. As an Augustinian Platonist very much opposed to the neo-Aristotelians, Henry believed that the body was actually part of the soul, and he restricted genuine knowledge to indubitable certitude concerning necessary objects. See Steven P. Marrone, *Truth and Scientific Knowledge in the Thought of Henry of Ghent* (Cambridge, MA: Medieval Academy of America, 2013); cf. Hugh G. Gauch, *Scientific Method in Practice* (Cambridge: Cambridge University Press, 2003), 52–57. Perhaps more germane, practically, Henry was also a dedicated defender of the secular clergy over the mendicant friars (especially the Franciscans), a cause that reached its zenith in his ultimately successful campaign to require everyone to confess at least once a year even the same sins already confessed to a monk.

metaphysics contributed to the early modern tendency to set God and humans, revelation and reason, intellect and will in opposition.[19] As important and germane as these questions are even for our topic, however, I will limit my scope to Scotus's discussion of grace, merit, and justification.

Original Sin

One could hardly be an ecclesiastical teacher and deny original sin. However, Scotus's account, says Richard Cross, "is in every respect weaker than the standard Augustinian one accepted by most of his contemporaries." "The supernatural gifts of unfallen humanity were minimal, and their loss has only the smallest effect on human existence."[20] Where Augustine and Aquinas—Bonaventure as well—regarded sin as depravity (the corruption of a good substance), according to Scotus sin is not something real, like a quality, inhering in the sinner. "Sin is just a lack of rectitude in an *act*, not in a *person*."[21] This has important consequences for his view of justification. "Furthermore, the guilt attaching to sin, according to Scotus, consists merely in God's decision to punish a person for his or her sinful acts." When David says, "Blessed is the one whose transgression is forgiven, whose sin is covered" (Ps 32:1), "Scotus understands this to mean that God can will not to punish someone without any concomitant change in the sinner."[22] Notice the break with Aquinas here, who, following William of Auxerre and Lombard, placed remission of sins at the end of the process of justification; God forgives only those who are changed inwardly (by the infusion of grace and turning of the will). Scotus challenges the priority of infused grace altogether. But the shift is deeper still: "Persons can certainly have morally bad qualities or habits, but *sinfulness* cannot be one of these."[23] It is difficult to conclude that Scotus has any operative notion of inherent

---

19. On these larger questions, see especially Allan B. Wolter, *Scotus and Ockham: Selected Essays* (Allegany, NY: Franciscan Institute, 2004), with whom proponents of the Scotus Story fail to interact, much like they fail to interact with Richard Cross, Marilyn McCord Adams, or other specialists. The most important study in the last half-century appeared with William J Courtenay, *Capacity and Volition: A History of the Distinction of Absolute and Ordained Power* (Bergamo: Lubrina, 1990), esp. 11–21.

20. Cross, *Duns Scotus*, 83.

21. Duns Scotus, *Ordinatio* 4.14.1, n. 3 and n. 6; 2.37.1, n. 6, cited in Cross, *Duns Scotus*, 94–95.

22. Cross, *Duns Scotus*, 95–96, referring to Scotus, *Ordinatio* 4.14.1, n. 6; and 2.37.2, n. 22.

23. Cross, *Duns Scotus*, 95–96, referring to Scotus, *Ordinatio* 4.14.1, n. 6; and 2.37.2, n. 22. Cross here describes Scotus's view as "wholly legal or forensic," perhaps as a way of drawing our attention to a connection to the Reformation. Regardless of his intention, this is an inaccurate definition. Scotus does indeed view sin as a character of an act rather than an inherent habitus

depravity (whether original or actual) as requiring divine judgment. In every case, the reason for justice or mercy is the grace that God gives it by a mere act of will. In short, we do not sin because we are sinners; we are sinners because we sin—and only the act itself can be called sinful.

Scotus also held distinctive views on human nature before the fall. He rejects the Augustinian conception on several counts. First, he denies the traditional Augustinian idea that Adam's original integrity was due to the grace added to nature; rather, this so-called *donum superadditum* was merited by Adam before the fall—by ungraced nature (*ex puris naturalibus*). Further, while Aquinas held that this first gift was lost in the fall, so that meriting it condignly was out of the question, Scotus believed that this first grace could, logically, be merited by us in the same manner. The fall "simply reduces us to our natural state," that is, to the condition of Adam before the addition of the supernatural gift (thus, of course, before the fall).[24] But again the real target of Scotus's criticism was Henry of Ghent. Along with Thomas Bradwardine (and later Gregory of Rimini), it was Henry who defended the Augustinian position against "the new Pelagians." However, Henry did not agree with Thomas's concept of a *donum superadditum*. Instead, he held that the *natural* condition of Adam and Eve before the fall was righteousness, with the will oriented toward God. While God's providential goodness and the help of his Spirit were necessary, there was no need for *grace* until this original rectitude had been lost, with the will now curved in on itself rather than delighting in God.[25] Original goodness is indeed a gift, but it is a gift intrinsic to nature as created (*donum concreatum*), rather than something added to it (*donum superadditum*). This is the view that the Reformers will embrace.[26]

In many important respects, the position that Scotus articulates is close to the view that Thomas Aquinas defends in the *Scriptus* but rejected in the *Summa*. Cross seems justified in concluding that "Scotus's

---

of a person, but this is not because of God's legal declaration but is due rather to the inherent *bonitas* of the act itself.

24. Cross, *Duns Scotus*, 97.

25. Cross, *Duns Scotus*, 96–97.

26. This rejection of the *donum superadditum* by the Reformers cannot therefore be attributed to their putative "nominalism," as Catholic critiques (including those of Milbank) suggest. Henry was a staunch Augustinian *critic* of "the new Pelagians" (especially Scotus) and was significantly Platonist in his metaphysics and epistemology. See Juan Carlos Flores, *Henry of Ghent: Metaphysics and the Trinity; with a Critical Edition of Question Six of Article Fifty-Five of the Summa Quaestionum Ordinariarum* (Leuven: Leuven University Press, 2006).

account of original sin is very different from the Augustinian one."[27] Scotus also rejects the doctrine of concupiscence.[28] The upshot of these moves is that God can hold us guilty for failing to have original justice but only because "God can impose obligations on us at will."[29] God's judgment does not correspond to anything in the sinner at all. This weak view of the fall is essential to Scotus's "strongly libertarian account" of free will.[30]

Grace and Free Will

A decisive break from Thomas's system is represented by Scotus's move away from an analogical view of human participation in God. At least at the conceptual level, some predicates applied to God and humans must be univocal (i.e., mean exactly the same thing). Although there are heated debates over the substance of Scotus's position as well as its implications, it seems clear enough that it was part of a general move toward viewing God as a being alongside other beings. Thus, human and divine agency were seen increasingly in competitive terms. The same was true of revelation and reason, grace and free will, with greater space given to autonomous human activity and the potential to act well by free will alone. William A. Frank notes that for Scotus both agents operate "with an independent, self-moving exercise of causality." Only by cooperating can God and free agents bring about a common effect.[31] Scotus uses the analogy of father and mother in the generation of a child.[32] Genuine freedom requires autonomous liberty to choose between various options. The will—both God's and ours—is sovereign and "a radically free, self-determining cause."[33] For Aquinas the more a human being acts, the more God's gracious efficient causality is needed; for Scotus, the more a human being acts, the less God acts—and vice versa. In short, God is not Being-Itself (or the source of beings who transcends being) but an actor among other actors.

---

27. Cross, *Duns Scotus*, 99.

28. Cross, *Duns Scotus*, 99.

29. Cross, *Duns Scotus*, 100.

30. Cross, *Duns Scotus*, 100.

31. William A. Frank, "Duns Scotus on Autonomous Freedom and Divine Causality," *Medieval Philosophy and Theology*, 2 (1992): 154–55.

32. Cross, *Duns Scotus*, 54, referring to Scotus, *Quod.* 5.3. Even Cross (who is not given to exaggerating Scotus's moves) points out that logically "it cannot be the case *both* that God knows free human actions, *and* that he is an autonomous co-cause of such actions."

33. Cross, *Duns Scotus*, 89.

Merit and Justification

Scotus's great Franciscan forebear Bonaventure had argued that "grace is a form given without merit, making someone who has it lovable and rendering their work good."[34] However, Scotus focuses once again on the actions rather than the person; Bonaventure's *gracious form* is replaced by Scotus with *virtuous acts*. God must accept as meritorious certain acts to which he has ordained an assigned value. The value, though, is assigned rather than inherent.[35] Like various bank notes made of the same material but of different values, it is only the designation or name given to the note that distinguishes five dollars from fifty. This is quite different from the thinking of Aquinas (in fact all of Scotus's predecessors), who maintains that God rewards a certain act because the person and thus the act *really are* meritorious due to infused grace. Thomas's epistemological intellectualism (i.e., the conformity of the will to reason) is grounded in and reinforces his ontological realism, while Scotus's voluntarism is inseparable from his protonominalism. Like other scholastics, Aquinas tried to strengthen Anselm's argument that, given God's free determination to save the elect, the death of Christ was the only way of accomplishing this while remaining just and merciful. Thomas's usual term is "fitting": neither necessary nor arbitrary. Scotus believes that Christ's merits make our merits possible, but he does not think that there is any reason to believe with Anselm that "God has to redeem us by Christ's death."[36] As a matter of fact, redemption does come through Christ's "satisfaction and merit," and Christ's merits make our merits possible.[37] However, the whole argument underlying the logical need for (or at least "fittingness" of) the God-Man is challenged.

Scotus insists, "We can merit both the gift of eternal life and an increase in grace." Even in the case of a major lapse, we may still restore this grace through the sacrament of penance.[38] Yet this belief is no longer grounded in the nature of things. Penance is not required

---

34. Rega Wood, "Ockham's Repudiation of Pelagianism," *The Cambridge Companion to Ockham,* ed. Paul Vincent Spade (Cambridge: Cambridge University Press, 1999), 354, referring to Bonaventure, *Sent.* II.27, dub. 2.

35. Cross, *Duns Scotus,* 103, referencing Scotus, *God and Creatures: The Quodlibetal Questions,* ed. and trans. Felix Alluntis and Allan B. Wolter (Princeton, NJ: Princeton University Press, 1975), 397–98.

36. Cross, *Duns Scotus,* 129.

37. Cross, *Duns Scotus,* 130–31.

38. Cross, *Duns Scotus,* 103.

because of something in God (viz., justice) or because of something in the sinner (viz., injustice); it is simply the divinely arranged system of assigned procedures and values. God is a debtor to no one, Scotus insists repeatedly. Of course, Aquinas made that point but grounded merit in God's debt to his eternal predestination. For Bonaventure, not even condign merit is pure proportionality between work and reward; rather, God has freely obligated himself "to reward condignly meritorious actions" with no such self-binding for congruent merits. Condignly meritorious acts "can only be performed by someone with the supernatural gift of grace."[39] Unlike both Bonaventure and Aquinas, Scotus rejects any view that places God under obligation of any kind to reward merits.[40] Whatever calculus God *decides* for rewards, there is no real connection to any inherent good that one possesses by participation in God's grace.

With Aquinas, Scotus teaches that everlasting life is merited condignly, but he believes that one may merit sanctifying grace (justification) congruently.[41] The key difference at this point is that in Scotus's scheme merit is suspended purely in God's decision to assign certain values to certain works, with no grounding in unconditional election or even grace as the accidental form in the soul. No infusion of grace, rendering the agent inherently good and in fact destroying inherent sin, is necessary according to this account.[42] In fact, infused grace can exist even without remission of sins, Scotus argued. For example, Adam had no sins to remit before the fall yet possessed infused grace (the *donum superadditum*).[43] In addition, Scotus argues that infusion brings about a real change in a person, while remission is merely an external change in God's mind with respect to the sinner.[44] Infusion and remission drift apart, like several things in Scotus's system that Aquinas had attempted

---

39. Cross, *Duns Scotus*, 104.

40. Cross, *Duns Scotus*, 104.

41. Cross, *Duns Scotus*, 105.

42. Alister McGrath helpfully contrasts Aquinas and the Scotist-nominalist scheme in terms of an *ontological* versus *covenantal* causality, respectively, in Alister E. McGrath, *Iustitia Dei: A History of the Christian Doctrine of Justification—The Beginnings to the Reformation* (Cambridge: Cambridge University Press, 1986), 49. I wonder if "covenantal" is too broad, however. After all, Aquinas could affirm that God's acceptance of the good works of those in grace is due to his free decision to give eternal life to the elect through their merits. In this sense, it is a covenant both with himself (in predestination) and with the *viator* (in following Christ's commands). Perhaps the best way to describe the contrast that McGrath highlights well here is in terms of a realist versus nominalist (or at least voluntarist) ontology.

43. McGrath, *Iustitia Dei*, 50.

44. McGrath, *Iustitia Dei*, 50.

to integrate.[45] Cross raises the obvious question: "Can the notion of merit survive this voluntaristic twist?"[46] What does merit mean if it is due merely to God's arbitrary decision in any case?

At last we are at the heart of our question: What does it mean for a person to be justified? Scotus returns to penance as the main locus for dealing with justification. On several points he differs with Thomas's construal. First, he argued that contrition (sorrow for offending God) is not necessary in order to receive penance; mere attrition (fear of penalty) is adequate.[47] Unlike contrition, attrition does not require sanctifying grace. While this weakening of penance is surely at odds with Aquinas, the real target is Henry of Ghent. Second, Scotus teaches that justification can be merited by a sufficiently intense attrition, even apart from the sacrament of penance.[48] While Lombard and Aquinas held that penance's efficacy depended on both inward contrition and the external sacrament, Scotus is now defending the idea that one may exhibit an inner fear of such intensity and genuineness that it merits justification not only apart from any sacramental action but apart from grace itself.

Scotus is convinced that he has saved himself from Pelagianism by saying that one can only earn justification *de congruo*, not *de condigno*: the very route that Aquinas took at first in the *Scriptus* but rethought in the *Summa*. Grounding merit in predestination, Aquinas felt, lessened the Pelagian blemish. Without eternal election or the necessity of an infused habit to ground it, Scotus backs away from condign merit. In any case, congruent merit fits better with his voluntarism. But does this save him from the charge of Pelagianizing? The effects of the fall are not total, he argues, leaving much of the powers of the intellect and will intact—enough to attain justifying attrition by one's own free will. These are good first steps. "Although by no means a total recompense for man's offenses against God, such acts were said to be 'fitting' and rewardable by God and that, in His mercy, God would accept them as sufficiently meritorious to dispose the sinner to receive grace which would elevate his attrition to contrition and complete the process of justification."[49] There is a greater emphasis, therefore, on "preparations for

---

45. Schmaus, *Dogma*, 6:73.

46. Cross, *Duns Scotus*, 103–04.

47. Charles P. Carlson, Jr., *Justification in Earlier Medieval Theology* (The Hague: Martinus Nijhoff, 1975), 123.

48. Carlson, *Justification in Earlier Medieval Theology*, 124.

49. Carlson, *Justification in Earlier Medieval Theology*, 124. Richard Cross is more eager to exculpate Scotus from the charge of Pelagianism: "Scotus is clear that attrition is congruously

grace," against which the Protestant Reformers would inveigh. Again, this merely natural attrition is insufficient for the condign merit that we need for eternal life, but congruent merit is a good start. Do what you can, and God will take notice. The maxim *facientibus quod in se est Deus non denegat gratiam* (God will not deny his grace to those who do what lies in them) was in long use—at least since Bonaventure. In Aquinas's treatise on grace in the *Summa*, it makes its appearance in the *objections* to his theses rather than expressing his own view. After all, Aquinas did not believe that anything worthy of acceptance lies in the sinner until God's gracious help moves him to seek the infused habit of justifying (i.e., sanctifying) grace.

To put the matter simply, Scotus wants to add another rung for the lowliest sinners to begin their ascent, while Thomas, Bonaventure, and most of the high scholastic theologians believed that only God's gracious and effectual assistance could lift them onto the ladder so that they could begin to climb with assisting grace toward meritorious acceptance. (This judgment is attenuated to some extent by Aquinas's argument that one may prepare oneself for initial grace by congruent merit. However, even here, Aquinas would reply that this preparation can only happen by God's helping grace and is therefore free of the semi-Pelagian charge.)

Cross judges, "As far as I can tell, Scotus holds that the value of the habit of grace is in no sense anything *intrinsic* to it." Consequently, without any injustice, "God could in principle damn someone with the habit."[50] Besides rendering God's will arbitrary, Scotus rejects Aquinas's insistence that effectual grace is required to bring about a meritorious work. It is enough that God provides sufficient (habitual) grace for everyone to act well by their own free will.[51] In the light of this emphasis

---

meritorious of grace. This is not—as has sometimes been suggested—a form of Pelagianism. As I have tried to make clear, Scotus does not believe that a congruously meritorious action such as attrition could ever be *sufficient* for grace. At the instant at which grace is given, the sinner could fail to receive it. But the Pelagian claim is that the sinner can earn grace without divine aid; in other words, that the sinner's actions are *sufficient* for grace. . . . Furthermore, this merit is done in cooperation with Christ" (Cross, *Duns Scotus*, 106). As we will see, these safeguards will be removed by Ockham and Biel.

50. Cross, *Duns Scotus*, 110–11. To add one more irony in the Radical Orthodoxy narrative: While highlighting (and in some ways, exaggerating) the contrast between Aquinas and Scotus, Milbank actually stands closer to Scotus with respect to predestination and effectual grace, doctrines that he routinely attributes to the Reformation (esp. Calvin). I have not located any place in his corpus where Milbank explains where and why he differs from the Augustinian stream of catholic Christianity on these points.

51. Cross, *Duns Scotus*, 111.

on God's freedom from contingent means, it should not surprise us that Scotus regards the sacraments as necessary (contingently) only by virtue of God's appointment rather than by any intrinsic value. Point by point, Scotus is dismantling the firewalls that Aquinas and other scholastics believed essential for guarding against Pelagianizing disaster.

However, we should not exaggerate Scotus's departure from Thomas.[52] In Scotus's scheme, God sets things up in such a way that whoever fulfills certain minimal terms will attain the first grace; in Thomas's, God predestines certain people to attain it. However, in both cases, there is a place for congruent merit even toward obtaining the first justification, not to mention condign merit of the increase and final justification (i.e., everlasting life). Even if (according to Aquinas) merit is by grace, the decisive question—which the Reformers will raise—is whether the two concepts are mutually exclusive. But even if we conclude that Aquinas's doctrine of merit is conceptually incoherent and a serious theological error, *semi-Pelagian* (much less *Pelagian*) is the wrong label to attach to it. The same cannot be said for Scotus—not to mention, William of Ockham.

WILLIAM OF OCKHAM (1285-1347)

The English Franciscan William of Ockham radicalized Scotus's distinctive theses. In fact, Scotists were among his sharpest critics, including Oxford colleague Walter Chatton, who defended metaphysical and epistemological realism. For his own part, Ockham believed that his system was the only way of resituating realism on a suitable foundation.[53] It suffices to say that with Ockham, we are furthest removed, thus far, from the Origenist or Neoplatonist trajectory represented by Eriugena

---

52. Joseph P. Wawrykow, *God's Grace and Human Action: 'Merit' in the Theology of Thomas Aquinas* (South Bend, IN: University of Notre Dame Press, 1995), 181–82. As noted in the previous chapter, Aquinas did accept congruent merit of the first grace. Further, as Wawrykow observes, "It is not immediately clear what exactly Thomas means by the divine ordination in this article on the possibility of merits," and this lack of clarity has led to widely divergent interpretations, including Otto Pesch's identification of Thomas's *ordinatio* with Scotus's *acceptio,* although Pesch recognizes that Aquinas emphasizes the intrinsic quality of grace in the person. But Wawrykow points out that Thomas has linked *ordinatio* to predestination and providential plan, not to a mere arrangement in time to accept certain acts for certain rewards. This is an important point that Pesch's argument overlooks.

53. We cannot explore Ockham's broader program here. See especially Allan B. Wolter, *The Concept of Univocity Regarding the Predication of God and Creatures According to William Ockham* (Allegany, NY: Franciscan Institute, 1952); and Wolter, *Scotus and Ockham: Selected Essays* (Allegany, NY: Franciscan Institute, 2004).

and Meister Eckhart, who was Ockham's contemporary. Necessarily confining ourselves in scope, I will begin with Ockham himself on the points most germane to grace and justification.[54]

At the beginning of the sixth Quodlibet, Ockham defines quite clearly his use of the distinction between God's absolute and ordained power. The distinction itself seems to have begun with Peter Damian in the eleventh century and attracted special interest in the debates over canon law. Is the secular ruler or the pope above the law and therefore able to suspend the established order at will? This of course raised the question as to God's absolute power over the order of nature and grace.[55] Ockham begins by clarifying that there are not actually two powers, nor does God do anything *inordinately*. The point of the distinction is simply that "there are many things God is able to do that he does not will to do, according to the Master of the Sentences, book 1, dist. 43. And these things God is said to be able to do by his absolute power."[56] As his appeal to Lombard shows, the distinction itself was in wide circulation and is unobjectionable for any theologian who affirms the relative contingency of creation as the result of a freely willed action.[57] To say that God does anything related to creaturely reality of necessity is to verge on the path of pantheism (or at least panentheism).

Ockham notes, for example, that even though baptism is ordained for salvation, God can and has in fact saved people (e.g., under the old covenant) without it. It is therefore impossible to be saved without baptism in an *ordinate* sense but possible for God in an *absolute* sense.[58]

On the basis of this definition he says, "I claim, first, that a human being is able by the absolute power of God to be saved without created charity." Whatever God can do *through* ordained means and instrumental causes, he can do directly *without* them. Thus, God can give eternal life without a created charity being infused into one's soul.[59]

---

54. For an excellent entry point to the secondary literature, see William J. Courtenay, *Ockham and Ockhamism: Studies in the Dissemination and Impact of His Thought*, Studien und Texte zur Geistesgeschichte des Mittelalters 99 (Leiden: Brill, 2008); William J. Courtenay, "Nominalism and Late Medieval Thought: A Bibliographical Essay," *Theological Studies* 33 (1972): 716–34.

55. See Lawrence Moonan, *Divine Power: The Medieval Power Distinction up to its Adoption by Albert, Bonaventure, and Aquinas* (Oxford: Oxford University Press, 1994).

56. William of Ockham, *Quodlibetal Questions*, vols. 1–2, *Quodlibets 1–7*, trans. Alfred J. Freddoso and Francis E. Kelley (New Haven, CT: Yale University Press, 1991), 6.1.1 (491–92).

57. See William J. Courtenay, "The Dialectic of Omnipotence in the High and Late Middle Ages," in *Divine Omniscience and Omnipotence in Medieval Philosophy*, ed. T. Rudavsky (Dordrecht, Holland: Reidel, 1984), 243–69.

58. Ockham, *Quidlibetal Questions*, 6.1.1, thesis 1 (491–92).

59. Ockham, *Quidlibetal Questions*, 6.1.2, thesis 1 (492).

But crucially, Ockham does not actually believe that ordinarily this is how things go. God *could* justify anyone he wants to apart from grace. However, he says, "I claim that, according to the laws now ordained by God, no human being will ever be saved or be able to be saved without created grace, and no human being will ever elicit or be able to elicit a meritorious act without such grace. And I hold this because of Sacred Scripture and the teachings of the Saints."[60]

Ockham acknowledges in the first objection and reply, "Perhaps you will object that the first thesis contains the error of Pelagius. . . . I reply that it does not. For Pelagius held that grace is not in fact required in order to have eternal life, but that an act elicited in a purely natural state [*in purus naturalibus*] merits eternal life condignly. I, on the other hand, claim that such an act is meritorious only through God's absolute power accepting it [as such]."[61] This is a remarkable admission. The difference with Pelagius hangs on a single and fragile thread. They both believe that God rewards even the first grace condignly, in a purely natural state, but Pelagius believes that it is because one is intrinsically worthy even apart from grace, and Ockham maintains that it is because God has simply decided to do it.[62] God could according to his absolute power refuse to reward an act even that was done by his grace with infused charity.[63] According to his ordained power and conditional necessity, though, "God of necessity accepts an act elicited out of charity."[64] It is "of necessity" because of God's obligation to his own rules. We should not be praised for possessing an infused charity that we did not pour into ourselves, "even though we might in some sense be praiseworthy if we dispose ourselves to receive this charity." "Likewise, [infused] charity is praiseworthy to the extent that it is a cause and principle of meritorious works."[65] In other words, you can either praise God (for infused charity) or praise your works (for their conformity to God's revealed calculus of reward). What you cannot do is praise God for your merits—the view of Aquinas. Remarkably, Ockham concludes from this argument

---

60. Ockham, *Quidlibetal Questions*, 6.1.2, thesis 2 (492–93).

61. Ockham, *Quidlibetal Questions*, 6.1.2, thesis 2, obj. and rep. (493).

62. Ockham, *Quidlibetal Questions*, 6.2.1, 494–95. Yet for the most part, God's ordained power is in force. Once God decrees something, it is no longer contingent. "For example, 'If Peter is predestined, then Peter will be saved' is necessary, and yet both the antecedent and the consequent are contingent." God did not have to elect Peter, but since he did, Peter must be saved.

63. Ockham, *Quidlibetal Questions*, 6.2.2, thesis 1 (495).

64. Ockham, *Quidlibetal Questions*, 6.2.2, thesis 2 (496).

65. Ockham, *Quidlibetal Questions*, 6.2.2, thesis 2, reply to main arg. (496–97).

that to affirm condign merit consistently, one must conclude with him that works springing forth from love are praiseworthy apart from any prior infusion of grace. If the Reformers had problems with Aquinas's account, they were appalled at Ockham's.

Eugenio Randi explains, "First of all, according to Scotus, the distinction can be applied not only to God, but *omni agenti per voluntatem et intellectum; potentia absoluta* does not describe just a logical possibility *ante ordinationem*, but the actual power of a subject of changing the rules of an *ordo*, providing he has power over it. Thus the king has an absolute power over the laws, because he is above the laws"[66] For Scotus, the distinction applies to both God and humans; for Ockham, to God alone, and for Henry of Ghent, to humans alone.[67] According to Peter of Atarrabia (or of Navarra), a ruler may suspend the *ordo* and exonerate a criminal: "The present *ordo* is simply overcome, but is still valid."[68]

Two radically different profiles of Ockham's teaching emerge in the secondary literature based on whether one privileges his statements regarding God's absolute or God's ordained power. For example, Gordon Leff suggests that for Ockham the uncreated gift of the Holy Spirit himself "suffices by God's absolute power for eternal life without any created gift."[69] But this ignores the firewall that Ockham installed between absolute and ordained orders. Regardless of what God *can* do, he has chosen to save only those who possess created grace.

What then is the difference between Ockham and the earlier tradition, especially Thomas, who also denied that God was bound by any absolute necessity to reward merits and also taught that certain acts are meritorious by God's decree?

First, Ockham adopts what his predecessors and most contemporary scholastics would have regarded as a semi-Pelagian account of God's predestination, based entirely on foreknowledge.[70] Rega Wood notes,

---

66. Eugenio Randi, "A Scotist Way to Distinguish Between God's Absolute and Ordained Powers," in *From Ockham to Wyclif*, ed. Ann Hudson and Michael Wilks (Oxford: Basil Blackwell, 1987), 45.

67. Randi, "A Scotist Way to Distinguish," 46.

68. Randi, "A Scotist Way to Distinguish," 50.

69. Gordon Leff, *Medieval Thought: Saint Augustine to Ockham* (Harmondsworth, UK: Penguin, 1958), 476–77.

70. Ockham, *Predestination, God's Foreknowledge, and Future Contingents*, trans. Marilyn McCord Adams and Norman Kretzmann (Indianapolis: Hacket, 1983). Cf. Rega Wood, "Ockham's Repudiation of Pelagianism," in *The Cambridge Companion to Ockham*, ed. Paul Vincent Spade (Cambridge: Cambridge University Press, 1999), 362–63.

"Ockham holds that there are generically good works that people in a state of sin should perform so that God might sooner confer on them the grace by which eternal life is merited. Such works dispose sinners for grace, but though they are good works, they are meritorious only in a qualified sense."[71] Recall that for Thomas merit—even of the condign sort—is preserved from Pelagianism only because it is grounded in God's unconditional election; some are chosen to eternal beatitude through a plan that includes an operative and cooperative grace to produce acts that merit such an end. Thomas is absolutely clear about this: the only reason that merit is not a Pelagian idea is that it is grounded in unconditional election. With Ockham, that grounding of merit in unmerited grace is now absent.

Second, earlier scholasticism had maintained that justification is founded on the presence in the soul of *uncreated* grace—namely, God himself (usually with the Holy Spirit as the bond of love, following Augustine). This divine presence did not necessarily entail any infused (created) *habitus*—that is, an ontological change.[72] But for Ockham, neither the uncreated Spirit nor created grace is absolutely necessary. Furthermore, he affirms an *actual* possibility of meriting the first grace by preparations *ex puris naturalibus* (according to pure nature).[73] Without a doubt, Aquinas would have regarded this as at least a semi-Pelagian move. In any case, one must say that in Ockham's hands the infused habit of grace and the divine acceptance of an act as meritorious drift apart from each other, and the latter becomes the more important.[74] Rega Wood warns against a facile conclusion: "Thus the masters at Avignon who accused Ockham of Pelagianism in the 1320s were mistaken when they claimed that according to Ockham either there was no habit of grace or it served no purpose."[75] Based on my quotes from Ockham above, Wood is correct. We should avoid conflating what he says about what God *can* do (*de potentia absoluta*) with what he thinks God in fact decides to do (*de potentia ordinata*).[76] Nevertheless, in view

---

71. Wood, "Ockham's Repudiation of Pelagianism," 361.

72. McGrath, *Iustitia Dei*, 48.

73. Even Rega Wood, who defends Ockham against the charge of Pelagianism in "Ockham's Repudiation of Pelagianism," notes that "Ockham does not hold that grace is necessary for virtue. He shares with Pelagius, and more importantly, with Aristotle, the view that created human nature functions properly for the most part" (352).

74. Wood, "Ockham's Repudiation of Pelagianism," 353.

75. Wood, "Ockham's Repudiation of Pelagianism," 354.

76. Like Marilyn McCord Adams, Wood gives considerable place to Ockham's debate with Peter Auriol, a fellow Franciscan who emphasized that God can only "save the lovable and damn

of his affirmation of meriting the first grace apart from grace itself, Marilyn McCord Adams is correct to conclude that Ockham's position is at least semi–Pelagian.[77]

Third, although Aquinas accepts the absolute–ordained distinction, Ockham built considerably more upon it (especially the absolute side), even more than Scotus. For all of the nominalists, observes Miyon Chung, "The only causal relationship between meritorious acts and salvation, therefore, is strictly covenantal, not ontological."[78] (I would add that the proper term here for their *foedus* is contract rather than covenant.) God has prescribed the value of such merit based on the terms of his *foedus*. It is now no longer the case, to borrow Ockham's analogy, that a silver coin has an inherent value and is therefore assigned that amount; on the contrary, God's assignation of value is what gives value.[79] To put it crudely, Ockham has removed divine judgment from the gold standard of realism (something truly in God and the individual). Merit and justification are grounded purely in an arbitrary assignation of worth.

Pope John XXII detested the Franciscans for their vow of poverty, and it was William of Ockham's defense of the order that drew an investigation into his theology, along with Meister Eckhart. Fifty-one theses of Ockham were judged Pelagian, though neither Ockham nor his system was ever condemned. He was only excommunicated by John XXII because he left the papal court at Avignon without permission and was exonerated by Pope Innocent in 1359. What is more intriguing, perhaps, is that after this episode Ockham's star rose in Paris at the heart of late medieval scholasticism and his influence spread considerably. One such follower, Gabriel Biel, pushed nominalism one step further toward the Pelagian badlands that would provoke Luther's reaction.

---

the detestable." It is the created form of grace that makes one loveable, Auriol argued, rather than God's own love and mercy. But Ockham says, quite properly, that this renders God's love absolutely necessary rather than a free expression of his own generous nature (Wood, "Ockham's Repudiation of Pelagianism," 355). Thus, if Ockham's position is extreme in a voluntarist direction, it would appear to be an overreaction, ironically, to an equally extreme position of an erstwhile *Scotist* who had come to adopt the *nominalist* views of Durandus! Thus, the narrative of Radical Orthodoxy—the Scotus Story—turns out once again to be a gross oversimplification of a more complex and fascinating history.

77. Marilyn McCord Adams, *William of Ockham*, 2 vols., 2nd ed. (South Bend, IN: University of Notre Dame Press, 1989), 1186–1297.

78. Miyon Chung, "Faith, Merit, and Justification: Luther's Exodus from Ockhamism *En Route* To Reformation," *Torch Trinity Journal* 6 (2003): 221.

79. Chung, "Faith, Merit, and Justification," 221.

GABRIEL BIEL (1420–95)

Dedicated to preaching, Biel nevertheless proved his mettle as a major theologian—in fact, he has been called "the last of the scholastics."[80] Recourse to his works was made repeatedly during the Council of Trent, and he was the only significant theologian of the medieval period never to have received any censure from the Vatican for his teaching, doubtless due in part to his constant defense of papal supremacy against conciliarists. Biel moved frequently during his studies: training first at Heidelberg, briefly at Erfurt, and later at Cologne, a long-standing bastion of Thomism. Cofounder (and later rector) of the relatively new University of Tübingen, Biel was also a devoted follower and supporter of the Brethren of the Common Life.[81] Through its network of schools and pattern of informal meeting for prayer and Bible study, this movement of practical piety was immensely popular in the late medieval period and included such notables as Nicholas of Cusa, Thomas à Kempis, and the Dutch pope Adrian VI, as well as Erasmus, Luther, and Ignatius of Loyola.[82]

Biel was the major theologian most proximate to Luther in time and place. In fact, the German reformer on many occasions singles him out, along with Ockham, as representing the "new Pelagianism" of the times, repeating earlier charges by highly regarded prelates. Luther and his opponent Johann Eck were both schooled in nominalism, and their instruction on Lombard's *Sentences* was based on the commentaries of Ockham and Biel.[83] Only one of them (viz., Luther) came to reject nominalism.

Absolute and Ordained Power Once More

Biel's nominalism has been taken in different directions by modern scholars, depending largely on whether one emphasizes the *absolute* or

---

80. Oberman, *The Harvest of Medieval Theology*, 9. For a critical edition of at least some of the works most germane to our topic, see the critical edition of Gabriel Biel, *Canonis Misse Expositio*, 4 vols., ed. William J. Courtenay and Heiko Oberman, Veröffentlichungen des Instituts für Europäische Geschichte, Abteilung für Abendländische Religionsgeschichte, Mainz, vol. 31 (Wiesbaden: Steiner, 1963–67).

81. Oberman, *The Harvest of Medieval Theology*, 10–15.

82. The reduction of Luther, much less the Reformation generally, to nominalism would be equivalent to explaining late nominalism as the creation of the Brethren of the Common Life. Yet the usual "Scotus Story" (*nouvelle*, Radical Orthodoxy, etc.) fails to even mention this highly influential movement and common thread that unites Luther and many of his greatest antagonists in terms of background.

83. Oberman, *The Harvest of Medieval Theology*, 18.

ordained side of the two orders.[84] As Scotus and Ockham underscored, God established a covenant (*pactum* or *foedus*) according to which God will not deny grace to those who do what lies within them (*facientibus quod in se est Deus non denegat gratiam*). If God were bound by the intrinsic worthiness of something or someone, the reward would be necessary. But God's contractual self-obligation also prevents rewards from being arbitrary. Johann Heinz notes of Biel's view that even before the first grace, "A person is able in his own strength to love God supremely, to avoid sin, and, out of the force of free will, to merit the grace *de congruo*, which God must grant necessarily according to the principle *facienti quod in se est* because on the basis of the *potentia ordinata* He cannot do anything else."[85] The mercy of God now means little more than God's having selected an order in which he makes himself a debtor to our merits.[86]

In contrast with the usual Scotus Story, the nominalism exemplified by Biel is hardly captive to a whimsical and arbitrary divine will. If anything, Biel's emphasis on the *potentia ordinata* excludes divine freedom and generosity. The order is firm and clearly spelled out. Consequently, as Oberman observes, any anxiety that this sort of teaching might inculcate could not be due to God's predictability but rather to the uncertainty as to whether one has happened to fulfill the obligations for being accepted.[87] According at least to Biel's nominalism, the ordained

---

84. Oberman, *The Harvest of Medieval Theology*, 31–35. On one side, Reynold Weijenborg argues that by underscoring that the infusion of grace (and therefore the church's sacramental system) was necessary according to God's ordained power (i.e., what normally holds true), Biel said nothing more than previous scholastics. On the other side, scholars such as Carl Feckes have argued (following Joseph Lortz) that nominalism represents an "extreme naturalism with a definite tendency to suppress the doctrine of grace." Basically, each interpretation emphasizes the role of one order or the other (Wijenborg, the ordained order, and Feckes, the absolute). According to Feckes, "The nominalist turns to faith as the only means of security in an uncertain, unknowable world"—uncertain and unknowable precisely because it is ruled by God's absolute power. Oberman judges, "This conclusion should be regarded as a fabrication, be it true or not; it is not derived from the sources themselves. . . . The issue of certitude and security, for all kinds of nontheological reasons, may have become so central that this has led to the questioning of the reliability of traditional physics, metaphysics, and theology." A third interpretation, represented by Paul Vignaux, sees both orders as a way of emphasizing God's freedom from any necessity and yet his free decision to *make himself* "a debtor of all those who possess infused grace."

85. Johann Heinz, *Justification and Merit: Luther vs. Catholicism* (Berrien Springs, MI: Andrews University Press, 1981), 141–42.

86. Oberman, *The Harvest of Medieval Theology*, 44.

87. Oberman, *The Harvest of Medieval Theology*, 45. Related to the two powers are God's two decrees. Both are eternal, but one is with respect to God's decision by which *he obligates himself* and the second is with respect to its temporal outworking by which *God obligates us*. According to the first, God has obligated himself to this plan even to the point of the incarnation; this obliges the sinner, in turn, to respond by actions that will merit final justification (Oberman, 46–47).

system, however grounded in God's arbitrary will, is final and perspic-
uous. The game comes with a clear and lengthy set of rules—and they
do not change.

Sin and Grace

Biel regarded concupiscence as part of the natural condition of
humans even before the fall.[88] To be sure, the fall has intensified the
struggle. However, original sin is "a certain outgrowth of natural
difficulties which can therefore be healed with natural medicines,"
Oberman relates. "Original sin has primarily a psychological, not an
ontological impact on the free will of man; it destroys the pleasure of
eliciting a good act and causes unhappiness and fear, thus changing the
direction of the will," but this does not "interfere with the freedom of
the will as such."[89] Consequently, there are myriad things that free will
can do, naturally, in order to dispose a person to the infusion of grace.
One thing is clear: "The impact of original sin and its consequences
leaves the freedom of the will intact."[90]

As with Scotus and Ockham, "We meet in Biel's anthropology a
dangerous approximation of fall and creation," Oberman observes.[91]
Biel locates the source of the human tragedy "in a lack of knowledge
which is not primarily explained as a result of his fall and loss of original
justice, but as a natural consequence of his status as creature."[92] To
put it differently, some of the obstacles to grace are already present in
human nature as created (viz., the inherent weakness of the lower self).
But this is already presupposed in Thomas's doctrine of a gift added
to nature (*donum superadditum*). If created nature is inherently unstable,
postlapsarian grace in Biel's account seems only to assist us in doing
what we could, with greater difficulty, already do.[93]

Gregory of Rimini considered Biel's position at least semi-Pelagian,
while Biel returned the favor, criticizing Gregory "for not having
sufficient confidence in man's potentiality *in puris naturalibus*." In fact,
Oberman concludes, "There is an explicit tendency toward naturalism,
as acts performed under the general influence of God are said to be

---

88. Oberman, *The Harvest of Medieval Theology*, 127.
89. Oberman, *The Harvest of Medieval Theology*, 129.
90. Oberman, *The Harvest of Medieval Theology*, 131.
91. Oberman, *The Harvest of Medieval Theology*, 68.
92. Oberman, *The Harvest of Medieval Theology*, 67–68, emphasis original.
93. Oberman, *The Harvest of Medieval Theology*, 47–49.

more completely in man's own power than those performed under the influence of created grace."[94] It should be obvious at this point how far we are from Aquinas's analogical perspective. A competitive view of double agency is now in full flower. The question is no longer how God effectually moves the will to act freely, but *who acts more, God or humans?*

Biel goes so far as to contend that if God's general providence in human affairs is maintained *in puris naturalibus*, we hardly require special grace at all. With the nominalist theologian Durandus, salvation was reduced to providence and providence to an essentially deistic "general influence of God."[95] Thus, while some nominalists like Ockham and Biel sowed the seeds of early modern naturalism, other *via moderna* theologians like Gregory of Rimini were its most vocal opponents. Gregory was opposed to various teachings of Ockham and other nominalists and "was probably responsible for the condemnations of 1347" against Ockham.[96] The situation becomes more complicated still when one considers that Renaissance humanism, with its Promethean view of the individual, was more indebted to the revival of Neoplatonism than to nominalism or other "schools." It would take us too far afield to pursue that point, but it is sufficient to include it as an aside over against jejune theories attending the Scotus Story.

Grace, Merit, and Justification

This pallid view of sin is the basis of the *facere quod in se est*: doing what you can toward attaining final blessedness.[97] Doing one's best is difficult, to be sure. "Nevertheless, Biel feels that this absolute love is

---

94. Oberman, *The Harvest of Medieval Theology*, 50. On Gregory's characterization of Biel's view as semi-Pelagian, see 50n63. There does seem to be a close relationship between Biel's view of nature and grace and his view of reason and faith. "The data of faith serve here only to complete experience and reason," Oberman summarizes (56). Similarly, grace supplements a nature that is capable at least of preparing for grace on its own.

95. Oberman, *The Harvest of Medieval Theology*, 50. It is worth noting that the figure to whom Oberman refers, Durandus de Saint-Pourçain (1275–1332), was also a nominalist, who, with regard to the Eucharist, rejected transubstantiation in favor of consubstantiation. Yet he was also a Dominican, beloved by many in his order, as well as a favorite of Avignon popes Clement V and John XXII. It was he, in fact, who was charged by the latter pope with the task of prosecuting the case against Ockham and his fellow Franciscans along with Eckhart. For an excellent study in the English language, see Isabel Iribarren, *Durandus of St. Pourçain: A Dominican Theologian in the Shadow of Aquinas* (New York: Oxford University Press, 2005).

96. Oberman, *The Harvest of Medieval Theology*, 204.

97. Oberman, *The Harvest of Medieval Theology*, 132. Oberman observes, "As far as we can see, the origins of the doctrine of the *facere quod in se est* go back to the *Ambrosiaster*, which interprets the justice of God as the merciful acceptance of those who seek their refuge with him: He would be unjust if he ignored them. This concept especially influenced the old Franciscan school, whose representative, Alexander of Hales, was Biel's teacher on this point."

within the reach of natural man *without the assistance of grace.*"[98] This basic assumption grounds Biel's view of grace, merit, and justification.

First, Biel's doctrine of predestination follows this Pelagianizing path. Oberman observes, "It is a reliable rule of interpretation for the historian of Christian thought that the position taken with respect to the doctrine of predestination is a most revealing indicator of the understanding of the doctrine of justification."[99] For Biel, who follows Ockham, even the election to grace is based on God's foreknowledge concerning those who do their very best.[100] The only exceptions are those who die in infancy, the Virgin Mary, and the apostle Paul, who were predestined eternally apart from merits. In terms therefore of the actual history of human beings, believers "live an existence conditioned by justification by works and by predestination *post praevisa merita*" (based on foreseen merits).[101] So the doctrine that Aquinas considered the bulwark against Pelagianism has been thoroughly demolished.

Just as Bradwardine opposed Ockham, Gregory of Rimini challenged Biel's tenets.[102] We must draw our belief in these doctrines from Scripture alone, not reason, Gregory concludes, which comes in sharp contrast with the speculative approach of Eriugena or Ockham and Biel. The testimony of the fathers is not normative since there is a divergence of opinion among them even on this point of predestination. "The Church does not establish scriptural truth," Gregory insisted, "but is a motivating cause for the acceptance of its claims. A theological truth exists prior to its official formulation by the Church and is in no way dependent upon it."[103]

Second, Biel's view of natural preparations for grace added further support to the *facere quod in se est.* Within a medieval frame, a high view of the efficacy of the sacraments went hand-in-hand with a high view of grace since the former was the vehicle of the latter. So it is not surprising that, as in Scotus and Ockham, for Biel the efficacy lies more in the recipient's will (e.g., intensity of penitence, disposition, and resolve)

---

98. Oberman, *The Harvest of Medieval Theology,* 133.
99. Oberman, *The Harvest of Medieval Theology,* 185.
100. Oberman, *The Harvest of Medieval Theology,* 189–90.
101. Oberman, *The Harvest of Medieval Theology,* 193.
102. Although several scholars place Gregory in the nominalist camp (with some justification concerning his rejection of Thomas's real distinction), Oberman highlights Gregory's independence of Ockham on several important points that lie beyond our scope. See Oberman, *The Harvest of Medieval Theology,* 197–98.
103. Oberman, *The Harvest of Medieval Theology,* 200–201.

than in the sacrament itself. For Augustine and Aquinas infant baptism was a capital example of prevenient grace, but the practice seems ill-suited to Biel's argument for natural preparations. "But as the quantity of grace granted in the sacrament of penance depends on the intensity of attrition or contrition," Biel argued, "so the quantity of baptismal grace depends on the disposition of the godparents and even of the administering priest himself."[104] For adults however the matter is clear-cut: doing what lies in oneself by nature, apart from grace, requires only God's general providence in upholding creation rather than restoring it, and doing one's best merits the first grace. Thus, Oberman judges, the concept of God's assisting grace "is thoroughly naturalized and barely distinguishable from man's natural endowments."[105] In fact, Biel criticized Gregory of Rimini for insisting (as had Thomas and the entire medieval tradition) that we require God's special assistance (*auxilium speciale*) to perform any good action. "Biel can therefore quite boldly say that grace does not prepare the sinner for the reception of this justifying grace since *grace is not the root but the fruit of the preparatory good works*."[106] It is not difficult to appreciate how far we have now drifted from Aquinas, much less Augustine, on the verge of Luther's era.

Third, with respect to justification directly, Biel takes an additional step beyond Scotus and Ockham, claiming that a sinner may merit justification *condignly* not only in a state of grace but *ex purus naturalibus*. What might be considered merely hypothetical in Scotus and Ockham has become an actual reality in Biel's thinking. Recall that, according to Scotus, even though being barely fearful of penalty (*parum attritus*) falls short of merit, "justification takes place through the sacrament, not *ex merito* but *ex pacto divino*" because such fear displays a will to receive the sacrament.[107] God will never fail to reward the smallest effort—just do what you can.

Fourth, despite this initial sign of Scotist sympathy for the slightest attempt, Biel sides with Lombard and Aquinas against Scotus on the

104. Oberman, *The Harvest of Medieval Theology*, 135.
105. Oberman, *The Harvest of Medieval Theology*, 138.
106. Oberman, *The Harvest of Medieval Theology*, 140–41, emphasis original. Oberman's quotation from Biel (141n66) is worth including: "Nam deus paratus est cuilibet disponenti se ad gratiam dare eam; ergo peccator disponens se recipit gratiam. Et quomodo disponet se ad recipiendum gratiam quam non habet nisi operando bona opera, licet nondum iustificatus? Neque enim potest se disponere ad gratiam per gratiam, alias haberet gratiam pruisquam haberet et hic est maximus huiuscemodi operum fructus. Has et multas alias utilitates bonas ferunt bona opera extra charitatem facta" S I 99 F. Cf. Lect. 59 P.
107. Oberman, *The Harvest of Medieval Theology*, 149.

question of whether mere attrition will suffice. He agrees with Scotus that the efficacy of penance lies not in the sacrament itself—the priest merely pointing out "that justification has already taken place." But "only contrition can delete the guilt and punishment of sin," not mere attrition.[108] Once again the key test for justification is whether one has done his very best, including at least the intention to confess to a priest at the first occasion. "This *facere quod in se est* is the necessary disposition for the infusion of grace and implies a movement of the free will, which is at once aversion to sin and love for God according to Eph. 5:14: 'Awake, O sleeper, and arise from the dead, and Christ shall give you light.'"[109] The traditional *ordo salutis*—with God first infusing grace, then moving the will to repentance, leading to remission—has been radically altered. The individual first repents, moves his or her own will, and then merits the infusion of grace and forgiveness.

It is important to remember that in all of this one is able *ex puris naturalibus* to love God above all else. Infused grace merely supplements but does not create this genuine love of God.[110] Neither baptism nor penance conveys this grace, according to Biel's highly voluntaristic and introspective account. While Scotus seems to have been motivated by more encouraging pastoral instincts, Biel thinks that the unregenerate are capable of doing more than attaining mere attrition. Further, he makes the sacrament of penance (especially the nonsacramental willing of the penitent) more integral to justification—without any loopholes. But this full and sincere contrition is entirely within the powers of the natural person, unaided by grace.[111] Without such sorrow, Biel constantly warns his congregation, no amount of good works will justify.[112] One can only conclude with Oberman that "the strictness of Biel's contritionism necessarily would enhance scrupulousness and despair."[113] The problem of what constitutes a genuinely justifying act of penance is only deepened by a "pan-European Donatist upsurge" centered especially in Bohemia and southern Germany, based on "the fear of the 'wicked priest.'"[114] In this context, how could one know that the priest who administered penance was himself pious, which

---

108. Oberman, *The Harvest of Medieval Theology*, 147, 150.
109. Oberman, *The Harvest of Medieval Theology*, 152.
110. Oberman, *The Harvest of Medieval Theology*, 153.
111. Oberman, *The Harvest of Medieval Theology*, 156.
112. Oberman, *The Harvest of Medieval Theology*, 157.
113. Oberman, *The Harvest of Medieval Theology*, 160.
114. Oberman, *The Harvest of Medieval Theology*, 221.

Lombard had made a prerequisite for the sacrament's efficacy? As long as the sinner's contrition is genuine, Biel counsels, it is beneath God's justice to punish the penitent for the priest's impiety.[115]

In short, penance—particularly the act of contrition—becomes an almost free-floating system of salvation. Divine election, the process of justification, effectual grace, baptism, Eucharist, and even the sacramental aspect of penance itself have faded into the background. The *habitus* of grace has not fallen out of the picture; in Biel's hands, it is crucial. Recall that the worth (*dignitas*) of a work is determined by its intrinsic good (*bonitas*). "To summarize Biel's doctrine of justification in one sentence: the habit of grace is the necessary bridge between *bonitas* and the *dignitas* which gives the *viator* a *de condigno* claim on his eternal salvation."[116] Whereas for Thomas infused grace is necessary even to perform a good work, for Biel it is only necessary to raise the act's meritorious status.

Grace is certainly needed once one is in a state of grace, Biel argues in semi-Pelagian fashion. Where Augustine pictures free will as a horse driven by grace, its rider, Biel suggests that "the driver is more like a second horse running side by side with the first (*concurrit*)."[117] And elsewhere Biel can even make free will the rider.[118] The habit of grace is not really necessary for the very good of the act itself. Grace merely makes easier what we can do by nature. Aquinas's analogical vision has vanished behind the clouds of a univocity that provokes the question, "Who does *more* in salvation?" with the *Palme d'Or* given to human beings.

The main problem, then, is that the intellect lacks the information the will needs to do its very best. "Not absence of grace, but improper cognition prevents man from acting rightly," as Oberman describes Biel's view. "The primary task of the Church is therefore not to provide grace, but to provide the Christian people with the proper information about God which necessarily leads to moral improvement."[119] As with Pelagius, for Biel grace comes into the picture at the level of God's generosity in accepting our works as meritorious.[120]

Yet even this gratuitousness is qualified by the earlier description of Biel's claim that God is obligated to reward such works condignly

---

115. Oberman, *The Harvest of Medieval Theology*, 221.
116. Oberman, *The Harvest of Medieval Theology*, 161.
117. Oberman, *The Harvest of Medieval Theology*, 162.
118. Oberman, *The Harvest of Medieval Theology*, 163.
119. Oberman, *The Harvest of Medieval Theology*, 164–65.
120. Oberman, *The Harvest of Medieval Theology*, 176.

by virtue of his ordained power (the *pactum*). To those who do their very best God *must* grant eternal life. Oberman judges, "It is clear that the emphasis falls on 'justification by works alone.' . . . It is therefore evident that Biel's doctrine of justification is essentially Pelagian."[121] At least on this point, the Roman Catholic church historian Joseph Lortz is correct in his "general observation that the Occamistic system 'as a matter of fact makes of grace a superfluous appendix.'"[122]

Mary as Exemplar of Condign Merit

So far I have not touched on Mariology, despite its importance particularly in later medieval theology. Even some of the first-generation magisterial Reformers, including Luther and Zwingli, held to Scotus's novel doctrine of Mary's immaculate conception and perpetual virginity. By themselves, such ideas do not determine one's doctrine of justification. However, at this point the topic becomes especially revealing with respect to divergent approaches to grace and justification.

The ancient church's motive in securing Mary's status as Mother of God or *Theotokos* (God-bearer) was christological: namely, an anti-Nestorian move to underscore that the one she bore is one person—God incarnate.[123] However, especially with Scotus, Mariology begins to drift away from Christology. She now becomes the great exemplar of one who cooperates with God and gains a meritorious reward.[124] Aquinas had argued that Mary's status could not have been merited, since the incarnation was above all merits and was even the basis for Mary's merits. However, Biel believed that she did merit it, even *de condigno*.[125]

On all of these points as well, Gregory, the *Doctor Authenticus*, was Biel's ardent critic. Mary was cleansed of all sin when she conceived Christ, Gregory allowed, but if she had been immaculately conceived, then she would not have been a sinner saved by grace.[126] Further, Scotus's teaching was unscriptural and, secondarily, unknown to the fathers, he urged.[127] The Thomists also firmly rejected the immaculate conception

---

121. Oberman, *The Harvest of Medieval Theology*, 177, emphasis original.

122. Oberman, *The Harvest of Medieval Theology*, 177, quoting Joseph Lortz, *Die Reformation in Deutschland*, 2nd ed., 2 vols. (Freiburg im Breisgau: Herder, 1941), 1:173.

123. See Jaroslav Pelikan, *The Christian Tradition: A History of the Development of Doctrine*, vol. 1, *The Emergence of Catholic Tradition (100–600)* (Chicago: University of Chicago Press, 1971), 287.

124. Oberman, *The Harvest of Medieval Theology*, 301.

125. Oberman, *The Harvest of Medieval Theology*, 299–300.

126. Oberman, *The Harvest of Medieval Theology*, 292. Chapter 9 is devoted to the exploration of Biel's Mariology.

127. Oberman, *The Harvest of Medieval Theology*, 290–91.

(which was not adopted as official dogma until 1854).[128] It is not surprising that the upsurge in Marian devotion and doctrinal elevation was due especially to Scotist-nominalist influences, since her role in salvation has always been used as a demonstration of human cooperation with God's grace. Biel's most ardent expressions of Marian devotion are found in his sermons, to which we turn briefly.

Justification in Biel's Preaching

Not in lecture halls but in churches are battles over the gospel won or lost, and there is no better test of a doctrinal system than in how it preaches. Unlike the mature Luther, Biel did not think of preaching as the proclamation of the word that produces faith but as "a 'consilium,' exhortation that prods the sinner onto the path of righteousness." For Biel, the preached Word was "the new Law."[129] Equating assurance of salvation with presumption, Biel's preaching discourages such confidence. After all, how could people know when they had done their very best, loving God above everything else, including their own salvation? The main thing is to remain now in a state of grace through penance.[130]

Biel's sermons emphasize, according to Oberman, "Christ has opened the doors of salvation, but now we have to enter through them by subjugating our *asinus*, the exterior man, to the rule of Christ, the law. Otherwise we would reap damnation from grace." Christ is still present among his people "but now first of all as judge."[131] Christ's work only makes salvation possible. However, "One can only profit from it by acquiring merits through fulfilling the law in its totality according to the example of Christ in his earthly life."[132] We can follow the life of Christ, so his life, not his inimitable death, is central for Biel. By this life Jesus provides an example, displaying "the possibility of man's elevation to the ranks of the blessed; this is the significance of the Ascension."[133] The Origenist (and Brethren of the Common Life) notes are evident here, as they are in the downplaying of the sacraments (and therefore grace) in favor of inner experience and moral resolve.

---

128. Even Hans Urs von Balthasar notes that the idea that Mary was immaculately conceived is rare in patristic literature (Balthasar, *Theo-Drama*, vol. 3, *The Dramatis Personae, the Person in Christ* [San Francisco: Ignatius, 1992], 321).

129. On this point, see Oberman, *The Harvest of Medieval Theology*, 22–23.

130. Oberman, *The Harvest of Medieval Theology*, 218–19.

131. Oberman, *The Harvest of Medieval Theology*, 225.

132. Oberman, *The Harvest of Medieval Theology*, 227.

133. Oberman, *The Harvest of Medieval Theology*, 234.

Biel does also emphasize Christ as the bridegroom who wants to enter the soul, but this habitation can occur only "after the requirements of the judge have been fulfilled."[134] "The God-directed Anselmian interpretation of Calvary is markedly less characteristic of Biel's position than the man-directed Abelardian understanding of the work of Christ."[135] Although the door is opened to salvation on account of Christ's merits, Biel quickly adds, "If we do not add our merits to those of Christ, the merits of Christ will not only be insufficient, but nonexistent."[136] The heart of the nominalist concept of the covenant is the idea of a testament to God's moral will. "We note here explicitly that this inheritance of Christ is not the remission of sins, but primarily the establishment of the New Law."[137]

Biel prods his parishioners by emphasizing Mary's cooperation with God's will and work, although she is the only person who was predestined eternally and unconditionally.[138] Mary's cooperation is extended into eternity with her glorification, becoming an advocate and source of merits for the living and the dead. Thus arise novel titles elevating her to "*Maria Co-Redemptrix, Mediatrix*, almost *Concreatrix*, and as we will have to conclude finally—to *Maria Spes Omnium*. It is in this last function of Mary, though derived from her intimate bond with Christ, that at the borderline where Mariology and justification meet, she occupies a position of priority."[139]

Biel describes Mary's entrance into heaven, with Jesus announcing that he has given to her "responsibility for compassion," while he will be "responsible for justice and truth." To come to Christ, one must go through his mother.[140] "Christ becomes more and more the severe judge," who "could not possibly hear the prayers of a sinner; what is needed therefore is a mediator with the mediator." "From eternity, God has provided one, thus erecting a new trinitarian hierarchy: the Virgin Mary hears the sinner, the Son hears his Mother, and the Father his Son."[141] Biel goes so far as to argue that by virtue of his deity, Jesus is not

---

134. Oberman, *The Harvest of Medieval Theology*, 228.
135. Oberman, *The Harvest of Medieval Theology*, 267.
136. Oberman, *The Harvest of Medieval Theology*, 268.
137. Oberman, *The Harvest of Medieval Theology*, 273.
138. Oberman, *The Harvest of Medieval Theology*, 302–3.
139. Oberman, *The Harvest of Medieval Theology*, 308.
140. Oberman, *The Harvest of Medieval Theology*, 311.
141. Oberman, *The Harvest of Medieval Theology*, 312.

really one of us in the way Mary is.[142] Consequently, he tends "to isolate the Virgin Mary as in herself the Hope of the World, in whom we can trust and have *fiducia* [trust] more than in Christ, *in contrast with Christ.*"[143] However, Biel also identifies Mary's role with that traditionally given to the Holy Spirit in applying Christ's work.[144] In short, "There is *only fiducia in Christ insofar as one has fiducia in Mary and her merciful influence on her Son.*"[145] Of course, intense Marian devotion was integral to medieval piety, but the dogmatic elevation of her person and work was just as integrally connected to the "new Pelagianism" that Gregory and other critics of these Mariological moves also opposed. It is no wonder, then, that Luther would often insist that if the truth about justification were recovered, all the other errors and superstitions would simply fall away.[146]

CONCLUSION

Far from being an aberration, Scotus represents a natural movement from Alexander of Hales to Bonaventure. As Charles Carlson argues, "The moment that an act of love is present, God rewards it with an infusion of justifying grace which perfects the movement of contrition." The full formula, *facere quod in se est*, was apparently used first by Ambrosiaster in the fourth century and became a formula in the work of the Franciscans, Alexander of Hales and Bonaventure.[147] The intent was pastoral, to bring the marginalized into the faith. But how do you know when you have done "your very best"? And does Scripture in fact teach that our very best is good enough, when all "fall short of the glory of God" (Rom 3:23)? That was Luther's anxiety, and he was hardly alone.[148] However, to whatever extent that Scotus disintegrated the medieval synthesis and that Ockham and Biel radicalized Scotus's innovations, many of the seeds that would grow into semi-Pelagianism had already been planted. Even Aquinas's brilliant synthesis and properly analogical metaphysics of grace were too riven with internal contradictions, such that one side of his thought could fully flower in Jansenism and another

---

142. Oberman, *The Harvest of Medieval Theology*, 319.
143. Oberman, *The Harvest of Medieval Theology*, 314.
144. Oberman, *The Harvest of Medieval Theology*, 319.
145. Oberman, *The Harvest of Medieval Theology*, 320.
146. Luther, "Against the Heavenly Prophets," in *LW* 40:85.
147. Carlson, *Justification in Earlier Medieval Theology*, 125–26, quote on 125.
148. Carlson, *Justification in Earlier Medieval Theology*, 127.

in semi-Pelagianism. Whatever else contributed to the eclipse of the biblical doctrine of justification, it was inextricably linked to the new sacrament of penance as formulated by Peter Lombard.

Luther recalls that from childhood he thought of Christ more as judge than as redeemer. He relates that his experience at Mass confirmed this view.[149] So did the Corpus Christi festival in Eisleben in 1515, as the sense of Christ's nearness filled him with dread.[150] Every time he looked at the crucifix or heard Jesus's name mentioned, he shuddered.[151] This emphasis, which we have seen in Gabriel Biel, would only be reinforced at Erfurt under his nominalist tutors.

---

149. Luther, *Table Talk*, in *LW* 54:234.
150. Luther, *Table Talk*, in *LW* 54:19–20.
151. Luther, "Genesis 45–50," in *LW* 8:188.

CHAPTER 6

THE ROAD FROM PENANCE TO CHRIST

> For nearly half a century, the Church was split into two or three obediences that excommunicated one another, so that every Catholic lived under excommunication by one pope or another, and, in the last analysis, no one could say with certainty which of the contenders had right on his side. The Church no longer offered certainty of salvation; she had become questionable in her whole objective form—the true Church, the true pledge of salvation, had to be sought outside the institution.[1]

These were the dire circumstances brought about by the Western Schism, as described in 1987 by no less than Joseph Cardinal Ratzinger, subsequently Pope Benedict XVI. The formal schism, which began in 1378, ended a century before Luther's Ninety-Five Theses, but only after leaving behind considerable disillusionment. Battles between papalists and conciliarists who believed that the pope should be subject to councils continued to the very eve of the Reformation with the Fifth Lateran Council (1512–17).

The rapacious, obscene, and acquisitive worldliness of the clergy, exemplified by successive popes who can be called Christian only with some sarcasm, had fostered cynicism. For the most sensitive souls, a crisis of conscience over whether the church in its present condition was more a pirate ship than the ark of salvation.

Sermons and pamphlets spread, excoriating the clergy and the hierarchy, including the pope. The preacher Michel Menot lamented,

---

1. Joseph Cardinal Ratzinger, *Principles of Catholic Theology* (San Francisco: Ignatius, 1987), 196.

"Never could less devotion be found in the Church." When someone in the audience asked why he did not do something about the abuses, Menot replied, "Friend, we do not have the man," and "I have no great hopes for the Church unless it be planted anew."[2] Pope Pius II lamented, "Christianity has no head whom all wish to obey. Neither the Pope nor the emperor is rendered his due. There is no reverence, no obedience." The masses regard "the Pope and Emperor as if they bore false titles and were mere painted objects." "Each city has its own king," he complained. "There are as many princes as there are households."[3] These comments were made more than sixty years before Luther's famous protest. By the turn of the sixteenth century, Erasmus could say, "The corruption of the Church, the degeneracy of the Holy See, are universally admitted. Reform has been loudly asked for, and I doubt whether in the whole history of Christianity the heads of the Church have been so grossly worldly as at the present moment."[4]

As we have seen, Lombard's stipulation that valid penance requires a faithful priest was upended by the various insurrections across Europe over the "wicked priests." From the fourteenth century on, cries for *reformatio in capite et in membris* ("reformation in head and members") were heard, to no avail. In Johan Huizinga's classic *The Waning Middle Ages*, he characterized the late medieval era as a time of profound pessimism and insecurity.[5] Given the story thus far, Hans Hillebrand is exactly right when he says that "there would have been a religious upheaval in the sixteenth century even if Martin Luther had died in the cradle."[6] Luther fought so hard not because he disregarded the church and its teachings but because he took them seriously.

But none of these corruptions can sufficiently explain the Reformation. Reformers had come and gone. The Brethren of the Common Life sought renewal by returning to the simple piety of the apostles, particularly the imitation of Christ. They criticized moral corruption and

---

2. Quoted in Heiko A. Oberman, *The Harvest of Medieval Theology: Gabriel Biel and Late Medieval Nominalism* (Durham, NC: Labyrinth, 1983), 324.

3. Heiko A. Oberman, Daniel E. Zerfoss, and William J. Courtenay, introduction to *Defensorium obedientiae apostolicae et Alia documenta*, by Gabriel Biel, eds. Heiko A. Oberman, Daniel E. Zerfoss, and William J. Courtenay (Cambridge, MA: Harvard University Press, 1968), 8.

4. J. A. Froude, *Life and Letters of Erasmus: Lectures delivered at Oxford 1893–4* (New York: Scribner's Sons, 1896), 284.

5. Johann Huizinga, *The Waning of the Middle Ages*, 1st ed. (New York: Doubleday, 1954), esp. ch. 2.

6. Hans J. Hillerbrand, *Men and Ideas in the Sixteenth Century* (Prospect Heights, IL: Waveland, 1984), 9.

abuses, avoiding doctrinal and liturgical questions as much as possible. Savonarola became a celebrity prophet in Florence only to become a laughing stock for his moralistic diatribes and fanciful eschatological predictions and pretensions. Wycliffe and Hus came closer to the issues that would characterize the Reformation, and Luther looked to Hus as a hero. However, it was Luther who sparked the Reformation. But why? What made his call to reform different? With this chapter we begin to answer that question.

Our story thus far has set the stage. Imagine a simple believer or even a pious priest who encounters second- or third-hand the complex labyrinth of scholastic distinctions regarding merit, penance, and justification that we have touched on only briefly. Add to this the subtle debates over the very meaning of these terms and their efficacy. It seems like a game so complicated that the referees cannot even agree on the rules. Yet these matters touch on personal salvation. Who are the true Christians, and what is the true church?

Following in the line of Luther's contemporary Johannes Cocclaeus, Heinrich Denifle (1844–1905) felt that he could explain the entire Reformation largely as a schism provoked by a profligate monk who crafted a theology suited to his allegedly antinomian principles. Hence Denifle's quote with which I began this story, charging Luther with either ignorance or malice in his description of medieval theology. Of particular offense, according to Denifle, was Luther's claim that none of his teachers had exposed him to any notion of the passive righteousness of God (i.e., a gift), but only to the active righteousness that God is, that God commands, and by which he judges.

It should be clear by now what Luther had in mind when he said that the only thing his teachers taught about the righteousness of God was that it condemns; he had learned nothing of gift of righteousness. Luther said,

> For they reduced sin as well as righteousness to some very minute motion of the soul. . . . And this tiny motion toward God (of which man is naturally capable) they imagine to be an act of loving God above everything else. . . . This is also the reason why there is, in the church today, such frequent relapse after confessions. The people do not know that they must still be justified, but they are confident that they are already justified; thus they come to ruin by their own

sense of security, and the devil does not need to raise a finger. This certainly is nothing else than to establish righteousness by means of works.[7]

This comment highlights the fact that the early Luther was not motivated by antinomianism but, on the contrary, by a lax view of repentance, which again becomes apparent in his criticism of indulgences in the Ninety-Five Theses.

REAL PENITENCE: THE STARTING POINT IN LUTHER'S JOURNEY

Our story has taken us from the evolution of public penances for serious crimes, heresy, and apostasy to a sacramental system of penance. And now it brings us to the most extreme form of ecclesiastical power over salvation: indulgences.

The Making of Indulgences

First, as we have seen, the patristic practice of church discipline evolved into a sacrament required for salvation. By comparison, baptism seemed dwarfed in significance, since it only sufficed for prior sins; for the remainder of one's life, penance was the sacrament for obtaining justification.

Second, Origen's concept of a postmortem continuing education before being welcomed into glory evolved into a dogma of purgatory. Penance now pertained chiefly to the remittance of temporal punishment (i.e., duration of suffering in purgatory).

Third, the idea gradually emerged that the good works of Mary and the saints were not only sufficient for their own salvation but accrued supererogatory merits that could be imputed to us. During the early persecutions, the lapsed (those who disowned Christ in order to preserve their life) who wanted to return could only do so with a special indulgence of the bishop. Examining each case on its own merits, he could determine if there had been sufficient repentance for restoration. Some even argued that the merits of the martyrs could be credited to

---

7. Charles P. Carlson, Jr., *Justification in Earlier Medieval Theology* (The Hague: Martinus Nijhoff, 1975), 132, quoting Gordon Rupp, *Righteousness of God: Luther Studies* (London: Hodder and Stoughton, 1968), 121f.

the lapsed. In later centuries these quite specific debates around church discipline evolved into a full-fledged sacrament, a new sun around which ordinary faith and practice orbited. *Everyone* was under a state of church discipline with the ever-present danger of "excommunication" by means of a mortal sin that could empty one's reservoir of infused grace and force one to begin the path to justification all over again. Even a venial sin, left unconfessed to a priest, could negate one's justification.

So, interestingly enough, the concept of imputed merits was far from unknown in the medieval church. The only question was whether Christ's imputed merits were sufficient. In any case, the dogma of the treasury of merit emerged by the middle of the thirteenth century, with the church as the keeper of this treasury.

Thomas Aquinas explained, "Now those things that are the common property of a number are distributed to the various individuals according to the judgment of him who rules them all. Hence, just as one man would obtain the remission of his punishment if another were to satisfy for him, so would he too if another's satisfactions be applied to him by one who has the power to do so."[8] A good summary of the view that came to be established in the wake of Thomas is found in the contemporary *Catechism of the Catholic Church* (1995),

> The "treasury of the Church" is the infinite value, which can never be exhausted, which Christ's merits have before God. They were offered so that the whole of mankind could be set free from sin and attain communion with the Father. In Christ, the Redeemer himself, the satisfactions and merits of his Redemption exist and find their efficacy. This treasury includes as well the prayers and good works of the Blessed Virgin Mary. They are truly immense, unfathomable, and even pristine in their value before God. In the treasury, too, are the prayers and good works of all the saints, all those who have followed in the footsteps of Christ the Lord and by his grace have made their lives holy and carried out the mission the Father entrusted to them. In this way they attained their own salvation and at the same time cooperated in saving their brothers in the unity of the Mystical Body.[9]

---

8. *ST* III, Q. 25, A. 1.
9. *CCC*, 1476–77.

At first Biel had rejected Thomas's argument that the church could transfer indulgences to the dead "on the grounds that the jurisdiction of the Pope is restricted to the living," Oberman relates. "Biel adds that if Thomas were right, the Pope would be able to liberate whomever he wants from the purgatorial prison and to empty purgatory by issuing plenary indulgences." But in 1477 Pope Sixtus IV announced his power to issue plenary indulgences that could be acquired for deceased loved ones, reducing their time in purgatory. After this decision, Biel happily affirmed the pope's jurisdiction over purgatory. Now he reasoned, "The Pope cannot empty purgatory since he liberates only those for whom a work of piety has been performed. Not a lack of love on the part of the Pope, but on the part of the faithful keeps the deceased in purgatory."[10]

In 1515, Pope Leo X announced a *full* plenary indulgence (i.e., covering all debts in purgatory) to fund the building of St. Peter's Basilica in Rome and entrusted the theatrical Dominican preacher Johann Tetzel with the mission to Saxony. Princes and city councils were generally open to the practice as long as they received a percentage of the proceeds. On October 31, 1517, Luther sent a letter to Albert the prince of Brandenburg and the archbishop of Mainz raising questions about the indulgence and this ignited the Reformation.

Luther's initial protest was provoked by his sense that the penitential system had made salvation too easy! People imagined that they were in a state of grace when they were not—carnal security was actually Luther's initial provocation. He noticed as people returned from having purchased one of Tetzel's indulgences that they no longer felt any need to repent.[11] Lifelong, daily, and deliberate repentance was thwarted by the cycle of flagrant sin, whispering in the ear of a priest, and saying a few "Hail Marys." The sale of indulgences merely added to this mockery, as if one could buy God off for a few guilders and return to the brothel.

Indeed, even before Luther came to understand justification as God's gift of Christ's alien righteousness, the first four of his Ninety-Five Theses asserted,

1. By saying "Poenitentiam agite" [Matt. 4:17], our Lord Jesus Christ wanted the entire life of the faithful to be *poenitentia*. 2. For the word

---

10. Oberman, *The Harvest of Medieval Theology*, 405.

11. Martin Brecht, *Road to Reformation, 1483–1521*, trans. James L. Schaff (Minneapolis: Fortress, 1985), 184.

cannot be understood concerning sacramental *poenitentia* (that is, confession and satisfaction which is administered by the ministry of priests). 3. But neither did he intend interior *poenitentia* alone; indeed, such interior *poenitentia* is nothing unless it produces various mortifications of the flesh. 4. Therefore *poena* [punishment for sin] remains as long as hatred of self (that is, true inner *poenitentia*) remains: right up to the coming of the kingdom of heaven.[12]

Ironically, the worry that he expresses here is that people "do not know that they must still be justified, but are confident that they are already justified," even though they continue in sin.[13] By "justification" here he means what every medieval theologian understood: the process of becoming righteous. The match that ignited the flame was not "justification by an alien righteousness."

Of course, Luther was hardly alone in this concern. As we have seen, there were widespread defections from penance by large groups in various cities who refused the ministrations of the "wicked priests." The "Babylonian captivity" in Avignon (1309–77) and the period of the Schism that followed (1378–1415) dealt a seismic blow to the medieval psyche. Regardless of the claims to which one yielded formal assent, it was hardly a universal sentiment that the church that they knew was the haven of infused *caritas*.

So Luther's protest did not begin as crisis of tortured subjectivity on the part of a monk obsessed with his individual salvation. In fact, his initial challenge was not sparked by the doctrine of justification but by the doctrine of repentance. Ironically, just as Lombard and other scholastics had treated justification under penance, Luther sort of stumbled into the former as he was working through the gross abuses related to the latter.

The Ninety-Five Theses were at first a private letter to the prince-archbishop questioning a practice that, he was convinced, made a mockery of God and gave false security to those duped by the indulgence. The theses hardly reflect Luther's mature understanding of justification. On the contrary, this list of propositions for university debate proves that Luther came to his understanding of God's gift of Christ's alien

---

12. WA 1:233, quoted in Timothy J. Wengert, *Law and Gospel: Philip Melanchthon's Debate with John Agricola of Eisleben over Poenitentia*, Texts and Studies in Reformation & Post-Reformation Thought (Grand Rapids: Baker, 1997), 15.

13. Quoted in Gordon Rupp, *The Righteousness of God* (London: Hodder and Stoughton, 1974), 121.

righteousness not first of all "in search of a gracious God," much less to satisfy libertine lusts, but out of a deep sensitivity to the seriousness of sin and God's righteousness. While according to most scholastics fear leads to love, Luther praised his abbot Johann von Staupitz in a 1518 letter, "Therefore I accepted you as a messenger from heaven when you said that *poenitentia* is genuine only if it begins with love for justice [righteousness] and for God and that what they consider to be the final stage and completion is in reality rather the very beginning of *poenitentia*."[14] Indeed, even when the Reformation was in full swing, the greatest crisis within the nascent evangelical movement was between Melanchthon and John Agricola over the relation of the law to *poenitentia*, and Luther stood squarely with the former over the perceived antinomian position of the latter.[15]

"Where Can I Find the Real God?"

We remember Luther because he went straight to the doctrine, and not just any doctrine but the doctrine of penance, whose practice involved every person. At first, he focused on indulgences, but he quickly realized that it was the tip of the iceberg.

Even though he had pointed out the mistranslations of the Latin Vulgate, including that of justification ("to make righteous" instead of the Greek's "to declare righteous"), Erasmus was ill-disposed to doctrinal debates. His heated exchange with Luther over free will and predestination displayed the path that the Catholic Reformation would take: amending the externals, emphasizing personal piety, unity, and correcting abuses. It was all the usual business of the Brethren of the Common Life. Doctrine and ritual are extraneous to the imitation of Christ. Erasmus made other excuses for not joining the evangelical Reformers (some of whom were his friends), but he made his own theological inclinations clear, especially after his debate with Luther over the freedom of the will. He was no Augustinian, much less a Lutheran. "One page of Origen is worth twenty of Augustine," he judged.[16]

---

14. *LW* 48:64–70 (WA 1:515).

15. Timothy J. Wengert recounts this controversy in illuminating detail in *Law and Gospel: Philip Melanchthon's Debate with John Agricola of Eisleben over Poenitentia* (Grand Rapids: Baker Academic, 1997).

16. Thomas P. Scheck, *Erasmus's Life of Origen: A New Annotated Translation of the Prefaces to Erasmus of Rotterdam's Edition of Origen's Writings (1536)* (Washington, DC: Catholic University of America Press, 2016), 73.

But these deeper controversies for which we remember Luther were not present at the beginning. The Luther of the Ninety-Five Theses was not a timid soul wondering how he could stand before a holy God but a prophet calling Israel to *true penitence*. For Protestants at least, this may seem like an unusual departure point, but in Luther's day the penitential system was the most visible, tangible, and all-encompassing network of saving machinery that the church had to offer. The question "How can I find a gracious God?" was provoked by the experience of this alleged sacrament. When salvation was quite literally being sold for money, who could fail to recognize the mockery that was being made not only of poor consumers but of God himself?

So Luther's initial protest was not excited by a discovery of free grace but by a sense that the church had come to the place where it no longer took God seriously. David Yeago has pointed out that the preoccupation of "the young Luther" was "not 'How can I get a gracious God?' but 'Where can I find the real God?' All the evidence in the texts suggests that it was the threat of idolatry, not a craving for assurance of forgiveness that troubled Luther's conscience."[17] Far from turning away from the catholic tradition, Luther was turning toward its Augustinian core. Especially in his 1518 sermons and the Heidelberg Disputation, he came to see the article of justification as (quite literally) the fleshing out of Christology: God is a very definite being, the one we come to know in the manger and hanging on a cross. God has made himself accessible to us, and he still descends to us in word and sacrament.

Countering Joseph Lortz's thesis that Luther's thinking was driven by subjectivism, Roman Catholic historian John Hessen argues persuasively that instead it was Christ as revealed in Scripture that possessed the Reformer.[18] While Luther, like many of his contemporaries, experienced anxiety over assurance of God's goodwill toward him, his concern was broader: Since we are "curved in" on ourselves, as Augustine put it, how can we be sure that we are not worshiping an idol, that we are not using rather than worshiping and enjoying God? It was a passion for discovering the *real* God, come what may.[19] But to make God a plaything? To suggest that God is easily placated by "doing what

17. David Yeago, "The Catholic Luther," *First Things* (March 1996): 17.

18. John Hessen, *Luther in katholischer Sicht: Grundlegung eines ökumenischen Gespräches* (Bonn: Röhrscheid, 1949), 21–24.

19. Yeago, "The Catholic Luther," 17.

you can" (or giving what you can), especially when the will is bound, as he learned from Staupitz? These are merely evasions of the real God.

Luther's protest progressed from indulgences and penance generally to idolatry and the righteousness of God. His original impetus was neither antinomianism nor merely an existential crisis of an anxious conscience. From his earliest treatises of reform to the very last, he emphasized the character of God, the nature of true worship, and the lives and callings of believers in the world. In fact, none of the Reformation confessions or catechisms, including Lutheran, begins with the question, "How can I, a sinner, be accepted by a just God?" After all, this question cannot even be provoked, much less addressed, apart from a wider theological horizon, much of which the Reformers were happy simply to receive as part of a legacy that they shared with the Greek and Latin churches.

Even Luther's wrestling with God shows that he was captive to the word of God throughout his awakening to the gospel. He was wrestling with the *real* God—or at least what he thought was the real God—even if he did not like what he found. God is holy, no one is righteous, and therefore God must condemn us all. The penitential system, particularly in Luther's day, felt like tissue paper meant to break the fall. Worse, it was "the broad way that leads to death." In short, God was not being taken seriously. It is enticing to reduce Luther's career to his "evangelical breakthrough." Evangelicals love conversion stories, and Luther embodied such dramatic autobiography. But in reducing Luther's story, we will miss the broader context and motivations that make Luther more than a forerunner of modernity's individualistic and subjective experiential-expressivism. Upon understanding the gospel, Luther hoped to liberate the curved-in self to look up to God in faith and out to neighbors in love.

Regardless of what one makes of Paul, or his consistency with Jesus, the Reformation was foremost a rediscovery of Pauline theology, in a long history of such Pauline *ressourcements*, though something more than a mere extension of the Augustinian legacy. No more than Prosper, Bradwardine, or Gregory of Rimini can the protest against the "new Pelagians" be explained by historical psychoanalysis of Luther's peculiar personality.

Even if we focus on Luther himself, he was a biblical scholar and preacher. Not merely a Paul specialist, he translated the whole Bible, wrote commentaries, and preached on practically every biblical book. We already begin to see some changes in his first lectures, which were on the Psalms. He may have come to Scripture longing to have his existential concerns addressed, but he was a profound exegete nonetheless. This grounding in Scripture from the original languages attracted interest from humanists not only in the North but also in Italy, as we will see in chapter 11. Wherever pockets of monks and secular clergy were learning Hebrew and Greek to study Scripture and the oft-neglected patristic sources, Luther and the other Reformers found a foothold. For centuries, lecturing and commenting on Lombard's *Sentences* was the rite of passage from pupil to master. The rite became commentaries on Romans. And in many of these cases, Luther became a rallying point for views that others had arrived at themselves.

If teachers were drawn to Luther, it was not because they identified with his inner struggle or were drawn to his social, political, or philosophical views but because they found in his message a clear articulation of their discoveries in Scripture. This much is a historical fact, however much one wishes to challenge his exegesis and theological conclusions. Like all of us, Luther had a personal story, both good and bad, but his story cannot explain why people of such different dispositions, personalities, background, and experiences felt and continue to feel a kindred spirit in the erstwhile Augustinian monk.

The Reformation controversy turned not only on fine points, however important, but on different paradigms. Of course, they did not disagree over the articles of the creed, yet different understandings of "the remission of sins" and "life everlasting" cast their shadow across every locus. Even common terms like sin, church, grace, faith, justification, and indeed salvation were understood differently. It is no wonder that *this* reform grabbed the hearts of the people, not just academics and clerics.

GRACE: FAVOR AND GIFT ON ACCOUNT OF CHRIST

One obvious example of the new paradigm is grace. It is not that the Reformers differed with the medieval tradition at every doctrinal point. However, their differences went to the very definition of grace itself.

Favor and Gift or Substance and Infusion?

We have seen that Aquinas moved justification from the locus on penance to his expansive treatment of grace. There he regarded grace as a medicinal substance (*gratia medicinalis*)—a "supernatural quality"— infused to heal the soul, and so the distinction was drawn between actual and habitual grace. This sanctifying quality is infused in baptism and, if lost, may be regained by the sacrament of penance.[20] The quality increases in cooperation with God's ongoing assisting grace. While the infused habit permanently inheres in the soul, this assistance is called "actual grace." God gives actual grace periodically to help the believer keep the passions under the control of the intellect so that the will may more easily choose the good.

Thus, grace was not understood chiefly as God's favor on account of Christ but as a created substance infused to cure the soul of vice, keep the passions in check, excite virtue, and assist the believer in producing condign merits worthy of eternal life. Remission of sins was included, but even this was based on the presence of intrinsic righteousness in the soul. Of course, none of this would have been possible without Christ's incarnation, life, death, resurrection, and ascension, but the Christ-event merely prepared the way for the believer's ascent. Justification was therefore treated under the work of the Holy Spirit rather than under Christology.

So what did Luther have in mind when he said that he had only been taught that God's righteousness is the active justice by which he punishes sinners? Luther had certainly studied Lombard closely.[21] Clearly, Luther could not have been referring to Aquinas. The Angelic Doctor had a robust notion of the gift of righteousness, although he essentially

---

20. True to the Anglo-Catholic spirit, John Milbank reflects a romanticized view of penance. Remarkably, in his view it was Luther who introduced a "contractual" approach that he inherited from nominalism, whereas penance was ordered to the exchange of gifts. Thus, he says, an "all too Protestant" perspective "does not see that Catholic (i.e., Christian) penance is as removed from the mere 'equivalence' of punishment as gift-exchange is removed from the mere equivalence of contract" (Milbank, "Paul Against Biopolitics," in *Paul's New Moment: Continental Philosophy and the Future of Christian Theology*, ed. John Milbank, Slavoj Žižek, and Creston Davis [Grand Rapids: Brazos, 2010], 57n71). Yet in *Being Reconciled: Ontology and Pardon* (London: Routledge, 2003), he says, "Likewise, the contagion of merit and intercessions, though it was still, and crucially, *a trade of sorts,* was an impossibility, a seeking to restore, by all and for all, the repayment of a debt due which is nothing but an infinite free accepting" (47). "For Aquinas," he says, "merit automatically elicits grace" (77). How does the *free gift* of Christ with all of his benefits become a "contract" in Milbank's account, while penance (admittedly and even "crucially, a trade of sorts"), with merit *automatically eliciting* grace, is the opposite of contract? Note that he is describing penance and merit according to Aquinas here, not in the wake of nominalism.

21. Like any theologian of the schools, Luther was expected to master Lombard's *Sentences,* which he did rather well between 1513–18. In *The Marginal Notes on the* Sentences *of Peter Lombard* (1509–10), *Dicta Super Psalterium* (1513–16), *Lectures on Romans* (1515–16), and the *Academic Disputations* of 1516 and 1517, he grew in his sophistication with the *Sentences.* See Denis R. Janz, *Luther and Late Medieval Thomism: A Study in Theological Anthropology* (Waterloo, ON: Wilfrid Laurier University Press, 1983), esp. 6–59.

reduced justification to sanctification. But Luther was not ignorant or maliciously misrepresenting what he had been taught, as Denifle and others have asserted. Rather, his particular criticism must derive from another source.

The teachers he had in mind were the disciples of Ockham and Biel. If anything, they exacerbated this anxiety over the "righteousness of God." The *via antiqua*, as defined by the moderns, was fading from memory. "The label 'nominalist,' however, must be used with extreme caution," as E. I. Saak warns, since the term emerged two centuries later.[22] Some *via moderna* theologians followed the Augustinian path of Bradwardine, Gregory of Giles, and Gregory of Rimini.[23] In fact, according to Saak, the *via moderna* was "the via Gregorii in the 1508 statutes of the University of Wittenberg" when it was founded, nearly a decade before Luther's arrival.[24] However, apart from Staupitz, this trail became largely moribund; "nominalists" generally followed the semi-Pelagian path of Scotus and Ockham—most notably, Gabriel Biel.

It was not by fine-tuning adjustments of the scheme, as medieval theologians had done time and again, but by a shift to an entirely different paradigm that Luther launched the Reformation. As Robert Preus explains, "Luther broke with the scholastic doctrine of grace" first by treating it under the second article (Christ's person and work) rather than the third article (the Spirit's work in the heart).[25] This is a crucial difference. When seen as a subset of Christology, grace is directly identified with Christ and what he has done for us. When treated as a subset of sanctification, grace is exclusively concerned with what happens within the individual. There are forms of Protestantism, especially pietism, that still repeat this mistake. Preus notes that Luther "saw God's grace as related first and foremost to the salvation and justification of a sinner for Christ's sake."

> He pointedly distinguished between grace and the gifts of grace. He rejected the notion of infused grace, as worked out by the scholastic

---

22. E. I. Saak, "Gregory of Rimini," in *Augustine Through the Ages: An Encyclopedia*, ed. Allan Fitzgerald and John C. Cavadin (Grand Rapids: Eerdmans, 1999), 406.

23. It is anachronistic to see Gregory of Rimini as a purveyor of "nominalism" as it came to expression in Ockham. Although he emphasized particulars, he remained an ontological realist, believing that particulars are instantiations of real essences.

24. Saak, "Gregory of Rimini," 406.

25. Similarly, it should be noted, Calvin criticized even Augustine, who "still subsumes grace under sanctification" (*Inst.* 3.11.15).

theologians, often in a synergistic or pelagian context, although into mid-career he used the metaphor of an infusion of grace and righteousness. After all, the metaphors of pouring (being poured and fullness) are common in Scripture in a variety of contexts (Eph 3:19, 5:18; Titus 3:6; Acts 9:17, 13:9; Rom 5:5; Jn 1:16), but the metaphors have to do with theological and spiritual realities and divine actions, not with philosophical, metaphysical, or physical referents.[26]

For Luther, these metaphors are equivalent to "give" or "apply," "not to an infusion of a quality which henceforth resides in man but a mighty, free, loving, giving act of God whereby He elects us in Christ, justifies, and forgives us for Christ's sake, blesses, sanctifies, and saves us—and all that freely given out of His grace in Christ." In short, says Preus, "What Luther and Melanchthon, in the Apology, objected to most strenuously in the Roman teaching was that grace was considered a 'quality' or essence, given the believer along with other 'finite gifts' and qualities, a quality with which a believer cooperates to obtain more grace."[27]

Luther insists that grace is first of all a *habitus*, but it is a disposition of God toward us rather than a disposition within us. Grace is first of all God's blessing (*favor*) expressed to those who deserve the very opposite. It is also a gift (*donum*) that regenerates and sanctifies inwardly. But this gift is not a created substance. Rather, grace must be defined constitutively around Christ. Grace is God's favor toward sinners *on account of Christ* (*propter Christum*), and the gift is nothing less than Christ himself with all of his benefits. For the Reformers, grace was not primarily something *in* believers but something *between* God and his people. Christ is not standing at a distance, infusing medicinal substances through the sacramental system. Rather, he is the Gift who brings every blessing—justification, sanctification, and glorification. Where for Rome, habitual and actual grace provide everything for attaining final glory, Luther insists that we already have everything—including final glory—secured for us through union with Christ. This contrast again underscores the difference between the two paradigms: for the Reformers, grace is given primarily to reconcile enemies, and for Rome, grace is given primarily to bring the bodily passions under the control of the mind. For the

---

26. Robert D. Preus, *Justification and Rome* (St. Louis: Concordia Academic Press, 1997), 46–47. See *LW* 34:168.

27. Preus, *Justification and Rome*, 49.

Reformers, salvation means first of all justification, with the fruit of love and good works; for Rome, salvation means first of all love and good works, with the result of final justification.

New Testament scholar John M. G. Barclay offers a helpful taxonomy. Differences over grace, he suggests, depend on different definitions derived from "perfecting" (taking to an extreme). These include grace as (1) superabundance (the scale is excessive and all-encompassing), (2) singularity ("the giver's *sole and exclusive* mode of operation is benevolence or goodness"), (3) priority (which always takes place prior to the recipient's initiative), (4) incongruity ("without regard to the worth of the recipient"), (5) efficacy ("that which fully achieves what it was designed to do"—emphasizing God's sovereignty), and (6) noncircularity ("it escapes reciprocity, the system of exchange or *quid pro quo* that characterizes sale, reward, or loan").[28] Barclay stipulates, "To perfect one facet of a gift-giving does not imply the perfection of any or all of the others."[29] One may, for example, perfect grace as *singular,* denying justice or "law" in God as Marcion did, without perfecting the other definitions.

Using this taxonomy we could say that Aquinas and Luther agree that grace is *superabundant, prior,* and *effectual,* and both deny that grace is *singular* (since God's justice as well as his mercy is satisfied), without agreeing on its *incongruity* and *noncircularity.* Aquinas can even say "that good works can also be seen as the 'cause' of glory because they are its 'meritorious cause.'"[30] Can one with consistency affirm the incongruity of grace alongside merit—of a condign sort? Yet not even this gets to the heart of the disagreement.

Grace Is Christ

"I lost touch with Christ the Savior and Comforter," Luther recalled of his life as a monk, "and made of him the jailor and hangman of my poor soul."[31] For the Reformers, no a priori definition of grace would suffice, even Barclay's helpful classification. For the magisterial Reformers, *sola gratia* was a subpoint of—or, better, another way of saying—*solo Christo.* Grace does not stand alone. Voluminous references

---

28. John M. G. Barclay, *Paul and the Gift* (Grand Rapids: Eerdmans, 2015), 70–75.

29. Barclay, *Paul and the Gift,* 75.

30. Joseph P. Wawrykow, *God's Grace and Human Action: 'Merit' in the Theology of Thomas Aquinas* (South Bend, IN: University of Notre Dame Press, 1995), 188, from *ST* I-II, Q. 5, A. 7; and I, Q. 23, A. 5.

31. James Kittelson, *Luther the Reformer* (Minneapolis: Augsburg Fortress, 1986), 79.

to "grace" and "what grace does" and "what grace is" did not impress the Reformers. Not even anchoring grace in God's eternal and unconditional election was sufficient unless it linked clearly to Christ and his sole mediation. Only in the light of Christ—who he is and what he has accomplished—can we understand what grace is and what it excludes. For the Reformers, the main point was that merit opposed not only grace but Christ. Everywhere they inveighed against the blasphemy of trying to add Christ's merits to those of Mary, the saints, and ordinary believers themselves. There simply is no such thing as "grace" hovering above or behind Jesus Christ.

So we miss a great deal if we imagine that the Reformers assumed nominalism's univocity of being and simply opted for God's agency over human actions. With respect to election and regeneration, they were on the same page as Aquinas in crediting them to God alone. They were also largely on the same page with respect to the progress in holiness. God does not act merely upon humans, or above them in fictitious decrees, but within them to effectually bring about their conformity to Christ. The principal disagreement does not hinge on who does more in salvation per se. In this respect, the magisterial Reformers did not diverge significantly from Aquinas's analogical account: grounded in unconditional election, God's grace not only makes genuinely free human response possible but brings it about. Thomas Aquinas would have been as opposed as the Reformers to the nominalists.

But the matter went deeper. It was not merely a question of whether God is credited with all of salvation, but whether Christ is sufficient as the meritorious basis of acceptance before God. Either merit or Christ had to go.

It is striking that Calvin could claim Chrysostom as the best exegete of the ancient church and translate Melanchthon's *Loci communes* into French even while acknowledging in both cases that he disagreed with their synergism. And yet, though Augustine was his muse, Calvin could openly and repeatedly lament his master's failure to understand justification as strictly forensic as forgiveness and imputation rather than as the process of sanctification. No recourse to strict Augustinian monergism could save the system from denying this central tenet—*solo Christo*—as long as the believer's love contributed to justification.

Thus, in Lutheran thinking *solo Christo*—that is, everything in salvation being on account of Christ (*propter Christum*)—is the basis for *sola gratia* and *sola fide*. It is on the basis not of faith but of Christ's saving deeds that God justifies sinners.[32] Not even the word and the sacraments have any independent salvific efficacy, but draw it from Christ and his cross. "The Lord's Supper is not a source of grace but a means of grace, what the Apology [to the Augsburg Confession] calls a 'sign of grace,' which not only points us to the one and only perfect sacrifice for sins, but connects and joins us through faith to that sacrifice which is the source of all graces, forgiveness, and salvation."[33] It is therefore wide of the mark to charge Luther with shifting the burden from one subjectivity (works) to another (faith). Not even faith had independent value or a role in salvation but was merely the graciously donated gift of looking outside of oneself to *Christ*. Even the gracious gift of the Holy Spirit came in Christ.

Heavily dependent on Luther, Calvin reached the doctrine of justification by way of the incarnation, life, death, and resurrection of Christ. Like Luther, he focuses especially on the sufficiency of Christ. He does not doubt that the medieval church proclaims Christ but worries they do not proclaim Christ alone.

> True, he is called a Redeemer, but in a manner which implies that men also, by their own free will, redeem themselves from the bondage of sin and death. True, he is called righteousness and salvation, but so that men still procure salvation for themselves, by the merit of their works. . . . True, they confess that we are washed from our sins by the blood of Christ, but so that every individual cleanses himself by washings elsewhere obtained. True, the death of Christ receives the name of a sacrifice, but so that sins are expiated by the daily sacrifices of men. True, Christ is said to have reconciled us to the Father, but with this reservation, that men, by their own satisfactions, buy off the punishments which they owe to the justice of God. When supplementary aid is sought from the benefit of the keys, no more honour is paid to Christ than to Cyprian or Cyricius. For, in making up the treasury of the Church, the merits of Christ and of martyrs are thrown together in the same lump.[34]

---

32. Preus, *Justification and Rome*, 49.

33. Preus, *Justification and Rome*, 50, quoting *Apology* 24.69, and citing 24.72, 92.

34. Calvin, "The Necessity of Reforming the Church," in *Selected Works of John Calvin: Tracts and Letters*, 7 vols., ed. Henry Beveridge and Jules Bonnet, trans. Henry Beveridge (Grand Rapids: Baker, 1983), 1:192.

Recalling his early years, he related,

> I believed, as I had been taught, that I was redeemed by the death
> of [God's] Son from liability to eternal death, but the redemption I
> thought was one whose virtue could never reach me. I anticipated
> a future resurrection, but hated to think of it, as being an event
> most dreadful. . . . They, indeed, preached of [God's] clemency
> toward men, but confined it to those who should show themselves
> deserving of it.[35]

Then he heard "a very different doctrine," he continues, which actually
"brought me back to its fountainhead," Christ.[36] At least the Galatians
sought justification through the law of Moses, but the pope and his party
mingle Christ's righteousness with works that God never commanded.
"The Galatians were not so grossly mistaken as to believe that they
were justified by observing the law alone," says Calvin. "They wanted
to mix Christ with the law, but even the smallest amount of righteousness cannot be attributed to the law without renouncing Christ and
his grace."[37] Henri Blocher comments, "One notices that John Calvin
already criticized special penitential exercises, as organized by 'several
Anabaptists' and the Jesuits, *Inst.* iii.3.2."[38]

The center of the gospel is not a process or the justification of the
sinner at the moment of conversion. It is not a question of who does
more in salvation: God or the sinner. This is why Roman Catholic
theologians are often at pains to defend against the charge of semi-
Pelagianism. For most, the principal frame of reference is Augustinian:
the priority and efficacy of grace. This is important for the Reformers
as well, but the primary concern for both Lutherans and the Reformed
is defending the sufficiency of Christ.

Not even human depravity and the undeservedness of grace play
a determinative role a priori in the Reformers' thinking. One may
even be, like Paul, "blameless" in the sense of major lapses according

---

35. Calvin, "The Necessity of Reforming the Church," 1:61.

36. Calvin, "The Necessity of Reforming the Church," 1:62.

37. John Calvin, *Commentary on Galatians*, in *Reformation Commentary on Scripture*, New Testament 10, *Galatians, Ephesians*, ed. Gerald Bray (Downers Grove, IL: InterVarsity, 2011), 174.

38. Henri Blocher, "Justification of the Ungodly," in *Justification and Variegated Nomism*, vol. 2, *The Paradoxes of Paul*, eds. D. A. Carson, Peter T. O'Brien, and Mark A. Seifrid (Grand Rapids: Baker Academic, 2004), 483n49.

to the law. However, *in the light of Christ*—all that he is and all that he has accomplished—our best works are "rubbish." Even if one went as far as the Catholic Jansenists or quietists and said that we can only let go and let God do everything, the Reformers would not be satisfied. This would be another form of works-righteousness: trusting in one's passivity!

For the Reformers, the gospel is not about what happens within us or to us; it is an announcement about who Christ is and what he has accomplished. How can one attribute the Reformers' doctrine to subjective introspection when its entire thrust calls people to look outside of themselves to Christ (*extra nos*)? As Luther puts it in the Smalcald Articles (1537),

> The first and chief article is this: Jesus Christ, our God and Lord, died for our sins and was raised again for our justification (Romans 4:24–25). He alone is the Lamb of God who takes away the sins of the world (John 1:29), and God has laid on Him the iniquity of us all (Isaiah 53:6). All have sinned and are justified freely, without their own works and merits, by His grace, through the redemption that is in Christ Jesus, in His blood (Romans 3:23–25). This is necessary to believe. This cannot be otherwise acquired or grasped by any work, law or merit. Therefore, it is clear and certain that this faith alone justifies us. . . . Nothing of this article can be yielded or surrendered, even though heaven and earth and everything else falls (Mark 13:31).[39]

Notice that this statement opposes merit not simply to grace but to Christ and from *solo Christo* to *sola fide*. In many Protestant defenses of these important qualifiers, each *sola* stands on its own. We believe in "faith alone" in opposition to "works." The Reformers would prefer to say: We believe in "Christ alone" in opposition to "ourselves." Only then does faith not slide into work and finds its proper place as the subject rather than the object.

Likewise, the logic of Calvin's argument in the *Institutes* (3.11–19) is as follows:

---

39. The Smalcald Articles, *Book of Concord: Confessions of the Evangelical Lutheran Church*, ed. and trans. Robert Kolb and Timothy Wengert (Minneapolis: Fortress, 2000), 295–328.

- To save us from judgment, the Son became flesh and merited our salvation (2.15–17).
- Thus, the righteousness by which we are saved is alien to us (3.11.2, etc.).
- Yet Christ must not only be given *for* us; he must be given *to* us (3.1.1).
- We are not only recipients of Christ's gifts but of Christ himself with his gifts (3.1.1; 3.1.4; 3.2.24; 4.17.11).
- Faith unites us to Christ (3.1.1), but it is the Holy Spirit who gives faith and it is Christ who always remains the sole ground of salvation rather than faith itself. In other words, faith is nothing in itself; it receives *Christ* and with him all treasures (3.11.7; 3.18.8). After all, "If faith in itself justified one by its own virtue, then, seeing that it is always weak and imperfect, it would be only partly effectual and give us only a part of salvation" (3.11.7).

Christ is not the basis merely of redemption, but of justification and sanctification. Everything that he accomplished for us outside us would be for naught unless the Holy Spirit unites us to Christ here and now through the gospel.[40]

Calvin, Trent, and Penance

Calvin argued, in his *Antidote to Trent*, that the council merges justification into sanctification. "The principal cause of obscurity, however, is that we are with the greatest difficulty induced to leave the glory of righteousness entirely to God alone." Calvin argues that the position of Trent is not Pelagian but semi-Pelagian. They preface their statement by extolling Christ but then leave him behind, repeating the line of the schools, "that men are justified partly by the grace of God and partly by their own works; thus only showing themselves somewhat more modest than Pelagius."[41]

In the same document Calvin argued that the so-called sacrament of penance, especially as formulated at Trent, diminished the importance of baptism. The council was interested more in "the chrism, the taper,

---

40. *Inst.* 3.1.1.
41. John Calvin, "Antidote to Trent," in *Acts of the Council of Trent: With the Antidote*, in *Selected Works of John Calvin: Tracts and Letters*, 7 vols., ed. Henry Beveridge and Jules Bonnet, trans. Henry Beveridge (Grand Rapids: Baker, 1983), 3:108.

the salt, the spittle than the washing with water, in which the whole perfection of Baptism consists." Penance has been "converted into a kind of spurious show."[42] In contrast, baptism "is the ordinary instrument of God in washing and renewing us; in short, in communicating to us salvation." "The only exception we make is that the hand of God must not be tied down to the instrument," he adds. "For when an opportunity of Baptism is wanting, the promise of God alone is amply sufficient," as in the example of the thief on the cross.[43] Again, the emphasis in Calvin's thinking falls on God's promise. God does not need us to be baptized in order to save us; we need baptism in order to be assured in our conscience by the sign and seal of God's gospel promise.

Where Trent has believers make up for their offenses through penance, Calvin counters, "Whenever the question relates to the forgiveness of sins, we must flee to Baptism, and from it seek a confirmation of forgiveness." After all, how can penance be considered a sacrament—that is, a means of God's grace—when it consists in satisfactions made by the believer that, if successful, yield absolution? In baptism, Christ himself absolves. It is his work and pledge. "What do the venerable Fathers say? Out of the trite rhapsodies of the sophists they restrict the promises of Baptism to the past, and the moment any one has sinned, burying all remembrance of Baptism, they enjoin him to rest in the fictitious Sacrament of Penance—as if Baptism were not itself a proper Sacrament of Penance."[44] And then they go on "to raise Confirmation above Baptism."[45]

As a distinguished Dominican theologian and prior of the Basilica in Lucca, Peter Martyr Vermigli was familiar with the growing dominance of Biel's ideas. Fleeing the Inquisition, he crossed the Alps and arrived at Strasbourg. Summarizing the nominalist thesis of "doing what you can," Vermigli notes that those who follow Ockham and Biel teach that even the unregenerate may merit justification congruently.[46] They appeal to patristic descriptions of repentance that include tears, alms, and fasting. "But these men do not understand what the fathers meant in those places, for they were concerned about ecclesiastical satisfactions

---

42. Calvin, "Antidote to Trent," 3:178.
43. Calvin, "Antidote to Trent," 3:180.
44. Calvin, "Antidote to Trent," 3:182.
45. Calvin, "Antidote to Trent," 3:183.
46. Peter Martyr Vermigli, *Locus on Justification*, in *Predestination and Justification: Two Theological Loci*, trans. and ed. Frank A. James III, Peter Martyr Library 8 (Kirksville, MO: Sixteenth Century Essays & Studies, 2003), 120.

[church discipline], not our own works by which God could be appeased or the forgiveness of sins deserved."[47] In other words, the fathers used public repentance as a form of church discipline in cases of serious crimes. They never intended the consciences of the Christian people to be bound by it, much less for it to be construed as a sacrament. But when Scotus and especially Ockham took a step beyond this, arguing that one may do good works prior to grace, Vermigli argues, they fall under the condemnation of the Second Council of Milevum (c. 416), which confirmed Augustine over Pelagius.[48]

THE PATH OF SALVATION: ASCENT OR DESCENT?

Before focusing directly on the Reformers' understanding of justification, there is one more "big-picture" contrast that should be summarized briefly.

Chapter 1 contrasted the trajectories of Irenaeus and Origen. We have seen that, despite the variety of formulations, medieval scholasticism generally agreed in seeing justification as a process of ascent—mystical, ethical, and intellectual—from this world of shadows known by the senses to the purely intellectual-spiritual realm. While Augustine's *ex nihilo* creation and the incarnation excluded the theory of emanation, even he was indebted to the exit-return cosmology of Neoplatonism. The debates that we have covered thus far are variations on a theme. Whatever the differences, these theories paired the ascent of mind and the process of justification.

If the Renaissance was a rediscovery of Plato (among other classical sources), it is not surprising that Christian humanists like Erasmus were especially fond of Origen. However, Pseudo-Dionysius had already cast his long shadow across medieval thought and practice. Quoted more times than any nonbiblical source in Aquinas's *Summa theologiae*, Pseudo-Dionysius was until the fifteenth century thought to have been the philosopher converted by Paul in Athens (recorded in Acts 17). Douglas Farrow points out that "the Dionysian Jesus is more akin to the cosmic

---

47. Vermigli, *Locus on Justification*, 121.
48. Vermigli, *Locus on Justification*, 123. As I have argued (along with Melanchthon, Vermigli, and Calvin), the church fathers were closer to the Reformers' view than Luther's comment suggests.

Christ of Origen than to that of Irenaeus."[49] Although his influence was just as great in the East, Orthodox theologian John Meyendorff acknowledges that the author (probably a fifth-century Syrian monk) was "clearly dominated by the Platonic opposition between the sensible and the intelligible" and "lacks the philosophical means to express the realities linked with the incarnation."[50] Elsewhere Meyendorff laments the impact on Byzantine theology of "the symbolic Gnosticism of pseudo-Dionysius."[51]

The Origenist trajectory of *askesis*—a struggle to attain unity with God by moral and intellectual ascent—was alive and well in the antischolastic and Hermeticist piety of figures like Nicholas of Cusa, another Brethren alumnus.[52] A key text for this Eckhartian (pantheistic or at least panentheistic) mysticism was the *Theologia Germanica*, from which Luther had to extricate himself over many years. In this scheme, the justification of the ungodly was not only irrelevant but the alternative to the ideal of the soul as a spark of the divine Good estranged by its bodily incarceration.

Nominalist Mystics?

Nominalism engendered its own type of mysticism. This is not supposed to be the case, according to reductionistic narratives, because nominalism created a wide gulf between God and the world. Apparently, mystics must be Neoplatonists, and nominalists must not be allowed into the Neoplatonist society.[53] In reality, however, these boundaries are not well-posted, much less followed. Where Biel differs most markedly from previous approaches is that the various stages central to monastic ascent (purgation, illumination, union) are now seen as *preparatory* to

---

49. Douglas Farrow, *Ascension and Ecclesia: On the Significance of the Ascension for Ecclesiology and Christian Cosmology* (Edinburgh: T&T Clark, 1999), 135.

50. John Meyendorff, *Christ in Eastern Christian Thought*, trans. Yves Dubois (Crestwood, NY: St. Vladimir's Seminary Press, 1987), 102–3.

51. John Meyendorff, *Byzantine Theology: Historical Trends and Doctrinal Themes* (New York: Fordham University Press, 1999), 119.

52. The Eckhardian spirituality was mediated especially through the *Theologia Germanica*. Several early Anabaptists were formed in this milieu. The tradition continued into the modern era especially through radical Catholic mystics and Protestant pietists like Jakob Boehme. Though well beyond our scope, it is worth noting that Eckhart, Cusa, the *Theologia Germanica*, and Boehme became celebrated forebears in the projects of Schelling, Hegel, Goethe, and other German (as well as English) idealists. See Ray C. Petry, ed., "German Theology (Theologia Germanica)" in *Late Medieval Mysticism*, Library of Christian Classics (Philadelphia: Westminster, 1957), 327–51.

53. For a discussion of some of these ironies, see Oberman, *The Harvest of Medieval Theology*, 330.

the infusion of grace for everyone. Contrition becomes the highest level before infusion.[54] By cleansing "the house of his soul" by sincere repentance and love for God above all, the sinner makes ready his or her heart for Christ. "This Christ-birth in the soul is not an exalted stage of perfection for a small privileged group, but necessary for the salvation of every Christian."[55] He can even say that "through man's decision to open the door of his heart, God is converted and moved to dwell in the soul through the gift of sanctifying grace."[56] Biel in fact describes his view as "Christ-mysticism," without which, he says, one cannot even be a beginner.[57]

Despite the democratizing emphasis, there is an aristocracy after all. For some who excel in doing what lies within them, there is, Biel says, "a special inhabitation of the Holy Spirit which no one can understand who has not experienced it." "This leads to a transformation of the soul which is not understood as an essential union, but as a union through love in conformity to the will of God, of higher quality than a mere adjustment to God's will." In fact, "The perfect Christian no longer needs psychological stimulation to love God; he lives already in God." Ironically, Biel comes to use language that Jean Gerson had criticized in the mystics Eckhart and Ruysbroeck: "The soul of the worthy participant is said to be changed into the body of Christ through a most intimate union. . . . On grounds of his participation in God, the soul is more truly in God than in the body."[58] Once again we see, then, the danger of simplistic narratives of "nominalism" as the undoing of Christian Neoplatonism. Even when the theory of Neoplatonism has been subverted, it remains in the spirituality of nominalists like Biel.

Luther surely had this ascent of mind/will in mind when he contrasted theologians of glory with theologians of the cross.[59] Although Erasmus said that one page of Origen is worth more than twenty of Augustine, Luther promised to bring Origen "back under the ban."[60] Of Pseudo-Dionysius, Luther concludes, "If one were to read and judge without prejudice, is not everything in it his own fancy and very much like a dream?" In fact, "He is downright dangerous, for he is

54. Oberman, The Harvest of Medieval Theology, 348.
55. Oberman, The Harvest of Medieval Theology, 349.
56. Oberman, The Harvest of Medieval Theology, 350.
57. Oberman, The Harvest of Medieval Theology, 352.
58. Oberman, The Harvest of Medieval Theology, 357–58.
59. See Walther von Loewenich, Luther's Theology of the Cross (Minneapolis: Augsburg, 1976).
60. Joseph W. Trigg, Origen (London: SCM, 1983), 256.

more of a Platonist than a Christian."[61] In his Heidelberg Disputation, the Reformer inveighs against the "theologians of glory," who seek to ascend to heaven instead of receive Christ as he descended to us in the manger and at the cross.[62] Luther focuses from this time forward on neither rationalism nor mysticism but the apocalyptic event of Christ. Although he would not prize the term "apocalyptic," Heinrich Bornkamm expressed Luther's new starting point well:

> The theology of the cross is not a theology which is contrived by the process of thinking. If we followed our ideas of the nature of the divine, we would imagine a quite different God: a great, mighty, victorious, indubitably loving, ingenious cosmic architect. But certainly not a God who allows his messenger, whom he sends for the salvation of the world, to go down to ignominious defeat, to suffer and die innocently. It is a theology that one can derive only from an actual event, or better, that one can believe only on the basis of the passion and the cross of Christ. . . . In that dereliction he became the brother of the loneliest and most derelict of men. No starry heaven, no marvel of creation, can make us so sure of it as the fact that Christ by the will of the Father took upon himself this uttermost affliction of soul.[63]

Odd Romance: Luther and the Neoplatonist Mysticism of the Theologia Germanica

The *Theologia Germanica* stood in the Eckhartian tradition of mysticism. It is clearly a manifesto for the theology of glory and was considerably influential in Anabaptist piety. But it is baffling to me at least that Luther not only translated this odd work into German but gave it such a glowing endorsement: "Next to the Bible and St. Augustine, no book has ever come into my hands from which I have learned more of God and Christ, and man and all things that are."[64]

Perhaps he was moved by the emphasis on humility in surrendering one's existence and will to God. Luther's earliest writings and sermons

---

61. Luther, "The Babylonian Captivity of the Church" in *LW* 36:109.

62. Gerhard O. Forde, *On Being a Theologian of the Cross: Reflections on Luther's Heidelberg Disputation, 1518* (Grand Rapids: Eerdmans, 1997), 5.

63. Heinrich Bornkamm, *The Heart of the Reformation*, trans. John W. Doberstein (New York: Harper & Row, 1965), 49–50.

64. Martin Luther, preface to *The Theologia Germanica of Martin Luther*, ed. and trans. Bengt Hoffman, Classics of Western Spirituality (New York: Paulist, 1980), 54.

do focus on justification through humility. In fact, abandonment of self and adherence to God's Word constituted his view of faith during this period. Jairzinho Lopes Pereira summarizes, "One cannot glorify God unless one does what one does not wish."[65] Denial, even hatred, of self is the way to union with God. The text also extolled the soul's passivity that figures prominently in Luther's theology. But we must also recall that with Luther more than any other sixteenth-century Reformer, we are dealing with a person in transition. Compared with the dry, complex, compromised, and increasingly implausible machinery of ecclesiastical absolution, the humid intimacy of the soul's direct experience of God may have brought refreshment. Some of Luther's earliest associates in the reform, such as Andreas Karlstadt, not only remained consistent devotes of *Theologia Germanica* but carried its implications to their logical extreme. Was this when Luther recognized the danger and crystalized his polemic against the way of ascent to the "naked God"?

Regardless of what Luther himself was thinking as he broke free from many of his late medieval assumptions, the more mature Luther of the Smalcald Articles (1537) had discovered a path entirely different from the mystical ascent. Steven Ozment observes, "Luther would not sympathize with an anthropology that endows man with a soteriologically significant 'eye' that can look into eternity," much less "the call for man to do the best that is in him if he hopes to achieve union with God." Ozment adds, "Even in the subtle mystical form of passive resignation—a 'doing' which is a 'doing nothing'—this is still allied to that semi-Pelagian *facere quod in se est*, which Luther overcame theologically in his first lectures on the Psalms (1513–16) and attacked explicitly in writings against the nominalists in 1516–17."[66] In fact, it was Andreas Osiander who in 1550 returned to the soteriological metaphysics of the *Theologia Germanica*, and when he did, despite being a notable colleague of Luther's, he found no sympathizers.[67]

---

65. Jairzinho Lopes Pereira, *Augustine of Hippo and Martin Luther on Original Sin and Justification of the Sinner* (Göttingen: Vandenhoek & Ruprecht, 2013), 406.

66. Steven E. Ozment, *Mysticism and Dissent: Religious Ideology and Social Protest in the Sixteenth Century* (New Haven, CT: Yale University Press, 1973), 24.

67. His views on justification (as an absorption of the soul into Christ's divinity rather than the imputation of righteousness) were condemned by Lutherans. In fact, Calvin added a sustained rebuttal to his final edition of the *Institutes* (3.2). In recent decades the so-called new interpretation of Luther, centered at the University of Helsinki and led by Tuomo Maanermaa, has argued that the Reformer's doctrine of justification was far from the idea of a forensic imputation of Christ's alien righteousness that became enshrined in the Lutheran and Reformed confessions. Rather, it was something much closer to deification as taught by the Christian East. As critics

Ironically, Luther's polemics against the Anabaptist "enthusiasts" target many of the views that had formerly impressed him. This is what Luther will attack as the mystic's ascent to behold the naked God (*Deus nudus*), apart from Christ as he is clothed in the gospel.[68] Adam and Eve were the first "enthusiasts," Luther said. "They were not satisfied with the divinity that had been revealed in the knowledge of which they were blessed, but they wanted to penetrate to the depth of the divinity"—in other words, to the hidden God rather than to the God who reveals himself in Christ as he is preached externally.[69]

Although Calvin was shaped by the medieval piety that was informed by Neoplatonic mysticism, Calvin had not been as drenched in it as Luther. French humanism was touching the austere colleges of the University of Paris, and soon the young reformer found himself in the circle of Jacques Lefèvre d'Étaples and others under the guidance of the bishop of Meaux and the protection of the king's sister. Philosophically, Lefèvre was a Neoplatonist Aristotelian, yet he was chiefly a biblical scholar and translator who had written on justification through faith alone before Luther. But unlike most of his humanist mentors, Calvin left the Roman church, barely escaping Paris for Switzerland with his friend and fellow reformer Nicholas Cop just after Cop delivered a reforming address (drafted by Calvin) as new rector of the university. That move was influenced by his reading of Luther.

Calvin's evaluation of the *Theologia Germanica* is less complicated. He judged that the work was "conceived by Satan's cunning" and could only "poison the church."[70] Plato at least realized that the aim of humanity is union with "God," Calvin says, but the Philosopher was incapable of seeing its true meaning, since he did not know Christ.[71] Calvin refers to Origen negatively and describes Pseudo-Dionysius's *Celestial Hierarchy* as initially impressive but ultimately "nothing but talk." "If you read that book, you would think a man fallen from heaven recounted, not what he had learned, but what he had seen with his

have pointed out, Maanermaa's interpretation of Luther is actually closer to the view of Osiander, and its sources are Luther's earliest writings. See my introduction, pp. 33–34. If my argument concerning Luther's early relationship to the *Theologia Germanica* is reasonably accurate, this would explain why Osiander as well as Anabaptists like Schwenckfeld felt betrayed as Luther moved on from this type of piety.

68. Steven D. Paulson, "Luther on the Hidden God," *Word and World* 19, no. 4 (Fall 1999): 363.

69. Luther, "Lectures on Genesis," in *LW* 5:42.

70. John Calvin, quoted in Bengt Hoffman, introduction to *The Theologia Germanica of Martin Luther,* trans. Bengt Hoffman, Classics of Western Spirituality (New York: Paulist, 1980), 26.

71. *Inst.* 1.5.11.

own eyes."[72] A later Genevan theologian Francis Turretin, would judge that "these things savor of Platonism and not of Paulinism."[73]

Calvin told Cardinal Sadoleto that "we are assailed by two sects: the pope and the Anabaptists." Although they seem quite different, he says, they are both dedicated to an enthusiasm that draws people away from the external word.[74] Both Reformers summarized the mystical way of ascent as a dangerous exploit—"seeking God outside the way," who is Christ embodied and delivered here and now through the fragile creaturely means he has chosen.

Calvin argues that Jesus does not merely help us ascend the ladder; rather, he *is* the ladder.[75] "The situation would surely have been hopeless had the very majesty of God not descended to us, since it was not in our power to ascend to him." Eckhart's scheme sees the preincarnate Logos in everyone establishing the link between the human and divine; Calvin, instead, refers to Christ assuming our human nature to make us sons of God. "Therefore, relying on this pledge, we trust that we are sons of God, for God's natural Son fashioned for himself a body from our body, flesh from our flesh, bones from our bones, that he might be one with us."[76] Ungrudgingly, God "took our nature upon himself to impart to us what was his, and to become both Son of God and Son of man in common with us."[77]

Among the magisterial Reformers, Zwingli stands out alone as an explicit disciple of Plato.[78] Early in his ministry (apparently before he had joined the reform) he had established a "Platonic Academy," modeled on Ficino's in Florence and his early notes display a remarkable debt to Origen, which helps to explain the lifelong friendship he enjoyed with Erasmus. The early Anabaptist leaders, some of whom had been students of Zwingli's informal academy, were certainly shaped by

---

72. *Inst.* 1.14.4. He adds, "Yet Paul, who had been caught up beyond the third heaven, not only said nothing about it, but also testified that it is unlawful for any man to speak of the secret things that he has seen. Therefore, bidding farewell to that foolish wisdom, let us examine in the simple teaching of Scripture what the Lord would have us know."

73. Francis Turretin, *Institutes of Elenctic Theology*, ed. James T. Dennison Jr., trans. George Musgrave Giger (Phillipsburg, NJ: P&R, 1992), 1:554.

74. Calvin, "Response to Sadoleto," in *Tracts Relating to the Reformation*, vol. 1, ed. and trans. Henry Beveridge (Edinburgh: Calvin Translation Society, 1844), 36.

75. Calvin, *Calvin's Commentaries*, vol. 17, Commentary on the Gospel according to John, trans. William Pringle (Grand Rapids: Baker, 1996), 80–81 (on John 1:51).

76. *Inst.* 2.12.1–2.

77. *Inst.* 2.12.2.

78. W. P. Stephens, *The Theology of Ulrich Zwingli* (Oxford: Clarendon, 1986), 14–15; cf. G. R. Potter, *Zwingli* (Cambridge: Cambridge University Press, 1977), 26–27.

Christian Neoplatonism, particularly the heritage of Eckhart and the *Theologia Germanica*.

I noted in chapter 1 the two patristic trajectories, which I identified as "Irenaean" and "Origenist."[79] Here I will only summarize a few points at which the Reformers are more "Irenaean."

First, they eschewed speculation in favor of following closely the Bible's narrative of creation, fall, redemption in Christ, gift of the Spirit, and age to come. Like Irenaeus, the Reformers' metaphysical presuppositions are typical of Christian thinkers of their day (with a default toward Plato), while the biblical drama pressed them to diverge from these assumptions along the way. Examples would include their understanding of terms like "flesh" and "Spirit," not to mention an emphasis on the horizontal-historical progress of redemption culminating in Christ rather than the vertical-contemplative ascent of the soul. With Irenaeus, Luther and Calvin emphasized God's descent in the incarnation and the gift of the Spirit in uniting us to his glorified humanity. We do not find God by our moral, intellectual, and mystical energy; he finds us and leads us to himself in a manger and on a cross. This creation-affirming logic, over against Gnosticism and Platonism of every stripe, underlies both the Reformers' critiques of concupiscence and the correlation of flesh and Spirit with physical-sensory and intellectual-spiritual.

The way of ascent is blocked by the Reformers at every turn. The object of faith is not merely "God," and certainly not "God-as-he-is-in-himself" as Eckhart's spirituality encouraged. Nor is the object Christ as the facilitator of union with God—as one among many intercessors—or as the supreme example to follow in order to be united with God.

---

79. I have expanded on this elsewhere: Michael Horton, "Atonement and Ascension," in *Locating Atonement*, ed. Oliver Crisp and Fred Sanders (Grand Rapids: Zondervan Academic, 2014), 226–50. Just as the differences between "Irenaean" and "Origenist" legacies can be exaggerated, their agreement can be overstated as well, as I think is evidenced in many *nouvelle theologie* and Radical Orthodoxy writers. To be sure, *Haer.* and *On First Principles* were written a half-century apart and for slightly different purposes (the one more polemical and the other more constructive), but both had Gnosticism in mind. Where Origen wanted to provide an alternative speculative system to the heresy, Irenaeus seems more impressed with the ability of the biblical narrative to speak for itself. Note Paul Ricoeur's comment: "Let us think about the scope of the revolution in the history of thought that this text [Irenaeus's *Haer.*] represents in relation to that Neoplatonism in which reality is a progressive withdrawal, an ineluctable beclouding that increases as we descend from the One, which is formless, to the Mind, which is bodiless, to the World Soul, and to souls which are plunged into matter, which itself is absolute darkness." Ricoeur asks, "Are we sensitive to the distance between this text" and Neoplatonic speculations? Ricoeur, *History and Truth*, trans. Charles A. Kelbley (Evanston, IL: Northwestern University Press, 1965), 111.

And predestination without the sufficiency of Christ is the deadliest of doctrines. Rather, the object of faith is the saving God incarnate *as he is clothed in his gospel*, Calvin says with Luther.[80] We should not "fly through the clouds," Calvin warns.

> Those who seek to see him in his naked majesty are certainly very foolish. That we may enjoy the light of him, he must come forth into view with his clothing; that is to say, we must cast our eyes upon the very beautiful fabric of the world in which he wishes to be seen by us and not be too curious and rash in searching into his secret essence.[81]

While the enthusiasts seek to ascend away from the body—away from the historical, homiletical, and sacramental—to find God within, for the Reformers the movement is the opposite: God descending to us in our flesh and uniting us to himself by his Spirit through the external means of preaching, baptism, and Eucharist. All of these emphases Calvin found in the New Testament and in Luther, as well as in Irenaeus and other patristic sources. An eager student of the church fathers, Calvin was influenced significantly by Augustine, the Cappadocians, Chrysostom, and Hilary.[82]

It should come as no surprise that as we get deeper into both Reformers' systems, additional similarities emerge with respect to justification. Most centrally, both emphasize the importance of Christ's humanity for our redemption in the idea of recapitulation: that is, Christ's "reheadshiping." The Word became flesh not simply to reveal God's love, nor to blaze the trail for our educative ascent of mind, nor

---

80. *Inst.* 3.2.32.

81. Herman Selderhuis, *Calvin's Theology of the Psalms* (Grand Rapids: Baker, 2007), 19, quoting Calvin on Ps 104:1 (*CO* 32, 85).

82. Irena Backus, "Calvin and the Greek Fathers" in *Continuity and Change: The Harvest of Later Medieval and Reformation History*, ed. Robert J. Bast and Andrew C. Gow (Leiden: Brill, 2000); Johannes Van Oort, "John Calvin and the Church Fathers," in *The Reception of the Church Fathers in the West: From the Carolingians to the Maurists*, ed. Irena Backus (Leiden: Brill, 1997); A. N. S. Lane, *John Calvin: Student of the Church Fathers* (London: Bloomsbury T&T Clark, 1991); Richard A. Muller, *The Unaccommodated Calvin*, Oxford Studies in Historical Theology (New York: Oxford University Press, 2001). Augustine ranks first, although he criticized Augustine on occasion for being too Platonist. See Calvin, *Commentary on John* 1:3 (*CO* 47, 4). These names remind us of the danger in exaggerating the contrast between Irenaean and Origenist trajectories as if they were explicit, much less watertight compartments. For most of its history, including the Reformation, Christian instruction and piety have been shaped significantly by Neoplatonism but always in a critical relation to this philosophical inheritance. On this spectrum Origen himself represents the least critical, but even he was attempting to give deference to Scripture.

only to offer his body as a sacrifice, but to fulfill the covenantal role that Adam abandoned.

Defining recapitulation directly, Calvin says that it is the Son's union with us and our union with him: the marvelous exchange.[83] "Our Lord came forth as true man and took the person and name of Adam," he says, "in order to take Adam's place in obeying the Father."[84] "How has Christ abolished sin? He achieved this for us by the whole course of his obedience." "In short," he adds, "from the time when he took on the form of a servant, he began to pay the price of liberation in order to redeem us."[85] We have seen this same statement in Lombard and Aquinas, so we should not see Calvin's remark as novel.[86] Nevertheless, the Reformers display a greater familiarity with patristic sources such as Irenaeus and a greater similarity not only in language here or there but in the whole structure of their soteriological scheme. Christ not only undoes Adam's fall and bears our judgment but by his meritorious obedience as the faithful Son of Man wins for us the right to eat from the Tree of Life.

The Reformers focus on what God has done, is doing, and will do *outside of us*, in history. An example of this emphasis on the objectivity of Christ's work *extra nos* is Luther's counsel to Melanchthon after one of the latter's bouts with introspective anxiety. This is the context of perhaps Luther's most oft-quoted remarks by friend and foe alike: "Sin boldly."

By itself the quote is misleading. While holed up in the Warburg, Luther received a letter from Melanchthon that read like a catalogue of questions concerning every detail of life in Wittenberg during his

---

83. "Such a gathering together as might bring us back to regular order, the apostle tells us, has been made in Christ. Formed into one body, we are united to God, and closely connected with each other. Without Christ, on the other hand, the whole world is a shapeless chaos and frightful confusion." Cited in Julie Canlis, *Calvin's Ladder* (Grand Rapids: Eerdmans, 2010), 235, from Calvin *Comm. Eph.* 1:10. Examples could be multiplied, including the following comparison by Canlis: First, Irenaeus (*Haer.* 3.19.1): "For it was for this end that the Word of God was made man, and He who was the Son of God became the Son of man, that man, having been taken into the Word, and receiving the adoption, might become the son of God." Then Calvin (*Inst.* 4.17.2): "This is the wonderful exchange which, out of his measureless benevolence, he has made with us; that, becoming Son of man with us, he has made us sons of God with him; that, by his descent to earth, he has prepared an ascent to heaven for us" (quoted in Julie Canlis, *Calvin's Ladder*, 236).

84. *Inst.* 2.12.3.

85. *Inst.* 2.16.5.

86. Peter Lombard, *The Sentences*, 4 vols., trans. Giulio Silano (Toronto: Pontifical Institute of Mediaeval Studies, 2010), 4:73–74: Not only at the cross, "but also from his very conception," Jesus began to merit "by his perfect obedience and will." Also in Aquinas's *De Veritate*, the final question (29) treats grace and merit, with the same conclusions as above: Christ could merit (a. 6), could merit for others (a. 7), and did so from the first moment of his conception (a. 8). See Wawrykow, *God's Grace and Human Action*, 137. Aquinas repeats this point in the *ST* III, Q. 48, A. 1, ad. 2. See Brian Davies, *The Thought of Thomas Aquinas* (Oxford: Oxford University Press, 1992), 334.

absence. There were particularly questions about marriage of priests and monks (whether to older widows, younger ones, or, forsooth, unmarried ladies!), how precisely Communion is to be administered, and so forth. Luther does his best to engage in the casuistry but concludes that there is not much exegesis either way to support hard-and-fast conclusions. It is almost as if Luther has regained his own sight of Christ:

> If you are a preacher of grace, then preach a true and not a fictitious grace; if grace is true, you must bear a true and not a fictitious sin. God does not save people who are only fictitious sinners. Be a sinner and sin boldly, for he is victorious over sin, death, and the world. As long as we are here we have to sin. This life is not the dwelling place of righteousness, but, as Peter says, we look for new heavens and a new earth in which righteousness dwells. It is enough that by the riches of God's glory we have come to know the Lamb that takes away the sin of the world. No sin will separate us from the Lamb, even though we commit fornication and murder a thousand times a day. Do you think that the purchase price that was paid for the redemption of our sins by so great a Lamb is too small? Pray boldly—you too are a mighty sinner.[87]

Perhaps Luther remembered how many confessors he had worn out by scrupulously cataloguing his sins. Given his experience—that only recalled and confessed sins are forgiven—Luther doubtless heard in the anxious shopping list of practical worries troubling Melanchthon (in part pressed on him by Karlstadt) the need to look away from such "fictitious sins" and focus on the one thing that really matters: Melanchthon is a mighty sinner with an even mightier Savior. Ready to return to Wittenberg, regardless of the danger, Luther had now moved fully and immovably from penance to Christ.

---

87. Luther, "To Philip Melanchthon, August 3, 1521," in *LW* 48:281–82.

CHAPTER 7

THE REFORMERS AND THE GREAT EXCHANGE

Mystical Union

What does it mean that the entire focus of our salvation is Christ and his redemptive work in history, apart from us, if we do not participate in that accomplishment? This was the question that Calvin raised at the beginning of book 3 of his *Institutes*. Here the *historia salutis* (history of redemption) and the *ordo salutis* (application of redemption) converge in the doctrine of union with Christ. Anyone who has as strong of a view of participation in Christ as Calvin can hardly be lumped with the nominalists.

We have seen that the initial impetus for the Reformation was really the question, "Who is God?" especially as provoked by the controversies over penance. Since we only know this God in Christ, a further question arises as to the meaning of grace especially as it appears in the Christ-event. Christ and what he has accomplished is the reference point for all of our faith and practice for the Reformers. From here, one question remains: How can we be united to Christ here and now? We cannot ascend to him by our mystical contemplation or works, but he has descended to us in our flesh. But how do we now become united to him so that our humanity is saved rather than left behind?

From this shared emphasis on Christ's reheadshiping, we should not be surprised to meet again a focus upon the "great exchange." After all, the key point in recapitulation is that all we have lost in union with Adam we have not only regained but surpassed in our union with Christ. Indeed, it can be argued that this motif is the broader frame of reference for the Reformers' treatment of justification. Puritan writer Thomas Goodwin represents the magisterial Reformation when he says that "being in Christ, and united to him, is the fundamental constitution of a Christian."[1] To the extent that "mysticism" is characterized by the goal of union with God, the Reformed tradition embraces a distinctly evangelical version: union with God the Father through the glorified humanity of the God-human Savior by the power of the Holy Spirit.

This chapter links with chapter 1, focusing on the "great exchange" as the encompassing motif for the application of redemption for the Reformers just as it was for many ancient Christian writers.

MEDIEVAL VERSIONS OF MYSTICAL UNION

We have observed various types of mysticism, all of them following the basic pattern of the ascent of the soul through the three stages of purgation, illumination, and union. Traditionally, this effort was central to monastic life, but nominalists such as Biel taught that it was essential for *every* person in order to be justified. Union with Christ is not the source but the goal. Not even sacraments were of any avail unless the tortures of deep sorrow are sufficient to appease God's wrath. Not all of his fellow Brethren of the Common Life adopted such extreme views. They often advocated a simple piety of following the example of Jesus toward one's union with God. Brethren (*devotio moderna*) piety was certainly Christ-centered but with Christ as a moral pattern more than a vicarious sacrifice.

In Eckhartian mysticism, the soul—which is *already* a spark of divinity—merges with the One like a drop of water in the ocean. This seems to be the basic template for early Anabaptist views of the mystical union, as is evident in Sebastian Franck, Hans Hut, Hans Denck, and Melchior Hoffman especially. Menno Simons was reproached by the Polish reformer Jan Laski and Calvin for his idea, taken from Schwenckfeld, of the "celestial flesh" that Christ assumed not from Mary but from heavenly substance.[2] Mary was merely a "channel" through whom the Son was born. Directly targeting this teaching, the Belgic Confession (1564) declared "against the heresy of the Anabaptists"

---

1. Thomas Goodwin, *Of Christ the Mediator,* in *The Works of Thomas Goodwin,* ed. Thomas Smith (1861–66; repr., Grand Rapids: Reformation Heritage, 2006), 5:350.

2. Early representatives of a similar view include the Gnostics and even Origen.

that the eternal Son became incarnate, "truly assuming a real human nature . . . being conceived in the womb of the blessed virgin Mary by the power of the Holy Spirit, without male participation."[3]

Furthermore, as noted already, early Anabaptist views of the Reformation's teaching on justification ranged from disinterest to rejection. Consequently, the entire Pauline interpretation (at least as Luther and Calvin understood it) of union with Christ was set aside in favor of a more nearly pantheistic union with God through *Gelassenheit* (yieldedness and humility), achieved through strict obedience to the communal law (*Ordnung*). In general, this type of piety reflects the influence of the *Theologia Germanica* as well as the Brethren of the Common Life, with Erasmus as a prime example.

Another type of medieval mysticism, more christocentric, was inculcated by Bernard of Clairvaux (c. 1090–1153). The Cistercian abbot and foe of Abelard wrote, "By faith alone he that is justified shall have peace. . . . Whatever you ascribe to merits lacks grace. Grace makes me justified freely."[4] Bernard's meditations on the marriage between Christ and the believer significantly influenced Luther and Calvin as they reflected on "the great exchange."

THE GREAT EXCHANGE AND UNION WITH CHRIST

Luther is famous for emphasizing the "marvelous exchange" of debts and riches in marital union with Christ. This doctrine of union with Christ was evident even in the early (pre-1517) Luther of the Psalms, Romans, and Galatians lectures. And he even recognized that he was

---

3. Belgic Confession, Article 18: The Incarnation, in *Ecumenical Creeds and Reformed Confessions* (Grand Rapids: Christian Reformed Church, 1979): "And he not only assumed a human nature as far as the body is concerned but also a real human soul, in order that he might be a real human being. For since the soul had been lost as well as the body he had to assume them both to save them both together. Therefore we confess, against the heresy of the Anabaptists who deny that Christ assumed human flesh from his mother, that he 'shared the very flesh and blood of children'; that he is 'fruit of the loins of David' according to the flesh; 'born of the seed of David' according to the flesh; 'fruit of the womb of the virgin Mary'; 'born of a woman'; 'the seed of David'; 'a shoot from the root of Jesse'; 'the offspring of Judah,' having descended from the Jews according to the flesh; 'from the seed of Abraham'—for he 'assumed Abraham's seed' and was 'made like his brothers except for sin.' In this way he is truly our Immanuel—that is: 'God with us.'"

4. Bernard of Clairvaux, *Serm.* 22 on the Canticles (PL 183.881), as quoted in Peter Martyr Vermigli, *Locus on Justification*, in *Predestination and Justification: Two Theological Loci*, trans. and ed. Frank A. James III, Peter Martyr Library 8 (Kirksville, MO: Sixteenth Century Essays & Studies, 2003), 230.

not an innovator here. He notes in his treatise, *Against the Antinomians*, "This doctrine is not mine, but St. Bernard's. What am I saying? St. Bernard's? It is the message of all of Christendom, of all the prophets and apostles."[5] Luther's advance on Bernard turned upon his recognition of marriage as first judicial—the imputation of our sin to Christ and his righteousness to sinners—and then as a growing relationship of trust, love, and good works in which the union is realized subjectively more and more. How could one be united to Christ for justification and not for regeneration and sanctification?[6]

Far from rejecting the believer's actual righteousness in sanctification, Luther says that Christ's imputed righteousness "is the basis, the cause, the source of all our own actual righteousness."[7] In *The Freedom of a Christian*, he writes, "We conclude, therefore, that a Christian lives not in himself, but in Christ and his neighbor. Otherwise he is not a Christian. He lives in Christ through faith, in his neighbor through love. By faith he is caught up beyond himself into God. By love he descends beneath himself into his neighbor. Yet he always remains in God and in his love."[8] Faith not only suffices for justification but is the constant source of the believer's renewal and service toward others. Faith not only justifies; it "unites the soul with Christ as a bride is united with her bridegroom," says Luther. "At this point a contest of happy exchanges takes place. . . . Is that not a happy household, when Christ, the rich, noble, and good bridegroom, takes the poor, despised, wicked little harlot in marriage, sets her free from all evil, and decks her with all good things?"[9] Not only justification but sanctification is granted in our union with Christ.

In the *Institutes* Calvin too displays his debt to Bernard—I count at least twenty-nine quotes in his section on mystical union.[10] There is no point in trying to distinguish Calvin from Luther (or vice versa) on

---

5. Martin Luther, "Against the Antinomians," in *LW* 47:110.

6. The prominence of the union motif in Luther is evident, for example, in his treatise, *The Freedom of a Christian* (*LW* 31:351).

7. Luther, "Two Kinds of Righteousness," in *LW* 31:298.

8. Luther, "Two Kinds of Righteousness," in *LW* 31:371. Cf. Cornelis P. Venema, "Heinrich Bullinger's Correspondence on Calvin's Doctrine of Predestination," *Sixteenth Century Journal* 17 (1986): 435–50.

9. Luther, "Two Kinds of Righteousness," *LW* 31:351

10. *Inst.* 3.20.1. On the number of references to Bernard, see François Wendel, *Calvin: Origins and Development of His Religious Thought*, trans. Philip Mairet (New York: Harper & Row, 1963), 127n43. For a thorough study of the influence of Bernard on Calvin, see Dennis J. Tambarillo, *Union with Christ: John Calvin and the Mysticism of St. Bernard* (Louisville: Westminster John Knox, 1994).

this point. While the humanist circle of Meaux (that included Jacques Lefèvre d'Étaples) brought him half way, Luther was Calvin's gateway into the Reformation. One of the best Roman Catholic interpreters of Calvin, Alexandre Ganoczy, correctly observed, "Proving his great independence of thought, he chose Martin Luther as the master to introduce him to the theological teachings of the reform."[11] He adds, "The first time that Calvin became thoroughly convinced of a theological perspective, it was Luther's perspective that triumphed," although he always retained his exegetical independence.[12] Bernard's influence is present as early as the 1536 *Institutes*, when Calvin was still devouring Luther. It is reasonable to speculate that the German reformer was therefore his gateway to Bernard and to the *unio Christi* motif more generally, although Calvin's own study of patristic sources and Scripture certainly shaped his inflection.

Independently of Luther, Vermigli had been steeped in Bernard. Indeed, as we have seen, the Italian evangelicals had uncovered the great exchange in all sorts of patristic sources. "Peter Martyr's theology is Patristic in a profound sense," observes Joseph C. McLelland. In fact, his 1559 *Defensio*—a treatise on the Eucharist, which shaped the Reformed doctrine both on the Continent and in the Church of England—"is actually a commentary upon the writings of the Fathers."[13] I have offered this "great exchange" motif as a broader ecumenical horizon not for the purpose of suggesting that all is well as long as all sides embrace the motif but because the doctrine of justification as Luther and the other magisterial Reformers taught it is the proper specification of what the exchange actually means. The imputation of Christ's alien righteousness through faith is not the only aspect, but it is essential for all of the others.

Although the great exchange was a prominent patristic motif, the Reformers deployed it after centuries dominated by the rising prominence of penance and theories of merit. One finds many references to union with Christ, including bridal imagery, in medieval writers, most notably in Thomas. The theme is especially prominent in commentaries on the Song of Songs. However, the primary emphasis in

---

11. Alexandre Ganoczy, *The Young Calvin*, trans. David Foxgrover and Wade Provo (Philadelphia: Westminster Press 1987), 93.

12. Ganoczy, *The Young Calvin*, 130, 135.

13. Joseph C. McLelland, *The Visible Words of God: An Exposition of the Sacramental Theology of Peter Martyr Vermigli, 1500–1562* (Grand Rapids: Eerdmans, 1957), 267.

scholastic theology—specifically that of Aquinas—is more Dionysian: union with God as the telos of the justifying process. The Reformers, by contrast, focus on union with Christ and see this union as the source rather than the goal of final salvation. This goal is not the eventual union of the elevated human intellect with the divine intellect, but the whole self united now to the whole Christ and, through him, to the Father. To risk oversimplification, the Reformers' view is Irenaean rather than Origenist.

Roman Catholic theologian Michael Waldstein offers a comparison of Thomas and Luther on this union motif.[14] Despite the impact of Augustine's *Spirit and Letter* on both figures, Waldstein notes, Aquinas's work nevertheless lacked the category of imputation or "alien righteousness."[15] As we have seen, Thomas also distinguished two senses of "righteousness": the justice of God by which he *condemns* the guilty and the justice by which he *makes the guilty righteous*.[16] So does Luther. "This spousal vision of justification does not seem to be a marginal part of Luther's teaching," Waldstein recognizes. "In this respect Luther stands in deep continuity with St. Thomas. . . . Faith, St. Thomas argues elsewhere, is the foundation of all spiritual goods, because it brings us into spousal union with Christ."[17]

But there is also a communal dimension.[18] Waldstein observes that Luther supplemented the individual emphasis of *Freedom of a Christian* with a corporate aspect: the whole church as Christ's spouse, especially in his commentary on the Psalms. Everything that belongs to Christ he shares with his whole church.[19] This is a fairly typical Roman Catholic way of assimilating Luther, which is usually followed by offering Thomas as a way of "getting that and more." However, notice in Waldstein's quote above that Thomas contrasts the phrase "condemns the guilty" with "makes the guilty righteous." This is clearly a category mistake. Paul regularly juxtaposes justification (declaring righteous)

---

14. Michael Waldstein, "The Trinitarian, Spousal, and Ecclesial Logic of Justification," in *Reading Romans with St. Thomas Aquinas*, ed. Matthew Levering and Michael Dauphinais (Washington, DC: Catholic University of America Press, 2012), 274–87.

15. Waldstein, "The Trinitarian, Spousal, and Ecclesial Logic of Justification," 337.

16. Waldstein, "The Trinitarian, Spousal, and Ecclesial Logic of Justification," 275–76.

17. Waldstein, "The Trinitarian, Spousal, and Ecclesial Logic of Justification," 279, from *Super Decretales*, para. 1.

18. Waldstein, "The Trinitarian, Spousal, and Ecclesial Logic of Justification," 280.

19. Waldstein, "The Trinitarian, Spousal, and Ecclesial Logic of Justification," 281, referring to Luther, *Selected Psalms I*, in *LW* 12:259ff.

with condemnation. If justification is the answer to sin's guilt and condemnation, then the action is forensic rather than transformative.

Luther's key difference with Thomas on this point is his rejection of *fides forma caritatis*: faith formed by love.[20] But, Waldstein asks, how can one affirm spousal union without love?[21] "Luther charges that his opponents 'reject Christ, this jewel; and *in His place they put their love*, which they say is a jewel.'"[22] Following a well-travelled path, Waldstein concludes that Luther failed to see divine and human agency in a "noncompetitive relation" as "a thinker trained in nominalist metaphysics."[23] God is not a being among beings, merely acting upon us. His causality "is creative."

> To the degree, therefore, in which God acts and causes, he creates, he sets the creature into *its own being and activity from within* rather than overwhelming it from without, canceling its own activity and threatening its being. A dim echo of this noncompetitive relation is found in spousal love. The impact of the two lovers on each other does not reduce the life and activity that is in each but increases it: "man can only find himself in a sincere gift of self" (*Gaudium et spes* 24:3). Once again, it seems to me that the Luther of the spousal texts would agree.[24]

In other words, if Luther were not a nominalist, he would have found Aquinas's spousal logic compelling and adequate.

But this misunderstands the Reformer's position. Luther has no trouble with love, even love infused, as a necessary grace in believers. (Certainly, later Lutheran and Reformed theologians wrote expansively on this theme.) On the contrary, he regards genuine love and its expression in good works as possible—in fact, inevitable—only on the ground of objective peace with God in justification. The word of God (specifically, the gospel) produces faith, faith produces love, and love produces good works. For Luther, mixing up that order serves no one. God is offended rather than satisfied, the believer has been deceived, and the neighbor is not served.

---

20. Waldstein, "The Trinitarian, Spousal, and Ecclesial Logic of Justification," 281.

21. Waldstein, "The Trinitarian, Spousal, and Ecclesial Logic of Justification," 282–83, referring to Luther's *Lectures on Galatians 1535: Chapters 1–4*, ed. Walter A. Hansen (St. Louis: Concordia, 1963), 136–37.

22. Waldstein, "The Trinitarian, Spousal, and Ecclesial Logic of Justification," 283, from Luther's *Lectures on Galatians*, 88.

23. Waldstein, "The Trinitarian, Spousal, and Ecclesial Logic of Justification," 285.

24. Waldstein, "The Trinitarian, Spousal, and Ecclesial Logic of Justification," 285.

Luther is not a hyper-Augustinian who, bathed in nominalist logic, merely opts for God over humans in doing bulk of the work. Rather, his problem is making the fruit the root and confusing justification with sanctification. Only when we are persuaded of Christ's trustworthiness for our entire salvation do we begin to love him—and in him begin to love the Father and the Spirit. Is this so disanalogous to marital love? Further, notice Luther's point. Even in Waldstein's quote, Luther laments the fact that Rome puts "their love" in the place of Christ. Of course Luther does not maintain that love is excluded from this union, but he insists that it is the fruit of trust in Christ. Since love is the summary of the law, justification by love is equivalent to justification by the law.

In the Reformers' writings the marital union of the believer to Christ is not merely a piece of devotional piety but attains a systematic role in delineating the blessings of salvation. The realism of this union, including the grace at work within believers, refutes any charge of nominalism. In his 1535 *Commentary on Galatians*, Luther wrote,

> Christ and I must be joined together so that He lives in me and I in Him—and what a wonderful way of speaking this is. For because He lives in me, whatever there is in me of grace, righteousness, life, peace, salvation, is all His but in such a way that it is mine through this inseparable union and conjunction which I have with Him through faith. Through this faith Christ and I are made one body, as it were, and spirit. Now because Christ lives in me there must be present with Him grace, righteousness, life, and salvation whereas the Law, sin, and death are absent; in fact, the Law is crucified and devoured and destroyed along with sin, death, and the devil. Thus Paul tries to draw us wholly away from ourselves and transplant us into Christ by faith in Him, so that in the matter of justification we think of nothing else but grace and separate this from the Law and works which must have no place in this matter.[25]

This, Luther says, is what is meant by the "blessed exchange." His description is vivid:

---

25. Luther, *Commentary on Galatians* 2:20, quoted in Robert Preus, *Justification and Rome* (St. Louis: Concordia Academic Press, 1997), 61. See *LW* 26:283–84. The *unio cum Christo* motif is important also in Luther, *Freedom of a Christian*, in *LW* 31:351–52.

With gratitude and a sure confidence, therefore, let us accept this doctrine, so sweet and filled with comfort, which teaches that Christ became a curse for us, that is, a sinner worthy of the wrath of God; that He clothed Himself in our person, laid our sins upon His own shoulders, and said, "I have committed the sins that all men have committed." Therefore He truly became accursed according to the Law, not for Himself, but as Paul says, for us. For unless He had taken upon Himself my sins, your sins, and the sins of the entire world, the Law would have had no right over Him, since it condemns only sinners and holds only them under a curse. Therefore He could neither have become a curse nor have died, since the cause of the curse and of death is sin, of which He was innocent. But because He took upon Himself our sins, not by compulsion but of His own free will, it was right for Him to bear the punishment and the wrath of God—not for His own Person, which was righteous and invincible and therefore could not become guilty, but for our person. By this fortunate exchange (*feliciter commutans*) with us He took upon Himself our sinful person and granted us His innocent and victorious Person. . . . We must look at this image and take hold of it with a firm faith. . . . Therefore we are justified by faith alone, because faith alone grasps the victory of Christ.[26]

Once more, then, we see the *solo Christo* at the heart of the Reformer's thinking. Faith is not something within the believer, a virtuous habit, that has an inherent efficacy. Rather, faith is simply the act of embracing Christ, who is our only virtue and moral worthiness before God. Faith merely "grasps the victory of Christ." "Now we must rightly teach faith," he says, "that through faith you are so closely joined together with Christ that you and He are made as one person which can never be separated but always remains united."[27]

The Nature of the Union

Robert Preus notes that Roman Catholic scholar George Tavard wonders how to square imputation with the great exchange. "How do we coordinate these two motifs in Luther's theology?" Tavard chalks this up to Luther's love of "dialectical contrasts." However, Preus counters,

---

26. Luther, *Commentary on Galatians* 3:13, quoted in Preus, *Justification and Rome*, 62–63.
27. Luther, *Lectures on Galatians*, in *LW* 26:166–68.

the mixing of metaphors is precisely what the great exchange encourages. Imputation is grounded in the great exchange.[28] "Rome did not discard the righteousness of Christ as playing no role in our justification," Preus observes. "Neither did Rome reject or object to the term 'impute,' which was a very common term in the vocabulary of scholastic theology. What Rome rejected was the joining of the two concepts."[29] According to Trent, Preus notes, Christ's righteousness is the "meritorious cause" (*causa meritoria*). "Essentially, that means that Christ's atoning work makes justification and sanctification by grace possible. Second, the righteousness of Christ's doing and suffering is not the righteousness by which we become righteous." What constitutes our justification (the *unica causa formalis*) "is not the imputed obedience and righteousness of Christ . . . but that by which He makes us righteous (*nos justos facit*), namely, that with which we being endowed by Him and are renewed in the spirit of our mind (Eph 4:23)."[30] There is thus "the divorce of any real, formal connection between Christ's work of redemption and the sinner's justification."[31] Preus's point is crucial, especially in displaying the fact that, ironically, it is Trent's position that severs the real ontological connection between Christ and the believer's salvation.

According to Preus,

> Trent followed the scholastic theology exemplified by Bonaventure, who taught that "neither to the resurrection nor passion [of Christ] can be attributed properly (*proprie*) the causality of justification or the remission of guilt," since justification is in a different category (*modo*) from Christ's passion and resurrection. It is obvious that Bonaventure did not consider the active obedience of Christ (Rom 5:15), His obedience to the Law and under the Law (which is clearly commensurate with man's disobedience to the Law), as a part of His righteousness and atonement. The scholastics made little of the active obedience of Christ as part of Christ's atoning work, and they restricted the merits of Christ to His death (Anselm; so also the *Catholic Catechism*, 1992).[32]

---

28. Preus, *Justification and Rome*, 62–63.
29. Preus, *Justification and Rome*, 64.
30. Preus, *Justification and Rome*, 65.
31. Preus, *Justification and Rome*, 65.
32. Preus, *Justification and Rome*, 66.

Luther's student Martin Chemnitz pointed this out against Diogo de Payva de Andrada (the Jesuit commentator on the Council of Trent): it is *not* a legal fiction because Christ's active obedience is actually imputed.[33] This again refutes the charge that the Reformers adopted nominalism's notion of an arbitrary decision of God. On the contrary, the righteousness imputed is real—that of Christ himself. Quenstedt argued, "For certainly our sins were extrinsic to Christ, and yet they could be imputed for punishment and guilt to Him and reckoned to Him."[34] In addition it is worth observing that Rome never denied that our sins were imputed to Christ at the cross. Consequently, the same question could be put to Rome: Is *this* imputation a legal fiction as well?

The great exchange provides the proper context in which to understand faith, then, as neither a meritorious virtue nor a general existential or voluntaristic stance but as a very specific act of clinging to Christ. On this point Preus comments, "Again in Romans 3:25 we are told that these great benefits are received through faith in His blood," faith being "the one means by which we *receive* Christ's righteousness, forgiveness, and the grace of God, the one means through which we are justified (*pistei*: Romans 3:28; Acts 26:18; *ek pisteōs*: Romans 3:30, 5:1; Galatians 2:16, 3:7–9, 11–12; *dia tēs pisteōs*: Romans 3:31)."[35] He appeals to the Formula of Concord:

> Faith is a gift of God whereby we rightly learn to know Christ as our Redeemer in the Word of the Gospel and to trust in Him, but solely for the sake of His obedience we have forgiveness of sins by grace, are accounted righteous and holy by God the Father, and are saved forever. . . . For faith does not justify because it is so good a work and so God-pleasing a virtue, but because it lays hold of and accepts the merit of Christ and the promise of the Holy Gospel.[36]

We have noted the remarkable number of times that the phrase "faith alone" appears in the church fathers—in direct connection with justification and over against works and merits. Even Origen inserted "alone" in Romans 3:28. Besides, as Melanchthon noted in the Apology, "If they

---

33. Preus, *Justification and Rome*, 66.
34. Quoted by Preus, *Justification and Rome*, 72.
35. Preus, *Justification and Rome*, 93.
36. Formula of Concord, Solid Declaration 2.10–12 and 3.13, quoted in Preus, *Justification and Rome*, 94–95.

dislike the exclusive particle 'alone,' let them remove the other exclusive terms from Paul, too, like 'freely,' 'not of works,' 'it is a gift,' etc., for these terms are also exclusive."[37] In short, works are opposed not only to grace or to gift in general, but to the gift of Christ in particular. United to Christ, we have all that we need in order to be justified before God.

The great exchange or union with Christ also attains a major place in Calvin's understanding of the gifts of salvation.[38] Calvin observes, "that mystical union" is "accorded by us the highest degree of importance, so that Christ, having been made ours, makes us sharers with him in the gifts with which he has been endowed." While our righteousness is indeed external to us—an alien righteousness that belongs properly to Christ rather than to us—Christ does not remain alien but joins himself to us and us to him. "We do not, therefore, contemplate him outside ourselves from afar in order that his righteousness may be imputed to us but because we put on Christ and are engrafted into his body—in short, because he deigns to make us one with him."[39] He rhapsodizes,

> This is the wonderful exchange which, out of His measureless benevolence, Jesus Christ has made with us; that, becoming Son of man with us, He has made us sons of God with Him; that, by His descent to earth, He has prepared an ascent to heaven for us; that, by taking on our mortality, He has conferred His immortality upon us; that, accepting our weakness, He has strengthened us by His power; that, receiving our poverty unto Himself, He has transferred His wealth to us; that, taking the weight of our iniquity upon Himself, He has clothed us with His righteousness.[40]

For Calvin as well as Luther, therefore, union with Christ and the marvelous exchange were interchangeable terms for the same reality. Earlier in the *Institutes* Calvin supplies one of the richest summaries:

> When we see that the whole sum of our salvation, and every single part of it, are comprehended in Christ, we must beware of deriving

---

37. Augsburg Confession, apology 4.73, quoted by Robert Preus, *Justification and Rome*, 99.
38. The best study on this subject is J. Todd Billings, *Calvin, Participation and the Gift* (New York: Oxford University Press, 2008). For the tradition after Calvin, see also J. V. Fesko, *Beyond Calvin: Union with Christ and Justification in Early Modern Reformed Theology (1517–1700)* (Göttingen: Vandenhoek & Ruprecht, 2012).
39. *Inst.* 3.11.10.
40. *Inst.* 4.17.2.

even the minutest portion of it from any other quarter. If we seek salvation, we are taught by the very name of Jesus that he possesses it; if we seek . . . purity in his conception . . . if we seek redemption, we shall find it in his passion; acquittal in his condemnation; remission of the curse in his cross; satisfaction in his sacrifice; purification in his blood; reconciliation in his descent to hell; mortification of the flesh in his tomb; newness of life in his resurrection; the inheritance of a celestial kingdom in his entrance into heaven; protection, security, and the abundant supply of all blessings, in his kingdom.[41]

Notice how not only justification but every aspect of our salvation is "comprehended in Christ," underscoring the point that it is the *solo Christo* that lies at the heart of the Reformers' concerns. In fact, he concludes the preceding statement, "In summary, since in him all kinds of blessings are treasured up, let us draw a full supply from him, and from no other quarter."[42]

Calvin's judicial emphasis with respect to *justification* is complemented by the organic imagery of union and ingrafting in relation to the *inner renewal* and communion with Christ, including his holiness. To be sure, justification is exclusively extrinsic—the imputation of Christ's alien righteousness—but, more generally, salvation also includes transformation. Yet here too, such sanctifying transformation rests on Christ and our union with him through faith rather than on an inner movement of the soul that makes union with God possible for all who cooperate meritoriously. For the magisterial Reformers, union with Christ is no longer conceived as the *goal* but as the *source* of sanctification.

Thus, commenting on John 17, Calvin explains, "Having been ingrafted into the body of Christ, we are made partakers of the Divine adoption, and heirs of heaven."[43] "This is the purpose of the gospel," he says, "that Christ should become ours, and that we should be ingrafted into his body."[44] (Hence, union has an intrinsically corporate, ecclesial dimension.) We are not first united to Christ and then justified on the

---

41. *Inst.* 2.16.19. Approaching the level of poetry, this paragraph was present from the first (1536) to the final (1559) edition.

42. *Inst.* 2.16.19.

43. Calvin, *Calvin's Commentaries*, vol. 17, Commentary on the Gospel according to John, trans. William Pringle (Grand Rapids: Baker, 1996), 166, commenting on John 17:3.

44. Calvin, *Commentary on the Epistle to the Romans*, trans. Ross MacKenzie, in *Epistles of Paul to the Romans and Thessalonians*, Calvin's New Testament Commentaries (Grand Rapids: Eerdmans, 1965), on Rom 1:9.

basis of his indwelling righteousness, but justified through faith by the imputation of Christ's alien righteousness. Nevertheless, one cannot grasp Christ without receiving all his benefits. Those who are justified are united to Christ and become fruit-bearing branches. Continuing this emphasis, John Owen writes, "There is no contemplation of the glory of Christ that ought more to affect the hearts of them that do believe with delight and joy than this, of the recapitulation of all things in him."[45]

According to critics like John Milbank, the Reformers' doctrine of justification resulted from an absolute "extrinsicism" in their view of the God-world relationship. Consequently, nominalism does not allow for what the church fathers considered the ultimate end of salvation: deification. This, according to Milbank, is the test of nominalist soteriology: whether it allows for the ontological glorification of the saints, and the Reformers, following Scotus and Ockham, fail the test.[46] However, for the Reformers extrinsic justification does not eliminate analogical participation in God as creatures, and the former becomes the secure basis for an exact identity between Christ's and our humanity. No one is united to God directly and immediately, the Reformers emphasized, but through faith believers are united to the God-human through his humanity, in the power of the Spirit working through the gospel. Thus, the intimate participation of the believer in Christ—even to the point of affirming "deification" as the greatest of all benefits (Calvin)—refutes the charge of nominalism.[47]

Calvin's understanding of union with Christ, then, is the same as the federal theology that followed in his wake, with Christ replacing Adam as our federal or covenantal head. It is not an abstract participation in being, says Owen, "as if it had been implanted in them by nature," but a personal union with the mediator of the covenant: "But Christ dwells principally on this, that the vital sap—that is, all life and

---

45. John Owen, "The Person of Christ," in *The Works of John Owen*, ed. William H. Goold (Edinburgh: Banner of Truth Trust, 1965), 1:372.

46. John Milbank, *Being Reconciled: Ontology and Pardon* (London: Routledge, 2003), 78; Milbank, *Beyond Secular Order: The Representation of Being and the Representation of the People* (Oxford: Wiley-Blackwell, 2013), 79, 80n142.

47. Contrary to the conclusions of the new Finnish school as well as T. F. and James B. Torrance, Luther and Calvin did not see divine and human agency in a competitive relation. Rather, they understood justification and regeneration to be unilateral divine actions (on the lines of Aquinas's operative grace), with sanctification as God's work of liberating and effectually bringing about the new obedience (Aquinas's cooperative grace). This latter move could not have been made if nominalist metaphysics had any determining effect on their system. The point was not to deny progressive renewal but to distinguish this from justification.

strength—proceeds from himself alone."[48] Given the Trinitarian emphasis of his doctrine of union, including a high view of the Spirit's role in uniting us to Christ, it is not surprising that his treatment suggests a more dynamic understanding. Whereas justification is a once-and-for-all and definitive verdict rendered at the moment that one embraces Christ through the gospel, we grow "more and more" into Christ and his body.

On the legal basis of the imputation of Christ's righteousness, believers can be united to Christ, confident that everything that belongs properly to him is given freely to us. In this marvelous exchange, all of our debts become his, and all of his riches become ours. And in our union with Christ, we actually receive these benefits to which his imputed righteousness entitles us. Not even in our sanctification, therefore, can we lodge confidence in our inherent holiness. "If you contemplate yourself, that is sure damnation."[49] In the *Institutes*, Calvin adds,

> Although we may distinguish [justification and sanctification], Christ contains both of them inseparably in himself. Do you wish, then, to attain righteousness in Christ? You must first possess Christ; but you cannot possess him without being made partaker in his sanctification, because he cannot be divided into pieces [1 Cor 1:13]. Since, therefore, it is solely by expending himself that the Lord gives us these benefits to enjoy, he bestows both of them at the same time, the one never without the other. Thus it is clear how true it is that we are justified not without works yet not through works, since in our sharing in Christ, which justifies us, sanctification is just as much included as righteousness.[50]

When discussing justification, Calvin cautions emphatically, "The question is not how we may become righteous but how, being unrighteous and unworthy, we may be reckoned righteous. If consciences wish to attain any certainty in this matter, they ought to give no place to the law."[51] Calvin recognizes here that justification need not be *confused* with sanctification by means of an all-encompassing ontology of union in order to recognize the *inseparability* of both legal (forensic) and

---

48. Owen, "The Person of Christ," 107, on John 15:1.
49. Owen, "The Person of Christ," 107.
50. *Inst.* 3.16.1.
51. *Inst.* 3.19.2.

organic (effective) aspects of that union. Possess *Christ* and you will have both the perfect righteousness of justification and the beginning of sanctification in this life.

Book 2 of the *Institutes* concentrates on "The Knowledge of God the Redeemer," elucidating all that God in Christ has accomplished for us *extra nos*—outside of ourselves. Christ's perfect person and work cannot be extended, completed, augmented, or improved. Our righteousness before God is alien: extrinsic, not inherent; perfect, not progressive. Yet "as long as Christ remains outside of us, and we are separated from him, all that he has suffered and done for the salvation of the human race remains useless and of no value for us. Therefore, to share with us what he has received from the Father, he had to become ours and dwell within us. For this reason, he is called 'our Head' [Eph. 4:15], and 'the first-born among many brethren' [Rom. 8:29]."[52]

As is often the case in church history, erroneous views provide an occasion for greater refinement and clarity. Andreas Osiander is a case in point. Although the influence of Origen is evident, the more direct influence on his thinking was the *Theologia Germanica*. Luther had slowly extricated himself from this influence, but some of his early colleagues—many of whom became Anabaptist leaders—did not. Although Osiander's views were roundly condemned by his fellow Lutherans, it was perhaps Calvin who drew the sharpest attention to them and in refuting them helped to define critical aspects of the Reformation consensus on justification. So concerned was Calvin with Osiander's views that he added eight sections of refutation to the 1559 edition of the *Institutes* (3.11.5–12).

It made little difference in Calvin's view to say that one was justified by cooperation with an infused righteousness or by the "essential righteousness" of Christ indwelling the believer. In either case the ground of justification would be an internal act of making righteous, rather than the imputation of an alien righteousness. "We too speak a great deal of mystical union," says Calvin. In fact, he complained that Erasmus's rendering of *koinōnia* as *societas* and *consortium* fell far short of the mystical union, so he chose *communio*.[53] "But Osiander has introduced some strange monster of 'essential' righteousness by which,

---

52. *Inst.* 3.1.1.
53. B. A. Gerrish, *Guilt and Grace: The Eucharistic Theology of John Calvin* (Minneapolis: Augsburg Fortress, 1993), 83. See Calvin's commentary on 1 Cor. 1:9 (*CO* 49:313).

although not intending to abolish freely given righteousness, he has still enveloped it in such a fog as to darken pious minds and deprive them of a lively experience of Christ's grace."[54] Besides indulging in "speculation" and "feeble curiosity," Osiander is faulted for "something bordering on Manichaeism, in his desire to transfuse the essence of God into men," with the additional speculation "that Adam was formed to the image of God because Christ had already been destined as the prototype of human nature before the Fall."[55]

Calvin accuses Osiander of several fatal conflations. First, he conflates Christ's divine *essential* righteousness with our righteousness, as if it were not "that righteousness which has been acquired for us by Christ," but rather "that we are substantially righteous in God by the infusion both of his essence and of his quality." Second, he conflates the believer's substance with God's, not only introducing a Creator-creature confusion but failing to recognize that "it comes about through the power of the Holy Spirit that we grow together with Christ, and he becomes our Head and we his members." The upshot is that justification is confused with regeneration and the believer is confused with the divine essence. We can still affirm a communion with Christ's person, Calvin counters, without surrendering the doctrine of forensic justification.[56] In Osiander's treatment, "To be justified is not only to be reconciled to God through free pardon but also to be made righteous, and righteousness is not a free imputation but the holiness and uprightness that the essence of God, dwelling in us, inspires."[57]

Justification and rebirth, Calvin counters, must be joined but never confused.[58] In addition, he criticizes Osiander's view that "faith is Christ" rather than an empty vessel that receives Christ.[59] Faith is the instrument through which we receive Christ, not to be confused with Christ (the material cause) himself.[60]

---

54. *Inst.* 3.11.5, in refutation of Andreas Osiander's *Disputation on Justification* (1550). Osiander was a Lutheran theologian whose views were finally rejected in the Book of Concord. Similarities with the view of justification advanced especially by the new Finnish perspective on Luther have been noted and will be discussed in ch. 12.

55. *Inst.* 3.11.5.

56. *Inst.* 3.11.5.

57. *Inst.* 3.11.6.

58. *Inst.* 3.11.6.

59. *Inst.* 3.11.7. The reference to Osiander is from his *Confession of the Only Mediator and of Justification by Faith* (1551). Faith is itself of no inherent worth, Calvin adds in this section; it only receives yet "can justify us by bringing Christ, just as a pot crammed with money makes a man rich."

60. *Inst.* 3.11.7.

In addition to these conflations, Osiander separates the two natures of Christ, Calvin judges, leading to a Nestorian Christology and an atonement doctrine that eliminates the saving humanity of Christ as mediator.[61] Calvin counters that not even Christ was justified by his essential righteousness as divine but by his obedience as a servant under the law.[62] Consequently, there can be no saving deity of Christ apart from the covenantal obedience that he rendered in his humanity as the Second Adam. "For if we ask how we have been justified, Paul answers, 'By Christ's obedience' [Rom. 5:19]. But did he obey in any other way than when he took upon himself the form of a servant [Phil. 2:7]? From this we conclude that in his flesh, righteousness has been manifested to us."[63] It is not surprising that the new Finnish interpretation of Luther presents an essentially "Osiandrian" Luther, following the usual modern path of creating a false choice between participation and forensic imputation and identifying justification with deification. Calvin already noted this: "Osiander laughs at those who teach that 'to be justified' is a legal term; because we must actually be righteous. Also, he despises nothing more than that we are justified by free imputation. Well then, if God does not justify us by acquittal and pardon, what does Paul's statement mean: 'God was in Christ, reconciling the world to himself, not imputing men's trespasses against them' [2 Cor 5:19]? 'For our sake he made him to be sin who had done no sin so that we might be the righteousness of God in him' [v 21]?" Calvin compares several New Testament texts to ordinary legal usage and then concludes, "Osiander objects that it would be insulting to God and contrary to his nature that he should justify those who actually remain wicked." To this Calvin replies with the familiar *simul iustus et peccator* (at the same time just and sinful), reminding Osiander that "they are always liable to the judgment of death before his tribunal" according to their own righteousness. The key, Calvin says, is to distinguish justification and inward renewal without divorcing them. Sanctification is always partial in this life. "But [God] does not justify in part but liberally, so that they may appear in heaven as if endowed with the purity of Christ. No portion of righteousness sets our consciences at peace until it has been determined that we are pleasing to God, because we are entirely righteous before him."[64]

---

61. *Inst.* 3.11.7.
62. *Inst.* 3.11.12
63. *Inst.* 3.11.12.
64. *Inst.* 3.11.11.

According to Calvin, Osiander, no less than Rome, denies this comfort to believers.[65] Only because justification is constituted by an imputed rather than an inherent righteousness are believers able "not to tremble at the judgment they deserve, and while they rightly condemn themselves, they should be accounted righteous outside themselves."[66] So we discern complementary emphases in Calvin's account: the righteousness of Christ that justifies us is "outside of us," although, by virtue of the mystical union, Christ himself—including his righteousness—cannot remain outside of us.

The Source and Means of the Union

Calvin's pneumatological emphasis is apparent in his treatment of the mystical union. The Spirit's mediation of Christ's person and work, not an immediate participation in the divine essence, is a critical aspect of his account. We are "one with the Son of God; not because he conveys his substance to us, but because, by the power of the Spirit, he imparts to us his life and all the blessings which he has received from the Father."[67] It is the Spirit who unites us here and now to Christ's work then and there so that his righteousness really becomes ours—though it is always *his* righteousness. Thus the Reformers would sympathize with Eastern theologians in rejecting *created grace* as an oxymoron. The Gift is Christ, who comes from the Father in the power of the Spirit. All else that we receive—redemption, justification, sanctification, glorification—is the fruit of belonging to Christ.

Apart from any virtues or actions that might improve our inherent moral condition, "Faith adorns us with the righteousness of another, which it seeks as a gift from God."[68]

> Faith then is not a naked knowledge either of God or of his truth; nor is it a simple persuasion that God is, that his word is the truth; but a sure knowledge of God's mercy, which is received from the gospel, and brings peace of conscience with regard to God, and rest to the mind. The sum of the matter then is this,—that if salvation

---

65. *Inst.* 3.11.11.
66. *Inst.* 3.11.11.
67. *Inst.* 3.11.11–12.
68. Calvin, *Commentary on the Epistle to the Romans*, trans. Ross MacKenzie, *Epistles of Paul to the Romans and Thessalonians*, Calvin's New Testament Commentaries (Grand Rapids: Eerdmans, 1965), 159.

depends on the keeping of the law, the soul can entertain no confidence respecting it, yea, that all the promises offered to us by God will become void: we must thus become wretched and lost, if we are sent back to works to find out the cause or the certainty of salvation . . . for as the law generates nothing but vengeance, it cannot bring grace.[69]

At the place where Rome spoke of infused habits of virtue, Calvin spoke of faith as a grasping or clinging to Christ and the gift of the Holy Spirit who creates this faith through the gospel.

At the same time, Calvin was concerned to keep faith from being perceived as the "one work" that we can perform in order to merit our justification. In itself, faith is nothing; its efficacy lies in its object, the person to whom it clings. Faith itself is imperfect, "for the mind is never so illuminated, but that many relics of ignorance remain; the heart is never so strengthened, but that much doubting cleaves to it."[70] Faith is partial and weak, so if we were justified by faith itself, our case would be as hopeless as if we merited faith by works.[71]

According to Calvin, faith *is* assurance. One did not look to Christ for justification and to oneself for assurance of being justified. Therefore, the popular thesis of the sociologist Max Weber—namely, that Calvinism engendered an activist spirit in the world by linking assurance of election to one's works—is untenable at least in relation to Calvin (and his heirs who equated faith and assurance in their confession). As Wilhelm Niesel reminds us, "The much discussed activism of Calvin is rooted in the fact that we belong to Christ and thus can go our way free from care and confess our membership in Christ; but it does not arise from any zealous desire to prove one's Christian faith by good works."[72] Not only at the moment of our justification but throughout the Christian life "all our works are under the curse of the law if they are measured by the standard of the law!"

---

69. Calvin, *Commentary on the Epistle to the Romans*, 171.

70. Calvin, *Commentary on the Epistle to the Romans*, 179.

71. *Inst.* 3.11.7. Doubtless, this emphasis was required not only for polemics against Rome but also against the perfectionistic teachings of the Anabaptists and even, as Wendel (*Calvin*, 263) observes, Zwingli's tendency to treat faith as perfect. Calvin may also have already begun to detect among Protestants a tendency to regard faith as the basis rather than the instrument of justification (sometimes encouraged by the use of the phrase justification *by* faith as shorthand for justification by Christ *through* faith).

72. Wilhelm Niesel, *The Theology of John Calvin*, trans. Harold Knight (Philadelphia: Westminster, 1956), 99.

But if, freed from this severe requirement of the law, or rather from the entire rigor of the law, they hear themselves called with fatherly gentleness by God, they will cheerfully and with great eagerness answer, and follow his leading. To sum up: Those bound by the yoke of the law are like servants assigned certain tasks for each day by their masters. . . . But sons, who are more generously and candidly treated by their fathers, do not hesitate to offer them incomplete and half-done and even defective works, trusting that their obedience and readiness will be approved by our most merciful Father, however small, rude, and imperfect these may be. . . . But how can this be done amidst all this dread, where one doubts whether God is offended or honored by our works?[73]

Once works are no longer presented to God for justification, they can be accepted despite their imperfections by a merciful Father for the sake of Christ.

Union with Christ does not provide a basis for God's discerning in us a righteousness imparted; rather, on the basis of justification we partake of Christ's vivifying life. The same act of faith that looks to Christ alone for justification looks to Christ alone for sanctification and glorification. The Christian life does not have two sources: one forensic and found in Christ alone and another moral and found in us. Forensic justification through faith alone is the fountain of union with Christ in all of its renewal. We are justified through faith, not through union with Christ. For Calvin the justified are united to Christ through faith and receive all his benefits by becoming members of his body, "although union with Christ cannot be regarded as the cause of the imputation of righteousness."[74]

Therefore, Calvin speaks of a "double grace" in fellowship with Christ:

Christ was given to us by God's generosity, to be grasped and possessed by us in faith. By partaking of him, we principally receive a double grace: namely, that being reconciled to God through Christ's blamelessness, we may have in heaven instead of a Judge a gracious Father; and secondly, that sanctified by Christ's spirit we may cultivate blamelessness and purity of life.[75]

---

73. *Inst.* 3.19.5.
74. Wendel, *Calvin: Origins and Development of His Religious Thought*, 258.
75. *Inst.* 3.11.1.

This double grace entails a "twofold acceptance": we are justified apart from works by the imputation of Christ's righteousness received through faith so that our works can be justified or accepted by the Father not as meritorious but as the fruit of justification and union with his Son.[76]

In this way, Calvin subverts the frequent Roman charge that such justification leaves no place for good works in the Christian life. On the contrary, it frees us to obey God and serve our neighbor without the fear of punishment for our short-comings. Justification in no way depends on an impartation of Christ's righteousness through union, yet the two are inseparable. "This alone is of importance: having admitted that faith and good works must cleave together, we still lodge justification in faith, not in works. We have a ready explanation for doing this, provided we turn to Christ to whom our faith is directed and from whom it receives its full strength."[77]

The believer does not keep one eye on Christ for justification and the other eye on his or her own works with the other but looks to Christ for both. "You cannot grasp [justification] without at the same time grasping sanctification also."[78] Although believers' imperfect works play no role in God's acceptance of us, they are now welcomed by the Father because their corruption "is buried in Christ's purity, and is not charged to our account."[79] Only when we give no place to our works in justification are our works themselves "justified." This distinction between our persons and our works being justified is assumed in the different ways that "justification" is used in Paul and James.[80]

Luther and Calvin hardly substituted union with Christ for justification; rather, they appealed to union with Christ as the umbrella term for the great exchange—both imputation (new status) and ingrafting (new life).[81] Of course, union with Christ can be considered the ground of both justification and sanctification in an important sense: as the

---

76. *Inst.* 3.17.4–5.
77. *Inst.* 3.16.1.
78. *Inst.* 3.16.1.
79. *Inst.* 3.17.10.
80. *Inst.* 3.17.11.

81. On this point, especially in relation to Calvin, see Billings, *Calvin, Participation and the Gift*, 22–30, 57–61. In chapter 2, Billings defends Calvin from Radical Orthodoxy's charge (especially Pickstock and Ward) that he presupposes a univocal metaphysics. Cf. Michael Horton, "Calvin's Theology of Union with Christ and the Double Grace" in *Calvin's Theology and Its Reception: Disputes, Developments and New Possibilities*, ed. J. Todd Billings and I. John Hesselink (Louisville: Westminster John Knox, 2012), 72–96; J. V. Fesko, *Justification: Understanding the Classic Reformed Doctrine* (Phillipsburg, NJ: P&R, 2008).

"marvelous exchange" in which Christ becomes our sin-bearer and we become the righteousness of God in him. Nevertheless, imputative justification must always be distinguished as the forensic ground of God's acceptance. To whatever extent Calvin may have refined the notion of a "double righteousness," he was elaborating a conclusion that Luther arrived at early on, in his *Sermon on the Double Righteousness* (1519).[82]

The Object of Faith

The object of faith is not merely "God," as the schools teach, Calvin argues, but the Triune God who has revealed himself in Jesus Christ as he is clothed in his gospel. Union with God is union with Christ, who is *God with us* and also *us with God*. To be in Christ is to live *in* God, not just *before* him, because Christ is the divine Lord and human servant of the covenant. "Ungrudgingly, he took our nature upon himself to impart to us what was his, and to become both Son of God and Son of man in common with us."[83]

Apart from this descent of God to us, Calvin argues, the beatific vision of God's majestic face would be deadly.

> The situation would surely have been hopeless had the very majesty of God not descended to us, since it was not in our power to ascend to him. Hence, it was necessary for the Son of God to become for us "Immanuel, that is, God with us," and in such a way that his divinity and our human nature might by mutual connection grow together. Otherwise the nearness would not have been near enough, nor the affinity sufficiently firm, for us to hope that God might dwell with us. . . . Therefore, relying on this pledge, we trust that we are sons of God, for God's natural Son fashioned for himself a body from our body, flesh from our flesh, bones from our bones, that he might be one with us.[84]

United to him, we now enter into the familiar relationship he enjoys with the Father, who has chosen and adopted us, and the Spirit, who indwells us, provoking us to cry, "Abba, Father!" This emphasis on union with *Christ* is a more evangelical version of the older spirituality.

82. Wendel, *Calvin: Origins and Development of His Religious Thought*, 261.
83. *Inst.* 2.12.2.
84. *Inst.* 2.12.1–2.

We live not only before God's face but in God himself, yet only because we are in Christ. There is no union of the believer or any part (including the intellect) with God but the uniting of the whole person to Christ the Mediator who is God as well as human.

To attempt direct union with God apart from Christ is to "seek God outside the way." It is to be trapped in a labyrinth, as one finds in Roman Catholic piety. So there is no moving on from Christ, as he is clothed in his gospel, to a higher truth or way of ascent. God has descended all the way down to us and accomplished everything we need in his Son. "The apostle does not say that he was sent to help us attain righteousness but himself to be our righteousness," Calvin reminds us.[85] In the *Institutes*'s prefatory address to the king of France, Calvin pleads the great exchange:

> For what is more consonant with faith than to recognize that we are naked of all virtue, in order to be clothed by God? That we are empty of all good, to be filled by him? That we are slaves of sin, to be freed by him? Blind, to be illuminated by him? Lame, to be made straight by him? Weak, to be sustained by him? To take away from us all occasion for glorying, that he alone may stand forth gloriously and we glory in him? When we say these and like things our adversaries interrupt and complain that in this way we shall subvert some blind light of nature, imaginary preparations, free will, and works that merit eternal salvation. . . . For they cannot bear that the whole praise and glory of all goodness, virtue, righteousness, and wisdom should rest with God. But we do not read of anyone being blamed for drinking too deeply of the fountain of living water.[86]

This message the pope considers novel and divisive. "But," Calvin explains to the monarch, "he who knows that this preaching of Paul is ancient, that 'Jesus Christ died for our sins and rose again for our justification,' will find nothing new among us."[87] Central to Christ's work is his death for our sins as if every page of Scripture were written in blood. All supernatural gifts are found in Christ alone by the Spirit alone, though working through means. That we are in Christ *and* that

---

85. *Inst.* 3.15.5.
86. Calvin, "Prefatory Address to King Francis I," in *Inst.* 13.
87. Calvin, "Prefatory Address to King Francis I," in *Inst.* 16.

Christ is in us are both due to the mediation of the Spirit. "But faith is the principal work of the Holy Spirit."[88] Faith receives justification and is active in love, yielding the fruit of good works. Since we are united to Christ through faith, this faith is the source not only of justification but also of sanctification and glorification.

Since Osiander, there have been attempts even in Protestant theologies to make this incorporation the basis for justification rather than vice versa. However, they always end up eliding the crucial distinction between Christ *for* us and Christ *in* us. According to classic Reformed treatments of this connection, Christ alone—his incarnation, obedient life, death, resurrection, and ascension—is the *basis* both for justification and union, but the *act* of justification is logically prior to union.[89] Nevertheless, Calvin concludes, once justification has provided the legal ground, all the gifts of God's grace are freely given in union with Christ.

> For in Christ he offers all happiness in place of our misery, all wealth in place of our neediness; in him he opens to us the heavenly treasures that our whole faith may contemplate his beloved Son, our whole expectation depend upon him, and our whole hope cleave to and rest in him. This, indeed, is that secret and hidden philosophy which cannot be wrested from syllogisms. But they whose eyes God has opened surely learn it by heart, that in his light they may see light [Ps 36:9].[90]

---

88. *Inst.* 3.1.4.

89. Louis Berkhof, *Systematic Theology* (Grand Rapids: Eerdmans, 1996), 452: "The mystical union in the sense in which we are now speaking of it is not the judicial ground, on the basis of which we become partakers of the riches that are in Christ. It is sometimes said that the merits of Christ cannot be imputed to us as long as we are not in Christ, since it is only on the basis of our oneness with Him that such an imputation could be reasonable. But this view fails to distinguish between our legal unity with Christ and our spiritual oneness with Him, and is a falsification of the fundamental element in the doctrine of redemption, namely, of the doctrine of justification. Justification is always a declaration of God, not on the basis of an existing condition, but on that of a gracious imputation—a declaration which is not in harmony with the existing condition of the sinner. The judicial ground for all the special grace which we receive lies in the fact that the righteousness of Christ is freely imputed to us."

90. *Inst.* 3.20.1.

CHAPTER 8

REFORMING JUSTIFICATION

For Aquinas justification is a movement from injustice to justice, from disorder to rectitude.[1] If he had said that *salvation* (rather than justification) includes this movement, the Reformers would have agreed. In fact, Aquinas's argument was left largely intact in Lutheran and Reformed systems: regeneration preceded justification, since one could not exercise saving faith while "dead in sin." It would be at least a semi-Pelagian position to say that faith is logically prior to regeneration. The problem is that Aquinas calls this new birth the *first justification*. In other words, forgiveness comes because one is no longer ungodly but has become inherently just.

In short, what Aquinas considered *final justification* obtained by meritorious cooperation with grace the Reformers considered a *present and unchanging status of justification* obtained by Christ's merits, received through faith. Justification, Thomas says, is remission plus infusion of created (habitual) grace.[2] By contrast, Calvin says, "Therefore, we explain justification simply as the acceptance with which God receives us into his favor as righteous. And we say that it consists in the *remission of sins* and the *imputation of Christ's righteousness.*"[3]

There is indeed still a real movement from ungodly to godly, but this is *sanctification*, which is not simply moving from worse to better but progressively realizing that we exist not "in Adam," or in ourselves, but are sharers in Christ's life, death, resurrection, and ascension by a marvelous union.

---

1. Alister E. McGrath, *Iustitia Dei: The History of the Christian Doctrine of Justification*, 3rd ed. (Cambridge: Cambridge University Press, 2005), 44–45.

2. *ST* I–II, Q. 82, A. 4, and I–II, Q. 81, A. 1.

3. *Inst.* 3.11.2, emphasis added.

LUTHER, AUGUSTINE, AND NOMINALISM

"At the close of the Middle Ages, a somber melancholy weighs on people's souls."[4] It was also a period of insecurity. "For the true future is the Last Judgment, and that is near at hand."[5] From the arguments thus far we can say at least what the Reformation was *not*. First, it was not a supernova appearing out of nowhere through the fertile mind and "tortured subjectivity" of a pious or impious monk. There are too many thinkers across time and place to lay the wreath or the blame at Luther's feet. Luther's experience was widely representative, at least of those who took seriously God, Scripture, and their relationship to God. Some experienced their own *Anfechtungen*—despair over the state of their soul, but many others were drawn to similar conclusions for other reasons. More than experience, the common factor was a rediscovery of primary sources, especially Scripture in the original languages and patristic literature, compared to which the wrangling of the schools seemed like a profound waste. Further, the thrust of the Reformers was to direct sinners outside of themselves to Christ *extra nos*.

Second, the Reformation cannot be explained as the inevitable result of Scotist and nominalist voluntarism. Milbank says that for Luther the Scotist "the will only 'inclines to God' under grace; the natural will has no natural orientation to God. But for Augustine, without the latter (always through grace) there is no will at all."[6] This misunderstands not only Luther but Augustine and Aquinas, for at this point Luther stands in their shadows. Luther believes that the will *is* naturally ordered for the vision of God. To be natural, it must retain this intrinsic lure. The problem is that sin has intervened and drawn the self inward (*incurvatus in se*—turned in on itself), so it cannot will this vision. Instead, it creates idolatrous substitutes. Failing to distinguish creation and the fall, Milbank thinks that any doctrine of the bondage of the will is necessarily a Manichean attack on nature. In this respect, he shows a surprising lack of familiarity with some of Augustine's deepest convictions—shared also by Luther.

Later Lutheran and Reformed theologians drew a sharp distinction between natural and moral inability. According to the former, humans

---

4. J. Huizinga, *The Waning of the Middle Ages: A Study of the Forms of Life, Thought and Art in France and The Netherlands in XIVth and XVth Centuries* (New York: Doubleday, 1949), 31.

5. Huizinga, *The Waning of the Middle Ages*, 38.

6. John Milbank, *Being Reconciled: Ontology and Pardon* (London: Routledge, 2003), 212n21.

are oriented toward God and have all the requisite faculties for fulfilling this telos, but according to the latter, humans are bound by sin. Consistent with much of Roman Catholic interpretation, Milbank's principal confusion lies in his recurring tendency to marginalize the damage of the fall: its total corruption, not in the sense of obliterating nature but of corrupting it and keeping it from fulfilling its design. Wherever one of the Reformers speaks of the total inability of humans to grasp "things heavenly" or to interpret the gospel properly, much less embrace it, Milbank thinks that he is talking about a vicious nature as such.

Third, if the Reformation was not the spawn of nominalism, it also cannot be explained as a mere revival of Augustinianism. With respect to justification specifically, the Reformers are both heirs and critics of Augustine. There is no doubt that the bishop of Hippo's work, especially his commentaries and anti-Pelagian writings, were a constant source of reviving *sola gratia* and *solo Christo* throughout church history. Faith itself is a gift, which God graciously gives to his elect throughout their pilgrimage. The sufficiency of Christ and of baptismal grace contrasts sharply with scholasticism's elaborate calculus of merit and penance. Even with respect to the scope of Christ's saving work, the formula "sufficient for the world, efficient for the elect only" shows the Augustinian provenance of much medieval thinking that Luther learned from his great mentor and head of the Augustinian Order in Germany, Johann von Staupitz.[7]

And yet, Augustine also laid the foundation for the medieval understandings of justification as a process of sanctification and faith as synonymous with love. Even the most ardent defenders of Augustinian doctrine such as Prosper, Gottschalk, Bradwardine, Gregory—and let us include Aquinas and Bonaventure—do not seem even to have entertained the idea of a purely forensic justification. The early Luther, like his mentor Staupitz, was an Augustinian predestinarian even while he had no inkling yet of Christ's alien righteousness being imputed. Yet, as we have seen, Chrysostom more nearly anticipates the Reformers' doctrine of justification on just these points, even as he affirms conditional election, though affirming faith as a gift of grace.

---

7. See for example Staupitz's tract, "Eternal Predestination and its Execution in Time," in *Forerunners of the Reformation: Illustrated by Key Documents*, by Heiko Oberman (Philadelphia: Fortress, 1981), 175–204.

The relation of Luther to the bishop of Hippo has been a subject of debate since the Reformation itself. It is significant that the first collection of Augustine's complete works, the Basel edition of Augustine's *Opera Omnia* by Johannes Amerbach, was published in 1506.[8] Andreas Karlstadt posted a thesis for debate on April 26, 1517 (four months before Luther's legendary "posting"). It was an invitation to debate "the Augustinian doctrine of grace."[9] Luther devoured Augustine's works and in fact observed that his devotion to Augustine had nothing to do with belonging to the Augustinian Order—he never knew anything about the church father, he said, until he stumbled upon his collected works.[10]

Much of the debate turns on when Luther's real turning point, his "breakthrough" in understanding justification as a forensic event, occurred. While some argue that it occurred between 1514 and 15, others think that it happened in 1518. Reflecting on it three years before his death, Luther himself said that it occurred in 1519. Especially in older Roman Catholic scholarship, the relationship is largely negative: Luther was a hyper-Augustinian who drew more on a "Manichean" Augustine in emphasizing moral depravity and the bondage of the will. That view has changed among many Roman Catholic scholars of Luther today. Jairzinho Lopes Pereira argues that "by the time Luther wrote the *Lectures on Romans* (1515–16) he was certainly in possession of his basic Reformation insights on justification. The way he used and interpreted Augustine's anti-Pelagian writings in his *Lectures on Romans* is sufficient to corroborate this claim."[11]

A major target of Pereira's critique is Alister McGrath's *Iustitia Dei*. In particular, he takes issue with the Anglican theologian's tendency to treat Luther as breaking with the whole tradition, including Augustine. In McGrath's narrative, says Pereira, "Augustine's doctrine of justification is the first discussion of the matter of major significance to emerge from the twilight of the Western theological tradition" and Luther's version was totally unknown in prior centuries.[12] McGrath also places too much weight on Luther's continuing nominalism as playing a role

---

8. Jairzinho Lopes Pereira, *Augustine of Hippo and Martin Luther on Original Sin and Justification of the Sinner* (Göttingen: Vandenhoek & Ruprecht, 2013), 300.

9. Pereira, *Augustine of Hippo and Martin Luther*, 301.

10. Luther, "Letter to Spalatin" in *LW* 48:24.

11. Pereira, *Augustine of Hippo and Martin Luther*, 463.

12. Pereira, *Augustine of Hippo and Martin Luther*, 218–35, referring to McGrath, *Iustitia Dei*, 38–39.

in his innovative view. Pereira argues persuasively that this is not quite right, that early Luther was simply following Augustine.

> Luther's use of Augustine in *Lectures on Romans* had taken a new orientation. The mystical ideas of the Church Father, largely exploited in *Dictata super psalterium* (written 1513–1515), under the guidance of Augustine's *Ennarationes in Psalmos*), was being replaced by a determined insistence on Augustine's anthropological and soteriological insights produced in the heart of the Pelagian controversies, especially during the long disputation with Julian of Aeclanum.[13]

"Only when one misunderstands Augustine can one maintain that Luther innovated in teaching that after Adam's Fall sin becomes part of a human's constitution and that this sin remains even after baptism."[14] Further, Luther's views concerning election and free will and the remaining concupiscence in believers (that is nevertheless not imputed) are Augustine's.[15]

According to Pereira, the typical Roman Catholic path of separating Luther from Augustine has been taken into the late nineteenth and twentieth century by Lutherans like Julius Köstlin (*The Life of Martin Luther*, 1881), and Pereira believes that McGrath follows Köstlin closely on this point.[16] Luther's movement from nominalism to the Reformation largely mirrors Augustine's transition from his pre- to post-Pelagian writings. "The young Luther's exegesis on the twins' case did not go beyond the Augustinian synthesis."[17] "Luther's doctrine of free will can be said to have gained systematic contours only by the 1520's in his harsh confrontation with Erasmus of Rotterdam. However, the main lines of his doctrine of free will were already present in his early Pauline commentaries, especially in his *Lectures on Romans*."[18]

The heart of Luther's criticism was that nominalism was not christocentric.[19] "Accordingly," says Pereira, "the young Luther's use of

---

13. Pereira, *Augustine of Hippo and Martin Luther*, 28.
14. Pereira, *Augustine of Hippo and Martin Luther*, 39.
15. Pereira, *Augustine of Hippo and Martin Luther*, 360–66.
16. Pereira, *Augustine of Hippo and Martin Luther*, 456. Ironically, Köstlin, a Lutheran professor at the Luther University Wittenberg-Halle, advances this typically Roman Catholic thesis in his *The Life of Martin Luther* (English, 1881).
17. Pereira, *Augustine of Hippo and Martin Luther*, 456.
18. Pereira, *Augustine of Hippo and Martin Luther*, 458.
19. Pereira, *Augustine of Hippo and Martin Luther*, 310.

Augustine basically had a clear purpose: to fight against the *monstrosa Theologia, cuius caput est Aristoteles et pedes Christus* ('monstrous theology which has Aristotle as its head and Christ as its feet').[20] Even as late as 1525, with his famous reposte to Erasmus (*Bondage of the Will*), there is little more than a typical Augustinian challenge to the Pelagianizing trend of his day. Writing to Spalatin, Luther divulged,

> What disturbs me about Erasmus . . . [is that] in explaining the Apostle, he understands the righteousness which originates in "works" or in "the Law" or "own righteousness" (the Apostle calls it that as referring to those ceremonial and figurative observances [of the Old Testament]. Moreover, he does not clearly state that in Romans chapter 5, the Apostle is speaking of original sin, although he admits that there is such a thing. Had Erasmus studied the books Augustine wrote against the Pelagians (especially the treatise On the Letter and the Spirit, On Merits and Forgiveness of Sinners, Against the Two Letters of the Pelagians, and Against Julian, almost all of which can be found in the eight volumes of his works), and he recognized that nothing in Augustine is of his own wisdom but is rather that of the most outstanding Fathers, such as Cyprian, Gregory of Nazianzus, Rheticus, Irenaeus, Hilary, Olympius, Innocent and Ambrose, then perhaps he would not only correctly understand the Apostle, but he would also hold Augustine in higher esteem than he has so far done. . . . I definitely do not hesitate to disagree with Erasmus on this point, because in Bible exegesis I esteem Jerome in comparison to Augustine as little as Erasmus himself in all things prefers Jerome to Augustine. Devotion to my Order does not compel me to approve of the blessed Augustine; before I had stumbled upon his books I had no regard for him in the least.[21]

This challenges McGrath's interpretation of Luther's autobiographical reflections on his "breakthrough." Writing in 1549, just three years before his death, the Reformer said that in 1519 he experienced a revolution in his understanding of the "righteousness of God" in Romans 3:19–20. But Pereira argues that Luther did not connect this breakthrough with the doctrine of justification taught in the *Lectures*

---

20. Pereira, *Augustine of Hippo and Martin Luther*, 310.
21. Luther, "Letter to Spalatin," in *LW* 48:24.

on Romans but with "his discovery of *mire et nova deffinitio iustitiae*, as a sudden happening, a sort of flash of insight into the true meaning of *iustitia Dei*."[22] McGrath suggests that Luther many years later compresses the development.[23] In *Lectures on Romans* Luther drew heavily on *De spiritu et littera*. Romans 3 does not concern the righteousness that God *is* but the imputation of righteousness.[24] The upshot is that, in Pereira's view, the mature Luther did not really change his Augustinian view of justification. Pereira's position finds support in eminent Luther scholars, especially those of the 1970s.[25]

Pereira mounts a compelling case that the early Luther was thoroughly Augustinian. However, he does so at the expense of recognizing the clear areas of departure even from his favorite church father. Pereira claims, "To maintain that Luther taught justification as a mere forensic declaration of righteousness is to misinterpret him."[26] To the claim that Luther excluded good works from justification: "He did not!"[27] For the most part, the basis for this aspect of Pereira's thesis is the new Finnish interpretation of Luther.[28] Throughout Pereira's study, passages in Luther that refer to humility, love, and good works are assumed to describe justification when in fact they describe conversion and the life of faith.

To be sure, early Luther was devoted to the later Augustine (anti-Pelagian writings) in part because he was convinced that he was facing the same threat in his day. Nevertheless, there is little to be gained by trying to make the early Luther a champion of his mature doctrine of justification. On all sides of the debate, the *Lectures on Romans* (as well as those on Galatians and the Psalms), not to mention the Ninety-Five Theses and the Heidelberg Disputation, represent an ordinary Augustinianism that clashed with the views of his nominalist teachers. Nominalists and humanists like Erasmus seemed to form a common flank against the biblical doctrines of sin and grace.

---

22. Pereira, *Augustine of Hippo and Martin Luther*, 296.

23. Pereira, *Augustine of Hippo and Martin Luther*, 296–97.

24. Pereira, *Augustine of Hippo and Martin Luther*, 297.

25. Pereira, *Augustine of Hippo and Martin Luther*, 35. Especially to be mentioned is Bernard Lohse's "De Bedeutung Augustins für den jungen Luther," *Kerigma und Dogma* 11 (1965): 116–35. According to Pereira, "By the 1970s the general opinion is that the *Lectures on Romans* contain the main line of Luther's reformation doctrine regarding issues such as Original Sin and the justification of the sinner."

26. Pereira, *Augustine of Hippo and Martin Luther*, 31.

27. Pereira, *Augustine of Hippo and Martin Luther*, 358.

28. The dependence is evident throughout but especially on 386–94.

But if this is as far as he went, we would never have had a Reformation, since this simply echoes the cries of Bradwardine, Rimini, Wycliffe, Staupitz, and others. It is where Luther diverges from Augustine that he triggers something really different—and dangerous, even to those sympathetic to his early message.

My position is therefore somewhere between McGrath and Pereira. Pereira is mostly right about the early Luther and his relation to Augustine but mostly wrong about the relation of early and later Luther. This is because, following the Finnish school, he focuses almost exclusively on the writings of the early Luther, which fail to distinguish justification from sanctification adequately. McGrath rightly highlights the mature Luther's differences on this point but goes too far in claiming that Luther's doctrine was completely unprecedented. There are many links of the mature Luther to Augustine. As we have seen, there are clear "Lutheran" emphases in Augustine's anti-Pelagian works, not only with respect to original sin, election, and free will but also regarding concupiscence in believers (a sort of *simul iustus et peccator*), the contrast between the merits of Christ and those of believers, and affirmations of *sola fide*. However, certainly by 1535 (*Commentary on Galatians*), Luther was teaching that justification was a strictly forensic declaration, not a process, and consisted in the forgiveness of sins and imputation of Christ's righteousness through faith alone. Whatever elements of this doctrine that we find in Augustine, and however one might argue that Luther was merely pushing Augustinianism to its logical conclusion, the fact remains that the two positions diverge on these points, Augustine implicitly and Luther explicitly. But we can only conclude that Luther's view was therefore a *novum* if we neglect such sources as John Chrysostom. If Augustine bequeathed to the German reformer a christocentric emphasis on *sola gratia* that included predestination and the bondage of the will, then Chrysostom (despite his disavowal of both doctrines) affirmed a view of justification much closer to Luther's (e.g., an instantaneous forensic event rather than an ethical process). This is not to make the patriarch Luther's principle source but is merely to observe that Augustinianism was a necessary but not sufficient presupposition. One reason for Luther's adoption of sola scriptura was that he found in Scripture, especially Paul, the most unambiguous teaching on the subject.

It is one thing to dismantle a system and another to put it back together with the right parts in the right places. The magisterial Reformers did not question everything. They were Reformers, not revolutionaries. They did not, like the Anabaptists, claim that the visible church had gone underground since the apostles. In fact, in varying degrees, they came to embrace the Reformation in part through reading the church fathers. Nevertheless, the changes that they made to the medieval doctrine of justification proved momentous and, after Trent's refusal to engage the arguments, church-dividing. The great tragedy is that the bishops of Rome, who had defended the faith against a string of heresies and justly earned the respect of the other churches, had been succeeded by wolves who exploited the office for their personal ambitions. The ignominy of having divided the Western church belongs to the four popes who presided over Trent, especially the one who reluctantly called it—Paul III.

Changes in Substance

The dogma that came to formal expression at the Council of Trent pressed a choice between a declaration that the sinner is just for the sake of Christ and inner renewal and transformation. The magisterial Reformers refused this choice, affirming both by distinguishing between justification and sanctification. This was, in nuce, the Reformation debate. The Reformers affirmed both justification and sanctification as key aspects of the "great exchange," while Rome collapsed justification into sanctification. Taken as a final verdict, justification has no real value in the Roman Catholic ordo salutis. It does not accomplish anything but merely acknowledges what the believer has done—or, more Thomistically, what God has already done in the believer by inwardly transforming him or her.

Even before we arrive at the late medieval (nominalist) distortions that Aquinas would have rejected, it is important to see that the Reformers already opposed the entire medieval way of thinking about justification, standing as it did in the shadow of the penitential system. The official Roman Catholic teaching still today is that "justification is not only the remission of sins, but also the sanctification and renewal of the interior man."[29] Initial justification in baptism cannot be merited, but an increase in justification and final justification are merited by cooperation with grace. Yet for the Reformers, faith is not a virtue that

---

29. CCC, 492, quoting the Council of Trent (1574), DS 1528.

must be completed by another virtue, charity, before it justifies; it is the empty hand that embraces Christ. Justice before God is not a movement of the soul from one moral state to another, but the declaration that the believing sinner is righteous for the sake of Christ alone. Rather than working toward the verdict of divine vindication, the believer leaves the court justified in the joy that bears the fruit of faith: namely, good works. In Scripture, especially in Paul, Luther discovered that the righteousness God is, which condemns us, is the same righteousness that God gives freely as a gift through faith in Jesus Christ (Rom 3:19–31). As Calvin puts it, "We say that [justification] consists in the remission of sins and the imputation of Christ's righteousness."[30]

Change in Priority

The magisterial Reformers were distinctive not only in their view of justification but in the high position they gave it. Obviously, if justification is basically sanctification, any distinct role of the former will be of limited value. Consequently, Roman Catholic teaching did not and to this day does not consider justification central to the gospel unless it is a synonym for renewal.

In contrast, along with Luther, Martin Bucer called justification "this chief article of religion."[31] Calvin regarded justification as "the primary article of the Christian religion," "the main hinge on which religion turns," and "the principal article of the whole doctrine of salvation and the foundation of all religion."[32] He explains, "For unless you first of all grasp what your relationship to God is, and the nature of his judgment concerning you, you have neither a foundation on which to establish your salvation nor one on which to build piety toward God."[33] All of the other abuses—pilgrimages, merits, satisfactions, penances, purgatory, tyranny, superstitions, and idolatry—flow from this corruption of the faith at its source. According to Peter Martyr Vermigli, "This doctrine is the hand, fountain, and mainstay of all religion. Therefore, we should be most sure and certain of this above

---

30. *Inst.* 3.11.2.
31. Quoted in Frank A. James III, introduction to *Predestination and Justification: Two Theological Loci*, trans. and ed. Frank A. James III, Peter Martyr Library 8 (Kirksville, MO: Sixteenth Century Essays & Studies, 2003), xxxiii.
32. *Inst.* 3.2.1, 3.11.1, and repeated in tracts, treatises, and commentaries.
33. *Inst.* 3.11.1.

all."[34] For many Roman Catholics, the Petrine office is of much greater importance in the ecumenical dialogue than justification. Even many Protestant traditions today would locate the chief point of variance with Rome at places other than justification: the roles of the pope, Mary, the saints, rituals, and so forth. But for the Reformers, justification was the chief divide, which may indicate as much cleavage with modern Protestantism as with medieval Catholicism.

As I argued in the previous chapter, the center and circumference of Reformation faith and practice turns on the person and work of Christ. This is why I have made so much (as did the Reformers) of the "great exchange." The heart of the evangelical message is Christ assuming our debts and clothing us in his righteousness. To be sure, this legal transfer is not the only aspect of the exchange, but without it the others (e.g., poverty for inheritance, death for life, corruption for renewal) are left suspended in midair.

NATURE, GRACE, AND FREE WILL: ANTHROPOLOGY IN REFORMATION PERSPECTIVE

"Do what you can? But you can't, and you won't," the Reformers responded to the entire trajectory of late medieval theology. The dispute over grace exposed deeper differences over sin. We need not go into detail. It will suffice to say that whereas the Council of Trent taught that the soul was wounded, the mind beclouded by the passions, and the will lacking an alacrity for the good, the Reformers held that the whole self, body and soul, was "dead in trespasses and sins" (Eph 2:1) with the will bound by original and actual sin. The Reformers would have challenged even an Augustinian interpretation of justification, but what they faced especially in nominalism was in fact a semi-Pelagian interpretation of original sin. According to the Reformers, neither the power of willing nor the freedom to will is removed; instead, what has been lost is the freedom apart from grace to desire what one cannot otherwise desire—namely, God in Jesus Christ as revealed in the gospel.

---

34. Peter Martyr Vermigli, *Locus on Justification*, in *Predestination and Justification: Two Theological Loci*, trans. and ed. Frank A. James III, Peter Martyr Library 8 (Kirksville, MO: Sixteenth Century Essays & Studies, 2003), 96–97.

Robert Preus explains the confessional Lutheran position on free will and grace. According to the Formula of Concord,

> It is evident . . . that the free will by its own natural powers can do nothing for man's conversion, righteousness, peace, salvation, cannot cooperate, and cannot obey, believe, and give assent when the Holy Spirit offers the grace of God and salvation through the Gospel. On the contrary, because of the wicked and obstinate disposition with which he was born, he defiantly resists God and His will unless the Holy Spirit illumines and rules him (Formula, Solid Declaration II, 18).

Man is "always doing penance, but never coming to repentance," as Luther puts it.[35] However, Preus explains, in Scripture "repentance is never partial, eclectic, or piecemeal but *total*," like forgiveness.[36] Of course, a diversity of moral character is evident to us as human beings, but Calvin reminds us (repeating Luther's contrast), righteousness before humanity (*coram hominibus*) is not the same as righteousness before God (*coram deo*).[37] Calvin rejected the view that Christ's sacrifice remits the guilt but not the punishment of sins.[38]

We have encountered the irony of Augustine, prince of monergists, who nevertheless helped to launch the idea of justification as a process of inner renewal, while Chrysostom, despite rejecting unconditional election, clearly affirmed justification as an immediate declaration of righteousness through faith alone. Thus, the categories of Pelagian, semi-Pelagian, semi-Augustinian, and Augustinian go only so far in helping us to understand differences over justification. In another irony, Thomas Aquinas formulates a doctrine of merit that Augustine would not have admired, yet only by becoming more of an Augustinian—grounding merit in predestination—than he was when he wrote the *Scriptus*.

Here is a third irony: Aquinas goes further than the Protestant Reformers in stressing the need for grace. While the Reformers held that human nature *as created* was capable intrinsically of fulfilling its vocation, Thomas insists that even before the fall Adam and Eve required

---

35. The Smalcald Articles 3.23, in *Book of Concord: Confessions of the Evangelical Lutheran Church*, ed. and trans. Robert Kolb and Timothy Wengert (Minneapolis: Fortress, 2000), 315.
36. Robert Preus, *Justification and Rome* (St. Louis: Concordia Academic Press, 1997), 42.
37. *Inst.* 3.12.2.
38. *Inst.* 3.4.30.

supernatural grace in order to obey in genuine love.[39] It will therefore not do for Protestant critics to declaim medieval (and contemporary Roman Catholic) theology as having a "weak view of grace," full-stop. Rather, it had a *different* view of grace—primarily as an infused substance to restore original justice (i.e., mastery of the lower self by the higher self) and assist the soul to cooperate toward final beatitude. Although the medieval Augustinians (including Aquinas) gave more place to merit than Augustine, they assumed a doctrine of merit grounded in the grace of God (especially predestination) and asserted this view often *in opposition to* the encroaching Pelagianism of the late Middle Ages.

Nature and Grace: Creation

According to Lutheran and Reformed exegesis, the Pauline contrast between Spirit and flesh is eschatological: the age of the Spirit intervening— breaking into—this present age of sin and death. This view breaks from the widespread—perhaps even dominant—view in the history of the church, which often followed Plato and Neoplatonism in reading this contrast in light of ontological differences between spirit and matter. Marriage is honorable in its own way, but virginity is superior in that it disavows bodily relations. Jerome wrote, "Reasonable and incorporeal beings are the highest of God's creatures, for not being clothed with bodies they are not the slaves of corruption. Since where there are bodies, there corruption is sure to be found."[40] There is something in the very nature of creation itself (viz., bodily constitution) that makes the fall virtually inevitable. The Reformers, however, would concur with Peter Brown: "The hierarchy of body and soul, which linked man both to the gods above and to the animal world below . . . concerned Paul not in the slightest."[41]

Formally, both parties embraced original sin, but in medieval theology the problem addressed by grace is chiefly this: "How does the upper soul or mind regain its control over the lower soul with its passions?" rather than "How can I, a sinner, be accepted and renewed by a holy God?" The latter was involved in the former, of course, but the medieval problem turned on how to repair something that was already

---

39. *ST* I-II, Q. 109, A. 4–5 (2:1126–27). This is not because the affirmed an autonomous space of secular nature but because the created order was suspended in divine love, not yet grace (i.e., mercy).

40. Jerome, *Letter 124: To Avitus*, in *NPNF*² 6:9.

41. Peter Brown, *The Body and Society: Men, Women, and Sexual Renunciation in Early Christianity* (New York: Columbia University Press, 1988), 48.

unstable in creation itself. From Augustine to the present day, Roman Catholic anthropology has focused considerable energy on grace as supplementing, elevating, and improving nature.

Even before the fall, there is a problem. In the *Summa*, Thomas says, "Now the gift of grace surpasses every capability of created nature, since it is nothing short of a partaking of the Divine Nature, which exceeds every other nature."[42] Human nature as created is incapable of partaking of the divine nature; such participation exceeds our nature. Human beings were not created to glorify God and to enjoy him forever. This is the supernatural end that required a supernatural gift added to nature to elevate it to this telos. This is why we required grace even before the fall. As Lossky noted, according to this view the only thing that was lost in the fall was the supernatural gift *added* to nature rather than nature itself being corrupted.[43] When the gift of rectitude was removed after the fall, the question became, "How do we get it back and move on?"

The Reformers, by contrast, did not believe that there was any inherent instability of the self's higher and lower powers or any problem with the passions as such. Their diagnosis turned not on any weakness in creation but in the complete deformation of nature in the fall. Thus, they were *more* affirming of human nature as such than Rome. Calvin explicitly rejects the idea of a *donum superadditum*.[44] Human beings were created to love, glorify, and enjoy God as their final end. This end was not something added to nature but is essential to—in fact, the most intrinsic aspect of—human nature as created.

Further for Calvin, as well as the other magisterial Reformers, not just the soul but the whole person is God's image.[45] The image of God "extends to the whole excellence" of human nature.[46] Even at this stage, Calvin conceives the image not chiefly as something within persons but as something between them: a covenantal and social interpretation that has recently been identified (perhaps exaggerating somewhat) "the birth of the relational imago."[47]

---

42. *ST* I–II, Q. 112, A. 1 (2:1140).
43. Vladimir Lossky, *The Mystical Theology of the Eastern Church* (Crestwood, NY: St. Vladimir's Seminary Press, 1976), 85–88.
44. *Inst.* 1.16.8.
45. *Inst.* 1.5.2.
46. *Inst.* 1.15.3.
47. Stanley Grenz, *The Social God and the Relational Self: A Trinitarian Theology of the Imago Dei* (Louisville: Westminster John Knox, 2001), 162. In this, Grenz follows David Cairns and Paul Ramsay.

Loss of Superadded Gift versus Corruption of Nature

The Neoplatonic residue in Augustine's anthropology understood the fall as an insurrection of the lower self, overthrowing the higher self. Nevertheless, Augustine was convinced by Scripture that the whole self is corrupted, including the mind and the will. With Aquinas, as we have seen, nothing of the somber concept of depravity has been weakened—except that its effects are mostly restricted to the will rather than the mind. There is little of Augustine's suspicion of reason's corruption in Aquinas. Johann Adam Möhler correctly highlights an important difference between Roman Catholic teaching and the anthropology of the Reformers. Representing the former, Möhler stresses the dualism between the "higher soul" (reason and free will) and the "inferior faculties of soul and bodily impulses."[48] This opinion, he says, "possesses the advantage of more accurately distinguishing between the two orders of nature and grace." "Adam's original justice" was "the attribute of pure nature, as it came from the hand of the Creator," but "his *internal sanctity* and acceptance before God" was "only the gift of supernatural grace."[49] So, according to the main scholastic view, all human beings are in exactly the same state as Adam and Eve before the fall *without the additional supernatural gift of grace.* This is why they are disordered, with the lower self overthrowing the reign of the higher self.[50]

Even before we arrive at nominalism, then, the course has been set toward logical entailments that distinguish high scholastic anthropology and soteriology: (1) Human nature as created is not capable of union with God apart from a supernatural gift. (2) Human nature is inherently unstable, requiring grace to keep the lower self under the control of the higher self. This concupiscence is not itself considered sinful (*pace* Augustine) but is a tendency of ungraced nature. Consequently, (3) the fall consists of a loss of both the superadded gift and the disorder resulting from the passions ruling the intellect.

Then when we come to Scotus, the *will* is left virtually unaffected by the fall. With a little instruction and encouragement, one can be

---

48. Johann Adam Möhler, *Symbolism: Exposition of the Doctrinal Differences Between Catholics and Protestants as Evidenced by Their Symbolical Writings,* trans. James Burton Robertson (New York: Crossroad, 1977), 25.

49. Möhler, *Symbolism,* 28.

50. Möhler, *Symbolism,* 53. Möhler goes so far as to say, "The conflict between reason and sensuality is caused by the two very heterogeneous essences, whereof man is composed, . . . for it is the nature of sensuality to be irrational."

moved to love God above all else. And by the time we arrive at Biel's writings, we find that sinners do not require grace to prepare to merit the first justification.

But by the time we reach Ockham, even the unregenerate are able to do enough good to merit congruently the first grace. So while the earlier scholastics (including Aquinas) had made sanctifying grace the sine qua non of final justification, Biel rendered sanctification, in Oberman's words, "barely distinguishable from man's natural endowments."[51] To be sure, nominalism removed the anti-Pelagian guardrails, but the trajectory that culminated at Trent began with the assumption that grace was the solution to the putative problem of *nature* rather than *sin*.

Although it is beyond our scope, the Renaissance provided another source of semi-Pelagian and even Pelagian confidence in human nature. Pico's *Oration on the Dignity of Man* is an anthem of this revival of Neoplatonism in an early modern key. Luther's engagement with Erasmus and Calvin's with the "modern Epicureans" heralded a new front on which the battle would be waged. If figures like Ficino, Pico, and Erasmus are representative, the turn to the self as an autonomous individual was due to the success of Christian Neoplatonists as much as nominalism. In fact, we have seen that Biel remains indebted to Neoplatonist mysticism. But the Reformers do not overreact against this Promethean impulse of early modernity by embracing gnostic fatalism.

According to the Reformers, just as the whole person (not just the mind or soul) is created in God's image, the whole person is fallen. Essentially, the root of all sin is idolatry, Luther believed, seeking one's own glory rather than God's, and it is motivated by ingratitude.[52] He despised such Ciceronian maxims as "virtue grows when it is praised."[53] This is just another form of self-love that masquerades as piety, much like the self-righteous posture of the Pharisees of Jesus's day, not to mention of the Roman church. Aristotle and the humanists speak of the virtue—the best in human beings *coram hominibus* (before fellow humans), but without faith in Christ, all of this is "doing good in an evil way."[54] All of this is to be found in Augustine, not to mention

---

51. Heiko Oberman, *The Dawn of the Reformation: Essays in Late Medieval and Early Reformational Thought* (Grand Rapids: Eerdmans, 1992), 139.

52. A good summary of this view is found in Pereira, *Augustine of Hippo and Martin Luther*, 297–99.

53. Pereira, *Augustine of Hippo and Martin Luther*, 420.

54. Pereira, *Augustine of Hippo and Martin Luther*, 431.

Scripture. For Augustine, the first sin "was not a sin of weakness, but a sin of *pride*."[55]

Total depravity did not mean for the Reformers that humans were as corrupt as they could possibly be but that there was no part of them that escaped the dominion of sin. The whole self loves the wrong thing: desiring objects, even that are good in themselves, more than God himself. The fall cannot be explained as an insurrection of the lower self against a pristine higher self; in fact, the treason began in their mind and spread from that beachhead into the whole person. As Calvin argues,

> For not only did a lower appetite seduce [Adam], but unspeakable impiety occupied the very citadel of his mind, and pride penetrated to the depths of his heart. Thus it is pointless and foolish to restrict the corruption that arises thence only to what are called the impulses of the senses; or to call it the "kindling wood" that attracts, arouses, and drags into sin only that part which they term "sensuality."[56]

Indeed, not even Lucifer is naturally evil. "For the depravity and malice both of man and the devil, or the sins that arise therefrom, do not spring from nature, but rather from the corruption of nature."[57] It would be a "Manichean error" to suggest otherwise. "For if any defect were proved to inhere in nature, this would bring reproach upon [God]."[58] In fact, Calvin extolls the dignity of human powers before the fall: "In this integrity man by free will had the power, if he so willed, to attain eternal life." He did not require supplemental grace to make him stand, for he "*could* have stood if he wished, seeing that he fell only by his own will."[59]

With the whole soul, human beings turned against God and plunged the race into helpless ruin. Nothing of this image has been destroyed, but the whole self exists in "frightful deformity" since the fall.[60] Thus the frequent assertion by some Roman Catholic theologians

---

55. Pereira, *Augustine of Hippo and Martin Luther*, 62. See also Jesse Couenhoven, *Stricken by Sin, Cured by Christ: Agency, Necessity and Culpability in Augustinian Theology* (New York: Oxford University Press, 2013), 373–74.

56. *Inst.* 2.1.9.

57. *Inst.* 1.14.3.; cf. 2.2.11.

58. *Inst.* 1.15.1.

59. *Inst.* 1.15.8, emphasis added.

60. *Inst.* 1.15.4.

that Reformation anthropology is quasi-Manichean, imputing evil to nature as such, turns out to be a caricature.[61] In fact, the truth is exactly the opposite. Regardless of whether they were correct, the Reformers were convinced that it was medieval teaching that displayed Manichean tendencies.

Consequently, grace is not given to solve the problem of nature but sin. Apart from a one-sided divine rescue that at once solved the problem of condemnation and corruption, there was no hope of salvation. In other words, the Reformers had a higher view of human nature's dignity before the fall and a more severe view of that nature's corruption after the fall.

Furthermore, medieval theology taught that this tendency of the sensual passions to cause disorder (concupiscence) is not a sin. How *could* God hold anyone responsible for a design flaw, or at least instability in human nature itself? Following Augustine, however, the Reformers disagreed. Concupiscence *is* sin—part of the condition of guilt and corruption that precedes and gives rise to sinful acts. Lust, selfishness, and greed, even embryonic, are venomous. Concupiscence is therefore not a tendency of human nature as such but of nature corrupted by original sin.

Luther wrote in 1521, "Paul calls that which remains after baptism, sin; the fathers call it a weakness and imperfection rather than sin. Here we stand at the parting of the ways. I follow Paul and you the fathers—with the exception of Augustine, who generally calls it by the blunt names of fault and iniquity."[62] The Augsburg Confession adds, "Concupiscence is not merely a corruption of the physical constitution, but the evil inclination of man's *higher capacities* to carnal things."[63] "Although sin in our flesh has not been completely removed or eradicated, [God] will not count or consider it (*rechnen noch wissen*)."[64] Melanchthon observes that "the inclination (*fomes*) to evil is not something neutral (*adiaphoron*),"

---

61. Many examples could be cited for this charge, but the description of Möhler's will suffice: Johann Adam Möhler, in *Symbolism*, 60–62, accuses Luther and Lutheranism in particular of being like "the Gnostics and the Manichaeans." While Matthias Flacius, whom he quotes, did veer in this direction with his idea that after the fall human nature is "satanic," he is hardly representative of the consensus found in the Book of Concord. This is odd for a volume that claims to base its descriptions on the symbols of the various churches.

62. Luther, "Against Latomus" (1521), in *LW* 32:220.

63. Preus, *Justification and Rome*, 35, emphasis added; quoting the Augsburg Confession, apology 2.24.

64. Preus, *Justification and Rome*, 36–37, quoting the Smalcald Articles, 3.13.1.

but is "truly sin (*vere peccatum*)."[65] Similarly, Vermigli argues, "I know there have been some who understand by 'flesh' the lower parts of the mind that are gross and wrapped in filthy lusts. But Paul excludes this meaning when he says, 'by the works of the law,' that is, by works commanded by God in the law, that must come from reason and not the strength of the inferior soul."[66] "Further, Scripture understands by 'flesh' the whole person, following the sense of the Hebrew, something we have explained more fully elsewhere."[67]

The Council of Trent begins well by condemning Pelagianism and affirming original sin, Calvin acknowledges. But then it condemns those who say that all sin—not just its guilt but its corruption—is swept away in baptism. Thus one cannot say that the believer is simultaneously justified and sinful, according to Trent, because baptism renders one inherently righteous at least in the beginning. "We assert that the whole guilt of sin is taken away in baptism," Calvin counters, "so that the remains of sin still existing are not imputed."[68] He adds,

> That this may be clearer, let my readers call to mind that there is a twofold grace in baptism, for therein both remission of sins and regeneration are offered to us. We teach that full remission is made, but that regeneration is only begun and goes on making progress during the whole of life. Accordingly, sin truly remains in us, and is not instantly in one day extinguished by baptism, but as the guilt is effaced it is null in regard to imputation.

Sin so remains in the elect that if God should count it, they could not stand in his judgment; but he doesn't count it for the sake of Christ's merits imputed.[69] "It cannot be denied without effrontery that repugnance to the Law of God is truly sin. But the Apostle affirms this of a disease remaining in the regenerate. It follows, therefore, that of its own nature it is sin, although it is not imputed and the guilt is abolished by

---

65. Quoted in Preus, *Justification and Rome*, 41, quoting the Augsburg Confession, apology 2.42.

66. Peter Martyr Vermigli, *Locus on Justification*, in *Predestination and Justification: Two Theological Loci*, trans. and ed. Frank A. James III, Peter Martyr Library 8 (Kirksville, MO: Sixteenth Century Essays & Studies, 2003), 98.

67. Vermigli, *Locus on Justification*, 99, referring to his Romans commentary, 222–66, esp. 225–45.

68. Calvin, "Antidote to Trent," in *Acts of the Council of Trent: With the Antidote*, in *Selected Works of John Calvin: Tracts and Letters*, 7 vols., ed. Henry Beveridge and Jules Bonnet, trans. Henry Beveridge (Grand Rapids: Baker, 1983), 3:85–86.

69. Calvin, "Antidote to Trent," 3:86.

the grace of Christ."[70] Trent declares that "free will was by no means extinguished in them, though weakened in its powers and under a bias."[71] In the debate between humanists like Erasmus and Luther, this point marks a decisive break.

Also like Augustine, the Apology distinguishes civil works (the external justice that is possible *coram hominibus*) from genuine righteousness before God (*coram Deo*) that comes from faith.[72] Especially against the Anabaptists, Calvin praises God's common grace toward "those whom the scriptures call 'natural men'" who were "nevertheless sagacious in earthly matters." "Let us, accordingly, learn by their example how many gifts the Lord left to human nature even after it was despoiled of its true good."[73]

Roman Catholic theologian Michael Schmaus recognizes clearly that for the Reformers the question was not whether human beings have any genuine agency. For Luther, what was lost in the fall was not "metaphysical freedom" but "eschatological freedom (the freedom of the children of God)."[74] We saw in the first two chapters that the Greek fathers were primarily defending metaphysical-psychological freedom against the deterministic cosmology of the Gnostics.[75] For theologians like Augustine and Aquinas, Schmaus observes,

> What man has lost through sin, according to Scripture, is this eschatological freedom. Weakened by his inclination towards evil, the sinner chooses evil rather than the good: he is so much under the power of sin that he must be called the slave of sin, which has taken root in his very existence. His will has been abandoned to evil, so that one can speak of a *servium arbitrium*. The liberty of fallen man is restored through grace alone. Thus it is that only one who is impelled by grace is really free.[76]

Luther was not interested in metaphysical freedom per se—that is, choosing freely between various options in daily life—"but only in the

---

70. Calvin, "Antidote to Trent," 3:87.
71. Calvin, "Antidote to Trent," 3:93.
72. Augsburg Confession, apology 4.33.
73. *Inst.* 2.2.15.
74. Michael Schmaus, *Dogma*, vol. 6, *Justification and Last Things* (London: Sheed and Ward, 1977), 13.
75. Schmaus, *Dogma*, 6:11.
76. Schmaus, *Dogma*, 6:14.

question of salvific action on man's part." The issue was not whether people had the freedom to choose red or white socks but whether they had the power to contribute to their salvation. "This is also what is meant by every theological text of the ancient Church which speaks of a loss of freedom due to sin," Schmaus notes, citing Prosper's *Indiculus*: "'All men lost their natural powers and their innocence in the sin of Adam. And no one is capable of rising from the depths of this loss by his own free will if the grace of the merciful God does not lift him up.'" Schmaus adds, "In the course of the text a statement of Pope Innocent I is cited which says that the sinner would have been stripped of his freedom for eternity, and remained forever under the power of his fall, if the coming of Christ had not graciously lifted him up."[77] The Reformers did not say anything more radical than this.

As to free will, Calvin says in his response to Trent that there is not a single scriptural passage that indicates we are merely weakened with respect to God; rather, we are dead in sins, "enslaved to the tyranny of sin," and so forth. The power to will certainly "remains in man." "For the fall of Adam did not take away the will, but made it a slave where it was free. It is not only prone to sin, but is made subject to sin."[78]

Grace comes not to coerce but to liberate the will to embrace Christ with all of his benefits. The delegates at Trent believe that grace does no more than make it easier for us to do what we could do on our own. "Paul claims the whole work for God; they ascribe nothing to him but a little help. But for what do they join man as an associate with God? Because man, though he might repudiate it, freely accepts the grace of God and the illumination of the Holy Spirit."[79] Like Luther, then, Calvin is describing existential (or ethical) freedom rather than metaphysical freedom. He rejects the charge "that the treachery of Judas is as properly the work of God as the calling of Paul."[80] God does not work sin in us, but only grace. After several citations from Augustine, he comments, "The hallucination [of the drafters at Trent] is in dreaming that we are offered a movement which leaves us an intermediate choice, while they never think of that effectual working by which the heart of man is renewed from pravity to rectitude."[81] On this point, it is difficult

---

77. Schmaus, *Dogma*, 6:17. In citing Prosper, Schmaus references "DS 239; cf. DS 243."
78. Calvin, "Antidote to Trent," 3:109.
79. Calvin, "Antidote to Trent," 3:110.
80. Calvin, "Antidote to Trent," 3:149, on canon 6.
81. Calvin, "Antidote to Trent," 3:111.

to believe that Aquinas would have agreed with Trent over Calvin. Trent at this point is following the nominalists (sufficient grace) rather than Aquinas (effectual grace). With Paul and Augustine we say that the will truly embraces Christ, as Calvin says, "because their will from being bad is turned to good."[82] "The whole may be summed up: Their error consists in sharing the work between God and ourselves." The will is free to choose what it wants, but it cannot choose what is alien to the disposition of the chooser. "Let us remember, therefore, that will in man is one thing and the free choice of good and evil another."[83]

This is a key point in Calvin's argument. Luther and Calvin do not believe that the power to will has been lost by the fall but only the power to will well in things heavenly, that is, to embrace Christ. Where Trent teaches that the fall has weakened the will and tilted it toward sin and unbelief, the Reformers are convinced that we are slaves of sin (John 8:34; Rom 6:18–20; 1 Cor 2:14) and "dead in trespasses and sin" (Eph 2:4). No amount of cooperation is possible apart from a unilateral act of God's grace.

It is crucial to see how much more Pauline the Reformers are even than Augustine in their anthropology. We have seen repeatedly how the flesh-Spirit contrast in Paul is interpreted in the light of a dualism between higher and lower worlds of which the self is a microcosm. In this Platonic anthropology, the battle between sin and grace is waged between the passions and the intellect. On this battlefield, the chief role of grace is to tamp down the embers of concupiscence before inflamed passions threaten to engulf the mind. Charles Raith II is exactly right when he says, "Calvin is less focused on the particular faculties of human nature (e.g., intellect, will, passions) and instead subsumes all the faculties under the one description of 'flesh' when speaking of the unregenerate, 'flesh' and 'spirit' when speaking of the regenerate." "Flesh" is simply the corrupt human nature due to original sin.[84] "Like Aquinas's *fomes*, these affections arise prior to the intellect, although Calvin speaks of them not in terms of 'lower' but rather 'deeper.'"[85] Unlike Aquinas, Calvin maintains that concupiscence is truly sin and there is no dis-

---

82. Calvin, "Antidote to Trent," 3:112.
83. Calvin, "Antidote to Trent," 3:113.
84. Charles Raith II, "Portraits of Paul: Aquinas and Calvin on Romans 7:14–25," in *Reading Romans with St. Thomas Aquinas*, ed. Matthew Levering and Michael Dauphinais (Washington, DC: Catholic University of America Press, 2012), 242.
85. Raith, "Portraits of Paul: Aquinas and Calvin on Romans 7:14–25," 243.

tinction between mortal and venial.[86] Appealing to Augustine, Calvin observes from Romans 7 that Paul admits his failure to keep the law. "But Aquinas still maintains that Paul commits condignly meritorious works and thus truly fulfills the law."[87]

Where Luther seemed to think that the image of God had been lost (or, according to Matthias Flacius Illyricus, had become satanic, though this view was repudiated), Calvin clearly affirmed the abiding image. It is "effaced" but "not destroyed."[88] Eventually the distinction emerged among Reformed writers between a natural ability (retained after the fall) and moral ability to attain righteousness (which has been lost). The whole self was turned to God and with the whole self Adam and Eve turned away from God. The image-likeness remains along with the office itself, but the office-bearer stands indicted. Embers of ethical beauty and glory still glimmer, but the children of Adam smear mud on themselves to cover these remnants of natural dignity in order to hide the reminder of their dependence and participation in God that would lead them to be thankful.[89]

In post-Reformation Reformed theology as well, grace is not something added to nature.[90] There is nothing to "fix" in creation, no weak spot to patch up, no inherent tendency to overcome. Grace is given not to make nature supernatural but to liberate nature from sin in order to be what it was intended to be all along.[91] There is one end, and it is naturally supernatural: to glorify and enjoy God forever. Human nature as it came from the hand of God is "very good." Grace (synonymous with mercy) is only necessary after the fall, not because of anything lacking in nature itself but because that nature has been corrupted, free will enslaved to unrighteousness and unbelief, and guilt imputed to the whole race.

Generally speaking, Lutheran and Reformed orthodoxy refined the Reformers' emphases, distinguishing more carefully between natural and moral inability, divine permission and direct causation, and so forth. Ironically, Aquinas was often appealed to with greater favor among Protestant theologians than their Roman Catholic counterparts.

---

86. Raith, "Portraits of Paul: Aquinas and Calvin on Romans 7:14–25," 252.

87. Raith, "Portraits of Paul: Aquinas and Calvin on Romans 7:14–25," 253–54.

88. *Inst.* 1.15.4.

89. *Inst.* 1.5.14.

90. See for example Francis Turretin, *Institutes of Elenctic Theology*, ed. James T. Dennison Jr., trans. George Musgrave Giger (Phillipsburg, NJ: P&R, 1992), 5.11.4, 9–10.

91. Herman Bavinck, *Reformed Dogmatics*, vol. 3, *Sin and Salvation in Christ*, ed. John Bolt, trans. John Vriend (Grand Rapids: Baker Academic), 578.

Language of infused habits was incorporated but distinguished from justification; the "light of nature," including some true knowledge of universals, was affirmed in spite of the comprehensive effects of sin.[92] The remnants of original good in human nature are not extinguished, but they cannot attain to saving understanding.

Explicitly nominalist theses do emerge in Protestant theology but not until the Dutch Remonstrant (Arminian) movement at the turn of the seventeenth century. James Arminius himself invoked the *facientibus*: "For if the expression be understood in this sense, to the one who does what he can (*potest*) by the first grace already conferred on him, then there is no absurdity in saying God will bestow further grace on him who profitably uses what is first."[93] Richard Muller sees this as justifying—at this point at least—the charge of "semi-Pelagianism," particularly since Arminius's construction of the phrase is the same as Biel's: namely, that God's grace can be resisted, and election is conditioned on human choice.[94]

INFUSION AND IMPUTATION

If human nature as created is not already oriented to God as its ultimate end, and the order between lower and higher powers is intrinsically unstable, then it makes sense that the fall would be considered a loss of the supernaturally added gift elevating nature to God and a dominion of the passions over the intellect (concupiscence). Consequently, grace is primarily going to be conceived in medicinal terms, as (a) restoring the superadded gift to elevate nature and (b) a healing of that disorder in the soul. In the thinking of Lombard and Aquinas, as in scholasticism generally, grace was conceived primarily as a spiritual medicine: a healing grace (*gratia sanans*) that also elevates nature beyond itself. "God so works in man that there are not two acts in this cooperation: one divine and the other human. Rather, it is a matter of one single act

---

92. See for example Canons of the Synod of Dort, Heads 3 and 4, in *The Psalter Hymnal: Doctrinal Standards and Liturgy of the Christian Reformed Church* (Grand Rapids: Board of Publications of the Christian Reformed Church, 1976), 102–9.

93. James Arminius, "Apology Against Thirty-One Theological Articles," *The Writings of James Arminius*, 3 vols., trans. James Nichols and William Nichols (repr., Grand Rapids: Baker, 1986), 2:20.

94. Richard A. Muller, "Grace, Election, and Contingent Choice: Arminius's Gambit and the Reformed Response," in *The Grace of God, the Bondage of the Will: Historical and Theological Perspectives on Calvinism*, ed. Thomas R. Schreiner and Bruce A. Ware (Grand Rapids: Baker, 1995), 2:261.

which fulfills at once the function of divine cooperation and the function of *gratia sanans*. . . . Thus the one grace-giving act of God brings it about that the human will performs a free salvific action."[95] Thus the collapsing of justification into sanctification seems inevitable. The idea of a purely forensic justification would not even occur to one holding these presuppositions. But with the advent of Scotus and Ockham, even the anti-Pelagian guardrails are removed.

Because of this wider metaphysical framework, Trent could never have affirmed the Reformers' propositions on justification and could not give the doctrine a prominent, much less central, role regardless of the definition. There were extensive treatments of and debates concerning the relation of nature and grace, predestination, grace and free will, and faith and sacraments. A prominent—perhaps even the most prominent—tradition in earlier scholastic theology even affirmed in resolute and consistent terms that the entire process of salvation/ justification was dependent on grace from start to finish. Yet seeing justification as a judicial verdict based exclusively on the imputation of Christ's righteousness, and distinguished from sanctification, does not seem to have occurred to Augustine or his medieval heirs.

All of this points to the importance of the different paradigms with which Thomas and the Reformers are working. Consequently, Thomas is convinced, our meriting is not opposed to God's grace, as if God and the believer were equal agents. Rather, just as we have our existence by participation in God, we have our adoption and salvation by participation in God's grace. Our merits are therefore nothing more than "faith working by love," the fruit of the Spirit's work in us, making us truly deserving (condignly) of God's saving benefits. Abraham is justified because his assent to God's word really is the beginning of sanctification, just as the tax-collector "went home justified" because he began to become obedient.[96] "Of course in seeing this justice in Abraham God simply looks upon what he himself has caused." Faith is "'the first act of justice which God works in us.'"[97] So reckoning is simply seeing things as they are.[98]

---

95. Schmaus, *Dogma*, 6:16.

96. *ST* II-II, Q. 4, A. 1, co; and Aquinas, *Romans* 4, lect. 1, para. 325. Quoted from Bruce D. Marshall, "*Beatus vir*: Aquinas, Romans 4, and the Role of 'Reckoning' in Justification," in *Reading Romans with St. Thomas Aquinas*, ed. Matthew Levering and Michael Dauphinais (Washington, DC: Catholic University of America Press, 2012), 220.

97. Marshall, "*Beatus vir*," 220, quoting Aquinas, *Romans* 4, lect. 1, para. 331.

98. Marshall, "*Beatus vir*," 220–21.

The Reformers are just as confident as Thomas that the inner grace of regeneration is required even for the exercise of faith, that the relation of divine and human agency is analogical (thus noncompetitive), and that there is no justification that is not accompanied throughout by continuing inner renewal. The obstacles between Aquinas and the magisterial Reformation can be narrowed down to these: the definition of justification and its relation to merit, penance and faith.

Justification Narrower than Salvation

We will recall that for Aquinas the stages of justification are (1) infusion of grace (ordinarily in baptism), (2) movement of free will, (3) contrition (genuine sorrow toward God), and (4) remission of sin. The Reformers reversed this order and called the whole process *salvation*, reserving "justification" for the event of divine declaration. Justification, Thomas says, is *remission plus infusion of created (habitual) grace*.[99] No, Calvin replied, *justification* does not include infused grace. "Therefore, we explain justification simply as the acceptance with which God receives us into his favor as righteous. And we say that it consists in the *remission of sins* and the *imputation of Christ's righteousness*."[100] According to Trent, in justification "we not only are reckoned to be just, but truly are just, and are rightly described as such."[101] Thus, according to this view, as Bruce Marshall explains, "The formal cause of our justification is that *iustitia* by which God makes *us* just or righteous, the justice he gives us rather than the justice he himself has and is."[102] For the Reformers, it is neither. Rather, the justice that Christ accomplished as our covenantal head is given to us by imputation.

Ever since the so-called Luther Renaissance led by Karl Holl, there has been a trend toward driving a wedge between Luther and later Lutheranism.[103] Accordingly, Melanchthon is seen as the real author of the imputation theory. This interpretation has been challenged decisively

---

99. *ST* I-II, Q. 82, A. 4, and I-II, Q. 81, A. 1.

100. *Inst.* 3.11.2, emphasis added.

101. Council of Trent, Session 6, Decree on Justification, in Heinrich Denzinger, *Compendium of Creeds, Definitions, and Declarations on Matters of Faith and Morals*, ed. Robert Fastiggi and Anne Englund Nash, 43rd ed. (San Francisco: Ignatius), para. 1529 (387).

102. Marshall, "*Beatus vir*," 217.

103. A recent defense of this view is Mark Seifried, "Luther, Melanchthon and Paul on the Question of Imputation: Recommendations on a Current Debate," in *Justification: What's at Stake in the Current Debates*, ed. Mark Husbands and Daniel J. Treier (Downers Grove, IL: IVP Academic, 2004), 137–52. The thesis is also at work in the new Finnish interpretation of Luther and in much of mainline Lutheran scholarship more generally.

in recent years. To be sure, there is development. Luther's 1515–16 *Lectures on Romans* demonstrate the work of an Augustinian teacher under the influence of Staupitz. Justification is still the righteousness that God imparts, making us righteous.[104] However, Luther steadily moves away from this traditional concept of justification as a process. It is hardly a Melanchthonian innovation,[105] although Melanchthon helped Luther to refine his understanding of the *iustitia alienum* with the concept of imputation.[106] R. S. Clark demonstrates that between 1513 and 1521 Luther moved away from viewing justification as gradual.[107] The change is obvious in the *Lectures on Galatians* (1535) and two disputations on justification (1536). In the second disputation, Melanchthon asks Luther if he thinks that imputation is the right concept and Luther replies, "I think this, and am most persuaded and certain that this is the true opinion of the Gospel and of the Apostles, that only by a gracious imputation are we righteous before God" (*sola imputatio gratuita sumus iusti apud Deum*).[108] This should be the final word against all attempts to distance Luther from forensic imputation.

By this time (1536), Calvin had completed his first edition of the *Institutes*. Thirty years later, in the first extended evangelical critique of Trent (*The Council of Trent and Antidote*), Calvin spent most of his ink on the sixth session on justification. Remarkably, he begins by representing faithfully Trent's arguments, precisely in its own terms. Nevertheless, he judges that that the assembly conflates justification and regeneration/sanctification because of a faulty anthropology.[109] The first justification in baptism is all of grace, but the second justification results from the ongoing cooperation of free will with God's grace, with the hope that one will attain—by the merits of Christ, the saints, and oneself—final justification at the Last Judgment. After preparing for grace, the soul attains justification, says Calvin, "which is not the mere forgiveness of sins, but also sanctification."[110]

---

104. Martin Luther, *Lectures on Romans*, in *LW* 25:151–52.
105. Carl Trueman, "*Simul peccator et justus*: Martin Luther and Justification" in *Justification in Perspective: Historical Developments and Contemporary Challenges*, ed. Bruce L. McCormack (Grand Rapids: Baker Academic, 2006), 88–92.
106. Lowell C. Green, *How Melanchthon Helped Luther Discover the Gospel* (Fallbrook: Verdict, 1980).
107. R. S. Clark, "*Iustitia Imputata Christi*: Alien or Proper to Luther's Doctrine of Justification?," *Concordia Theological Quarterly* 70 (2006): 269–310.
108. Quoted in Clark, "*Iustitia Imputata Christi*," 303.
109. Calvin, "Antidote to Trent," 3:94.
110. Calvin, "Antidote to Trent," 3:95.

Further, "No one can know with a certainty of faith . . . that he has obtained the grace of God. . . . Faith cooperating with good works, they grow and are justified more and more."[111] Thus, Trent decrees, no one can know with certainty that he or she is elect and will attain final justification. The justified who fall into sin "may again be justified . . . by the sacrament of penance," which is "a second plank after shipwreck of lost grace."[112] This penance includes "satisfaction by fasting, alms, prayer, and other pious exercises of the spiritual life."[113] Eternal life is therefore both a gift and "a reward faithfully to be paid according to the promise of God for their good works and merits." Believers are said "truly to merit the obtaining of eternal life in due time, provided they die in grace."[114] Hence, "For the righteousness which is called ours, inasmuch as by it inhering in us we are justified, is also the righteousness of God because infused into us by God through the merits of Christ."[115]

If the new Finnish interpretation puts forward a Luther preoccupied with Eastern deification more than forensic justification, others have seen Calvin's emphasis on union with Christ as a qualification of or even alternative to forensic justification.[116] Both approaches try to distance their respective reformer from his followers, particularly those who drafted the confessions. According to William M. Thompson, "Justification is already intrinsic and transformative" for Calvin because justification takes place through the Spirit's work of ingrafting into Christ.[117]

In this perspective, union with Christ broadens the doctrine of justification itself beyond merely forensic frontiers. Thompson quotes Barth's formula, "It is a declaring righteous which without any reserve can be called a making righteous."[118] Thompson admits that Calvin's critique of Osiander is "the most difficult and ambiguous text." Noting that "Osiander explains 'justify' as 'to make righteous,'" Calvin goes on to

---

111. Calvin, "Antidote to Trent," 3:98.

112. Calvin, "Antidote to Trent," 3:100–101.

113. Calvin, "Antidote to Trent," 3:101.

114. Calvin, "Antidote to Trent," 3:102.

115. Calvin, "Antidote to Trent," 3:103.

116. Thomas F. and James B. Torrance have written prolifically along these lines. More recently, see Charles Partee, "Calvin's Central Dogma Again," *Sixteenth Century Journal* 18 (1987): 191–99; cf. Partee, *Theology of John Calvin* (Louisville: Westminster John Knox), 2010), 40–42, 136–41; William Evans, *Imputation and Impartation: Union with Christ in American Reformed Theology* (Eugene, OR: Wipf and Stock, 2009).

117. William M. Thompson, "Viewing Justification Through Calvin's Eyes: An Ecumenical Experiment," *Theological Studies* 57 (1996): 447–66, at 452.

118. *CD* IV/1, 95.

refute the idea.[119] The only reason that this is a "difficult and ambiguous text" for Thompson is that it clearly and unmistakably contradicts his thesis. Thompson merely repeats his assertion that Calvin did not reduce justification to forensic imputation. "An autonomous 'becoming righteous' seems to be the target."[120] Thompson relates, "Barth's guidance in interpreting Calvin was crucial to me."[121] Another Barthian theologian, Charles Partee, says that Calvin "helpfully proposes the 'union with Christ' theme as unusually central and rich in the *Institutes*."[122] "It is hard to see how there could be any real this-worldly justification without this transforming indwelling."[123] These attempts to transform Calvin into Barth are legion over the last half-century, especially in the wake of Thomas and James Torrance, but they are tangentially related to the primary sources.

Astonishingly, Thompson looks to Cardinal Newman as offering a helpful mediating role. "Newman's key theme is the divine indwelling as the basis of justification. A greater attentiveness to that indwelling, he thought, would overcome Protestant 'extrincisim' and Catholic works-righteousness where and when they occur."[124] Though Newman is too harsh in his critique of Luther, "his view of the central role of the divine indwelling as the key seems exactly right," Thompson judges.[125] He adds,

> John Wesley is also helpful; his work mediates here as well. I have discovered that Roman Catholics instinctively find him appealing. The patristic theme of divinization is clearly strong in various of his writings as well as the teaching of the Christological mystics of the 17th century. Accordingly, Wesley articulated a clearly transformative interpretation of justification: "You are really changed; you are not only accounted, but actually made, righteous."[126]

---

119. Thompson, "Viewing Justification Through Calvin's Eyes," 452, referring to *Inst.* 3.13.5.

120. Thompson, "Viewing Justification Through Calvin's Eyes," 453. For a helpful critique of Newman's description, see Alister McGrath's *Iustitia Dei*, 2.121–34.

121. Thompson, "Viewing Justification Through Calvin's Eyes," 453, referring to *CD* IV/1, 95; IV/3.2, 539–54.

122. Thompson, "Viewing Justification Through Calvin's Eyes," 453n25.

123. Thompson, "Viewing Justification Through Calvin's Eyes," 453.

124. Thompson, "Viewing Justification Through Calvin's Eyes," 453.

125. Thompson, "Viewing Justification Through Calvin's Eyes," 453n26.

126. Thompson, "Viewing Justification Through Calvin's Eyes," 454, quoting John Wesley, "The Menace of Antinomianism," in *John Wesley*, ed. Albert C. Outler, Library of Protestant Thought (NY: Oxford University Press, 1964), 381.

However, Thompson has simply conflated Calvin's comments about salvation in general with justification in particular. Of course, Christ indwells us by his Spirit, conforming us to his image. He is even quite happy to acknowledge glorification (calling it "deification") as the consummate blessing of salvation.[127] But these are gifts of salvation in addition to and even based upon justification rather than justification itself. Calvin is quite clear that the basis of justification is *not* the indwelling Christ but the imputation of his righteousness. The Spirit unites us to Christ by giving us faith, which first justifies and then begins the process of sanctification. So also Wesley here is simply affirming with the Reformers that those who are justified by an alien righteousness *are also really changed* in sanctification.[128]

Thompson notes favorably the new Finnish approach to Luther. He quotes Luther's exegesis of 2 Peter 1:4:

> Through the power of faith, [Peter] says, we partake of and have association or communion with the divine nature. This is a verse without parallel in the New and the Old Testaments, even though unbelievers regard it as a trivial matter that we partake of the divine nature itself. But what is the divine nature? It is eternal truth, righteousness, wisdom, everlasting life, peace, joy, happiness, and whatever can be called good. Now he who becomes a partaker of the divine nature receives all this, so that he lives eternally and has everlasting peace, joy, and happiness, and is pure, clean, and righteous, and almighty against the devil, sin, and death.[129]

From this statement Thompson concludes, "Any attempt to conceive of justification in simply forensic terms breaks down here. So, consequently, does any attempt to associate the intrinsic dimension of participation exclusively with sanctification."[130] But this is wishful thinking. Luther has no difficulty affirming a variety of gifts in salvation without confusing them with justification. In any case, Thompson hopes to see a similar move in Calvin studies succeed.[131] He says that the Council of

---

127. Calvin, *Calvin's Commentaries*, vol. 22, *Epistle of Paul to the Hebrews* and *The Catholic Epistles*, trans. John Owen. (Grand Rapids: Baker, 1998), 371.

128. Wesley taught that justification was the imputation of Christ's righteousness in "The Lord Our Righteousness" (1765), in *The Works of John Wesley* (Grand Rapids: Baker, 1996), 5:237.

129. Thompson, "Viewing Justification Through Calvin's Eyes," 454, from *LW* 30:155.

130. Thompson, "Viewing Justification Through Calvin's Eyes," 455.

131. Thompson, "Viewing Justification Through Calvin's Eyes," 455.

Trent "wrongly, I think," thought that the Reformers "hold a simply forensic-extrinsicist view of justification."[132]

But there is no reason from the primary sources to conclude that Trent misidentified the Reformers' view on this point in the slightest, especially since Calvin's response to Trent repeats the position that the council anathematized. At no point did Melanchthon, Calvin, or Martin Chemnitz in their lengthy responses suggest that they had been misunderstood as teaching that justification is an exclusively forensic imputation. If they had done so, the Reformation would have ceased, and there would have been little reason to continue the division.

First, the magisterial Reformers argued that justification is a legal or forensic term.[133] Although Luther felt the inextricable connection between doctrine and experience, he did not arrive at his conclusions simply out of his own "tortured subjectivity," as some modern interpreters suggest.[134] Rather, it was spurred by the renaissance of biblical languages. Peter Martyr Vermigli, proficient in Hebrew as well as Greek, points out in reliance on the lexicon of Rabbi David Kimhi (1160–1235), "*Hitsdiq* is a forensic verb, because it looks to judgments; likewise, this word *hirshiah*, meaning 'to declare one wicked.' Then 'to justify means that through judgment, words, witness, or assertion one counts the other person just.'"[135]

Jacques Lefèvre d'Étaples (1455–1536), an eminent French humanist and biblical scholar (who made the first French translation of the Bible from the Latin Vulgate), arrived at an evangelical interpretation of justification a decade before Luther. Erasmus made important textual contributions that paved the way for recovering the original meaning of justification as well as other terms, such as repentance (versus penance). Johann von Staupitz helped shape Luther's development and recommended Luther as a professor of Bible in the university. None of these figures left Rome, but they laid the tracks for the Reformation.

---

132. Thompson, "Viewing Justification Through Calvin's Eyes," 459.

133. For a helpful study of the Reformed interpretation of the doctrine, see J. V. Fesko, *Justification: Understanding the Classic Reformed Doctrine* (Phillipsburg, NJ: P&R, 2008).

134. Attempts to psychoanalyze Luther to explain his "evangelical breakthrough" reached its hagiographical limits in Erik H. Erikson, *Young Man Luther: A Study in Psychoanalysis and History* (New York: W. W. Norton, 1962). Krister Stendahl's *Paul: Among Jews and Gentiles* (Minneapolis: Augsburg Fortress, 1976) followed this thesis, which has become a largely unexamined assumption among advocates of the New Perspective(s) on Paul (esp. James D. G. Dunn and N. T. Wright).

135. Vermigli, *Locus on Justification*, 88. James notes, "Martyr is following the analysis of Rabbi David Kimhi, *Sefer Hashorashim* (Book of Roots) (ספר השורשים), in *Radicum Liber sive Hebraeum Bibliorum Lexicon*, ed. Biesenthal and Lebrecht (Berlin, 1847)," 88n4.

Luther therefore did not appear out of nowhere, suddenly seeing things in the biblical text heretofore undisclosed to mortal minds.

Melanchthon and Calvin devoted themselves to learning Greek and Hebrew, and other Reformers took such studies as their primary field. Erasmus praised the Reformed theologian Oecolampadius for having "the upper hand among us" in language studies and made him the Hebrew consultant for Erasmus's Greek New Testament. Through the next century, most of the pioneering Hebrew and Greek scholars of the period were Lutheran or Reformed. Regardless of one's verdict concerning their conclusions, the Reformers were biblical exegetes of the first rank. Their conclusion on this point at least has been vindicated by contemporary exegetes, including Roman Catholic specialists, as we will see in volume 2. But if this is accurate, then not only nominalism but also Augustine and the entire medieval tradition went down the wrong path. If justification *means* "legal declaration" rather than "movement from injustice to justice," then one wonders how this central plank of the Tridentine rejection of forensic justification can continue to receive dogmatic approval.

Second, the divine act of justification is a judicial verdict consisting in the gift of an "alien righteousness" through faith alone because of Christ alone. In fact, Melanchthon and Calvin influenced each other (Melanchthon influenced even Luther) in working out the refinements of this common evangelical position.[136] This righteousness "consists in the remission of sins, and in this: that the righteousness of Jesus Christ is imputed to us."[137] According to this evangelical interpretation, justification is not a process of transformation from a condition of sinfulness to a state of justice. Believers are *simultaneously* justified and sinful.[138] Sin's dominion has been toppled, but sin still indwells believers.[139] Consequently, whatever works believers perform will always fall short of that righteousness that God's law requires; nevertheless, they are accepted as fully righteous already through faith in Christ.

The question here is not whether God's grace-gift includes renewal as well as imputation. From Christ we receive "two kinds of righteousness,"

---

136. See, for example, Richard A. Muller, *The Unaccommodated Calvin: Studies in the Foundations of a Theological Tradition* (New York: Oxford University Press, 2001), 126–27. Calvin, however, sharply criticized Melancthon's later synergistic turn, which the orthodox (Gnesio) Lutherans also rejected.

137. *Inst.* 3.11.2.

138. *Inst.* 3.3.10.

139. *Inst.* 3.3.11.

Luther insists in a famous sermon by that title: passive righteousness, which is properly Christ's and is imputed to the believer, and active righteousness, which consists in the sanctified activity of believers—love and good works. It is therefore insufficient when the better scholastics like Aquinas recognize passive righteousness if they still interpret this gift as an infused ability to attain final justification by meritorious obedience.

Even with respect to imputation, the focus is not on the mechanism as an end in itself. In addition to sober exegesis, the Reformers argue that the importance of affirming imputation rather than impartation or infusion lies in the fact that imputation alone provides a righteousness (viz., Christ's) able to withstand divine judgment. The existential anxiety is an important pastoral concern, but assurance is not the heart of their argument. The argument is more objective. Even with God's assistance, our sanctification is only partial in this life. It is not only what we do but what we leave undone that requires satisfaction. Even if penance were a biblically sanctioned sacrament, it could provide no more than remission for moral wounds to the soul; it could not give one a status of "righteous" before God.

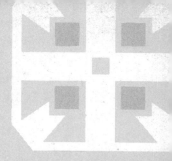

CHAPTER 9

A NEW DIRECTION
Word, Faith, and Works

In the medieval *ordo*, union with God was the goal of salvation; for the Reformers, union with God *in Christ* is salvation's source. This massive paradigm shift affects the consciousness of the average Christian in his or her daily experience. Similarly, the Reformation shifted the direction of reaching this union. Rather than grace-empowered works acquiring an increase of justification with the hope of final justification, the order for the Reformers was God's effectual word (particularly the gospel), which creates faith and then, as the fruit of faith, good works. It is a mistake therefore to represent the Reformation as a debate over grace versus works full stop. Rather, it was a debate over whether works are the fruit of faith or the root, whether faith itself is a kind of work in that, in its justifying activity at least, it is actually love.

Criticisms that see the Reformation doctrine as mired in nominalist "extrinsicism" overlook the deeply sacramental outlook of the Reformers.[1] Justification is not something that happens from afar, as Calvin notes,[2] as mere assent to the truth of certain doctrines. Nor is it based on an inward striving according to an "inner light." Rather, Christ himself is present and active in the Word and the sacraments with the Holy Spirit. In the words of the Heidelberg Catechism concerning justifying faith, "The Holy Spirit creates it by the preaching of the holy

---

1. E.g., John Milbank asserts that Reformation soteriology is based on a "nominalist univocal metaphysics" with no "real, inward reworking of our nature." He continues, "The pathetic gesture of truth" is mere assent to "a neat set of propositions about [Christ's] saving significance." Milbank, *Beyond Secular Order: The Representation of Being and the Representation of the People* (Oxford: Wiley-Blackwell, 2013), 79–80.

2. *Inst.* 3.1.1–3.

gospel and confirms it by the use of the holy sacraments."[3] The signs (creaturely words, water, bread and wine) are united by the word and Spirit to the reality they signify so that Christ truly gives himself to all who receive him. Christ is present in faith because he is present in his word.

The incarnation provides the ontological basis for this union of sign and reality. God himself became flesh without loss to his deity. Christ is God yet is also fully human. If spiritual realities cannot be given through physical means, then the incarnation would have been impossible. "For in his flesh was accomplished man's redemption," Calvin argues.[4] He employs the realistic language of the patristic era to affirm this bond created by the Spirit between *signum* and *res*. "Christ communicates his riches and blessings to us by his word," writes Calvin, "so he distributes them to us by his sacraments."[5]

The Reformers differed among themselves over the sacraments, and this was largely due to Christological differences. As Carl Trueman has observed, the debate between Luther and Zwingli reflected radically different Christologies.[6] However, Bucer, Calvin, Vermigli, and other magisterial Reformers shaped the tradition in a quite different direction than Zwingli's implicit Nestorianism (separating the two natures of Christ and therefore the sign from the reality), while Zwingli's emphasis (shared by erstwhile associates of Luther such as Andreas Karlstadt) was taken still further by the Anabaptists. Despite their differences, Luther and Calvin shared a considerable consensus in their emphases. "Both Reformers kept to a middle road, or rather a synthesis," Yves Congar notes, "and each in his own way insisted on a close relationship between an external 'instrument' of grace . . . and the activity of the Spirit."[7] Another Roman Catholic scholar Kilian McDonnell, OSB, observes of Calvin, "Rather than denying the real presence" in the Eucharist

---

3. Heidelberg Catechism, Q. 65, in *The Psalter Hymnal: Doctrinal Standards and Liturgy* (Grand Rapids: CRC Board of Publications, 1976), 31–32.

4. Calvin, *The Gospel according to John*, trans. T. H. L. Parker, ed. David W. Torrance and Thomas F. Torrance, Calvin's New Testament Commentaries 4 (Grand Rapids: Eerdmans, 1959–72), 1:167.

5. Calvin, "Form for Administration of the Sacraments" in *Selected Works of John Calvin: Tracts and Letters*, 7 vols., ed. Henry Beveridge and Jules Bonnet, trans. Henry Beveridge (Grand Rapids: Baker, 1983), 2:115.

6. Carl Trueman, "The Incarnation and the Lord's Supper," in *The Word Became Flesh: Evangelicals and the Incarnation*, ed. David Peterson (Carlisle, UK: Paternoster, 2003), 227–50.

7. Yves Congar, *I Believe in the Holy Spirit*, trans. David Smith (New York: Crossroad, 1997), 138.

"he presupposes it. None of the Reformers defended it more forcibly than Calvin."[8]

For Calvin, faith and the sacraments are as integrally related as the soul and the body. Just as obtaining Christ through faith alone does not cancel the instrumentality of the proclaimed gospel, "so neither do we exclude the Sacraments, the nature of which is the same, as they are the seals of the gospel."

> First, then, if there are any who deny that the Sacraments contain the grace which they figure, we disapprove of them. . . . We acknowledge that the Sacraments are intended, not only to maintain but to increase faith. But these horned gentry mean something else; for they pretend that the Sacraments have a magical power, which is efficacious *without faith*."[9]

In Calvin's understanding, "without faith" is equivalent to "without Christ," since faith clings to Christ's person together with all of his benefits. Trent descends into the sophism that "even unbelievers receive the grace which is offered in the Sacraments, provided they do not reject it by opposing other obstacles—*as if unbelief were not in itself obstacle enough*." While denying that they confer salvation apart from faith, he says that "they are not empty and naked signs of a distant grace."[10] In short, Calvin says, Rome binds God to earthly means, while the Anabaptists disallow that God can freely bind himself to them.[11]

THE SACRAMENTAL WORD

Especially in reaction to the Anabaptists' emphasis on the Spirit's speaking directly through an "inner word," Luther declared, "Where Christ is not preached, there is no Holy Ghost who creates, calls, and gathers the Christian church, without which no one can come to Christ the Lord."[12]

---

8. Killian McDonnell, OSB, *John Calvin, The Eucharist and the Church* (Princeton: Princeton University Press, 1967), 224.

9. John Calvin, *Selected Works of John Calvin: Tracts and Letters*, vol. 3, *Acts and Antidote*, 7 vols., ed. Henry Beveridge and Jules Bonnet, trans. Henry Beveridge (Grand Rapids: Baker, 1983), 174 on canons 4–6, emphasis added.

10. John Calvin, *Acts and Antidote*, 175, emphasis added.

11. *Inst.* 4.1.5.

12. Luther, Article 3, in *Luther's Large Catechism*, trans. F. Samuel Janzow (St. Louis: Concordia, 1978), 73.

Not only is *sola fide* bound to *solo Christo* in the Reformers' thinking, but, as Eberhard Jüngel points out, so too is *sola scriptura*, which in connection with justification especially is better identified as *solo verbo*.[13] The Reformers were actively engaged in vernacular translations of the Bible, in making the Scriptures widely available, and in encouraging regular reading and meditation on Scripture. However, when they spoke of the power of the word, they usually had in mind its public proclamation.

God created the world by his powerful word (Gen 1:3, 6; cf. Ps 33:6; 148:5; Heb 11:3). As the Great King, his speech does not merely describe reality but creates it (Isa 55:11). This is what the Reformers have in mind when thinking about the power of the Word to create the world of which he speaks. Thus even justification is not an abstract declaration that someone is righteous because he or she believed in Christ. Rather, God's decree announcing Christ's work effects faith in us to embrace it as good news for us all. Far from being a mere assent to propositions, faith is created by hearing the good news announcement. Christ creates faith by proclaiming himself to us, and therefore justification, sanctification, glorification, and all the realities of the age to come are thereby gifted to us in him. The new creation, like the old, is *spoken* into being (2 Cor 4:6). Thus, "The gospel is the power of God unto salvation" (Rom 1:16), not because the gospel provides a wise course for living or attaining righteousness or for being converted but because it *effects* righteousness and conversion. The Reformers had a deeply apocalyptic view of the word as a divine decree that breaks into this present evil age like a thunderbolt but with massive historical effects. This understanding of the word as "living and powerful" (Heb 4:12) lies at the heart of the Luther's and Calvin's understanding. Just as God declared the world into being out of nothing, so he declares the sinner to be righteous without any merits (Rom 4:17). When God declares someone righteous, he or she *is* so. Then the process of sanctification *must* begin, as the continuing effects of that gospel word.

The Reformers discerned, in Romans 10 especially, a contrast between the way of ascent through works and God's descent to us in Christ not only in the incarnation, an event of the past, but here and now through his word. Where the word is present, Christ is present

---

13. Eberhard Jüngel, *Justification: The Heart of the Christian Faith* (London: Bloomsbury T&T Clark, 2006), 204–10.

(Rom 10:3–16). "So faith comes from hearing [the message], and hearing through the word of Christ" (v. 17).

God's words really are his own, as are ours. But God's external word (as external grace) comes *to us* from *outside of ourselves* to judge and to justify. In this way, mysteriously and through the work of the Spirit, the Christ outside of us, sacrificed for our sins and raised for our justification, unites us to himself. What has happened to him and by him must now happen to us because we are united to him forever. The Spirit accomplishes this not by a secret inner word but by a public, social, and audible event of judgment and grace. United to Christ the head, believers are necessarily and simultaneously members of his body, the church.

The Reformers referred to preaching as the "sacramental word" (*verbum sacramentale*) from the conviction that this speech (especially the gospel), based on the canonical word, is itself saving—a means of grace, not just a means of information or exhortation. The sacramental word is essential in Reformation theology. Otherwise, the work of Christ becomes separated from justification, the latter being a private and inner experience of the individual. Somehow, Christ and his cross and resurrection are essential facts in which to believe, but justification becomes indistinguishable from the experience of conversion, which is often (especially in pietism and revivalism) accomplished by us through various steps. By a Protestant route, we return to a medieval *processus iustificationis*.

By contrast, the emphasis on the word, especially the gospel, proclaimed as the event that links us by the Spirit's power to Christ and his benefits ensures the real presence of Christ in the event of our justification. There is simply no space here for any extrinsic relation to God, despite the repeated criticism. Extrinsic justification simply means that the righteousness in which we boast is Christ's and not our own; it does not mean that we bear no metaphysical relation to God in Christ (both in nature and in grace).

Through a word outside of us, the Christ who has saved us outside of us, comes to us, and joins us to his body. He is the hypostatic Word in whom we exist (Col 1:16–20). Our response does not create this saving event but clings to it, embraces it, and rests in it for justification. In other words, the fact that justification is not only *sola fide, solus Christus*, and *sola gratia* but also *solo verbo* distinguishes divine and human agency without setting them in a competitive relation. Through faith, the believer's existence is so bound up with Christ that he or she can say truly, "For me to live is Christ" (Phil 1:21).

SIGNS AND SEALS OF THE PROMISE

There is no uniform sacramental doctrine in the patristic era, but there is a strong enough consensus to affirm that they held what has come to be called a realistic view. That is to say, when the New Testament speaks of the sacraments—in this case, baptism—as bringing remission of sins, death of the old self, and entrance into Christ's risen life, forgiveness, and the gift of the Spirit, it is not speaking merely in figurative terms.

Origen comes closest to a merely symbolic view when he argues that "baptism in the Holy Spirit" has nothing to do with water baptism. Following his usual allegorical interpretation, the "waters above" (the Spirit) are contrasted with the "waters below." Visible baptism is one thing, but genuine baptism into Christ's death and resurrection is another.[14] "Therefore," he adds, "those who are hastening to baptism ought to take care as a matter of first importance that they should first die to sin."[15] It is no wonder that many Christians in Origen's time put off baptism until they could accomplish this. And even then, as we have seen, baptism only has reference to *past* sins, so something else will have to deal with future sin.

Other patristic sources, especially in the East, held a more straightforward reading of the passages but were loath to formulate detailed accounts of how this happens. Baptism is a means of grace but does not save apart from faith. Gregory of Nyssa, for instance, says that the water in baptism and the bread and wine in Communion—ordinary substances—are only means of grace by the operation of the Spirit, who works where he will "by some unseen power and grace." Therefore, "It is not the water that bestows [grace] (for in that case it were a thing more exalted than all creation), but the command of God and the visitation of the Spirit that comes sacramentally to set us free."[16] Augustine, especially

---

14. Origen, *Commentary on the Epistle to the Romans*, vol. 1, *Books 1–5*, trans. Thomas P. Scheck (Washington, DC: Catholic University of America Press, 2001), 355.

15. Origen, *Commentary on the Epistle to the Romans, Books 1–5*, 358.

16. Gregory of Nyssa, *On the Baptism of Christ*, in *NPNF*[2] 5:519.

in his anti-Pelagian works, teaches that the sacraments are an outward sign of inward grace. While we can speak of them as conferring grace, apart from receiving the reality through faith, they are just signs.

Luther is emphatic that the sacraments actually accomplish salvation *and* equally emphatic that faith is necessary for receiving the reality that they convey. In a sermon on dying, he assures, "It is of the utmost importance that we highly esteem, honor, and rely upon the holy sacraments, which contain nothing but God's words, promises, and signs. This means that we have no doubts about the sacraments or the things of which they are certain signs, for if we doubt these we lose everything." Many say on their deathbed that Christ wiped out sin in general, or the sins of some, but not of them in particular. The sacraments assure them, "I did this *for you.*" But "the sacraments will be completely fruitless," he says, "if you do not believe the things that are indicated, given and promised to you." "Faith must be present for a firm reliance and cheerful venturing on such signs and promises of God. What sort of a God or Savior would he be who could not or would not save us from sin, death, and hell? Whatever the true God promises and effects must be something big."[17]

The Spirit creates faith through the Word, says Calvin. "But the sacraments bring the clearest promises."[18] "For baptism attests to us that we have been cleansed and washed; the Eucharistic Supper, that we have been redeemed."[19] Calvin saw in both Roman Catholic and Anabaptist views a common tendency to treat sacraments as human works. However, Calvin argues, "In Sacraments God alone properly acts; men bring nothing of their own."[20] God is the promise-maker. "Baptism testifies to us our purgation and ablution; the Eucharistic supper testifies our redemption. Water is a figure of ablution [washing], and blood of satisfaction."[21] Thus, there is no antithesis of grace and sacraments as means of grace.

Though he did not take it as far as the Anabaptists, Zwingli also assumed a dualism between sign and reality, spirit and matter, God's work and the church's ministry. "For faith springs not from things accessible to

---

17. Martin Luther, in his sermon "Preparing to Die" (1519) in *LW* 42:109–10.
18. *Inst.* 4.14.5.
19. *Inst.* 4.14.22.
20. Calvin, "Antidote to Trent," in *Acts of the Council of Trent: With the Antidote*, in *Selected Works of John Calvin: Tracts and Letters*, 7 vols., ed. Henry Beveridge and Jules Bonnet, trans. Henry Beveridge (Grand Rapids: Baker, 1983), 3:176.
21. *Inst.* 4.14.22.

sense nor are they objects of faith," he insisted.[22] However, Calvin early on rejected the contrast between "flesh" and "Spirit" as equivalent to "matter" and "spirit."[23] In short, he saw the physical aspect as the means chosen by God for delivering and strengthening the spiritual communion with Christ.[24] Once again, Calvin's conclusion was grounded in the incarnation: "For in his flesh was accomplished man's redemption."[25]

And, once again, it becomes clear that all of the *solae* converge on *solo Christo*. We do not ascend to God by reason, experience, or work, Luther argues; instead, we receive God in Christ hanging on a cross.[26] For Calvin as well as Luther, the repeated refrain is "Christ as he is clothed in the gospel."[27] Even the clarity and magisterial authority of Scripture alone is related inseparably to the fact that we receive salvation outside of ourselves, in Christ. Nor is *sola fide* a way of basing justification on an act of faith; rather, through the gift of faith alone we cling to Christ. The sacraments, too, are God's works, signs and seals of the gospel promise. And because we are reconciled to God in Christ alone, through the faith that the Spirit creates through the gospel and confirms through the sacraments, all glory is due to the triune God alone. Separate the other *solae* from *solo Christo* renders them entirely different claims. To convey the efficacy of the means of grace, Calvin often uses the verb *exhibēre*, which means to present, confer, or deliver.[28] The same view is summarized later in the Westminster Standards, referring to the sacraments as "effectual means of salvation."[29] This objectivity affirmed the scriptural emphasis on the baptism and the Lord's Supper as deepening our assurance of union with Christ and communion with his

---

22. Zwingli, *Commentary on True and False Religion*, ed. Samuel Macauley Jackson and Clarence Nevin Heller, trans. Samuel Macauley Jackson (Durham, NC: Labyrinth, 1981), 214. Of course, if followed consistently (which, happily, he did not do), one wonders how faith could come by *hearing* (Rom 10:17).

23. Calvin, *Calvin's Commentaries*, vol. 19, *Commentaries on the Epistles of Paul to the Galatians and Ephesians*, trans. John Owen (Grand Rapids: Baker, 1996), 224–25 (on Gal 6:6).

24. Willem Balke, *Calvin and the Anabaptist Radicals*, trans. William J. Heynen (Grand Rapids: Eerdmans, 1981), 53.

25. Calvin, *The Gospel according to John* 1:1–10, trans. Parker, 167.

26. Luther, "Heidelberg Disputation," in *LW* 31:38.

27. *Inst.* 3.2.32.

28. Calvin's view is nicely summarized in answer 65 of the Heidelberg Catechism: "The Holy Spirit produces [faith] in our hearts by the preaching of the holy gospel [Rom 10:17; 1 Pet 1:23–25] and confirms it through our use of the holy sacraments [Matt 28:19–20; 1 Cor 10:16]." The Heidelberg Catechism, LD 23, Q. 61, in *Ecumenical Creeds and Reformed Confessions* (Grand Rapids: CRC Publications, 1988).

29. Westminster Confession of Faith, 27; Shorter Catechism, 91–93; Longer Catechism, 161–64.

body. Nevertheless, the sacraments themselves do not effect this great work; the Spirit works through them as he pleases, and they cannot save apart from faith in Christ.

Over against nominalist and Neoplatonist dualism, Calvin critiques Trent's seventh session by insisting upon the interdependence of faith, word, and sacraments.[30] In other places I have explored Calvin's sacramental theology and, in particular, his view of the Eucharist.[31] I have only said enough here, I hope, to explain the crucial connection for the Reformers between justification and the external, visible, audible, and public means of grace through which believers are united to Christ and his redemptive work. In Reformation theology, the official ministry of word and sacrament is not set over against grace and justification. On the contrary, rather than works they are means of grace. If we want to be assured of our justification, we will do so by finding Christ where he has promised to give himself to us: in the preached word, in baptism, and in the Supper. It is the Son's incarnational descent and the Spirit's work of making us share in his ascent that ground the Reformers' thinking, despite critical differences concerning the way these mysteries operate.

JUSTIFICATION AND FAITH

The magisterial Reformers agreed that faith is the sole instrument of this justification, in contrast with all human virtues, works, and merits. Here, many have gone astray in their interpretation, claiming that Luther merely substituted one subjective act (faith) for another (love). In so doing, God's acceptance remains conditional, they argue.[32] However, once again, this misunderstands Luther's fundamental point. Not because of faith's intrinsic value (understood as a theological virtue) but because of *what it grasps*—namely, Christ—is faith the sole instrument of justification.

In Luther's Galatians lectures, he points out, "If faith does not justify without love, then faith is vain and useless, and love alone justifies." Why not then simply say "justified by love"?[33] Further, if love is the

---

30. Calvin, *Acts and Antidote*, 174, on canon 5, emphasis added.
31. Michael Horton, *People and Place* (Louisville: Westminster John Knox, 2008), 99–152; cf. *The Christian Faith* (Grand Rapids: Zondervan, 2011), 751–827.
32. Among many examples that could be cited, I have in mind especially Karl Barth, T. F. and James B. Torrance, and, most recently, Douglas A. Campbell.
33. Luther, *Lectures on Galatians 1535: Chapters 1–4*, ed. Walter A. Hansen (St. Louis, MO: Concordia, 1963), 136.

summary of the law, as Jesus and Paul affirm with Moses, then is not "justified by love" equivalent to "justified by the law"? However, when union with Christ—the marital "exchange"—is the dominant rubric, to say that faith is a condition is no more legalistic than is the bride's agreement to be married to the groom—her trust in his love and faithfulness to his promise. However, in this case, there is no symmetrical exchange of gifts. We come with debts and corruption and Christ brings his riches and Holy Spirit. In both cases, the focus is the great exchange, which is nothing less than Christ giving himself and his benefits to us, and receiving our liabilities as well. Jono Linebaugh shows persuasively that for Luther Christ is not only the object but is present in faith, giving himself to the sinner.[34] In the same way, Calvin says, "As regards justification, faith is something merely passive, bringing nothing of ours to the recovering of God's favor but receiving from Christ that which we lack."[35] Unlike love, faith merely receives. We come "empty-handed," he says.[36]

The value, then, is not the hand but what is received, Vermigli argues. "Suppose there were a beggar with a loathsome and leprous hand by which he received alms from one who offered them. Surely that beggar is not helped by the loathsomeness or leprosy of his hand, but by the alms he receives with it, whatever kind of hand he has."[37] "For as 'to justify' comes by way of judgment or accounting, to ascribe righteousness to someone and not make him just in reality, so 'to believe' is not (in truth) to make the words and promises of anyone sure and firm, but to think and determine within ourselves that they are such."[38] From the verb 'aman is the noun emunah: simply to reckon as certain and firm.[39] "Moreover," adds Vermigli, "if faith itself is considered our work, we cannot be justified by it, since as a work it is imperfect and flawed, far beneath what the law requires. But we are said to be justified by

---

34. Jonathan A. Linebaugh, "The Christo-Centrism of Faith in Christ: Martin Luther's Reading of Galatians 2:16, 19–20," *New Testament Studies* 59 (2013): 534–44. Luther writes, "If it is true faith, it is a sure trust and firm acceptance of the heart. It takes hold of Christ in such a way that Christ is the object of faith, or rather not the object but, so to speak, the One who is present in the faith itself" (*LW* 26:129).

35. *Inst.* 3.13.5.

36. *Inst.* 3.11.7, 10, 18; cf. 2.7.8.

37. Peter Martyr Vermigli, *Locus on Justification*, in *Predestination and Justification: Two Theological Loci*, trans. and ed. Frank A. James III, Peter Martyr Library 8 (Kirksville, MO: Sixteenth Century Essays & Studies, 2003), 96.

38. Vermigli, *Locus on Justification*, 88–89.

39. Vermigli, *Locus on Justification*, 90.

[faith] because through it we take hold (*apprehendimus*) of the promises of God and the righteousness and merits of Christ, and apply them to ourselves."[40] The Father sent Christ to accomplish what we could not, Vermigli argues. He did not send the Spirit in this instance to help us fulfill the law, but sent Christ to fulfill it for us.[41]

This oft-repeated point counters the caricature of Douglas Campbell and many others today who conclude that the magisterial Reformers and their heirs taught a contractual and conditional view of justification. To be sure, faith is the condition of justification in the way that receiving a gift is the condition of possessing it. And even this condition is fulfilled by God's gracious gift. Faith then is *not* a smaller work that merits justification. It is not a qualifying work at all; it is casting oneself upon God's mercy in Christ. It is not because of any virtue inhering in faith itself, but due entirely to the virtue of what is grasped, that one is justified. In their view, faith is the instrument, not the basis, of justification.

This orientation stood in sharp contrast not only with Rome but with the radical Protestants.[42] Though more radical in other ways, Anabaptist views on justification were similar to Rome's.[43] Both understood justification as a process of inner transformation rather than as God's free acquittal of sinners for the sake of Christ and his imputation of Christ's righteousness to their account.

The fourth article of the Augsburg Confession teaches that human beings "cannot be justified before God by their own strength, merits, or works, but are freely justified for Christ's sake, through faith, when they believe that they are received into favor, and that their sins are forgiven for Christ's sake, who, by His death, has made satisfaction for our sins." One of the clearest summaries of the evangelical doctrine of justification is found in chapter 13 of the Westminster Confession:

---

40. Vermigli, *Locus on Justification*, 96.
41. Vermigli, *Locus on Justification*, 103–104, commenting on Rom 8:3.
42. *Inst.* 3.3.14: "Certain Anabaptists of our day conjure some sort of frenzied excess instead of spiritual regeneration," Calvin relates, thinking that they can attain perfection in this life.
43. Thomas A. Finger, *A Contemporary Anabaptist Theology: Biblical, Historical, Constructive* (Downers Grove, IL: InterVarsity, 2004), 109. Contemporary Anabaptist theologian Thomas Finger observes, "Robert Friedmann found 'A forensic view of grace, in which the sinner is . . . undeservedly justified . . . simply unacceptable' to Anabaptists. A more nuanced scholar like Arnold Snyder can assert that historic Anabaptists 'never talked about being "justified by faith."'" Finger believes that Anabaptist soteriological emphases (especially on divinization) can bring greater unity especially between marginalized Protestant groups (Pentecostals and Quakers) and Orthodox and Roman Catholic theologies of salvation (110). Finger observes that recent Anabaptist reflection is no more marked in its interest in this topic than its antecedents, with discipleship ("following Jesus") and the inner transformation of the believer as central (132–33).

Those whom God effectually calls, he also freely justifies: not by infusing righteousness into them, but by pardoning their sins and by accounting and accepting their persons as righteous; not for anything wrought in them or done by them, but for Christ's sake alone; *not by imputing faith itself, the act of believing, or any other evangelical obedience to them as their righteousness*; but by imputing the obedience and satisfaction of Christ unto them, they receiving and resting on him and his righteousness by faith; which faith they have not of themselves, it is the gift of God. Faith, thus receiving and resting on Christ and his righteousness, is the sole instrument of justification; yet is it not alone in the person justified, but is ever accompanied with all other saving graces, and is no dead faith, but works by love.

The justified may fall into grave sin and "fall under God's Fatherly displeasure," but they "can never fall from the state of justification."[44] Notice what the confession excludes from the ground of justification: not only anything "done by them" but "anything wrought *in them*," even by God himself. Again, the question is not merely monergism versus synergism. Not even God's regenerating grace, though necessary to believe in Christ, is the basis for justification. Not because one is regenerated or because grace is at work in the soul but "for Christ's sake alone" is one justified.

The Heidelberg Catechism too emphasizes that this divine verdict has Christ's righteousness, not ours, as its basis. Through faith alone we who "have grievously sinned against all the commandments of God and have not kept any one of them" are nevertheless regarded as though we had never sinned and had perfectly kept the commands. Not even the gift of faith itself can be considered the ground of justification but simply the empty hand that receives it.[45] Similar summaries can be found in the Anglican Thirty-Nine Articles and the London/Philadelphia (Baptist) Confession. Yet with the longest decree at the Council of Trent, Rome officially anathematized this understanding.[46]

Drawing on key confessional passages, Robert Preus points out that Lutherans distinguish but do not separate regeneration from justification.

---

44. Westminster Confession of Faith, in *The Book of Confessions* (Louisville: PCUSA, 1991), ch. 13, emphasis added. This last point differs from the Lutheran view, with the possibility of finally apostatizing and thus losing one's justification.

45. The Heidelberg Catechism, LD 23–24, Q. 60–64, in *Psalter Hymnal*, 30–31.

46. *Canons and Decrees of the Council of Trent: Original Text with English Translation*, trans. H. J. Schroeder, OP (St Louis: Herder, 1960), 43, 45–46.

The moment faith is brought into the picture of a sinner's justification before God, regeneration is brought into the picture, too; for regeneration is the gift of faith. Justification by faith *involves* regeneration to faith (cf. Apology IV, 117). Apparently some confusion developed over Melanchthon's linking justification to regeneration so closely. The Formula of Concord (Solid Declaration II, 19) cleared up this difficulty: "Since the word 'regeneration' is used in place of 'justification,' it is necessary to explain the term strictly so that the renewal which follows justification by faith will not be confused with justification."[47]

At issue here is, on one hand, the recognition (with Aquinas and, indeed, Scripture and the whole tradition) that, in order to believe, those "dead in trespasses and sins" (Eph 2:1) must be regenerated—made alive—and, on the other hand, the distinction between this inner renewal and justification. This is why the citation from the Westminster Confession above excludes from the *ground* of justification "anything wrought in us," while nevertheless acknowledging that regeneration precedes faith. Like the Lutherans, the Reformed were refining their account in such a way as to account for both of those important points. Although one must be regenerated in order to believe, regeneration is not *the reason* for justification.

The need to distinguish justification and regeneration more clearly was pressed upon the Lutherans particularly because of the teachings of Andreas Osiander and because of Trent. The Formula of Concord (Solid Declaration 3.17) especially set out to clarify the definition: "Accordingly the word 'justify' here means to declare righteous and free from sins and from the eternal punishment of these sins on account of the righteousness of Christ which God reckons to faith (Phil. 3:9). And this is the usual usage and meaning of the word in the Holy Scriptures of the Old and New Testaments."[48] It is *iustitia aliena*. "It is a righteousness that comes from God (Rom 1:17), but it is not His essential righteousness."

Nor the righteousness by which He redeems them from their sins. Rather, this divine righteousness revealed in the Gospel is the

---

47. Robert Preus, *Justification and Rome* (St. Louis: Concordia Academic Press, 1997), 65, referring to Apology, Art. 4, and Formula of Concord, 3–6.
48. Quoted by Preus, *Justification and Rome*, 57.

righteousness of His Son Jesus Christ. But again, it is not Christ's essential righteousness, the righteousness of His divine nature. It is rather the righteousness of Christ, the God Man, which He fulfilled and accomplished and acquired for us. It is the saving righteousness [dikaiosynē] of His obedience [dikaiōma, hypakoē] to the Father (Rom 5:18–19; Phil 2:8; Heb 5:8), His obedience under the Law (Gal 4:4), by which He obeyed the Law as our Substitute [hyper hēmōn], and obeyed the will of the Father to die innocently as our Substitute, and thus to redeem us (Gal 3:13).[49]

Preus notes, "Luther's discovery of the meaning of 'righteousness' in Romans 1:17 was a discovery also of the *justitia aliena* which was at the heart of justification."[50]

We are therefore a great distance from discourse on substances, causes, habits, infusions, and various subsets of each. Justification is a particular gift that we have in Christ alone, received through faith alone. It is a legal decision but not a legal fiction. Unlike the arbitrary decree of the nominalist deity, this justification is the most real event imaginable. Its ground is the covenantal obedience, faithfulness, and merits of God incarnate. This righteousness—the Messiah's faithfulness—is really imputed or credited to real sinners. We are no longer in the ambit of created substances but of an exchange between persons: rags for a robe, debts for an inheritance, curse for blessing, death for life, condemnation for justification. Everything that we had in Adam, which included our own debts, is transferred to Christ, and everything that he possesses is transferred to his people. Even the faith to embrace Christ comes with, and is strengthened by, the gift of Christ himself as he is delivered through his word and sacraments.

Lutheran and Reformed orthodoxy would return to some of these categories of high scholasticism (such as infused habits), not (*pace* Ritschl) because they were diverging from the purity of Luther's putative "postmetaphysical" system but because debates—internal and external—pressed confessional theologians to articulate the transformative aspect of salvation (viz., regeneration/sanctification). Here talk

---

49. Preus, *Justification and Rome*, 59.

50. Preus, *Justification and Rome*, 59–60. The same is true of the Reformed tradition, as in the Canons of the Synod of Dort, Heads 3 and 4, Articles 4 and 11, where the language of infused habits is used in relation to regeneration. The Holy Spirit by the gospel "infuses new qualities into the will, which, though heretofore dead, He quickens" (Art. 11, *Psalter Hymnal*, 105).

of "infused habits" could be used as long as they did not encroach into justification territory. Further, we must not assume that these categories meant precisely what they meant in a system like that of Aquinas, since some of the underlying assumptions (especially anthropological) were quite different.[51]

FAITH AND WORKS

"Because of justification," according to Puritan theologian William Ames, "the defilement of good works does not prevent their being accepted and rewarded by God."[52] Again, the Reformation did not oppose faith to works in an abstract way but with respect to the concrete question of how one is justified. Counterintuitively, genuinely good works are possible only by justification apart from works. This teaching of justification cannot be used to defend moral carelessness, according to the Heidelberg Catechism, "for it is impossible for those who are engrafted into Christ by true faith not to bring forth the fruit of gratitude."[53] The gospel creates faith and faith yields the fruit of good works. The Reformers insisted that if we confuse this order, we lose both faith and works in the process.

The restriction of the "works of the law" in Paul to ceremonies (i.e., boundary markers separating Jews from gentiles) is far from being a new perspective. We have seen that this was the tack taken by Origen in order to allow *some* works to merit justification—namely, spiritual works (performed through the Spirit)—as opposed to external observances. "They prate that the ceremonial works of the law are excluded, not the moral works . . . [but] let us hold as certain that when the ability to justify is denied to the law, these words refer to the whole law," Calvin says.[54]

Calvin thinks that the Origenist line adopted by Trent denigrates the Old Testament believers and breaks the continuity of the Abrahamic

---

51. It is for this reason that I find unpersuasive the attempt to display commonalities between Aquinas and Calvin on justification and merit in Charles Raith II, "Portraits of Paul: Aquinas and Calvin on Romans 7:14–25," in *Reading Romans with St. Thomas Aquinas*, ed. Matthew Levering and Michael Dauphinais (Washington, DC: Catholic University of America Press, 2012), 238–61; cf. Raith's longer essay, *Aquinas and Calvin on Romans: God's Justification and Our Participation* (New York: Oxford University Press, 2014). On many related points, Augustine is a common debt. However, the paradigms of discourse at least on justification are too different to allow such facile attempts at synthesis.

52. William Ames, *Marrow of Theology*, trans. John D. Eusden (Durham: Labyrinth, 1983), 171.

53. The Heidelberg Catechism, LD 23–24, Q. 60–64, in *Psalter Hymnal*, 30–31.

54. *Inst.* 3.11.19; cf. 3.19.3.

covenant, which was founded on God's promise as opposed to the works of the law. On Romans 1:17 he says, "Whereas many think there is under these words a secret comparing of the Old with the New Testament, that is more subtle than firm." On the contrary, Paul is highlighting the unity that we have with our old covenant forbearers "from faith to faith." "From faith to faith" for Thomas Aquinas and Nicholas of Lyra was hardly historical; it is individualized and allegorized to mean the movement from *fides informis* to *fides formata*.[55] As Luther pointed out, this is ridiculous: for one, how could anyone be justified by unformed faith (mere assent to propositions, in Aquinas's view)—it is not actually faith at all.[56]

Luther inveighed especially against the Scotist and nominalist idea that even apart from grace one is capable of loving God above all else and therefore of meriting justification.[57] "The [Old Testament] fathers had the same faith as we," Luther says. "There is only one faith, though it may have been less clear to them, just as today the scholars have the same faith as the laymen, only more clearly."[58]

Carlson has referred to "the quiescence of the Pauline doctrine of justification in the Middle Ages." These writers tended to see Paul's debate over "works of the law" simply as "records of controversies in the apostolic Church in which the issues had long since been settled and held no contemporary urgency."[59] Who after all is arguing today that people need to be circumcised? "And in this frame of reference," as Carlson notes, "justification seems to pertain only to the removal of original and prior actual sin. After this occurrence, works are enjoined to 'fulfill' the faith which alone no longer suffices to maintain the state of grace gained in justification, but must 'work by love.'"[60] Calvin directly rejects even Augustine's interpretation of this passage. Paul is not referring to justification, the Reformer says, but the fruit of justification: for those justified through faith alone (as Paul has argued up to this point), what matters are not exclusionary policies (like circumcision

---

55. Charles P. Carlson, Jr., *Justification in Earlier Medieval Theology* (The Hague: Martinus Nijhoff, 1975), 74.

56. Carlson, *Justification in Earlier Medieval Theology*, 74, quoting Luther's *Lectures on Romans*, in WA 56:172ff.

57. Carlson, *Justification in Earlier Medieval Theology*, 75n136.

58. Carlson, *Justification in Earlier Medieval Theology*, 76, quoting Luther's "Lectures on Romans," in WA 56:173.

59. Carlson, *Justification in Earlier Medieval Theology*, 76.

60. Carlson, *Justification in Earlier Medieval Theology*, 69.

and dietary laws) but "faith working by love." In fact, this passage merely confirms the Reformation's insistence that the gospel produces faith, which justifies, and the fruit is love and good works.[61]

Whereas Luther affirms the necessary *link* between faith and love (as well as obedience), Bruce Marshall thinks that the Reformer believes that faith *is* love.[62] But this is wishful thinking on Marshall's part. According to Luther, it is not because faith *is* love but because faith grasps *Christ* that it necessarily yields love and good works. "Therefore," Luther said, faith "is also a very mighty, active, restless, busy thing, which at once renews a man, gives him a second birth, and introduces him to a new manner and way of life, so that it is impossible for him not to do good without ceasing. For as naturally as a tree bears fruit good works follow upon faith."[63] I must say that perhaps the most confusing element in all of these controversies for me is the apparent inability of Roman Catholics (as well as Orthodox and many Protestants) to affirm two distinct things as inseparable without making them one and the same thing.

The whole Reformation debate comes down to this: according to the Reformers, salvation includes *both* a purely forensic justification *and* a regenerating and sanctifying renovation, while Rome *rejects* the former by simply assimilating it to the latter. We receive a "twofold grace" in union with Christ—justification and sanctification—as Calvin argues at the beginning of book 3 of the *Institutes* and as Luther had in "Two Kinds of Righteousness." However, even within this union there is a logical dependence of sanctification on justification. If our assurance of the latter depended on the former, we would indeed be presumptuous to consider ourselves regenerate, as Trent alleges. Indeed, he adds in his *Antidote*, "So long as we look at what we are in ourselves, we must tremble in the sight of God, so far from having a firm and unshakable confidence of eternal life. I speak of the regenerate; for how far from righteousness is that newness of life which is begun here below?"[64]

---

61. See Calvin on Rom 3:28 for his criticism of the "faith working through love" interpretation, directly rejecting Augustine and Rabanus, in *Calvin's New Testament Commentaries*, vol. 8, *Romans and Thessalonians*, trans. Ross Mackenzie (Grand Rapids: Eerdmans, 1996), 79–80. Also see Calvin on Rom 3:21.

62. Bruce Marshall, "Justification as Declaration and Deification," *International Journal of Systematic Theology* 4, no. 1 (2002): 3–28. See Michael Allen, *Justification and the Gospel: Understanding the Context and Controversies* (Grand Rapids: Baker Academic, 2013), 49–52.

63. Martin Luther, *Commentary on Romans*, trans. J. Theodore Mueller (Grand Rapids: Zondervan, 1954), xvii.

64. Calvin, *Acts and Antidote*, 115.

Justification and sanctification are constantly conjoined and cohere, but from this it is erroneously inferred that they are one and the same. . . . We acknowledge, then, that as soon as any one is justified renewal also necessarily follows: and there is no dispute as to whether or not Christ sanctifies all whom he justifies. It were to rend the gospel and divide Christ himself to attempt to separate the righteousness which we obtain by faith from repentance. The whole dispute is as to the *cause* of justification.[65]

He adds,

For they again affirm that we are truly righteous and not merely counted so. I, on the contrary, while I admit that we are never received into the favour of God without being at the same time regenerated to holiness of life, contend that it is false to say that any part of righteousness (justification) consists *in quality* or in the habit which resides in us and that we are righteous (justified) only by gratuitous acceptance.[66]

Calvin simply does not understand why Trent forces such a false choice: either justification as forgiveness and imputation alone or reject sanctification and repentance. "It is just as if they were to say that forgiveness of sins cannot be dissevered from repentance, and therefore repentance is part of it."[67] Trent's argument is tantamount to saying that the claim that one sees with his eyes he denies that he can hear as well. We encounter the same argument today, for example from John Milbank, who tirelessly repeats the charge that among "the peculiar errors of Protestantism" is the view that Christ "extrinsically makes them good, without real, inward reworking of our nature."[68] "For the Reformation," he says, "salvation came primarily by the pathetic gesture of 'faith' and no longer through the infused habit of charity."[69] But of course Lutheran and Reformed traditions have a robust view of regeneration and sanctification, which also belong to *salvation*, so this

---

65. Calvin, *Acts and Antidote*, 116, emphasis added.
66. Calvin, *Acts and Antidote*, 117.
67. Calvin, *Acts and Antidote*, 118.
68. John Milbank, *Beyond Secular Order: The Representation of Being and the Representation of the People* (Oxford: Wiley-Blackwell, 2013), 79.
69. Milbank, *Beyond Secular Order*, 225.

is pure caricature. Their scholastic theologians even spoke of infused habits without apology, as long as they were not conceived as the basis for justification.[70]

For Calvin the inseparable bond between justification and sanctification was found in his emphasis on union with Christ. To be united to Christ through faith is to receive all the benefits of his incarnation, obedience, death, resurrection, and glorification. Yet it is no less the case that for him justification was the foundation for sanctification.[71] Canon 10 of Trent's sixth session condemns the view "that we are formally righteous by the obedience of Christ" even though "They formerly asserted in their decrees that the righteousness of God was the only formal cause of justification."[72] Canon 11 rejects justification through faith as if it were opposed to works, but Calvin replies, "It is therefore faith alone which justifies, and yet the faith which justifies is not alone."[73]

Calvin appeals to Augustine and Bernard, among others, for his conclusion that we find all of our justifying righteousness in Christ and none in ourselves.[74] The law of God arraigns us before God's judgment,

---

70. For example, the phrase even appears in a Reformed symbol. The Canons of Dort teach that in regeneration the Holy Spirit "infuses new qualities into the will" (Art. 11, *Psalter Hymnal*, 104). It also condemns the view "that in the true conversion of man no new qualities, powers, or gifts can be infused by God into the will" and that faith therefore "is not a quality or gift infused by God but only an act of man" (Third and Fourth Heads, Rejection of Errors, para. 6, p. 108). Here the Reformed are drawing on Thomistic teaching to refute the Arminians.

71. Here I am taking some exception to the view articulated well by Craig B. Carpenter, "A Question of Union with Christ? Calvin and Trent on Justification," *Westminster Theological Journal* 64 (2002): 363–86. "However, Calvin's view is not most fully articulated in his 'Antidote to the Council of Trent—1547,' as Rome's view is by the Council's official decrees" (371). "The question might then be raised: to what extent does appealing to Calvin promote a rapprochement between Protestants and Roman Catholics?" At least it "leads one to doubt that, if he were alive today, he would level his polemic against Roman Catholic soteriology on the precise sequence of salvation's renovative and juridical aspects in the believer. This, however, is precisely what many Protestant apologists who identify themselves with Calvin have historically done and what some are doing with respect to ECT and 'The Gift of Salvation.' Just as he did in his own day, I suspect that Calvin would spend more energy challenging Rome's view of sin and depravity, on the one hand, and of union with Christ, on the other, always underscoring the controlling significance of this union for every saving benefit, including justification by faith" (386). Carpenter is correct to see union with Christ as the overarching framework, but Calvin typically introduces this topic whenever the objection is raised that a purely forensic justification leaves no room for sanctification. Carpenter even acknowledges that one must turn to the 1559 *Institutes* (beginning of book 3) for an explicit treatment of union with Christ but tries to read too much of it into the *Antidote*. Calvin simply saw no tension between invoking union with Christ and seeing justification as the basis for sanctification within that *ordo salutis*. The *Antidote* itself does a fine job of underscoring that point.

72. Calvin, *Acts and Antidote*, 151.

73. Calvin, *Acts and Antidote*, 152.

74. *Inst.* 3.12.3.

leaving us with no hope. Because of our turpitude, the law cannot provide the righteousness that it commands. "Removing, then, mention of law, and laying aside all consideration of works, we should, when justification is being discussed, embrace God's mercy alone, turn our attention from ourselves, and look only to Christ. . . . If consciences wish to attain any certainty in this matter, they ought to give no place to the law."[75]

What then do we make of the host of passages that speak of being judged according to works? Vermigli responds that, in adducing passages from the Gospels, the papal party treats as causes what are in fact antecedents. One example is Matthew 25:35, where the sheep are welcomed as those who cared for their persecuted brothers and sisters. "Yet Christ does not in fact mention these things [they did] as causes, but rather as antecedents: 'Come you blessed of my Father, possess the kingdom prepared for you since the beginning of the world.' The true cause of our felicity is that we are elected and predestined by God to an eternal inheritance. . . . For no one can be so ignorant as not to know there are two principles of things: one by which they exist, the other by which they are known."[76] Repentance follows faith.[77] The prodigal returned conceiving all sorts of preparations and satisfactions that might curry his father's favor (Luke 15:11–17). However, the father would not allow such servile relationship but met the son when he was still a long way off, embraced him in his arms and held a feast.[78]

The Reformers did not simply oppose human actions (works) and divine actions (grace) in an abstract (indeed, nominalist) manner. Markus Bockmuehl seems to ascribe a similar interpretation to the Reformers when he says, "But Paul's point in the whole chapter is not so much that Abraham was a scoundrel before he was justified, but that he was *not circumcised*. . . . The Reformers' application of this principle to the idea of earning God's favor with good works may well be true *by extension*, but it is not what is intended here in the first place."[79]

But the Reformers never held that Abraham was a scoundrel. In any event, their point did not require that he be unsavory. Paul's statement that Abraham was justified before he was circumcised serves his

75. *Inst.* 3.19.2
76. Vermigli, *Locus on Justification*, 135, referring to Aristotle, *Analytica posteriora* 19.99b.17ff.
77. Vermigli, *Locus on Justification*, 136.
78. Vermigli, *Locus on Justification*, 137.
79. Markus Bockmuehl, "Aquinas on Abraham's Faith in Romans 4" in *Reading Romans with St. Thomas Aquinas*, ed. Matthew Levering and Michael Dauphinais (Washington, DC: Catholic University of America Press, 2012), 43.

larger argument that *no works of the law* provided a condition for his justification—which entails that gentiles cannot now be excluded. More specifically, the Reformers understood Scripture to oppose the merits of believers to the merits of Christ. In contrast with Marcion and many liberal theologians today, they did not believe that God was only loving and merciful; they knew that he was also just and righteous. Not only did transgressions have to be punished, but God's law had to be fulfilled. And just as this righteousness had been lost in Adam, it had to be fulfilled by a human representative.

The Reformers did not therefore do away with the notion of merit. Luther, Calvin, and the other Reformers speak repeatedly of Christ having merited our salvation. There is therefore no "legal fiction" involved. Justification is not a bare declaration without any foundation in reality, as Scotus and Ockham taught. Furthermore, Calvin attributes this not only to Christ's atoning sacrifice (which would only have yielded forgiveness) but to his lifelong obedience (meriting a positive status by fulfilling the law in our place). This is one of Calvin's criticisms of Osiander. Our Savior not only had to be fully human and sinless in order to be the *appropriate sacrifice for sin*; in that humanity he had to *fulfill all righteousness*.

Thus justification is not only forgiveness (i.e., not imputing our sins to us), but the positive imputation of Christ's merits. As François Wendel observes, "Calvin goes on to point out that it is by the obedience of Christ that we are justified, but that he could not have manifested that obedience except in his quality as a servant; that is, according to his human nature."[80] In his obedience, he offered his merits, and in handing his body over to death, he offered himself as a sacrifice for sin. All of this he could do only as a human servant. Christ discharged the office of covenant head, claiming by right (condign merit) that status of perfect justice which he shares with his body.

Calvin believed that the Epistle to the Romans can be summarized as saying "that man's only righteousness is through the mercy of God in Christ, which being offered by the Gospel is apprehended by faith."[81] There will be rewards, but "it is an absurd inference to deduce merit

---

80. François Wendel, *Calvin: Origins and Development of His Religious Thought*, trans. Philip Mairet (Durham: Labyrinth, 1987), 260.

81. Calvin, *Commentaries on the Epistle of Paul the Apostle to the Romans*, trans. and ed. John Owen (rep., Grand Rapids: Baker, 1996), xxix–xxx.

from reward."[82] Calvin was aware of the exegesis of Romans 2:13 ("For it is not the hearers of the law but the doers who are justified") that defended justification (at least, final justification) by works. "They who pervert this passage for the purpose of building up justification by works deserve most fully to be laughed at even by children," he wrote. It is obvious from Paul's argument that the passage's purpose is to show that the Jews were in fact under the law's curse along with the gentiles for *failing to do* what the law requires, "so that another righteousness must be sought."[83] Not only the ceremonies but the whole law—including the moral law—is included when Paul opposes the law to faith as the way of justification.[84] "For if there be any righteousness by the law or by works, it must be in men themselves; but by faith they derive from another what is wanting in themselves; and hence the righteousness of faith is rightly called imputative."[85] Thus, once more, faith as the means turns us outside, to Christ, whereas works (even faith as a virtuous basis, much less identified with love) drives us deeper into ourselves.

Also echoing Luther—and, more importantly, Paul—Calvin insists that the logic of works-righteousness (what Luther called a "theology of glory") is opposed to the logic of righteousness through faith alone. Intuitively, we know that good people go to heaven and bad people go to hell; that God cannot declare someone righteous who is at that moment inherently unrighteous. We have to examine the actual state of affairs and judge people by what we see. However, the gospel is counterintuitive. Here, God's promise must override our moral sensibilities, which judge by appearances. With Abraham, faith clings to a promise, against all human "possibilities":

> All things around us are in opposition to the promises of God: He promises immortality; we are surrounded with mortality and corruption: He declares that he counts us as just; we are covered with our sins: He testifies that he is propitious and kind to us; outward judgments threaten his wrath. What then is to be done? We must with closed eyes pass by ourselves and all things connected with us, that nothing may hinder or prevent us from believing that God is true.[86]

---

82. Calvin, *Commentaries on the Epistle of Paul the Apostle to the Romans*, 90.
83. Calvin, *Commentaries on the Epistle of Paul the Apostle to the Romans*, 95–96.
84. Calvin, *Commentaries on the Epistle of Paul the Apostle to the Romans*, 151.
85. Calvin, *Commentaries on the Epistle of Paul the Apostle to the Romans*, 155.
86. Calvin, *Commentaries on the Epistle of Paul the Apostle to the Romans*, 180.

When Paul speaks of Christ being crucified for our sins and raised for our justification in Romans 4:25, Calvin observes, "For if justification means renovation, then that he died for our sins must be taken in the same sense, as signifying that he acquired for us grace to mortify the flesh, which no one admits. . . . He therefore still speaks of imputative justification."[87] No more than the careless unbeliever does "the Pharisee" know this peace with God through justification.[88] There are no "preparations" of our own that can give us "access" to God.[89]

The Council of Trent cites Paul's reference in Galatians 5:6 to "faith working by love" in support of the distinction between unformed and formed faith. The former is mere assent, but it does not become justifying until it becomes formed by love. But here Paul is not talking about justification but about its fruit. "For if love is the fruit and effect of faith," Calvin argues, "who sees not that the informal [unformed] faith which they have fabricated is a vain figment?" Mere assent is not faith at all. Here Paul is talking about sanctification, not justification.[90]

According to Calvin, the direct referent of "faith operating through love" (πίστις δι' ἀγάπης ἐνεργουμένη) is not justification, but the identifying marker that one belongs to Christ; it is not the demand for circumcision, which has been the occasion for exclusivism and division, but faith that designates one a member of the covenant—a faith that works not by proud pretensions but by love. If we are justified by grace alone, in Christ alone, through faith alone, then how can we exclude gentiles? It is at this point where Calvin (like Luther) comes off as a "new perspective" exegete. "Faith working by love" is not the definition of justification, however, but of the practical (ecclesiological) implication.

Karla Wübbenhorst observes that "Calvin is undoubtedly a disciple of the Lutheran evangelical movement," and nowhere is this clearer than in his "teaching on justification."[91]

In his comments on Romans 3:21 and 5:5, Calvin explicitly rejects Augustinian exegesis. Romans 5:5 speaks of the love of God being shed abroad in our hearts by the Holy Spirit. Augustine interprets

---

87. Calvin, *Commentaries on the Epistle of Paul the Apostle to the Romans*, 186.
88. Calvin, *Commentaries on the Epistle of Paul the Apostle to the Romans*, 187.
89. Calvin, *Commentaries on the Epistle of Paul the Apostle to the Romans*, 188.
90. Calvin, *Acts and Antidote*, 119.
91. Karla Wübbenhorst, "Calvin's Doctrine of Justification: Variations on a Lutheran Theme," in *Justification in Perspective; Historical Developments and Contemporary Challenges*, ed. Bruce L. McCormack (Grand Rapids: Baker Academic, 2006), 99.

"the love of God" in the "active sense"—as *human beings' love for God*. Calvin remarks that "Augustine . . . is mistaken in his view" and that "love is . . . to be taken here in . . . a passive sense"—as *God's love for human beings*—a wonderful truth of which Christians become more and more convinced as the Holy Spirit increases their faith. Augustine is one of those of whom Calvin says, "They place the efficacy of justification in love, though in words they ascribe it to faith."[92]

Also at Romans 3:21 Calvin adds,

> It is not unknown to me that Augustine gives a different explanation; for he thinks that the righteousness of God is the grace of regeneration; and this grace he allows to be free, because God renews us, when unworthy, by his Spirit; and from this he excludes the works of the law, that is, those works by which men of themselves endeavor, without renovation, to render God indebted to them. . . . But that the Apostle includes all works without exception, even those which the Lord produces in his own people, is evident from the context.

Critics say that the word "only" cannot be inserted here, he continues. "But if justification depends not either on the law, or on ourselves, why should it not be ascribed to mercy alone? And if it be from mercy only, it is then by faith only."[93]

Not even love can be added to (or be made a perfection of) faith, the Reformers insisted. After all, the command to love is the *summary* of the law. "It were long and troublesome to note every blunder, but there is one too important to be omitted," Calvin continues. "They add, 'that when catechumens ask faith from the Church,' the answer is, 'If you will enter into life, keep the commandments' (Matt. 19:17)."

> Wo to their catechumens, if so hard a condition is laid upon them! For what else is this but to lay them under an eternal curse, since they acknowledge with Paul that all are under a curse who are subject to the law (Gal iii.10)? But they have the authority of Christ!

---

92. Wübbenhorst, "Calvin's Doctrine of Justification," 107.
93. Wübbenhorst, "Calvin's Doctrine of Justification," 110–11.

I wish they would observe to what intent Christ thus spoke. This can only be ascertained from the context, and the character of the persons. He to whom Christ replies had asked, "What must I do to have eternal life?" Assuredly, whoever wishes to merit eternal life by works has a rule prescribed to him by the law: "This do and you will live." But attention must be paid to the object of this as intimated by Paul, viz., that man experiencing his powers, or rather convinced of his powerlessness, may lay aside his pride and flee all naked to Christ. There is no room for that righteousness of faith until we have discovered that it is in vain that salvation is promised us by the law. . . . But so preposterous are the Fathers of Trent that while it is the office of Moses to lead us by the hand to Christ (Gal iii.24), they lead us from the grace of Christ to Moses.[94]

So once again Trent is condemning a view that nobody (at least among the Reformers) holds. Faith itself does not save. Christ saves through faith, and even that is a gift. "Hence it is that faith, however imperfect, nevertheless possesses a perfect righteousness, because it has respect to nothing but the gratuitous goodness of God."[95]

This last comment leads us to the question of the nature of faith. As we have seen, Luther was not the first to insert *alone* in Romans 3:28. It is there even in Origen, as a manifest implication of Paul's argument, and my quotations in chapters 1–2 demonstrate the repeated affirmations of justification through "faith alone" across a wide spectrum of patristic sources. But the *sola* was even included in New Testament *translations* before Luther. Michael Schmaus notes, "The translation of the Bible that appeared in 1483 had rendered Galatians 2:16: 'justified only by faith.' Three Italian editions of Scripture (Genoa, 1476; Venice, 1583 and 1546) offered a similar translation. In a gloss to 1 Timothy 1:8, Thomas Aquinas had explained that justification is not the result of fulfilling the law, but is received through faith alone."[96] "In his work 'On Justification' [*De justificatione* 1.25, in *De controversiis*, vol. 4], Cardinal Bellarmine cited a series of Fathers and Church documents as witnesses to the formula 'by faith alone.'" And yet, in line with Trent, Schmaus

---

94. Calvin, *Acts and Antidote*, 120.
95. Calvin, *Acts and Antidote,* 125.
96. Michael Schmaus, *Dogma*, vol. 6, *Justification and Last Things* (London: Sheed and Ward, 1977), 29.

adds, "In the light of this usage it is clear that the formula should not be taken literally, without adverting to its full sense."[97]

We have seen that the majority consensus of the high scholastics was that faith is incomplete (mere assent) until it is perfected by love. When the Reformers refer to *sola fide,* however, they are saying that not only the beginning but the continuation and completion of salvation is due entirely to that union with Christ that we obtain through faith. Even Schmaus interprets the concordance between Paul and James in the way that Melanchthon, Calvin, and other Reformers had done. James is not opposed to Paul, he says, for the context is different. The community had accepted justification by faith alone, but believed mistakenly that works "are altogether superfluous," so James is warning them that such faith is "ineffective."[98] In short, Reformation theologies give a large place to hope and love alongside faith; sanctification alongside justification. But faith remains the sole medium of that union with Christ that renders believers beneficiaries of all gifts.

The question is not temporal but logical. Of course, there are virtues present alongside faith in the act of justification. Trust implies humility, hope, and indeed even love. In fact, there could be no conversion (repentance and faith) without regeneration (call it an infusion of grace, if you will). Augustinian theologies, whether Roman Catholic or Protestant, have emphasized that point, in fact, over against semi-Pelagianism for many centuries. The difference is that in the Roman Catholic view the logical *dependence* of justification on regeneration entails justification-*as*-regeneration. Ordinarily for most couples, one hopes, love is a prerequisite for marriage; however, they are not married through love but through some sort of official and legal ceremony in which vows are exchanged. While the Reformation view revels in transformation as well as imputation, alternative views press a false choice between them.

---

97. Schmaus, *Dogma*, 6:29–30.
98. Schmaus, *Dogma*, 6:30–31.

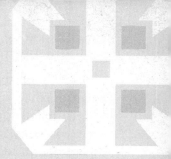

CHAPTER 10

LAW AND GOSPEL

A Tale of Two Covenants

Like two breasts, the Old and New Testaments are united by the fact that "both hold out rewards for those who labour," Gabriel Biel preached.[1] But the new law justifies because Christ calls us to interior and voluntary acts. The righteousness of Christians must exceed that of the scribes and Pharisees both in the number of acts and the sincerity with which they are performed; assisted as we are by effective sacraments, the new law carries greater obligation. "In short, the Law of Christ is the fulfillment of the Law of Moses inasmuch as it implies the interiorization of righteousness." Thus for Biel, Oberman says, "The righteousness of the New Law is in the full sense of the word legal righteousness."[2] "Whereas the literal sense of the Law—that is the Law without grace—kills, the spiritual sense of the Law conforms to the Gospel, which is the same Law—except for the ceremonial and judicial laws—but now with grace."[3] The eternal rest to which Jesus invites in Matthew 11:28 is a "free" gift indeed, but only for those who "prepare themselves, taking into consideration the necessary conditions attached to this promise."[4] "Christ has fulfilled and perfected the law of Moses in order that He might be imitated. The New Law is the *Lex imitationis*, necessary for salvation." In short, the Old and New Testaments "fall in the same category: '*Lex*.'"[5]

---

1. Heiko A. Oberman, *The Harvest of Medieval Theology: Gabriel Biel and Late Medieval Nominalism* (Durham, NC: Labyrinth, 1983), 112.
2. Oberman, *The Harvest of Medieval Theology*, 112–13.
3. Oberman, *The Harvest of Medieval Theology*, 114–15.
4. Oberman, *The Harvest of Medieval Theology*, 117.
5. Oberman, *The Harvest of Medieval Theology*, 118–19.

In addition to the legalism of the nominalist *pactum*, the pietistic emphasis of the Brethren of the Common Life once again suggests itself. Origen reigns supreme in the *devotio moderna*. The Pauline contrast between old and new covenants, letter and Spirit, law and gospel are understood in terms of a difference between formal rites and heart-religion, doctrine and love, creeds and deeds, outward circumcision and circumcision of heart, public worship and private or at least informal service. Especially where the Brethren emphasis was felt (Erasmus being a prime example), the complicated rules were reduced to one: love. This call to love God and neighbor in imitation of Christ is the gospel, or new law, according to this powerful strand of medieval teaching. The Reformers pointed out that genuine love for God and neighbor may be simpler than a thousand rules, but it is not any easier to follow. In contrast with at least some (less Origenist) patristic sources, what one rarely finds in medieval treatments is any recognition of a hermeneutical distinction between the law and the gospel (or promise) as two different principles, much less covenants, that run from Genesis to Revelation.

If the justification of the ungodly lies at the heart of the gospel, then the careful distinction between law and gospel is essential, especially in preaching. The Reformation doctrine of justification is not only culled from a handful of proof texts; it rests on important distinctions that they believed to be essential for the biblical writers themselves. On the basis of the law-gospel distinction, the Reformed tradition developed a more redemptive-historical narrative with distinct covenants providing the coordinates and contexts for the interplay of law and gospel. After summarizing the development of the law-gospel distinction and its theological and exegetical significance, I will turn to the rise of federal theology, principally provoked by this doctrine.

THE LAW-GOSPEL DISTINCTION

I have argued that we misunderstand the Reformation if we reduce it to a simple slogan, "grace, not merit" or "faith, not works." Everything that the Reformers had to say about justification (as well as other topics) orbited around and was in fact drawn from the center: *solo Christo*. This is just as true when we come to another distinction that had profound ramifications for justification and for exegesis of the relevant passages in Scripture. Luther acknowledged that distinguishing the law and the gospel in practice is one of the most difficult things to do. Whoever can do it well, he said, should be given a doctorate.[6]

Development of the Distinction

The ancient teachers, such as Origen and Chrysostom, drew remarkably different conclusions because of how they understood law and the gospel, works and faith. They were not always clear or consistent, but the explicit stipulation of this distinction and its importance is often evident. In addition to the many quotations that I included in chapters 1 and 2, Justin Martyr writes to his Jewish interlocutor in *Dialogue with Trypho* (c. 150),

> We do not trust through Moses or through the law; for then we would do the same as yourselves. . . . For I have read that there shall be a final law, and a covenant, the chiefest of all, which it is now incumbent on all men to observe, as many as are seeking the inheritance of God. For the law promulgated at Horeb is now old, and belongs to yourselves alone; but *this* is for all universally . . . and the covenant is trustworthy, after which there shall be no law, no commandment, no ordinance. . . . For the true spiritual Israel, and descendants of Judah, Jacob, Isaac, and Abraham (who in uncircumcision was approved of and blessed by God on account of his faith, and called the father of many nations), are we who have been led to God through this crucified Christ, as shall be demonstrated while we proceed.[7]

Justin contrasts law and promise, correlating the ministry of Moses and the new covenant, even tracing the latter to Abraham and the promise of a worldwide family in Christ. We are "no longer purified by the blood of goats," he adds, "but by faith through the blood of Christ, and through his death."[8]

Over against the Gnostics, especially Marcion (who attributed the Old Testament to an evil, lawgiving Creator), Irenaeus says that only through faith in the promise of God can we "acknowledge that both the Mosaic law and the grace of the new covenant, as both fitted for the

---

6. Luther, *Dr. Martin Luthers Sämmtliche Schriften*, vol. 9 (St. Louis: Concordia, n.d.), col. 802.

7. Justin Martyr, *Dialogue with Trypho* 13 (*ANF* 1:199–200).

8. Justin Martyr, *Dialogue with Trypho* 13 (*ANF* 1:200).

times [they were given], were bestowed by one and the same God for the benefit of the human race." It is not a simplistic and abstract opposition between Old and New Testaments, as the Marcionites imagine, but a distinction between types of covenants that accounts for the distinction between law and promise: "For all those who are of a perverse mind, having been set against the Mosaic legislation, judging it to be dissimilar and contrary to the doctrine of the Gospel, have not applied themselves to investigate the causes of the difference of each covenant."[9] He concludes, "There is but one author, and one end to both covenants. . . . But one and the same householder produced both covenants, the Word of God, our Lord Jesus Christ, who spoke with both Abraham and Moses, and who has restored us anew to liberty, and has multiplied that grace which is from Himself."[10] The one "given in order to liberty" is greater "than that given in order to bondage; and therefore [the new covenant] has also been diffused, not throughout one nation, but over the whole world." The same Christ promised in the law has appeared in the new covenant. "Moreover, we learn from the Scripture itself that God gave circumcision, not as the completer of righteousness, but as a sign, that the race of Abraham might continue recognizable."[11]

In fact, Irenaeus saw clearly that the Abrahamic covenant was a promise distinct from the law-covenant of Sinai. "Abraham himself, without circumcision and without observance of Sabbaths, 'believed God, and it was imputed unto him for righteousness; and he was called the friend of God.'" The same is true of Lot, Noah, Enoch, and all of the patriarchs before Moses, who "were justified independently of the things above mentioned, and without the law of Moses. . . . As also Moses himself says to the people in Deuteronomy: 'The LORD thy God formed a covenant in Horeb. The LORD formed not this covenant with your fathers, but for you.'"[12] Abraham's faith and ours "are one and the same: for he believed in things future, as if they were already accomplished, because of the promise of God; and in like manner do we also, because of the promise of God, behold through faith that inheritance in the kingdom."[13] This account contrasts sharply with Origen's, where there is no distinction in covenants or principles of law and gospel but only one

---

9. *Haer.* 5.1211–12 (*ANF* 1:434).
10. *Haer.* 4.9.1–2 (*ANF* 1:472).
11. *Haer.* 4.16.1 (*ANF* 1:480).
12. *Haer.* 4.16.2 (*ANF* 1:481), quoting Deut 5:2.
13. *Haer.* 4.21.1 (*ANF* 1:492).

continuous covenant of law with differing degrees of spiritual empowerment. Comparisons with E. P. Sanders's description of "covenantal nomism" in ancient Judaism are striking, as I pick up in volume 2.

We have also seen (chapters 1 and 2) affirmations of a clear distinction between law and gospel in the ancient church besides that of Irenaeus. While, according to a Marcionite interpretation, law and gospel are intrinsic opposites that represent rival deities, Yahweh and Christ, Origen interprets it as referring to nothing more than the external rituals separating Jews from gentiles as opposed to the opportunity to merit salvation by an internal obedience attended by a greater influx of the Spirit. Chrysostom, we have seen, avoids both extremes and understands, in the broadest sense, "law" as "works" and "gospel" as a promise of blessing apart from works, in Christ alone, through faith alone. This was the Reformers' interpretation as well, over against the more Origenist approach to the biblical (especially Pauline) distinction. Once again, the Reformation view proves less reductive than the dominant alternative. The ceremonies (like circumcision) are *included*, but the *whole law* is intended by the phrase "works of the law."

Augustine devotes an entire treatise to the relation between law and gospel: *On the Spirit and the Letter*. Pelagius repeatedly protests that he believes in the necessity of grace, but this grace is merely "referring to teaching, revelation, the opening of the eyes of the heart, the showing of things to come, pointing out satanic snares, and enlightening by the manifold and ineffable gift of heavenly grace." "The purpose of all such help, of course, is to make us learn the divine precepts and promises," Augustine summarizes. "All this is therefore only a locating of God's grace in the law and teaching!"[14]

In addition to anathematizing "anyone who denies original sin," the Council of Carthage (418) condemns those who say "that the grace of justification is given that we may more easily fulfill through grace what we are commanded to accomplish through free choice, as though we could still fulfill the divine commands, though not as easily, even if grace were not given. When he spoke about the observance of the commandments, the Lord said not, 'Without me you can do only with great difficulty,' but 'Without me you can do nothing' [John 15:5]."[15]

---

14. Quoted in J. Patout Burns, *Theological Anthropology*, Sources of Early Christian Thought (Philadelphia: Fortress, 1981), 66–67.
15. Quoted in Burns, *Theological Anthropology*, 57, 59.

However, medieval scholasticism conflates the law and gospel, making Christ another Moses. Even for Aquinas, the difference between law and gospel is one of degree: from shadows to reality, implied truth to explicit truth, severity to greater leniency. And it corresponds to Old and New Testaments, respectively.[16] The goal of the law "is to bring man to that end which is everlasting happiness."[17] "This 'everlasting happiness,'" Matthew Levering explains, "is our perfect unity with God and neighbor."[18]

The reference to the new covenant as the "new law" goes all the way back to an offhand remark by Justin Martyr in the paragraph above, where he sees "law" simply as a synonym for covenant rather than referring strictly to the Sinai covenant. However, Aquinas helped to make it a hermeneutical as well as theological fixture, especially in question 106 of the *Summa*. There he says that the "chief element" of the new law is "the grace of the Holy Ghost bestowed inwardly. And as to this, the New Law justifies."[19] The new law does not (like the old) "work wrath . . . because as far as it is concerned it gives man sufficient help to avoid sin."[20] In terms of external works, the old law is more burdensome; in terms of inward works, the new law is more burdensome.[21]

As the most recent *Catholic Catechism* (1994) expresses, the gospel is "the new law" in that "it works through charity; it uses the Sermon on the Mount to teach us what must be done and makes use of the sacraments to give us grace to do it."[22] This new law *is* the gospel—namely, the love of God and neighbor more effectively fulfilled because we have sacraments that cause rather than foreshadow grace. And Christ is a new Moses. Gabriel Biel may have pressed this assimilation of the gospel to the law as far as it could go, but the paradigm was shared across the entire Middle Ages, even though it was a radical departure from the earlier Augustinian consensus. This paradigm, more than anything else, provoked the Reformation. Once more, this underscores how incomplete our understanding is of the Reformers' concerns if we reduce it to a difference over the definition of justification or the

---

16. *ST* III, Q. 1, A. 2; cf. III, Q. 8, A. 6, and III, Q. 7, A. 13, ad. 3.

17. *ST* I-II, Q. 98, A. 1.

18. Matthew Levering, *Engaging the Doctrine of the Holy Spirit: Love and Gift in the Trinity and the Church* (Grand Rapids: Baker Academic, 2016), 297.

19. *ST* I-II, Q. 106, A. 2 (2:1105).

20. *ST* I-II, Q. 106, A. 2 (2:1105).

21. *ST* I-II, Q. 106, A. 4 (2:1112).

22. *CCC*, 477.

relation of faith and works. These were of course crucial questions, but this one—the relation of law and gospel—generated them all.

According to his own account, Luther came to see this distinction first in Romans and soon afterward discovered it in Augustine's *Spirit and Letter.* "As the Reformers saw it," Otto Weber notes, "Paul was really understood here . . . [as] the distinction between law and Gospel, between the letter and the spirit, was brought to full theological validity."[23] Like its interpretation of "Spirit" and "flesh," the Origenist interpretation of the Pauline "letter" and "Spirit" contrasted the literal (correlative to the body and history) with the spiritual (correlative to the intellect). Luther detected this presupposition in his vitriolic critic, Jerome Emser. He said that the Dominican preacher had built his argument on the sand provided by "Origen, Jerome, Dionysius, and some others."[24] Paul is not talking about two levels of interpretation; rather, he is comparing the old and new covenants.[25] He quotes Augustine saying, "The letter is nothing but law without grace."[26]

Article 4 of the Apology of the Augsburg Confession (1531) states, "All Scripture ought to be distributed into these two principal topics, the Law and the promises." This is not a distinction between Old and New Testaments, the article adds, since the free remission of sins in Christ is found along with the law in the Old Testament.[27] The fourth article of the Formula of Concord states, "We believe, teach, and confess that the distinction between the Law and the Gospel is to be maintained in the Church with great diligence."[28]

The gospel is not an easier and more simplified law; it is not law— that is, a conditional promise depending on the personal fulfillment of the law's conditions. Rather, the gospel is an announcement of what God has done in his incarnate Son to reconcile us to himself. In fact, Luther defines the gospel by a gloss of Romans 1:3–4: "The Word is the Gospel of God concerning his Son who was made flesh, suffered, rose

---

23. Otto Weber, *Foundations of Dogmatics,* trans. by Darrell L. Guder (Grand Rapids: Eerdmans, 1981), 1:88.

24. Luther, "Against 'Goat' Emser," in *LW* 39:175.

25. Luther, "Against 'Goat' Emser," in *LW* 39:182. Calvin follows the same argument in *Calvin's Commentaries,* vol. 22, *Commentary on the Epistles of Paul the Apostle to the Corinthians,* trans. William Pringle (Grand Rapids: Baker, 1981), 172–74.

26. Luther, *LW* 39:182.

27. F. Bente and W. H. T. Dau, ed. and trans., *Triglot Concordia: The Symbolical Books of the Evangelical Lutheran Church* (St. Louis: Concordia, 1921), Apology 4, 2.5 (135).

28. *Triglot Concordia,* FC Epitome 5, 2.1 (503ff).

from the dead, and was glorified through the Spirit who sanctifies."[29] Timothy Wengert explains, "Further, Melanchthon and Calvin (along with Luther) reject the narrowing of 'works of the law' to the ceremonies." In comments he added in 1528 to the *Scholia* on Colossians 2:17, "Melanchthon warned the readers specifically against Origen and others (=Erasmus) who imagine that the Decalog 'or, as they say, *opera moralia*' justify."[30]

In short, the law and the gospel differ not merely in degree but in category. Yet it goes deeper than a mere cataloguing of Scripture into indicatives and imperatives. *God* is the speaker, and he is doing different things through the words he employs. There are commands in the New Testament and gospel promises in the Old. In fact, the law of Christ—essentially, love of God and neighbor (Luke 10:27)—is nothing new; it is the essence of the moral law as described by Moses (Deut 6:5; Lev 19:18). The law is only opposed to the gospel with respect to the question, "How can I be saved?" God's commands do not condemn inherently. Rather, the law is the expression of God's moral will; therefore, the law condemns only when it is transgressed. Yet especially in Paul, the law that condemns is associated with its role in a covenant whose principle is "Do this and you shall live." In other words, the law functions either as a condition for blessing (in a covenant based on it) or as an imperative for the way in which the blessed are to walk (in a covenant based on Christ's mediation). For the justified, the law becomes an ally of the gospel in sanctification. Yet, still, the law commands, and the gospel alone saves, renews, and empowers.

When Paul speaks of the condemning law, he has in mind the Sinai covenant Israel failed to keep (and the moral law gentiles know by nature). This is evident in the way that he reaches for Leviticus 18:5—the law as principle of inheritance—in Galatians 3 and Romans 10. Those who are "under the law"—that is, look to it as the condition of their blessing—are "under a curse," not because of the law itself but because they failed to keep it (Gal 3:10, quoting Deut 27:26). There is one verdict for Jew and gentile alike: the whole world is guilty before God (Rom 3:19). Yet when Paul turns in the same discourse to imperatives

---

29. Luther, "Freedom of a Christian," in *LW* 31:346.

30. Timothy J. Wengert, *Law and Gospel: Philip Melanchthon's Debate with John Agricola of Eisleben over Poenitentia*, Texts and Studies in Reformation & Post-Reformation Thought (Grand Rapids: Baker Academic, 1997), 194.

for the Christian life, they are the commands of the Decalogue—albeit from the eschatological perspective of the new creation that has dawned with Christ, the new heart with the fruit of the Spirit that the prophets anticipated. Here the imperatives function not as conditions for inheriting the promise but as the "reasonable service" of those who have been rescued from this evil age and united to Christ.

Furthermore, Luther is sensitive to the condition of the hearer as well as the way texts are preached. One who is confident in Christ's sufficiency could hear the command, "You shall have no other gods before me," as an assurance that God's jealousy bespeaks his love. By contrast, one who is anxious before God may even hear a promise like John 3:16 as accusation: "Christ died for the world, but not for me," and "if I do not believe, then I am condemned already, yet I do not know whether I have that kind of faith." Apart from faith in Christ, one will hear a passage such as Christ's discourse on the last judgment (Matt 25) either as condemning or as confirming a false sense of having fulfilled the command, as in the case of the "goats." In Christ, however, one will hear even Matthew 25, if preached properly, as a call to live out rather than attain our union with Christ and therefore with each other ("my brothers and sisters," v. 40).

God's speech is always an interpersonal affair, establishing a relationship through judgment and forgiveness. Everything that Christ has accomplished is applied directly by the Spirit through the gospel. Among other negative effects, to confuse the law and the gospel, especially in preaching, is to lead hearers to imagine that the former is easy and the latter is difficult. According to Luther and other Reformers, this concern reflected the teaching and preaching they had experienced.

However, different nuances opened up into open confrontation even within Luther's inner circle. Philip Melanchthon's first open attack on John Agricola came in 1527. Melanchthon saw the law as preparing for the gospel and thought that the law had a positive place both to drive sinners to Christ and to guide them. Agricola's view of the law was entirely negative: it closes off all hope and can only be heard by the human being as a horrible burden.[31] Is this not what Luther meant when he said that the law always accuses? But surely this is only when we seek our life from it. Based on Psalm 51, Melanchthon's catechetical work

---

31. Wengert, *Law and Gospel*, 58–74.

taught that the law provokes us to true sorrow and not merely fear of punishment. "Where there is no fear, there can be no faith," he said in his 1523 comments on the Decalogue.[32] Like other refinements, this was an important qualification of some of Luther's tendencies (taken to an extreme by Agricola) to treat the law only as a terror. But especially with Agricola in mind, Melanchthon insisted that faith is *not* "fleshly security and despising of the wrath of God."[33] Then in 1527 he "made a passing reference in the preface to 'many' who teach forgiveness and faith without *poenitentia*," which can only be considered "a foolish dream."[34]

Agricola's opposition between law and gospel veered perilously close to Marcionite territory. Remember that for the magisterial Reformers, there is no intrinsic opposition between the law (commands) and the gospel (promises). In fact, the former conspires with the latter by driving us out of ourselves to cling to Christ.

Admittedly, Luther's hyperbolic rhetoric about the opposition of Moses and Christ sounds Marcionite at times, but he qualifies it in other places by underscoring that Moses's ministry was in service to Christ's. The law is good since it "reveals and teaches how to recognize sin" and tells us how to love: "Such works of love toward the neighbor should flow forth in meekness, patience, kindness, teaching, aid, and counsel, spiritually and bodily, free and for nothing, as Christ has dealt with us."[35] The law *as such* is not condemning but rather just, acquitting the righteous and judging the wicked. "The Law does not work lust" in the righteous, since sin is no longer the dominating power. It is "not the fault of the Law" that we are revealed by it as sinners.[36] In fact, "The Law is established [fulfilled] *in us* when we fulfill it willingly and truly. But this no one can do without faith."[37] However, when we seek justification, the opposition between law and gospel is total.

But Agricola turned *law* into an inherently negative category and swept every ceremony under this category as merely external and oppressive. Not only at the point of justification but *in toto*, Agricola declared, the law has no role to play in the life of the believer. On one side stands faith, Christ, and the gospel; on the other, all commands

---

32. Wengert, *Law and Gospel*, 78.
33. Wengert, *Law and Gospel*, 78.
34. Wengert, *Law and Gospel*, 79.
35. Luther, "Against the Heavenly Prophets," in *LW* 40:82–83.
36. Luther, *Commentary on the Epistle to the Romans*, trans. J. Theodore Mueller (repr., Grand Rapids: Kregel, 1979), 111.
37. Luther, *Commentary on the Epistle to the Romans*, 80.

and ceremonies.[38] Agricola kept returning to 1 Timothy 1:8–11: "Now we know that the law is good, if one uses it lawfully, understanding this, that the law is not laid down for the just but for the lawless and disobedient, for the ungodly and sinners, for the unholy and profane." The law is for those without the Spirit, not for believers. "Agricola categorically denied any role for works, good or bad, in the life of the believer," according to Timothy Wengert. "He excluded any common ordering of the Christian life. Christians live by grace alone."[39] "If you believe, you will be holy even in sin. . . . If you sin, be happy; it should have no consequence."[40]

Melanchthon collided with Agricola repeatedly during these years. First, Melanchthon was stupefied at Agricola's disdain for all outward regulations. There must be Sunday services, rules for singing and fasting, that are laid down not by necessity but for common order.[41] Only fanatical spirits want to get rid of all external ordinances.[42] The 1527 Visitation Articles "relentlessly attacked Agricola's understanding of *poenitentia* and law."[43] The preaching of the law is useful not only to drive to Christ but for the believer's daily mortification. According to Melanchthon, "The preaching of the law rouses [a person] to *poenitentia*."[44]

Believers too need to learn fear of God, Melanchthon argued, so that they do not mistake faith for carnal security.[45] Faith only comes from a contrite heart.[46] Without this fear, the gospel is not full of peace and comfort.[47] The law plays an important role in arousing not only legal but also evangelical-filial fear.[48] We move back and forth constantly between law and gospel, "from *mortificatio* to *vivificatio*."[49] Regarding 1 Timothy 1:9, he "explicitly censured those who, when they hear that we are not justified by our own powers or deeds, live the most impure lives. 'They will incur great punishment from God.'"[50]

---

38. Wengert, *Law and Gospel*, 86.
39. Wengert, *Law and Gospel*, 86.
40. Wengert, *Law and Gospel*, 87.
41. Wengert, *Law and Gospel*, 87.
42. Wengert, *Law and Gospel*, 88.
43. Wengert, *Law and Gospel*, 97.
44. Wengert, *Law and Gospel*, 97.
45. Wengert, *Law and Gospel*, 97.
46. Wengert, *Law and Gospel*, 98.
47. Wengert, *Law and Gospel*, 98.
48. Wengert, *Law and Gospel*, 99.
49. Wengert, *Law and Gospel*, 100.
50. Wengert, *Law and Gospel*, 101.

Luther stood with Melanchthon in this controversy.[51] By 1529, Luther himself had stepped in, contributing his own two catechisms, in the place of the many others, including Agricola's. This was "a turning point," says Wengert, and things only worsened with the so-called Antinomian Controversy, during which Luther condemned Agricola's view explicitly in several treatises. After this, Agricola's influence disappeared.[52] By 1534 Melanchthon was adding another "use of the law": the so-called third use, to guide believers.[53] The category appears in his Romans commentary, which also emphasized justification as strictly forensic. It is the law's terrifying accusation, not its normative commands, that has been eliminated in the new covenant.[54]

This "third use of the law" (to guide believers), confessed in the Formula of Concord (1577), appears for the first time on the Reformed side in Calvin's Romans commentary (1540), after he had read either Melanchthon's 1534 Romans commentary or the second edition of his *Loci communes*, which Calvin translated into French.[55]

Zwingli affirmed justification through faith alone, but his center of gravity was the new life that believers have in Christ. He was wary of saying, with Luther, that the law frightens us with condemnation and leads us to despair. Rather than law and gospel, Zwingli's order was first the gospel, then the law. Those who know God as merciful in Christ will love his law. "I understand gospel here to be everything which God has made known to us through his own Son. It is also gospel when he says: You shall not be angry with one another." So everything in Scripture may be considered "gospel."[56] At the same time, Zwingli stressed (with Luther prior to the antinomian controversy) that the law is not for believers, since they look to Christ alone and are guided by the Spirit.[57]

However, all of the other Reformed leaders not only agreed with Luther's distinction but with its importance. Peter Martyr Vermigli said that "we wish to affirm that Gospel should be distinguished from law

---

51. Wengert, *Law and Gospel*, 103.
52. Wengert, *Law and Gospel*, 153.
53. Wengert, *Law and Gospel*, 195. Melanchthon still uses two in the Romans commentary of 1532. "In the 1534 *Scholia*, however, a clear shift has taken place." Now he speaks of three uses.
54. Wengert, *Law and Gospel*, 186–87.
55. Wengert, *Law and Gospel*, 206. Wengert even supposes that Calvin may have first gleaned it from Melanchthon's Colossians commentary.
56. Stephens, *The Theology of Ulrich Zwingli*, 164–65.
57. Stephens, *The Theology of Ulrich Zwingli*, 166–67.

and law from Gospel. But this cannot be done by those who ascribe justification to works, and confuse them."[58] Zwingli's successor Heinrich Bullinger concurred, including an article in the Second Helvetic Confession on the distinction: "The Gospel is indeed opposed to the Law. For the Law works wrath and pronounces a curse, whereas the Gospel preaches grace and blessing."[59]

Theodore Beza, Calvin's successor, wrote a confession that was published in Geneva in 1558. He addressed "the means which the Holy Spirit uses to create faith in the heart of the elect." His answers, of course, were the Word and the sacraments, and these discussions therefore follow. But the discussion of "The Word" itself is divided into two parts: *law* and *gospel*:

> We divide this Word into two principal parts or kinds: the one is called the "Law," the other the "Gospel." For, all the rest can be gathered under one or the other of these two headings. What we call Law (when it is distinguished from Gospel and is taken for one of the two parts of the Word) is a doctrine whose seed is written by nature in our hearts. . . . What we call the Gospel ("Good News") is a doctrine which is not at all in us by nature, but which is revealed from Heaven (Mt.16:17; Jn.1:13), and totally surpasses natural knowledge. By it God testifies to us that it is his purpose to save us freely by his only Son (Rom.3:20–22), provided that, by faith, we embrace him as our only wisdom, righteousness, sanctification and redemption (1Cor.1:30).[60]

---

58. Peter Martyr Vermigli, *Locus on Justification*, in *Predestination and Justification: Two Theological Loci*, trans. and ed. Frank A. James III, Peter Martyr Library 8 (Kirksville, MO: Sixteenth Century Essays & Studies, 2003), 115. See Joseph McLelland, introduction to *Early Writings: Creed, Scripture, Church*, by Peter Martyr Vermigli, ed. Joseph C. McLelland, trans. Mariano Di Gangi and Joseph C. McLelland, Peter Martyr Library (Kirksville, MO: Sixteenth Century Essays & Studies, 1994), 85: McLelland notes that for Martyr "the sum of that teaching is Law and Gospel." A recurring emphasis is that "the polarity of Law and Gospel is a constant in revelation" (85).

59. Wilhelm Niesel, *Reformed Symbolics: A Comparison of Catholicism, Orthodoxy and Protestantism*, trans. David Lewis (Edinburgh: Oliver and Boyd, 1962), 217. Cf. Michael Horton, "Calvin and the Law-Gospel Hermeneutic," *Pro Ecclesia* 6, no. 1 (1997): 27–42. Set on the course for the Carthusian order, Bullinger entered the University of Cologne at the age of 15. As debates over Luther's Ninety-Five Theses reached him, he determined to study Scripture as well as the church fathers and medieval theologians and only then to examine Luther's arguments. Besides Luther's works, Melanchthon's *Loci communes* won him over. He was now a devoted "Martinist." He took a teaching position in Kapel, Switzerland, where he instructed monks in the "new learning" and thereby came to Zwingli's attention.

60. Theodore Beza, *The Christian Faith*, trans. James Clark (Lewes, UK: Christian Focus, 1992), 40–50.

Beza goes on to warn, "We must pay great attention to these things. For, with good reason, we can say that ignorance of this distinction between Law and Gospel is one of the principal sources of the abuses which corrupted and still corrupts Christianity." Why is this? People always turn the law into something easy and the gospel into something difficult, as if the gospel were "nothing other than a second Law, more perfect than the first." Beza then devotes a great deal of space to distinguishing the law from the gospel. The law is in us by nature; the gospel is "from above." "Having carefully understood this distinction of the two parts of the Word of God, the Law and the Gospel, it is easy to understand how and to what end the Holy Spirit uses the preaching of the one and the other in the Church." We do not know our sinfulness. "This is why God begins with the preaching of the Law," and after discussing this point more fully, he concludes, "There then is the first use of the preaching of the Law." But "after the Law comes the Gospel" in preaching. The "third use" Beza discusses under the heading, "The other fruit of the preaching of the Law, once the preaching of the Gospel has effectually done its work," and he argues that because the believer's relation to the law has changed, it simply directs instead of inspiring fear and doubt.[61]

The distinction is just as clear and important in later Reformed writings of theologians as diverse as Zacharius Ursinus, whose *Commentary on the Heidelberg Catechism* begins with the law and the gospel as "the two parts of the Word of God."[62] The distinction was a staple also of Puritan preaching and writing. In William Perkins primer for preachers, he advised, "The basic principle in application is to know whether the passage is a statement of the law or of the gospel. For when the Word is preached, the law and the gospel operate differently."[63]

The Meaning of the Distinction

It is not surprising to see influences of Melanchthon on Calvin. They developed a close friendship and worked hard together to keep the

---

61. Beza, *The Christian Faith*, 51.

62. Zacharius Ursinus, *Commentary on the Heidelberg Catechism*, 2nd Am. ed. (Columbus: Scott & Bascom, 1852), 1–3.

63. William Perkins, *The Art of Prophesying and the Calling of the Ministry* (1606; repr., Edinburgh: Banner of Truth, 1996), 54. A few Puritans diverged from this pattern. Some rejected the law altogether at least as having any relevance for the believer, while others (especially Richard Baxter and John Goodwin) assimilated the gospel to the law. The labels "antinomian" and "neonomian" were used frequently during this period. The controversy erupted again in the eighteenth century. See Sinclair Ferguson, *The Whole Christ: Legalism, Antinomianism, and Gospel Assurance—Why the Marrow Controversy Still Matters* (Wheaton, IL: Crossway, 2016).

evangelical movement from splitting. Even after Melanchthon moved in a more synergistic direction with the final edition of his *Loci communes*, Calvin translated the work into French (offering a brief disclaimer on the synergism in his preface). By the way, this fact as well as Calvin's appreciation for Chrysostom exhibits the Reformer's priorities. Without downplaying his predestinarian monergism, Calvin considered such matters as the law-gospel distinction front and center.

Like Melanchthon, Calvin continued to speak of law and gospel in two senses: (1) as referring to the Old Testament and New Testament and (2) as referring to condemnation and justification. This significant distinction is found explicitly in Paul, who uses law in both senses within the same sentence: "But now the righteousness of God has been manifested *apart from the law*, although *the Law and the Prophets* bear witness to it" (Rom 3:21, emphasis added).

As noted above, Calvin's definition of the law's three uses comes from Melanchthon's as well. Calvin too accepts Aquinas's threefold division into moral, civil, and ceremonial laws. The moral law (i.e., the Decalogue) is a written statement of the natural law: duties inscribed on the human conscience. Thus the moral law is eternal and unchanging, reflecting God's own righteous character, while the civil and ceremonial laws were supplements or addenda to it.[64] These laws specific to the Mosaic economy are no longer in force.[65] "It is a fact that the law of God which we call the moral law is nothing else than a testimony of natural law and of that conscience which God has engraved upon the minds of men."[66] The second table of the Decalogue prescribes an "equity" (justice tempered by love) that transcends the theopolitical laws of Israel and may observed by many different constitutions, laws, and forms of government.[67]

Further, Calvin's pedagogical use of the law (viz., to drive us to Christ)f is identical to Luther's. The scholastics speak of the gospel as a "new law," Calvin laments. They use phrases like "the law of the gospel" and therefore "fancied Christ another Moses, the giver of the law of the gospel, which supplied what was lacking in the Mosaic law."

---

64. John Calvin, preface to *Commentaries on the Four Last Books of Moses*, vol. 1, trans. Charles W. Binham (repr., Grand Rapids: Baker, 1996), xvii.

65. *Inst.* 4.20.14–16.

66. *Inst.* 4.20.16.

67. *Inst.* 4.20.16.

This is "in many respects a most pernicious opinion!"[68] Instead, the first use of the law is "to shut us up deprived of all confidence in our own righteousness, so that we may learn to embrace [God's] Covenant of Grace, and flee to Christ, who is the end of the law."[69] According to Paul, Calvin adds, "The difference between the Law and the Gospel lies in this: that the latter does not like the former promise life under the condition of works, but from faith. What can be clearer than the antithesis?"[70] Of course, if we are talking about *the Law*, the first five books of the Bible, the Pentateuch, there is gospel in it. But if we are thinking about "that part only which was peculiar to [Moses's] ministration, which consisted of precepts, rewards, and punishments," then it is completely distinct from the gospel. Indeed, leading sinners to despair of themselves and flee to Christ "was the end or design of the Mosaic dispensation." "And whenever the word law is thus strictly taken, Moses is by implication opposed to Christ: and then we must consider what the law contains, as separate from the gospel."[71] When the believer's conscience seeks repose, the law must be excluded, Calvin insists.[72]

At every point, Calvin reflects Luther's emphasis with respect to the law's condemning function. The law is a mirror,[73] pronouncing a curse on all violators,[74] and "only begets death; it increases our condemnation and inflames the wrath of God." He adds, "The law of God speaks, but it does not reform our hearts. . . . For in the Gospel God does not say, 'You must do this or that,' but 'believe that my only Son is your Redeemer; embrace his death and passion as the remedy for your ills; plunge yourself beneath his blood and it will be your cleansing."[75] "The Law holds all men under its curse. From the Law, therefore, it is useless to seek a blessing."[76]

Even the best precepts cannot change a person. Nor can one say that justification comes by love. If that is what "faith working by love"

---

68. *Inst.* 2.8.7.

69. Calvin, preface to *Commentaries on the Four Last Books of Moses*, trans. Charles William Bingham, *Calvin's Commentaries*, vol. 2 (Grand Rapids: Baker, 1996), xviii.

70. Calvin, *Selected Works of John Calvin: Tracts and Letters*, vol. 3, *Acts and Antidote*, ed. Henry Beveridge and Jules Bonnet, trans. Henry Beveridge (Grand Rapids: Baker, 1983), 156 and 250.

71. Calvin, *Calvin's Commentaries*, vol. 19, *Commentaries on the Epistle of Paul the Apostle to the Romans*, trans. John Owen (Grand Rapids: Baker, 1996), 186–87 (on Rom 6:6).

72. *Inst.* 3.11.17; cf. on Calvin, *Calvin's Commentaries*, vol. 21, *Commentaries on the Epistles of Paul to the Galatians and Ephesians*, trans. William Pringle (Grand Rapids: Baker, 1996), 88.

73. Calvin, *Commentaries on Romans* 10:8 (19:386–87).

74. *Inst.* 2.9.4.

75. Calvin, *Sermons on Isaiah's Prophecy and the Death and Passion of Christ*, trans. T. H. L. Parker (London: James Clarke, 2002), on Isa 53:11.

76. Calvin, *Commentaries on Galatians* 3:10 (21:88).

(Gal 5:6) means, then Paul is contradicting everything he said before. After all, "sincere love of God" is the summary of the whole law.[77] Calvin observes that one "may indeed view from afar the proffered promises, yet he cannot derive any benefit from them."

> Therefore this thing alone remains: that from the goodness of the promises he should the better judge his own misery, while with the hope of salvation cut off he thinks himself threatened with certain death. On the other hand, horrible threats hang over us, constraining and entangling not a few of us only, but all of us to a man. They hang over us, I say, and pursue us with inexorable harshness, so that we discern in the Law only the most immediate death.[78]

The law promises conditionally, while the gospel covenants on the basis of Christ's fulfillment of all conditions in the believer's place. "The promises of the Law depend on the conditions of works while the Gospel promises are free and dependent solely on God's mercy."[79] Calvin also anticipates the emerging Reformed distinction between law and gospel in terms of "two covenants," which he identifies as "Legal and Evangelical."[80]

At the same time, Calvin follows Melanchthon in warning against reducing the law to its first use—to threaten. "Readers must be put on their guard in this matter; for I see many make the mistake of acknowledging no other use of the Law than what is expressed here," in spite of many Pauline passages that continue to exhort believers to order their lives by its rule while refusing to seek righteousness by it.[81] This "third use" is not a back door to seeking justification by obedience. Whenever the conscience seeks peace with God, the law operates in its first use to send the believer back to Christ. However, the believer's relationship to the law has changed because of the mediation of Christ rather than Moses so that "it is not what it formerly was: it may no longer condemn and destroy their consciences by frightening and confounding them."[82]

---

77. Calvin, *Commentaries on Romans* 3:21 (19:386–87).
78. *Inst.* 2.7.4.
79. *Inst.* 3.11.17.
80. Calvin, *Commentaries on Galatians* 4:24 (21:137–38). He makes the same point in *Commentaries on Romans*, 298.
81. Calvin, *Commentaries on Galatians* 3:19 (21:90).
82. *Inst.* 2.7.14.

This is why Calvin calls the third use the "chief or principal use," since the law now has no other office than to guide believers, "even though before God's judgment seat it has no place in their conscience."[83] "For the law is not now acting toward us as a rigorous enforcement officer who is not satisfied unless the requirements are met," but is rather pointing out "the goal toward which throughout life we are to strive." Before, the law accused, but now it has a different purpose: "Now, the law has power to exhort believers. This is not a power to bind their consciences with a curse," but to point the way toward divinely approved service.[84]

Even in its third use, the law can only direct; it cannot give the power to obey its commands. Believers continue to look to the law for direction and to the gospel for assurance. Only the gospel promises can move us to grateful obedience, says Calvin, referring to David in Psalm 51:

> He lays hold not only of the precepts, but the accompanying prom-
> ise of grace, which alone sweetens what is bitter. For what would
> be less lovable than the Law if, with importuning and threatening
> alone, it troubles souls through fear, and distressed them through
> fright? David especially shows that in the Law he apprehended the
> Mediator, without whom there is no delight or sweetness.[85]

Even repentance takes on a different color for the believer. While the law does drive sinners to repentance, clinging to Christ in faith, it is also true that the gospel leads to repentance. It is not only fear of God's wrath but filial wonder at God's provision in Christ that draws us away from our idols. Thus, "The beginning of repentance is a sense of God's mercy."[86]

LAW-GOSPEL AND FEDERAL THEOLOGY

Especially in Reformed theology, the law-gospel distinction evolved into a two-covenant scheme. The original covenant with Adam in Paradise was a "covenant of works," also called a covenant of creation, law, or life. Like this covenant, the one sworn by Israel at Sinai was

---

83. *Inst.* 3.11.2.
84. *Inst.* 2.7.12–13.
85. *Inst.* 2.7.12.
86. Calvin, *Calvin's Commentaries*, vol. 13, *Daniel 7–12, Hosea*, trans. Thomas Myers and John Owen (Grand Rapids: Baker, 1979), on Hos 6:1.

based on the principle, "Do this and you shall live; transgress and you will die." There was a range of views as to the extent to which the Mosaic economy could be compared with the covenant of works in Eden, but all parties agreed that the terms of the Sinai covenant were different than the Abrahamic promise fulfilled in the new covenant.

Consequently, Reformed exegetes increasingly used the phrase "law and gospel" interchangeably with the "two covenants" to which Paul refers in Galatians 4:22. We must "observe how the covenant of the law [*foedus legale*] compares with the covenant of the gospel [*foedus euangelicum*]," Calvin says.[87] On Galatians 4:22, Giovanni Diodati (Hebrew professor at Geneva's academy and translator of the first Italian Bible) observes that there are "two kinds" of children "according to the two doctrines or covenants propounded by God to humankind: namely, the law and the gospel."[88] The two families are easily discerned, according to Olevianus: "The false ones talk about free will, merits and satisfaction, and so are puffed up with pride," while the true children place all confidence in the Father and his inheritance "not because of our merits or those of any other creature but because his Son was made a man for our sake and bought us with the price of his blood. We have done nothing to deserve this but merely receive what God has freely offered and given in Christ. Thus Christ is not just our savior in part but completely."[89] David Dickson, chair of divinity at Glasgow in the seventeenth century, further explains that they refer to "the covenant of works represented by Hagar" and "the covenant of grace or faith, represented by Sarah."[90]

In order to appreciate the way classic Reformed exegesis of the most relevant passages works, it helps to understand its broader framework. It touches directly, for example, on how one interprets "works of the law," law and promise, and other Pauline terms.

While essential, the law-gospel distinction itself is static. For instance, what happens when we are preaching through Deuteronomy and meet its inexorable demands and threats? Most basically, one should be able to

---

87. *Inst.* 2.11.4.

88. Jean Diodati, *Annotations on the Bible*, in *Reformation Commentary on Scripture*, New Testament 10, *Galatians, Ephesians*, ed. Gerald Bray (Downers Grove, IL: InterVarsity, 2011), 158.

89. Kaspar Olevianus, *Sermons on Galatians*, in *Reformation Commentary on Scripture*, New Testament 10, *Galatians, Ephesians*, ed. Gerald Bray (Downers Grove, IL: InterVarsity, 2011), 158–59.

90. David Dickson, *Brief Exposition of Galatians*, in *Reformation Commentary on Scripture*, New Testament 10, *Galatians, Ephesians*, ed. Gerald Bray (Downers Grove, IL: InterVarsity, 2011), 160.

distinguish the law from the gospel and recall that life is not to be sought in the law. However, the passages require otherwise. They *do* promise life on the basis of obedience. What do we do with such imperatives?

It becomes essential to be able to distinguish not only law and gospel but different covenants in which the law is functioning. The Sinai covenant did not offer an antithetical path to justification in Scripture; it was never intended to give justification and everlasting life in the first place. Sinai was a temporary covenant, promising "long life in the land," with fruitful wombs and vineyards by obedience to a covenant that had Moses for its mediator. The complex web of laws, ceremonies, and institutions served collectively as a typological sketch of the everlasting kingdom but could not—and was never intended to—bring it about. The Abrahamic covenant stands behind Sinai as the promise that is realized in Jesus Christ. Furthermore, the specific commands change from one covenant to another. The many purity stipulations about clothes, food, menstruation, and so forth, belong to a covenant that has since passed from history.

Development of the Two-Covenant Scheme

The distinction between *covenants* of law and promise is evident as far back in the tradition as Irenaeus.[91] The bishop of Lyon identified six epochs in redemptive history but grouped them under two covenants: Sinai and the new covenant.[92] The first he identified as a period—"the law of works"—reigning from Moses to John the Baptist.[93]

Significantly, Irenaeus did not confine this law of works to the ceremonies but to the entire ministry of Moses where obedience was the condition of life. The covenant of grace, which was promised to Abraham through his single offspring, Christ, is the basis for the new covenant, which he calls a "new economy of liberty."[94]

Importantly, this emphasis on distinct covenants was part of a strategy to refute the ahistorical speculations of Gnosticism. Ever since,

---

91. For relevant passages, see esp. *Haer.* 3.10.4; 3.12.11; 4.11.2; 4.14.2; 4.25.1; 4.31.1; and 4.38.1 (*ANF* vol. 1). See Everett Ferguson, *Backgrounds to Early Christianity*, 2nd ed. (Grand Rapids: Eerdmans, 2003), 92, 288, 292, 405, 425, 468–69, 507–8, 524–27, 547–50; cf. J. Ligon Duncan, "The Covenant Idea in Irenaeus of Lyons: An Introduction and Survey," in *Confessing Our Hope: Essays in Honor of Morton Howison Smith on His Eightieth Birthday*, ed. J. A. Pipa Jr. and C. N. Willborn (Taylors, SC: Southern Presbyterian Press, 2004).

92. *Haer.* 3.12.12, *ANF* 1:434–35.

93. *Haer.* 4.25.1, *ANF* 1:496.

94. *Haer.* 3.10.4, *ANF* 1:425.

an interest in covenant theology has gone hand-in-hand with an interest in the historical development of God's plan from promise to fulfillment. And the story of Abraham, with the promise of a worldwide family, has been a central feature of that broader narrative.

Besides Augustine's *De spiritu et littera* (*On the Spirit and the Letter*), his *Civitas Dei* (*City of God*) contains influential seeds for the two covenants: "The first covenant was this, unto Adam: 'Whensoever thou eatest thereof thou shalt die the death,'" which is why all his children "are breakers of God's covenant made with Adam in paradise."[95]

It is by closer attention to the dynamism of the history of redemption that the Reformed tradition developed its covenant theology in a way that actually made the law–gospel distinction more structurally significant.

Although Luther also made use of the argument, the first appearance of a special emphasis on the covenant motif is in the anti-Anabaptist polemics of Zurich under Ulrich Zwingli. Some of his students, including Conrad Grebel and Felix Manz, moved increasingly in an Anabaptist direction. Finally, during his so-called "second disputation" in 1523, Zwingli offered a vigorous defense of infant baptism. This was followed by several additional treatises on the subject.[96] "Christian people are also in the gracious covenant with God, in which Abraham stood," he argued. Therefore, "It is clearly proved that our children are no less God's than Abraham's."[97]

Zwingli's case for infant baptism rested largely on the unity of a single covenant of grace spanning the whole of redemptive history.[98] This argument had significant hermeneutical implications. On one hand, it underscored the fundamental coherence of both testaments, the continuity of the New Testament with the Old. On the other hand, it meant that the diversity of covenants in Scripture, particularly the Old Testament, could be marginalized. For example, how does one account for the differences between the covenant that Yahweh alone

---

95. Augustine, *City of God*, ed. David Knowles; trans. Henry Bettenson (New York: Penguin, 1972), 16.28 (688–89). In addition, there is some evidence of this type of thinking among Roman Catholic theologians at the time of the Reformation. See Aaron Denlinger, *Omnes in Adam ex pacto Dei: Ambrogio Contarini's Covenantal Solidarity and His Influence on Post-Reformation Reformed Theologians* (Göttingen: Vandenhoeck & Ruprecht, 2010).

96. See W. P. Stephens, *The Theology of Ulrich Zwingli* (Oxford: Clarendon, 1986), 206–17.

97. Quoted by Stephens, *The Theology of Ulrich Zwingli*, 209.

98. Zwingli pursues this line of argument in *Baptism, Rebaptism, and Infant Baptism* (1525), *A Reply to Hubmaier* (1525), *A Refutation* (1527), and *Questions Concerning the Sacrament of Baptism* (1530).

swears to Abraham, ratified in a vision of the LORD passing through the pieces in Genesis 15, and the covenant that Israel swears at Mount Sinai, with Moses sprinkling blood on the people "in accordance with the words that you have spoken, 'All this we will do'" (Exod 24:8)? Zwingli did not distinguish these covenants clearly and tended to blend them together into a single covenant of grace. Furthermore, he emphasized the human side of the covenant, which made it easier of course to blend the Abrahamic and Sinai covenants.[99] In short, Zwingli's failure to see a distinction between law and gospel was at least consistent with (if not a motivating factor of) his tendency to conflate different covenants. Bullinger's embrace of the law-gospel distinction helped him to become one of the pioneering theologians of a protofederal theology, particularly evident in his *Decades*.

With the apostle Paul, Calvin went so far as to identify "law and gospel" with the "two covenants" (the Sinaitic and Abrahamic).[100] This move reflects the crucial transition from "law and gospel" to the scheme of the covenant of works and the covenant of grace. "The contradiction between the law and faith [in Gal 3:7–14]," wrote Calvin, "lies in the cause of justification. The law is not of faith because it has a completely different way of justifying people. . . . We are not concerned with whether believers should keep the law to the best of their ability—we all agree with that—but whether they obtain righteousness by their works, which is impossible."[101] The "two covenants" are "legal and evangelical."[102]

Already by the late sixteenth century, Reformed theologians (e.g., Beza, Ursinus, Olevianus, Rollock, Perkins, etc.) were distinguishing explicitly between two covenants: a *covenant of works* (also called the covenant of law, nature, or life) made with Adam as the federal head of the human race and a *covenant of grace* made with believers and their children. The first covenant required Adam's personal fulfillment of the stipulations, on the basis of which he and all of his posterity would

---

99. Stephens, *The Theology of Ulrich Zwingli*, 215.

100. Calvin, *The Epistles of Paul the Apostle to the Galatians, Ephesians, Philippians and Colossians*, ed. David W. Torrance and Thomas F. Torrance, trans. T. H. L. Parker (Grand Rapids: Eerdmans, 1965), 85–86: "legal and evangelical." "For the legal covenant makes slaves and the evangelical covenant free-men" (86). He has already labored the law-gospel distinction throughout, especially 53–69.

101. John Calvin, *Commentary on Galatians*, in *Reformation Commentary on Scripture*, New Testament 10, *Galatians, Ephesians*, ed. Gerald Bray (Downers Grove, IL: InterVarsity, 2011), 102.

102. Calvin, *Commentary on Galatians*, in *Reformation Commentary on Scripture*, 10:160.

be confirmed in righteousness, immortality, and glory. The presence of the elements of an ancient treaty—alongside references such as Hosea 6:7, "But like Adam they transgressed the covenant"—supports the contention that the original relationship between God and humanity was determined by this covenant.[103]

In addition to other passages, federal theologians especially point to Romans 5:12–21, with its explicit contrast between the covenantal headships of Adam and Christ: specifically, the imputation of original sin and justification, respectively. In this view, Christ perfectly and personally fulfilled all righteousness as the "last Adam," bore the sanctions on behalf of his elect, and rose again as the head of his body. Even repentance and faith are gifts dispensed by the Spirit through this unchangeable oath. Furthermore, united to Christ, all believers are not only justified but are renewed inwardly, sanctified progressively, and will one day be raised bodily in the likeness of their ascended head. These are not conditions that the believer must fulfill in order to be justified but the conditions that God himself gives along with justification by uniting sinners to Christ. With some differences in nuance, Lutheranism's distinction between law and gospel finds its corollary within Reformed theology in the distinction between the covenant of works and the covenant of grace.

One of the most succinct statements of this scheme of the two historical covenants is found in the seventh chapter of the Westminster Confession of Faith:

> The distance between God and the creature is so great, that although reasonable creatures do owe obedience unto him as their Creator, yet they could never have any fruition of him, as their blessedness and reward, but by some voluntary condescension on God's part, which he hath been pleased to express by way of covenant. The first covenant made with man was a covenant of works, wherein life was promised to Adam, and in him to his posterity, upon condition of

---

103. Among the myriad sources that could be cited to this point, see Peter Van Mastricht, *Theologia Theoretico-Practica*, vol. 3 (*Editio nova*: Utrecht and Amsterdam, 1725; repr., Morgan, PA: Soli Deo Gloria, 2002), xii, 23, 289–90, etc.; Johannes Cocceius, *Summa Theologiae ex Scripturis repitita* 22.1, cited in Heinrich Heppe, *Reformed Dogmatics*, ed. Ernst Bizer, trans. G. T. Thompson (London: Allen & Unwin, 1950; repr., London: Wakeman Great Reprints, 2002), 281; Herman Witsius, *The Economy of the Covenants*, 2 vols., trans. William Crookshank (London: R. Baynes, 1822; repr., Escondido, CA: Den Dulk Foundation, 1990); 1:135–61; Edward Fisher, *The Marrow of Modern Divinity* (Ross-shire, UK: Christian Focus, 2009), 75–76.

perfect and personal obedience. Man, by his Fall, having made himself incapable of life by that covenant, the Lord was pleased to make a second, commonly called the covenant of grace: wherein he freely offered unto sinners life and salvation by Jesus Christ, requiring of them faith in him, that they may be saved, and promising to give unto all those that are ordained unto life, his Holy Spirit, to make them willing and able to believe.[104]

This system is also explored thoroughly by Herman Witsius (1636–1708), John Owen (1616–83), and Francis Turretin (1623–87) among many others.

Defining the Two Covenants

By the dawn of the seventeenth century, a consensus emerged around a distinction between the covenant of creation and the covenant of grace. Yet behind these two covenants stood a third: the *covenant of redemption*. This is an eternal pact between the persons of the Trinity for the salvation of the elect from the mass of condemned humanity. Reformed theologians pointed out that Jesus speaks of having been given a people by the Father before all ages (John 6:39–44; 10; 17:1–5, 9–11).[105]

In addition, Paul speaks of God's "eternal purpose in election" (Rom 8:28–31; 9:11; Eph 1:4–5, 11; 3:11; 2 Tim 1:9), and the writer to the Hebrews speaks of the "unchangeable oath" that rests on God's promise rather than on human activity (Heb 6:17–20) and represents Jesus as announcing in his ascension, "Behold, I and the children God has given me" (Heb 2:13). Thus, lying behind the covenants with human beings in history, it is this eternal covenant, grounded in the free love and mercy of the Trinity, that gives the covenant of grace its absolute and unconditional basis. According to these theologians, it is this covenant of redemption that lies behind both the *historia salutis* (the history of God's redeeming acts) and the *ordo salutis* (the application of redemption). "For those whom he foreknew he also predestined to be conformed to the image of his Son, in order that he might be the firstborn among many brothers. And those whom he predestined he also called, and those whom he called he also justified, and those whom he justified he also glorified" (Rom 8:29–30). The Father elects, the

---

104. *Westminster Confession of Faith*, 7.1–3.
105. See J. V. Fesko, *The Trinity and the Covenant of Redemption* (Ross-shire: Mentor, 2016).

Son redeems, and the Spirit calls the elect to faith, through which they are justified, sanctified, and kept until their glorification. A remarkable consensus was held on this federal scheme across episcopal, presbyterian, and independent divides both on the Continent and in Britain.

COVENANT OF CREATION (LAW)

Zacharius Ursinus, primary author of the Heidelberg Catechism, begins his commentary on the catechism by stating in usual fashion that the whole of Scripture may be gathered into two headings, "Law and Gospel."[106] Caspar Olevianus, coauthor of the Heidelberg Catechism, sees in the original covenant's prohibition the essence of the whole law—love of God and neighbor.[107] And in this state Adam, and his covenant heirs, could expect royal entrance into the consummation, the Sabbath rest of God himself, and everlasting confirmation in righteousness. In the words of the Formula Consensus Helvetica, "The promise annexed to the covenant of works was not just the continuation of earthly life and felicity," but of a confirmation in righteousness and everlasting heavenly joy.[108]

William Perkins went out of his way in both theological writings and commentaries to link the law-gospel distinction to the covenant of works and the covenant of grace, even linking the Sinai covenant to the former.[109] In his Galatians commentary, he emphasizes, "For the two testaments, the law and the gospel, are two in nature, substance, or kind. And the difference lies not in the presence or absence of the Spirit." The "papists," he says, "establish a third testament compounded of both," by their confusion of law and gospel. Yet for Paul these remain distinct. "And here lies the difference between the law and the gospel. The law is from Sinai; the gospel, from Zion or Jerusalem."[110]

---

106. Zacharius Ursinus, *Commentary on the Heidelberg Catechism*, trans. G. W. Willard (1852; repr. Phillipsburg, NJ: P&R, n.d.), 1.

107. Caspar Olevianus, *De substantia foederis gratuiti inter Deum et electos*, 169, cited in Heppe, *Reformed Dogmatics*, 294.

108. Heppe, *Reformed Dogmatics*, 295.

109. William Perkins, *The Golden Chain*, in *The Works of William Perkins*, ed. Ian Breward, Courtenay Library of Reformation Classics 3 (Appleford, UK: Sutton Courtenay, 1970), 211–12.

110. William Perkins, *Commentary on Galatians*, in *The Works of William Perkins*, ed. Paul M. Smalley (Grand Rapids: Reformation Heritage, 2015), 302–3. There were differences over the question of whether (and, if so, to what extent) the Sinai covenant was a "republication" of the covenant of works. Geerhardus Vos offers a nuanced approach to this question when he says that "Scripture repeatedly sets the old and new covenants in opposition with each other (cf., e.g., Heb 8:8). To be sure, in such places the opposition is not directly between the covenant in Christ and that in Adam but between the new dispensation of the covenant of grace and the old. However,

Warnings against confusing the gospel with the law went hand-in-hand with those against turning the covenant of grace into a covenant of works. It seems that the two distinctions were interchangeable. Peter van Mastricht (1630–1706) warns against those (chiefly Rome) who would turn the gospel into a "new law." The "works of the law" demand "most punctilious obedience ('cursed is the man who does not do all the works therein')." Only in this context, says Mastricht, can we possibly understand the role of Jesus Christ as the "fulfiller of all righteousness."

> Heb. 2.14–15 (since the children are sharers in blood and flesh, he also in like manner partook of the same; that through death he might bring to nought him that hath the power of death, that is, the devil). . . . If you say the apostle is speaking of a covenant not in Paradise, but the covenant at Sinai, the answer is easy, that the Apostle is speaking of the covenant in Paradise so far as it is re-enacted and renewed with Israel at Sinai in the Decalogue, which contained the proof of the covenant of works.[111]

Mastricht argues further:

> Synonyms of the covenant of works are extant in the NT Rom. 3.27 (where is the glory? It is excluded. By what manner of law? Of works? Nay: but by a law of faith) Gal. 2:16 (knowing that a man is not justified by the works of the law save through faith in Jesus Christ . . . because by the works of the law shall no flesh be justified).[112]

In addition to the exegetical arguments, Mastricht adduces the intrasystematic importance of the doctrine:

---

one must bear in mind that the old dispensation of the covenant of grace bore a legal character for Israel as a nation and, therefore, *in its external form* once more kept the covenant of works in view, although the core of what God established with Israel was of course the continuation of the Abrahamic revelation of the covenant of grace" (Geerhardus Vos, *Reformed Dogmatics*, vol. 2, *Anthropology*, trans. and ed. Richard B. Gaffin, Jr. [Bellingham, WA: Lexham, 2012], 36, emphasis added). Later he adds, "The covenant with Israel served in an emphatic manner to recall the strict demands of the covenant of works. . . . This law was not, as Cocceius meant, simply a form for the covenant of grace. It truly contained the content of the covenant of works." Hence, it was "a ministry of condemnation," which was nevertheless essential for the realization of the covenant of grace in Christ. The law itself is not "an independent covenant of works," but it is also "not a summary of the covenant of grace" (130).

111. Cited in Heppe, *Reformed Dogmatics*, 290.

112. Cited in Heppe, *Reformed Dogmatics*, 289–90.

To very many heads of the Christian religion, e.g., the propagation of original corruption, the satisfaction of Christ and his subjection to divine law Rom. 8.3–4 (what the law could not do, in that it was weak through the flesh, God, sending his own Son in the likeness of sinful flesh and for sin, condemned sin in the flesh, that the requirement of the law might be fulfilled in us, who walk not after the flesh, but after the Spirit) Gal. 3:13 (Christ redeemed us from the curse of the law, having become a curse for us . . .), we can scarcely give suitable satisfaction, if the covenant of works be denied.[113]

Even those who found themselves on opposite sides in many debates, like Cocceius and Voetius, jointly emphasized the absolute and unconditional foundation of the covenant and saw the law–gospel distinction as integral for its preservation.[114] According to Cocceius (1603–69),

Man who comes upon the stage of the world with the image of God, exists under a law and a covenant, and that a covenant of works. . . . When further we say that he who bears the image of God given in creation was established under God's covenant, we do not mean that he has a right to the communion and friendship of God, but that he is in that state in which he ought to ask the right to the communion and friendship of God and to make it stable and so to have the offer of God's friendship, if he obeys His law.[115]

---

113. Heppe, *Reformed Dogmatics*, 290.

114. Heppe, *Reformed Dogmatics*, 290–91, from Cocceius, *Summa Theologiae ex Scripturis repitita* 22.1.

115. Cocceius, *Summa Theologiae ex Scripturis repitita* 22.1, cited in Heppe, *Reformed Dogmatics*, 281. Cf. Witsius, 1.2.1: "The covenant of works is the agreement between God and Adam created in God's image to be the head and prince of the whole human race, by which God was promising him eternal life and felicity, should he obey all his precepts most perfectly, adding the threat of death, should he sin even in the least detail; while Adam was accepting this condition" (cited in Heppe, *Reformed Dogmatics*, 283). The terms were that "he should by this natural holiness, righteousness and goodness possess a blessed state of life" (Eglin, *De foedere gratiae* 2.10, cited in Heppe, *Reformed Dogmatics*, 283). For a somewhat baroque explanation: "According to this the covenant of works retained the following four connections (Wyttenbach Tent. II, 571): 'The act by which a first party demands something from a second is called *stipulatio*; the act by which it assigns good to it, *promissio*; while the act by which the second party takes upon itself to supply what the first had demanded is called *adstipulatio* and where it asks for the promise, *restipulatio*. Thus in any covenant there are four acts, two belonging to the party initiating the covenant, and two to that which accepts the covenant offered. In God's covenant with the first man all four covenant acts are discernible. Whereas God has demanded of man perfect keeping of the law, we have discerned the *stipulatio* in it, and whereas He promised man life in heaven and has already conferred the greatest happiness in this world, we discern the *promissio*. On the other side as long as man studied to keep God's law, *adstipulatio* was being given by him to God's demand. Had

This covenantal arrangement is "God's pact with Adam in his integrity, as the head of the whole human race, by which God requiring of man the perfect obedience of the law of works promised him if obedient eternal life in heaven, but threatened him if he transgressed with eternal death; and on his part man promised perfect obedience to God's requirement."[116]

The point that this covenant was made "with Adam in his integrity" is crucial. Prior to the fall, humanity in Adam was neither *sinful* nor *confirmed* in righteousness. He was on trial: would he follow his covenant Lord's pattern of working and resting, subduing and reigning, or would he go his own way and seek his own good apart from God's Word? Created for obedience, he was entirely capable of maintaining himself in a state of integrity. In this perspective, love and law are not antitheses; law prescribes in concrete terms what love looks like in relation to God and fellow humans. As Irenaeus's account explains, Adam was created good but immature, and he had a vocation to fulfill. In Adam, humanity was on trial covenantally. Would he pass—and we in him—from the trial of service into the glorious reward of sons? This original trial sets the scene for the history of Israel, climaxing in Christ as the Second Adam, and the entire Bible was read and preached according to this typological structure of promise and fulfillment.

Herman Witsius's widely influential *Economy of the Covenants* (1677) reflects the mature consensus in organizing Scripture according to its own internal covenantal principle by recognizing the covenant of works and the covenant of grace. Confusion at this point would mean confusion of law and gospel—the very confusion that Paul lamented in Romans 10 concerning his fellow Jews and that he criticized with such vehemence in Galatians. Wilhelmus à Brakel observed the importance of the distinction between law and gospel as bound up with that between the covenant of works and the covenant of grace. "Acquaintance with it is of the greatest importance, for whoever errs here or denies the existence of the Covenant of Works will not understand the Covenant of Grace."[117]

---

he persisted therein vigorously and non-stop, he might in the end have asked a good promise of God and so *restipulatio* would have ensued" (295).

116. Heppe, *Reformed Dogmatics*, 283, citing Heidegger.

117. Wilhelmus à Brakel, *The Christian's Reasonable Service*, 4 vols. (Grand Rapids: Reformation Heritage, 1999), 1:355.

COVENANT OF GRACE (GOSPEL)

Once this Second Adam has successfully fulfilled the Adamic covenant ("For their sakes I sanctify myself that they may be truly sanctified"), the benefits of this feat are dispersed by the Spirit according to a *gracious* covenant. Thus the terms of the divine benediction are reversed. Instead of acknowledging the inherent goodness, truth, and beauty of sinners, the Father pronounces those qualities on the basis of the inherent justice of another (*iustitia alienum*), his Son. It is a true judgment rather than a legal fiction because the requisite covenantal righteousness is fully present in the covenantal head (in fulfilling the creation covenant) and therefore belongs to his body by incorporation.

Like the covenant of creation (or works), this covenant is made between God and human partners—in this case, fallen Adam, Seth, Abraham, and David. In this covenant, provisions are made for offenders, based on another fulfilling the legal covenant on their behalf. Thus, the federal theologians commonly contrasted the covenant of works and the covenant of grace in terms of its basic principle: "Do this and you shall live" versus "Live and you will do this." It is precisely this contrast that, according to the Reformed theologians, energizes so much of Pauline theology. Jesus is the faithful Israelite who fulfilled the covenant of works so that we could through his victory inherit the promises according to a covenant of grace. This gracious covenant is announced in Eden after the fall as the so-called *protoeuangelion* (Gen 3:15).

The Abrahamic covenant rather than the Mosaic covenant establishes the terms according to which people from every nation now share in the Israel of God. In this context we can better understand passages like Jeremiah 31:32, where God pledges a "new covenant" that is "not like the conditional covenant that Israel swore at Sinai, and Galatians 3:17–18, "This is what I mean: the law, which came 430 years afterward, does not annul a covenant previously ratified by God, so as to make the promise void. For if the inheritance comes by the law, it no longer comes by promise; but God gave it to Abraham by a promise." Through Jeremiah, God prosecutes the terms of the Sinai covenant: "And the men who transgressed my covenant and did not keep the terms of the covenant that they made before me, I will make them like the calf that they cut in two and passed between its parts" (Jer 34:18). Once again, this curse-formula fits the terms of Sinai: the people swearing the oath, assuming its sanctions, in sharp contrast with the Abrahamic promise in Genesis 15.

Thus in the covenant of grace God restores in his new creation what was lost in the old creation and could not be recovered according to the original principle that was established in nature and at Sinai. But because of the covenant of grace, and the Messiah's having fulfilled the covenant of works, "There remains a Sabbath rest for the people of God" (Heb 4:1, 9). There also remains a place for the law. In fact, it is only because of justification and the covenant of grace that the law can actually be a delight. The Westminster Confession teaches that believers are still obligated to the law, "but not as a covenant of works" (7.6). In other words, the law no longer functions as the basis of acceptance. The same emphasis is found seminally in Augustine's comment, "It is not therefore by the law, nor is it by their own will, that they are justified; but they are justified *freely by His grace*—not that it is wrought without our will, but our will is by the law shown to be weak, that grace may heal its infirmity; and that our healed will may fulfill the law, *not by compact under the law*, nor yet in the absence of law."[118] "Compact" here is *foedus*, the same word for "covenant."

Covenant theology has always therefore been eschatologically oriented, convinced that creation was the beginning rather than the goal of human existence. Humankind was created to pass through the probationary period and attain the right to eat from the Tree of Life. The telos of human existence was not fully present in creation but held out as a future reward. Humankind would lead creation in triumphal procession into the consummation, represented by the Tree of Life. Adam was to imitate God's sovereign session and, as a creature, to climb the steps of eternal glory, claim the prize for himself and his posterity, and take his place as vassal-king under the great Suzerain. Only in the fulfillment of the covenant of creation by the second Adam is the destiny of the image-bearer finally attained and dispensed through the covenant of grace. In this way, all of human history should be read in the light of Christ's advent, life, death, resurrection, and exaltation to the right hand of the Father.

---

118. Augustine, *A Treatise on the Spirit and the Letter*, in *NPNF*[1] 5:89.

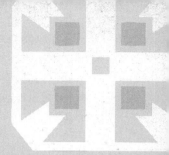

CHAPTER 11

THE TRIUMPH OF NOMINALISM

"The Reformation teaching of justification by faith alone (*sola fide*) exemplified a great deal of continuity with the nominalist tradition. This continuity centered on the imputation of Christ's righteousness."[1] This critique by Reformed theologian Hans Boersma is representative of a particular narrative that I have glanced at periodically but will now address focally in this chapter. According to this story, the Reformation was a prime carrier of the nominalism that has emptied into the gulf of postmodern nihilism. Although the label has been discredited by specialists, through the labors especially of scholars associated with Radical Orthodoxy, nominalism has become in recent decades a very clear and well-defined late medieval school with a united program of dismantling a participationist metaphysics.[2] Though the term is now corrupted by historical anachronisms, I will continue to use it here to refer to a univocal metaphysics associated with Ockham and Biel.

This genealogy has a somewhat lengthy heritage, beginning at least with Joseph Lortz as well as Henri de Lubac and the so-called *nouvelle théologie*. With more expansiveness and less nuance and engagement with primary sources, John Milbank and other scholars associated with the label "Radical Orthodoxy" assert frequently that "late medieval nominalism,

---

1. Hans Boersma, *Heavenly Participation: The Weaving of a Sacramental Tapestry* (Grand Rapids: Eerdmans, 2011), 92; cf. Boersma, *Nouvelle Théologie and Sacramental Ontology* (New York: Oxford University Press, 2013).
2. On the discrediting of the label, see Alister E. McGrath, *Iustitia Dei: A History of the Christian Doctrine of Justification*, vol. 1, *Beginnings to 1500* (Cambridge: Cambridge University Press, 1985), 166–70. "Nominalism" was not coined until long after Ockham and Biel and there never was a nominalist school per se. Besides, the term fails to distinguish figures who diverged widely even over questions related directly to univocity and analogy.

the protestant reformation and seventeenth-century Augustinianism . . . completely privatised, spiritualised and transcendentalised the sacred, and concurrently, reimagined nature, human action and society as a sphere of autonomous, sheerly formal power."[3] For Milbank and others, the Reformation's doctrine of justification is only the tip of the nominalist iceberg that the church struck fatally as the late Middle Ages gave way to the dawn of modernity.[4] Given the scope of the present work, I will confine my engagement to the doctrine of justification.

WAS LUTHER A NOMINALIST?

Luther's studies at Erfurt (1501–5) brought him into the center of the *via moderna*, with Jodocus Trutvetter and Bartholomew Arnoldi of Usingen.[5] His earliest work was *Randbemerkungen zu Gabriel Biel* (1509–10), and he sided with Ockham on universals.[6] Heiko Oberman is right: "Luther was a nominalist, there is no doubt about that."[7] Luther is his own witness on this account: "I demand arguments, not authorities. That is why I contradict my own school of Occamists, which I have absorbed completely."[8] But this statement points to the complexity of the relationship: he absorbed it completely and also rejected it. We must allow Luther the privilege of telling us at least what he thought about nominalism after his turnabout, and his *Disputation against the Scholastics* is almost exclusively focused on this school.[9]

---

3. John Milbank, *Theology and Social Theory: Beyond Secular Reason* (Oxford: Wiley-Blackwell, 2006), 9. See also John Milbank, *Beyond Secular Order* (Oxford: Wiley-Blackwell, 2013), 28–48; John Milbank, Graham Ward, and Catherine Pickstock, "Suspending the Material: The Turn of Radical Orthodoxy," in *Radical Orthodoxy: A New Theology*, ed. John Milbank, Graham Ward, and Catherine Pickstock (London: Routledge, 1999), 3: "The central theological framework for radical orthodoxy is participation as developed by Plato and reworked by Christianity, because an alternative configuration perforce reserves a territory independent of God. The latter can lead only to nihilism (though in different guises)."

4. See James K. A. Smith and James H. Olthuis, eds., *Radical Orthodoxy and the Reformed Tradition: Creation, Covenant and Participation* (Grand Rapids: Baker Academic, 2005).

5. On Luther's nominalist formation, see (in addition to Oberman) David C. Steinmetz, *Luther and Staupitz: An Essay in the Intellectual Origin of the Protestant Reformation* (Durham, NC: Duke University Press, 1980); Gordon Rupp, *The Righteousness of God: Luther Studies* (London: Hodder and Stoughton, 1953), esp. 87–89; Miyon Chung provides a good overview of Luther's movement away from Nominalism in "Faith, Merit, and Justification: Luther's Exodus from Ockhamism *En Route* to Reformation," *Torch Trinity Journal* 6 (2003): 210–39.

6. Gordon Rupp, *The Righteousness of God: Luther Studies* (London: Hodder and Stoughton, 1953), 88.

7. Heiko Oberman, *Man Between God and the Devil* (New Haven, CT: Yale University Press, 2006), 122.

8. Oberman, *Man Between God and the Devil*, 120.

9. Miyon Chung, "Faith, Merit, and Justification: Luther's Exodus from Ockhamism *En Route* To Reformation," *Torch Trinity Journal* 6 (2003): 213.

We require subtlety and attention to primary sources to tease out where nominalism continued to influence Luther's thinking despite his vehement denunciation of the system. This is especially true in relation to Luther as a transitional figure who was in transition himself and was a more occasional than systematic thinker. Critics often focus on "dualism" as the tie that binds the Reformation to nominalism: church versus state, God's agency versus human agency, sacred versus secular, revelation versus reason, and so forth. This is an ironic charge coming from advocates of Neoplatonism, especially since Reformed theology (especially in the Dutch tradition) has been distinctively polemical against "dualism" especially of the Platonic/Neoplatonic variety. However, this charge assumes that *distinctions* are *separations*, which is certainly not characteristic of the Lutheran or Reformed treatment of these topics. In fact, more than Radical Orthodoxy, the Reformers affirmed the temporal city, common grace, and common callings in the world. With these cautions, we can more carefully analyze the influence of nominalism.

We do see evidence of the continuing influence of nominalism in Luther on various topics—for example, in some of his treatments of the relation between church and state (correlated with soul and body, Christ and Satan). This, we have seen, follows Biel. However, when he hears this antithesis from radicals like Thomas Müntzer, Luther becomes more nuanced; in *On Temporal Authority* (1523), Luther instead sees the church and the state as "God's two hands" guiding both salvation and providence. Luther's mature thinking has no autonomous secular realm. God maintains his lordship over everyone and every place and time, but he does so in different ways with different ends and means. Luther carried his respect for Augustine as the greatest interpreter of Scripture throughout his days, and the bishop's *City of God* shaped Luther's views of the "two governments" obviously far more than nominalism.

Luther's vituperations against "Whore Reason" are too sweeping to be an accurate reflection of nominalism and are more representative of typical humanist criticisms of scholasticism. Luther's suspicion of philosophy was due to his conviction that *on all hands* theology had become captive to theories considered reasonable to the natural person rather than to revelation. Aristotle's *Physics* had been put to bad use in Thomas's subjection of grace to the causal transition from movement to rest, and the philosopher's *Ethics*—especially at the hands of his nominalist teachers—had backed the assumption that people become good by doing good things. Nominalism was even more committed to aspects of Aristotelian philosophy than earlier scholastics, ignoring, for example, Aquinas's caution against following Aristotle at this point.

On other points, Luther's fulminations against Aristotle appear to have a generally humanist rather than nominalist inspiration. Even here, though, Luther's criticism was not universal. In his 1520 "Open Letter to the Christian Nobility," he thought that Aristotle's *Rhetoric*, *Logic*, and *Poetics* should remain standard textbooks.[10] It is when Aristotelian theories are used by scholastics to subvert justification that the Reformer becomes unsettled. As Erasmus displays, the appeal to philosophical over scriptural arguments extols virtue and freedom of the will in heavenly matters, Melanchthon complains.[11] Lacking serious engagement with the sources, narratives of this sort miss Luther's point. Erasmus was the archdefender of voluntarism in that debate, after all. As we have seen, especially in chapter 8, the emphases in the Reformers that Milbank and others attribute to nominalism (e.g., God's freedom and sovereignty in predestination and justification as well as the bondage of the will) are thoroughly Augustinian.

Melanchthon was better-versed in Aristotle and admired the philosopher. Timothy Wengert observes, "In 1528 he would attack not the Scholastic exegetes' use of Aristotle in interpreting the Scripture, but their inept use of the rhetorical and dialectical tools that Aristotle provided."[12] In terms of method, terminology and categories, Lutheran and Reformed orthodoxy were Aristotelian. But this says nothing about the content, including how much they agreed with specific views of Aristotle, particularly on metaphysical and ethical questions. However, most of the formative figures of Protestant orthodoxy after the magisterial Reformers themselves were inclined toward Aristotle even on many of these matters, while others preferred Plato. Melanchthon's influence no doubt contributed, but there were many other Reformers who did not exhibit the hostility toward Aristotle and scholasticism that characterized humanists more generally.

---

10. Martin Luther, "An Open Letter to the Christian Nobility of the German Nation Concerning the Reform of the Christian Estate" (1520), in *Works of Martin Luther*, vol. 2, trans. C. M. Jacobs (Philadelphia: A. J. Holman, 1915), 4.

11. Timothy J. Wengert, *Law and Gospel: Philip Melanchthon's Debate with John Agricola of Eisleben over Poenitentia*, Texts and Studies in Reformation & Post-Reformation Thought (Grand Rapids: Baker, 1997), 85.

12. Wengert, *Law and Gospel*, 85.

Luther does not exhibit the philosophical interest or perhaps even sufficient expertise to propose a sophisticated account of the relation between revelation and reason in the abstract. His provocations were pastorally-motivated. Both mystics and nominalists sought to penetrate heaven itself to behold the naked God, Luther thundered.[13] In context, his attacks on reason were identical to his fulminations against "enthusiasm": it is not reason or experience per se that are the problem, but the arrogance of human beings in preferring to follow their own autonomous conjectures rather than the express word of God. Otherwise, as Bruce D. Marshall notes, Luther shares many similarities with Aquinas on the larger questions of faith and reason.[14]

To be sure, Luther's account of how Christ is present in the Lord's Supper is still very much indebted to nominalist physics.[15] Yet even at the point where Luther is most beholden to nominalism—consubstantiation over transubstantiation—there are obvious differences. Right or wrong, Luther was driven by exegetical and theological arguments centered on the incarnation. And one can hardly contrast these views in terms of their relative concordance with reason. Even by Aquinas's reckoning, the dogma of transubstantiation is entirely improbable in terms of natural reason. Oberman explains that, like Aquinas himself, Thomists insisted, "Obedience, and thus action of will, is the only possible reaction to a presentation of this doctrine. Faith is a much more reliable form of knowledge than so-called scientific knowledge can be since it has as its object God, who is more infallible than any human object or inquiry ever could be."[16] The content of Scripture is of no consequence to its acceptance, but the will submits to the infallible authority of its divine author. "The beginning of faith is, therefore, assent to the veracity of the Christian faith, that is, assent to the Bible in its entirety."[17] When Luther argues similarly, why is he singled out for ranking Scripture about rational speculation?

There is a version of the distinction between God revealed and hidden, but unlike Luther's version it corresponds to past and future events

---

13. Timothy F. Lull, *Luther's Basic Theological Writings* (Minneapolis: Fortress, 1989), 30–49.

14. Bruce D. Marshall, "Faith and Reason Reconsidered: Aquinas and Luther on Deciding What Is True," *The Thomist* 63 (1999): 1–28.

15. Thomas M. Osborne, "Faith, Philosophy, and the Nominalist Background to Luther's Defense of the Real Presence," *Journal of the History of Ideas* 63:1 (2002): 63–82.

16. Oberman, *The Harvest of Medieval Theology: Gabriel Biel and Late Medieval Nominalism* (Durham, NC: Labyrinth, 1983), 71.

17. Oberman, *The Harvest of Medieval Theology*, 74.

rather than to God's hiddenness *in* his revelation.[18] Furthermore, for Biel divine revelation is essentially information and exhortation.[19] This is far removed from Luther's performative and sacramental conception of the Word as "living and active," creating the world of which it speaks.[20] We must get beyond similar terminology and inquire as to what Luther is doing with concepts and categories he learned in the schools.

One may also discern the specter of the *potentia Dei absoluta* hovering over Luther's distinction between the hidden and revealed God in *The Bondage of the Will*. Historians of ideas are often tempted to find easy explanations for theological positions by locating them on the map of regnant philosophical schemes. Peter Harrison does this by discerning the specter of nominalist voluntarism (at least with respect to God) in the emphases of Luther and Calvin, especially (1) God's radical freedom and inscrutable will and (2) the idea that acts are good because God commands them, not vice versa.

> It follows that apparently virtuous acts carried out by human agents derive their goodness not from any putative inherent worth, but because God chooses to regard them as meritorious. The reformers' commitment to voluntarism thus explains in part their attitude to good works. For Calvin, even the redemptive work of Christ was efficacious only because of God's free decision to accept it as gen-uinely meritorious. Calvin's voluntarist inclinations also provide a partial explanation of his difficult and counterintuitive doctrine of election, according to which God preordains who will be saved and who will be damned. What is just and moral is to be understood in terms of the divine will, and not the reverse.[21]

The argument makes perfect logical sense, if only the Reformers had actually made it. Not even Luther equated the "hidden God" with Ockham's "absolute power" (*de potentia Dei absoluta*). Gordon Rupp points out that where nominalists appealed to the absolute power as a launching pad for speculation, for Luther absolute power is the limit to

---

18. Oberman, *The Harvest of Medieval Theology*, 78.

19. Oberman, *The Harvest of Medieval Theology*, 70.

20. I explore this emphasis in Luther and Calvin in *People and Place: A Covenant Ecclesiology* (Louisville: Westminster John Knox, 2008), 35–98.

21. Peter Harrison, "Philosophy and the Crisis of Religion," in *The Cambridge Companion to Renaissance Philosophy*, ed. James Hankins (Cambridge: Cambridge University Press, 2007), 245.

human reasoning; we only know God as he has accommodated himself to us in Christ through the gospel, and this "ordained power" is wholly antithetical to nominalism's Pelagianizing tendencies.[22] Again, Augustine's influence is sufficient to account for these emphases in Luther and the other magisterial Reformers. Indeed there is even a more Dionysian (Christian-Neoplatonist) reserve about imagining that we can know God's essential being.

Luther's screeds against "scholasticism" are directed entirely at nominalism. "It is arguable," according to Willem van Asselt and Eef Dekker, "that Luther in fact opposed a new strand of thought in his immediate predecessors and contemporaries. If this line of argument is correct, Luther was in fact a defender of the genuine medieval Augustinian position against a 'modern' [nominalist] paradigm."[23] In fact, they point out that Henri de Lubac "portrays Luther and Calvin as medievals reacting against the new paradigm!"

> Its background is this: in the Augustinian, medieval anthropology, man is essentially made for and directed toward God, i.e., cannot find his fulfillment in the creaturely realm. This picture was almost all-pervasive from Augustine onward. Somewhere in the transition from the Middle Ages to Renaissance a new way of looking at reality arose. Nature was seen now as an independent, autonomous "basement," upon which the first floor might be built. Nature's finality is not seen any longer as aimed at a transcendent grace, but aimed at an immanent, natural fulfillment.[24]

Thus, ironically, the principal thesis on which Milbank and other Radical Orthodoxy writers build does not support their contention that the Reformers were the carriers of nominalism into modernity. In fact, "One of the first straightforwardly applying this divorce between nature and grace is Cajetanus (1469–1534), the cardinal before whom Luther was to appear in 1518."[25] Cajetan is also the culprit in Milbank's

---

22. Gordon Rupp, *The Righteousness of God* (Cambridge: Hodder and Stoughton, 1953), 91; cf. 30, 248–49.

23. Willem J. van Asselt and Eef Dekker, introduction to *Reformation and Scholasticism: An Ecumenical Enterprise* (Grand Rapids: Baker Academic, 2001), 36–37.

24. Van Asselt and Dekker, introduction to *Reformation and Scholasticism*, 37.

25. Van Asselt and Dekker, introduction to *Reformation and Scholasticism*, 37.

narrative: the first "Thomist" to interpret the Angelic Doctor in a pro-
tonominalist direction.[26]

But the Reformers did not share Cajetan's nominalism. "Luther and
Calvin adhered to the Augustinian picture of mankind as essentially,
not only accidentally, related to God."[27] If the dominant interpretation
of Aquinas is correct, then (*pace* de Lubac and Milbank), he did in fact
teach two orders of purpose: a natural and supernatural end. And if this
is true, then the Reformers were more Augustinian and therefore antid-
ualistic than Aquinas. There is one end of human existence, "to glorify
God and to enjoy him forever," as the first answer of the Westminster
Shorter Catechism puts it.

Luther was a complicated figure with many debts besides nominalism, including the Brethren of the Common Life and the Eckhartian
tradition of German mysticism, both of which were as likely sources as
nominalism to tilt him in a more individualistic direction. As Charles
Taylor notes, "This devotion put more emphasis on private prayer, on
introspection; even encouraging the keeping of a journal."[28] None
of the proponents of the Luther-nominalism thesis make a point of
Luther's even more clearly avowed relation to the Neoplatonist mysticism of the *Theologia Germanica*. "Next to the Bible and St. Augustine,
no book has ever come into my hands from which I have learned more
of God and Christ, and man and all things that are," Luther puffed in
its 1518 preface.[29]

Given his antipathy to mysticism as a theology of glory, his emphasis
on God's descent to us in the incarnation and the cross, and the favor
that the "enthusiasts" accorded to *Theologia Germanica*, why would
Luther in the midst of the Reformation hail this work of Eckhartian
Neoplatonism as second only to Scripture itself? This is at least as
important a question as the ongoing influence of nominalism, since
Luther explicitly acknowledged its continuing impact on his thinking.
Though beyond our scope here, such an exploration would complicate
the narrative that casts Luther as a supporting actor in the Scotus Story.
Luther's championing of *Theologia Germanica* should have merited for

---

26. John Milbank, *Beyond Secular Order: The Representation of Being and the Representation of the People* (Oxford: Wiley-Blackwell, 2013), 103. He repeats this charge in many places.

27. Van Asselt and Dekker, introduction to *Reformation and Scholasticism*, 37.

28. Charles Taylor, *A Secular Age* (Cambridge: Harvard University Press, 2007), 70.

29. Martin Luther, preface to *Theologia Germanica* (1518), in *The* Theologia Germanica *of Martin Luther*. Classics of Western Spirituality (New York: Paulist, 1980).

him a more favorable role—not as a pioneer of nihilistic modernity but one of the last defenders of that Christian Neoplatonism which Radical Orthodoxy writers insist can alone resist the lure of nihilism. But this too would be an oversimplification of a rather complex and evolving figure. As I have argued, Luther increasingly repudiated the Origenist ascent of mind. Yet it would be at least as important to understand the lingering impact of Neoplatonism as nominalism on his thinking.

When we come to the question of justification specifically, it is all the more erroneous to correlate Luther's teaching with nominalism. Lacking any serious engagement with primary sources, the approach of Radical Orthodoxy and many sympathetic to this genealogical narrative (such as Hans Boersma and Peter J. Leithart) basically resurrect Joseph Lortz's 1939 thesis, with little or no interaction with the substantial secondary literature refuting it.[30]

First, Luther discovered his understanding of justification as a Bible professor. Hardly alone, Luther was the beneficiary as well as a catalyst for the return to sources, especially the church fathers and the Bible. Luther was indebted to Erasmus's publication of the Greek New Testament (1516). In addition, "Lorenzo Valla's notes on the text of the New Testament, published by Erasmus in 1503 as *Annotations on the New Testament*, thus drew attention to the different implications of the Latin and Greek terms for repentance—respectively *poenitentia* and *metanoia*."[31] The same was true with respect to justification: *dikaiosis* and its cognates vs. *iustificare*.

Second, despite superficial similarities of language, Ockham's construal of God's decision to accept those who are not inherently righteous is as far from Luther's view as possible. "I claim, first," said Ockham, "that a human being is able by the absolute power of God to be saved without created charity." Whatever God can do *through* ordained means and instrumental causes, he can do directly *without* them. Thus, God can give eternal life without there being a created charity infused into one's soul.[32] Yet what Ockham has in mind is far from Luther's thinking. On the contrary, it shows that God "is able to give eternal life without

---

30. See Joseph Lortz, *The Reformation in Germany*, 2 vols. (London: Darton, Longman and Todd, 1968), published in German in 1939. Heiko Oberman refutes this thesis in various places but especially noteworthy is his argument in "'Iustitia Christi' and 'iustitia Dei': Luther and the Scholastic Doctrines of Justification," in *The Dawn of the Reformation: Essays in Late Medieval and Early Reformational Thought* (Grand Rapids: Eerdmans, 1992), 104–25.

31. Harrison, "Philosophy and the Crisis of Religion," 243–44.

32. William of Ockham, *Quidlibetal Questions*, 6.1.2, thesis 1, 492.

such [sanctifying or infused] grace *to someone who does good works.*" As long as they *do what lies within them,* those who are not in a state of grace may merit eternal life. Paul, for example, was given the beatific vision apart from any antecedent habit of grace "as the principle of meriting," even at the moment that he was on his way to persecute the Christians.[33] Further, "The will is able to elicit a meritorious act on its own. Therefore, by God's absolute power a will placed in a purely natural state is able to elicit a meritorious act." Since charity is not within our power, and "nothing is meritorious except that which is within our power," the power of the free will to choose the act is itself sufficient. "Therefore, God could accept such an act, elicited by the will, in the absence of the grace in question."[34]

Luther never taught that by an act of free will one could choose to love God above all else and thereby merit justification even apart from any inherent grace. On this question, he would have agreed with Aquinas: inherent and effectual grace is required even to desire to love God. Luther wrote,

> It is always necessary that the substance or essence of a person be good before there can be any good works and that good works follow and proceed from a person who is already good. Christ says in Matthew 7:18: "A good tree cannot bear bad fruit, nor can a bad tree bear good fruit." . . . The fruit does not make the tree good or bad but the tree itself is what determines the nature of the fruit. In the same way, a person first must be good or bad before doing a good or bad work.[35]

Strictly speaking, according to the Reformers, God's gracious work within the sinner is a necessary prerequisite for justification, since it is through faith that one embraces Christ, and this faith is itself the gift of God. However, regeneration is not the basis of justification in their view.

In the Reformation view, in sharp contrast with nominalism, one gift (forgiveness) cannot be had without the other (regeneration). This is not because regeneration causes forgiveness, as Aquinas would say, but

---

33. William of Ockham, *Quidlibetal Questions,* 6.1.2, thesis 1, 492–93, emphasis added.

34. William of Ockham, *Quidlibetal Questions,* 6.1.2, Thesis 1, 493.

35. Martin Luther, *The Freedom of a Christian,* trans. M. Tanvik (Minneapolis: Augsburg Fortress, 2008), 74–75.

because justification is not the *only* divine act and gift of union with Christ. Everyone who is justified is being sanctified. The basis for both aspects is always Christ himself. Luther's disagreement with Aquinas was on whether to call this inherent and effectual grace *justification* and therefore whether *merit* was an admissible category at all. Ockham's interest in affirming justification as a decree apart from inherent grace was designed to undergird a semi-Pelagian scheme, to encourage sinners to do whatever they can and this would suffice. Nothing could be further from Luther's conception, as he made clear enough in his *Against Scholastic Theology*, which is aimed directly at Ockham and Biel. The sinner is not justified *necessarily* or absolutely by any inherent grace, according to Ockham, because his or her *actions* are sufficient to justify.

Third, contrary to the many characterizations of Biel's doctrine of justification as forensic, he insists that according to God's ordained power no one will be justified apart from created grace. None of the nominalists held that justification was a forensic declaration apart from a change in the sinner.[36] The *pactum* of Ockham and Biel is pure law. "Indeed," McGrath notes, "the *modernus* Gabriel Biel explicitly contrasts a forensic justification before a secular judge with justification as a transformation in relation to God, the spiritual judge."[37] Whatever arbitrary divine decisions Biel may or may not have thought God to make, *justification* was for him a process of moving from injustice to justice. Unlike Aquinas, Biel emphasizes human initiative over God's effectual grace. Infused grace is not regarded by the nominalists as effectual grace but as an aid to free will. In other words, it tends toward semi-Pelagianism. Oberman adds,

> The acceptation by God, however, is not the exterior declaration or *favor dei* of later Protestant orthodoxy; it is the coming of the Holy Spirit himself. In justification, therefore, two gifts are granted: (1) created grace, necessary according to God's revealed will, as the *ratio meriti*; (2) the Holy Spirit, necessary in an absolute sense, as the *ratio acceptationis*. . . . Christ the judge is watching over every *viator* closely to observe whether he is indeed preparing his soul for his inhabitation. . . . This being the case, it does not surprise us that we found no trace of a distinction between justification and sanctification.[38]

---

36. Oberman, *The Harvest of Medieval Theology*, 353.
37. McGrath, *Iustitia Dei*, 51.
38. Oberman, *The Harvest of Medieval Theology*, 354, 356.

Fourth, Scotist/Ockhamist *acceptio* (acceptance) is not Luther's concept of imputation. While Ockham has no real basis for God to reward such actions with justification apart from his mere will, Luther holds that God's justifying verdict is grounded entirely in the perfect obedience and satisfaction of Christ. Luther rejects the nominalist account of nonimputation. For Luther, the remission of sin is not an arbitrary declaration; justification is a positive declaration that is based on the *reality* that Christ has fulfilled the covenant's obligations and this status is imputed to the believer. Ockham's view may indeed be characterized as a "legal fiction." Recall that for Scotus, remission of sin is merely an external change in God's mind with respect to the sinner.[39] However, Luther's view is just as realistic as the Thomistic doctrine; Luther's is simply that *Christ's righteousness imputed* is the basis for God's acceptance rather than *created grace infused* along with the righteousness of Christ, Mary, the saints, and the believer herself imputed. How could one assert that the former is less real than the latter? From the Reformers' perspective, Thomas's formulation rendered Christ insufficient while Ockham's rendered Christ unnecessary.

There is no generic metaphysical "extrinsicism" guiding the Reformers' doctrinal reflections. They certainly do not hold that the world or anything in it is autonomous but insist as resolutely as Aquinas, Augustine, and Scripture that human beings exist in and through God's agency. The world is not related to God merely as an effect of a cause, but as a dependent system of creatures who draw their life from God's loving goodness. Even with respect to sin and grace, the Reformers affirm *both* forensic, extrinsic, and declarative *and* renewing, intrinsic, and sanctifying aspects of union with Christ. Indeed, the very concept of union with Christ that the Reformers work out is inimical to the conception of the God-world relation in nominalist metaphysics. The Reformers hold that original sin involves both the imputation of guilt and corruption; salvation involves both the imputation of Christ's righteousness (justification) and renewal in Christ (sanctification). The inner renewal is not the ground for the verdict, but it is inseparable from it. One cannot be justified apart from regeneration and sanctification.

For the Reformers, imputation is not a mere verdict to regard sinners as righteous. It is the opposite of such an arbitrary decree since it is based

---

39. McGrath, *Iustitia Dei*, 1:50.

on the real righteousness of Jesus Christ, incarnate God, who fulfilled the law and won for himself and his posterity the right to eat from the Tree of Life. In fact, this doctrine of justification is further removed from nominalist provenance than Thomism. God *could not* simply acquit the guilty by royal whim without violence to his simple nature. God's inherent justice requires the condemnation of the ungodly. It is the Reformers who took this fact with the utmost seriousness. If God chooses to have mercy on sinners, the satisfaction of his justice is not only fitting but morally necessary. God is not free to save sinners simply by ignoring their wrongs. By locating this debt in God's justice rather than simply his honor, the deepest possible connection was made between God's decision to show mercy and the work of Christ as the only way of God's being "just and the justifier of the one who has faith in Jesus" (Rom 3:26). The Christ-event is grounded not only in God's will but in God's being: once God freely determines to save sinners, he *must* do so in a way that satisfies his love and his righteousness.

Even with respect to guilt and justification, it is not simply *acts* but the *person* who is the object of God's imputation. Any Augustinian (including Aquinas) holds that original sin is both a moral corruption inherited *and* a legal debt that requires judicial punishment. If the imputation of Christ's righteousness reflects an "extrinsicism" that Augustinian tradition disallows, then an inherited legal liability to judicial punishment for *Adam's* sin must be no less illicit. Or those who force a choice between extrinsic condemnation/justification and inherent corruption/sanctification misunderstand the tradition.

Fifth, even after his initial break with nominalism, Luther continued to move further away from it, and this movement needs to be taken into account when interpreting earlier and later works. Miyon Chung has provided a useful summary of Luther's development in relation to nominalism. Luther did not make any use of the absolute/ordained powers, Chung points out. "He eventually divorced himself completely from the Scholastic anthropology and soteriology and developed a decisively Christocentric doctrine of justification that is often characterized by the principles of 'sola fide' and 'sola gratia.'"[40] Luther's early (pre-Reformation) theology incorporates nominalist epistemology and "the notion of a covenant (*pactum* or *testamentum*) between God and man."[41]

---

40. Chung, "Faith, Merit, and Justification," 225.
41. Chung, "Faith, Merit, and Justification," 225, citing McGrath, *Reformation Thought,* 58.

Biel went beyond Ockham, arguing that according to his ordained power, God is bound to reward merits that are accrued even by the unregenerate, who are nevertheless able by their free will to love God and do what lies within them.[42] So if the unregenerate cease sinning, God is obliged to give the first grace (merit *de congruo*).[43] However, already in Luther's pre-Reformation work on Biel, *Randbemerkungen* (1509–10), Luther moves away from the nominalist view, identifying infused grace with the Holy Spirit, although such uncreated *caritas* is essential to justifying faith.[44]

Luther is basically an Augustinian of the *via antiqua* sort on this point. In his *First Lectures on the Psalms* (1513–15) a christocentric focus emerges, but conversion and justification are still interchangeable terms.[45] "Hence the fact that God has made Himself our debtor is because of the promise of Him who is merciful, not because of the worth of meritorious human nature. He required nothing but preparation, that we might be capable of this gift."[46] But there is no mention of the two powers or for merit *de condigno* in his *pactum*, and he explicitly rejects the *facientibus*.[47] Yet a person "may well prepare himself on the basis of fitness [*de congruo*] because of this promise of God and the covenant of His mercy."[48] "Preparation" is basically humility, recognizing one's sinfulness and need for God's grace over against reliance on works.[49]

Next, in the *Lectures on Romans* (1515–16), Luther criticizes the Ockhamists for introducing contingency into predestination.[50] This critique pushes him further away from the whole scholastic scheme of justification and free will, with reliance on Augustine.[51] There are references to Christ's righteousness as alien but given to us apart from the law.[52] Chung relates, "The concept of *habitus*, then, needs to be replaced with 'the righteousness' that 'depends on the imputation of God.' Righteousness is not a 'quality' or 'the essence of a thing itself,'

---

42. Chung, "Faith, Merit, and Justification," 225, quoting Heinz, 141–42.
43. Chung, "Faith, Merit, and Justification," 225, citing McGrath, *Iustitia Dei,* 1:83, 89.
44. Chung, "Faith, Merit, and Justification," 226.
45. Chung, "Faith, Merit, and Justification," 226–27.
46. Chung, "Faith, Merit, and Justification," 227.
47. Chung, "Faith, Merit, and Justification," 227–28.
48. Chung, "Faith, Merit, and Justification," 228 from Luther, *Psalms* (1513–15), in *LW* 11:397; WA 4:262.
49. Chung, "Faith, Merit, and Justification," 228–29.
50. Luther, Lectures on Romans in *LW* 25:372–3. This is still a typically Augustinian concern.
51. Luther, *Lectures on Romans,* in *LW* 25:258–78.
52. Luther, *Lectures on Romans,* in *LW* 25:252–56.

but that which comes 'only by the imputation of a merciful God through faith in His Word.'"[53] Yet he still speaks of preparation in terms of repentance and humility, crying out for grace.[54] "This idea is communicated in terms of a 'progress of justification' until it reaches its perfection [LW 25:18–19]. In [Romans] 1:17, faith is portrayed as a journey from 'unformed to formed faith or from beginning to perfect faith.'"[55]

In short, during this period we have a movement toward faith in Christ as justifying, over against relying on one's own righteousness, and even an imputation over against an infusion, but with lingering categories of operative and cooperating grace, preparation, and justification as a process. The earliest sermons (1510–16) "are notably ethical in content," notes Chung.[56] There remains an emphasis on humility and the work of the law in producing it.[57]

With the *Disputation against the Scholastic Theology* (1517), we recognize a decisive break. Chung agrees with Leif Grane that this "demonstrates Luther's complete exodus from the *via moderna*." "In theses 57 and 93 Luther specifically denounced Ockham: 'God cannot accept man without his justifying grace. This in opposition to Ockham.' 'There is a kind of subtle evil in the argument that an act is at the same time the fruit and the use of the fruit. In opposition to Ockham, the Cardinal, Gabriel.'"[58]

> For Luther, the grace of God is necessarily active and living, thereby negating the possibility of the remission of sin by God's absolute power without the presence of grace. Human beings in their natural state are utterly incapable of loving God. Apart from grace, the will is incapable of doing any good such as fulfilling the law. Grace in essence is a "director" or "mediator" of the will that reconciles the law with the will. This treatise, therefore, manifests no dependence on Ockhamist soteriology.[59]

Luther's *Lectures on Hebrews* (1517–18) now emphasize the role of faith. "Also, humility is now identified with Christ's humility in the

---

53. Chung, "Faith, Merit, Justification," 231, referencing *LW* 25:274–75.
54. Chung, "Faith, Merit, Justification," 232.
55. Chung, "Faith, Merit, Justification," 232, referencing *LW* 25:152.
56. Chung, "Faith, Merit, Justification," 232.
57. Chung, "Faith, Merit, Justification," 232–33.
58. Chung, "Faith, Merit, Justification," 233–34, quoting *LW* 31:14.
59. Chung, "Faith, Merit, Justification," 234.

Incarnation and crucifixion. The humility of Christ, in turn, is what transforms a person and produces a belief or faith in God. Not only is faith prior to works, but it also makes good works possible."[60] According to Chung, "*Lectures on Hebrews*, therefore, ostensibly attests Luther's complete dismissal of the *quod in se est*."[61]

In the *Lectures on Galatians* (1519), humility as preparation is absent and the *simul iustus et peccator* makes its debut.[62] From this thorough survey, Chung concludes with some irony, "Perhaps it can be said that Luther took Ockham's 'razor' principle to its logical conclusion by piercing through the enormously complex and opaque Scholastic doctrine of saving faith."[63] Carl R. Trueman discerns a clear change in Luther's 1519 sermon, "Two Kinds of Righteousness," which emphasizes Christ's alien righteousness that becomes ours the moment we trust in Christ.[64] As soon as 1520 with *The Freedom of a Christian*, his formulation becomes clearer still as union with Christ becomes a crucial motif. The earlier idea of a proleptic justification, with some confusion between justification and renewal, is now absent.[65]

NOMINALISM AND THE OTHER REFORMERS

Finally, if Luther were corrupted by nominalism, how does one explain the Reformation more generally? In contrast with Luther as well as those who had a significant hand in the theology of Trent, most of the Reformers were not schooled in nominalism at all. Martin Bucer was a traditional Dominican trained in the Dominican monastery in Heidelberg. Bucer studied a year of dogmatics at Mainz and returned to Heidelberg in 1517, where he first met Luther at the Heidelberg Disputation. A survey of his library shows that it was stocked with all of Aquinas's works.[66] Bucer's mentor, Beatus Rhenanus, was a classics scholar trained at the University of Paris under Jacques Lefèvre d'Étaples, who, besides arriving independently of Luther at *sola scriptura*

---

60. Chung, "Faith, Merit, Justification," 234.
61. Chung, "Faith, Merit, Justification," 235.
62. Chung, "Faith, Merit, Justification," 235–36.
63. Chung, "Faith, Merit, Justification," 236.
64. Carl Trueman, "*Simul peccator et justus:* Martin Luther and Justification" in *Justification in Perspective; Historical Developments and Contemporary Challenges*, Bruce L. McCormack (Grand Rapids: Baker Academic, 2006), 77. See *LW* 31:298–99.
65. Trueman, "*Simul peccator et justus*," 77.
66. Martin Greschat, *Martin Bucer: A Reformer and His Times* (Louisville: Westminster John Knox, 2004), 25.

and justification through faith alone, was a noted Aristotelian—and Neoplatonist.

Ulrich Zwingli's friendship with Erasmus was nourished by a common love of Plato, and his successor, Heinrich Bullinger, was trained at Cologne—a center of Thomism with nominalism excluded by statute. Intrigued by Luther's Ninety-Five Theses, Bullinger turned to a close study of Scripture and the church fathers, especially Chrysostom and Jerome as well as Gratian's *Decretum*, where he found no mention of a sacrament of penance. After reading Melanchthon's *Loci communes* in 1522, Bullinger declared himself a "Martinian" (after Martin Luther), and as head of the cloister school in Kappel, he instituted a program for the monks in biblical languages and exegesis. Peter Martyr Vermigli was a Thomist, trained at Padua alongside Cardinals Contarini, Pole, and Seripando. Guillaume Farel, who initiated the Geneva reformation, was trained at the University of Paris and, with Jacques Lefèvre, became part of the Meaux circle around the reform-minded bishop Guillaume Briçonnet. Through Lefèvre's influence, Farel was appointed to teach grammar and philosophy at the College Cardinal Lemoine, eventually becoming regent of the college, and was appointed diocesan preacher by Briçonnet before he had to flee to Switzerland. There is no evidence of any nominalist connection.

Though some have tried in vain to locate Calvin in the Paris classroom of the nominalist John Maior, Calvin rarely entered into the debates that roiled medieval Thomists, Scotists, and Ockhamists, and when he did, he frequently sided with Aquinas and "the better scholastics."[67] His screeds against "the schoolmen" were directed chiefly at contemporaries at the Sorbonne.[68] "The basic opposition of Luther and Calvin to scholasticism is often confined to late medieval nominalism in its semi-pelagian form," note Willem J. van Asselt and Eef Dekker.[69] In its extreme voluntarism, late medieval nominalism had in fact based

---

67. Calvin's actual engagements of scholastic theologians reveal a range of sympathy, depending on the argument and point of view. For example, acknowledging the debate between intellectualism and voluntarism briefly in the *Institutes*, he advised that it was a false choice: that the whole self is involved in every determination. One may conclude that this is philosophically naïve but not that it is voluntarist (much less nominalist). But the idea of Calvin as either a nominalist or as an opponent of scholastic method is not supported by the evidence. See, e.g., Richard A. Muller, *The Unaccommodated Calvin: Studies in the Foundations of a Theological Tradition* (New York: Oxford University Press, 2001), 45–46; and Paul Helm, *John Calvin's Ideas* (Oxford: Oxford University Press, 2006).

68. Van Asselt and Dekker, introduction to *Reformation and Scholasticism*, 40.

69. Van Asselt and Dekker, introduction to *Reformation and Scholasticism*, 36.

predestination on a view of God's absolute will as sovereign even over God's nature. However, with the vigor of any Thomist, Calvin attacked this view directly as "a diabolical blasphemy" that would render God the author of evil and render us balls that he juggles in the air.[70] While all things are subject to God's decree, Calvin said, evil and sin are attributed to Satan and human beings.[71] "And we do not advocate the fiction of 'absolute power'; because this is profane, it ought rightly to be hateful to us. We fancy no lawless god who is a law unto himself."[72] Whether he was targeting Scotus is debatable, but he certainly had in mind the extreme voluntarism represented by Ockham and especially Biel, which was popular at the Sorbonne where Calvin had studied.[73]

So much for Calvin's voluntarism.[74] The one citation in Harrison's summary—to the effect that Christ's death was efficacious because God accepted it as such—omits its context in the *Institutes* 2.17.1, as well as the fact that Aquinas had said the same thing, alongside nearly every other major scholastic theologian. Harrison asserts that "Calvin's voluntarist inclinations also provide a partial explanation of his difficult and counter-intuitive doctrine of election, according to which God preordains who will be saved and who will be damned." Yet in the same essay he acknowledges that, though he finds the idea repulsive, this was the view of Paul and Augustine, who can hardly be said to have been shaped by Ockhamist voluntarism.[75]

Calvin was not a philosopher and only entered upon such ground when soteriological questions were involved. For example, on the

---

70. *Inst.* 3.23.2 and 3.23.4–5. See also Calvin, *Sermons on Job*, trans. Arthur Golding (Edinburgh: Banner of Truth Trust, 1993), 415: "And undoubtedly whereas the doctors of the Sorbonne say that God hath an absolute or lawless power, it is devilish blasphemy forged in hell, for it ought not once to enter into a faithful man's head."

71. *Inst.* 2.4.2.

72. *Inst.* 3.23.2.

73. Scouring Calvin's critical references to the "two powers," David C. Steinmetz argues that the *potentia absoluta* against which he inveighs is an arbitrary and lawless power. See Steinmetz, "Calvin and the Absolute Power of God," in *Journal of Medieval and Renaissance Studies* 18, no. 1 (1988): 65–79.

74. This is contrary to the thesis of Willem J. van Asselt, J. Martin Bac, and Roelf T. te Velde, trans. and eds., *Reformed Thought on Freedom: The Concept of Free Choice in the History of Early-Modern Reformed Theology* (Grand Rapids: Baker Academic, 2010), who interpret Scotus very differently (and favorably) from his critics. They maintain that Scotism provided the ground for affirming genuine contingency over determinism and that while Luther and Calvin remained in the thrall of Thomist/Aristotelian determinism, Reformed orthodoxy followed the Scotist path. Richard Muller challenges this thesis convincingly in *Divine Will and Human Choice: Freedom, Contingency, and Necessity in Early Modern Reformed Thought* (Grand Rapids: Baker Academic, 2017), esp. pt. 3.

75. Harrison, "Philosophy and the Crisis of Religion," 231, 236–37.

question of whether the intellect or will is the determinative faculty, Calvin eschews the complex debates and simply says that it is a false choice: the will and the intellect are mutually engaged in every act. After reviewing some of the distinctions and debates, he concludes, "Though these things are true, or at least plausible, still, as I fear they are more fitted to entangle by their obscurity than to assist us, I think it best to omit them."[76]

Calvin thought of divine and human agency in analogical terms, much like Aquinas. According to Randall Zachman, there is "nearly universal agreement" that Calvin is an "analogical and anagogical theologian."[77] The Reformed orthodox followed Aquinas's doctrine of analogy over Scotus, Richard Muller observes, and "the denial of univocity, taken together with the typical affirmation of an analogy of being, opened the way for the Reformed orthodox to argue a doctrine of the divine attributes that affirmed both the transcendence of God and the intimate relationship of God to the world order."[78] "The soul cannot elicit acts of the understanding and will," Turretin argues, "unless renewed by supernatural dispositions and habits."[79] Thus, "We obtain the new birth, from which acts of faith and love flow forth (1 Jn. 4:7; 5:1)."[80] "The movement of efficacious grace is properly to be called neither physical nor ethical, but supernatural and divine."[81] The Spirit infuses "the supernatural habits of faith and love."[82]

Seminal theologians such as Vermigli, Musculus, Zanchi, Turretin, and Owen were soaked in Aquinas, and it is not exaggerating to say that the intellectual culture of Continental and British Calvinism was more Thomistic than most Counter-Reformation theologians.[83] John Owen

---

76. *Inst.* 1.15.6–8.

77. Randall Zachman, "Calvin as Analogical Theologian," *Scottish Journal of Theology* 51, no. 2 (1998): 162.

78. Richard Muller, "'Not Scotist': Understanding of Being, Univocity and Analogy in Early Modern Reformed Thought," *Reformation and Renaissance Review* 14, no. 2 (2012): 139. See also Muller, *Post-Reformation Reformed Dogmatics*, 4 vols. (Grand Rapids: Baker Academic, 2003), 1:234: "Scotus, the nominalists after him, and virtually all of the formulators of Protestant theology denied the Thomist analogia entis and declared that no proportion exists between the finite and the infinite (*finite et infiniti nulla proportio*)." Cf. Muller, *Post-Reformation Reformed Dogmatics*, 3:109.

79. Francis Turretin, *Institutes of Elenctic Theology*, ed. James T. Dennison Jr., trans. George Musgrave Giger (Phillipsburg, NJ: P&R, 1992), 2:523.

80. Turretin, *Institutes of Elenctic Theology*, 2:523.

81. Turretin, *Institutes of Elenctic Theology*, 2:524.

82. Turretin, *Institutes of Elenctic Theology*, 2:524.

83. Harm Goris, "Thomism in Jerome Zanchi's Doctrine of God," in *Reformation and Scholasticism: An Ecumenical Enterprise*, ed. Willem J. van Asselt and Eef Dekker (Grand Rapids: Baker Academic, 2001), 121–40; and Sebastian Rehnmann, "John Owen: A Reformed Scholastic

displays "some preference for John of Damascus (c. 675–740)" as well as Bernard of Clairvaux. "When Duns Scotus is referred to in *A Dissertation on Divine Justice*, the references are all negative since Owen is here restating the Thomist argument of the absolute necessity of satisfaction, strengthened by Suarez." He is explicitly opposed to Ockham and Biel, favoring Henry of Ghent, Alexander of Hales, and Bonaventure. "However, the most important of the medieval scholastics for Owen was Thomas Aquinas." In this respect he was typical of the Reformed orthodox.[84] In one of the most heated Reformed debates of the seventeenth century, both interlocutors—Voetius and Cocceius—opposed the nominalist interpretation of the absolute-ordinata scheme. "Even if God could actualize his power in other possible worlds, he does not have the power to act beyond his essential righteousness," they concurred. Instead, they followed Thomas.[85]

"John Calvin was more sympathetic to pagan philosophy, perhaps on account of his humanist background," Harrison notes. Yet he too was generally suspicious.[86] "Even Calvin's beloved Augustine was chided for having been 'excessively addicted to the philosophy of Plato.'"[87] Justification and transubstantiation were the fields where the Reformers thought philosophy had taken over.[88] Melanchthon returned to Aristotle, though, and most Lutherans (and Reformed) followed.[89] Just at this time, among other treasures of classical thought, the Renaissance had rediscovered the skeptics of the Academy. "This ancient philosophy according to its leading Renaissance proponent, Michel de Montaigne, 'presents man naked and empty, acknowledging his natural weakness, fit to receive from above some outside power; stripped of human knowledge, and all the more apt to lodge divine knowledge in himself,

---

at Oxford," on pp.181–203 of the same volume. See also Richard A. Muller, *Divine Will and Human Choice: Freedom, Contingency, and Necessity in Early Modern Reformed Thought* (Grand Rapids: Baker, 2017).

84. Rehnmann, "John Owen: A Reformed Scholastic at Oxford," 192.

85. Willem J. van Asselt, "Cocceius Anti-Scholasticus?" in *Reformation and Scholasticism: An Ecumenical Enterprise*, ed. Willem J. van Asselt and Eef Dekker (Grand Rapids: Baker Academic, 2001), 248–49. Not even Scotus fits Radical Orthodoxy's portrait, since "Scotus's emphasis on the *potentia absoluta* does not need to be problematic when it is related to his doctrine of synchronic contingency. In addition, Scotus underlined that the *potentia absoluta* is not allowed to contrast with God's essential attributes" (249n52).

86. Harrison, "Philosophy and the Crisis of Religion," 236–37.

87. Harrison, "Philosophy and the Crisis of Religion," 237, quoting Calvin, *Calvin's Commentaries*, vol. 17, Commentary on the Gospel according to John, trans. William Pringle (Grand Rapids: Baker, 1996), 31 (1:3).

88. Harrison, "Philosophy and the Crisis of Religion," 237.

89. Harrison, "Philosophy and the Crisis of Religion," 241–42.

annihilating his judgment to make room for faith.'"[90] Such a resource may have attracted sympathy from nominalists who walled off reason from faith, but it was scorned by all of the Reformers as the gateway to "Epicurean" infidelity.

While Calvin was reticent to engage in detailed questions of philosophical theology, Reformed orthodoxy drew heavily on medieval categories and issues particularly to refute a host of new challenges, especially from the Jesuits, Molinists, Socinians, and Arminians. For the most part, their conclusions reflect early medieval and Thomist influences rather than Scotist options. In sharp contrast with their Roman Catholic contemporaries, they showed no interest in nominalism, and in fact even those with a voluntarist (Franciscan/Scotist) leaning turned to Aquinas concerning analogy, concursus, double agency, and other important categories.[91]

The Radical Orthodoxy thesis is not susceptible to acknowledging multiple factors and multiple accounts that do not fit neatly into either the genealogy of either Neoplatonism or nominalism. Since the Reformation obviously does not fit well into the former, it *must* belong to the latter. But such a heavy-handed and a priori template does not do justice to the sources.

It is true of course that the Reformation produced unintended consequences that had negative as well as positive effects on emerging modernity. Yet history is complicated and even if we were to confine ourselves to the history of ideas, it seems implausible to imagine that the West would be a glorious domain of Christian Neoplatonism had Scotus, Ockham, and Luther never been born.

Why, for example, is it not just as plausible that unintentionally Aquinas's theory of transubstantiation fundamentally undermined realism by positing accidents without substantial foundation? Aristotelian realism requires the belief that accidents are always accidents of something in particular. If you take away the substance, then the accidents are hovering in midair. As Reformed theologians argued, transubstantiation was not a scriptural mystery that transcended reason; rather, it contradicted Scripture, the senses and reason. Could it be that it was actually those who endorsed such a view who pushed faith and reason apart from each other? Furthermore, advocates of the Scotus Story (as it

---

90. Harrison, "Philosophy and the Crisis of Religion," 242.
91. See Muller, *Divine Will and Human Choice*, chs. 5–8.

reaches the Reformers) seem to forget the Renaissance, which itself was a revival of Neoplatonism (Christian and pagan).

At a time when numerous leading theologians on the Roman Catholic side were explicitly committed to nominalism, not a single reformer or refiner of Reformed orthodoxy in the sixteenth and seventeenth centuries attempted to incorporate the ideas of Ockham or Biel, even those purged of their Pelagianizing theses. The broad consensus of Reformed scholasticism was given to Aquinas's analogical view of participation over against Scotus and especially nominalist departures.[92]

THE COUNCIL OF TRENT

As for the entrance of nominalism into early modernity, de Lubac placed the blame as much upon Tridentine theologians and neo-Thomists as upon the Reformers and their heirs. Milbank makes an effort to do the same, focusing on Michael Baius and other extreme cases as aberrations, while simply dismissing the Reformation traditions as nominalist in one sweep. Luther and his staunchest opponents like Johannes Eck were trained in nominalism, as we have seen. The only difference on this score is that Luther rebelled against it. As for the other Reformers, we have seen that Ockham had no special influence on their thinking. If indeed nominalism fashioned a secular age, what then was its carrier? Until such interpreters interact with the actual sources and answer this question with more than an assumed metanarrative, there is no basis for entertaining their repeated attacks on the Reformation.

It would be just as ridiculous to identify Trent as the gateway to secularism. However, the balance of this chapter argues that particularly on the point of justification, Trent's relationship with nominalism is far more certain and widespread.

Augustinianism at Trent

One way of exposing the nominalist sources of Tridentine theology is by a process of elimination. Were the delegates sent to Trent basically

---

92. See Richard Muller, "'Not Scotist': Understanding of Being, Univocity and Analogy in Early-Modern Reformed Thought," *Reformation and Renaissance Review* 14, no. 2 (2012): 127–50; cf. Steven J. Duby, "Election, Actuality and Divine Freedom: Thomas Aquinas, Bruce McCormack and Reformed Orthodoxy in Dialogue," *Modern Theology* 32 (2016): 325–40.

Augustinians who were seeking to avoid the Scylla of Pelagianism and the Charybdis of the Reformers' teaching?

In the line of archbishop of Canterbury Thomas Bradwardine, the *via Augustini moderna* continued through Gregory of Rimini, who opposed nominalist theologian Peter Aureol and became a bridge between Oxford Scotism and Paris scholasticism. Gregory became the general of his Augustinian Order of Hermits and was eventually given the title *Doctor authenticus*.[93] Johann von Staupitz, vicar general of the Augustinian order in Germany, wrote moving treatises on predestination, grace, and justification.[94] Luther considered Gregory a major forerunner, and although he regarded Staupitz as the one who set him on his path, his mentor did not embrace the Reformation. We can regard these figures as "forerunners of the Reformation" in only a qualified sense. While they advocated for the priority of grace, the centrality and sufficiency of Christ, and the role of faith in receiving Christ with all of his benefits, they regarded justification as a process of conversion from sinner to saint. In other words, they were Augustinians. Consequently, they were the most vociferous critics of Ockham and Biel, particularly when it came to soteriological questions, although they were still working with the mistaken translation of "to justify" as *iustificare*, "to make righteous." Luther's innovation at this point was due to the recovery of the Greek New Testament associated with Erasmus and others.

This tradition of late medieval (or early modern) Augustinianism was not limited to the North. There were similar circles in Italy, especially among Benedictine monasteries, wholly independent of Luther. The movement grew out of a fascination with biblical and patristic scholarship and attracted some of the best and brightest young minds of Italy. Some were members of the so-called *spirituali*, evangelically minded Reformers who would become sympathetic to the concerns of Luther, Bucer, and Calvin.

Tracing the movement in detail, Barry Collett unearths a distinct piety and theology that emphasized the "benefits of Christ" and salvation by grace alone through faith alone.[95] Sharing the humanists' interest

---

93. See James L. Halverson, *Peter Aureol on Predestination: A Challenge to Late Medieval Thought* (Leiden: Brill, 1998).

94. Johann von Staupitz, "The Eternal Predestination of God," in *Forerunners of the Reformation: The Shape of Late Medieval Thought*, ed. Heiko Oberman (Philadelphia: Fortress, 1966), 151–64.

95. Barry Collett, *Italian Benedictine Scholars and the Reformation: The Congregation of Santa Guistinia of Padua*, Oxford Historical Monographs (Oxford: Clarendon, 1985).

in returning to the sources, these monks were also critical of scholastic theology, including nominalism. The circle included Cardinal Gasparo Contarini, who in 1536 was commissioned by Pope Paul III to head a committee for reform. The result was his *Consilium de Emendanda Ecclesia*, which fell on deaf ears when Paul IV succeeded. Paul IV even placed the work on the *Index* in 1539. Contarini continued his labors at the Regensburg conference, attended by Luther, Melanchthon, and Calvin, but his concessions (especially on justification through faith alone) made him suspect thereafter (eventually leading to his assassination).

Another important member of the *spirituali* was Peter Martyr Vermigli. At Padua he had become proficient in Aristotle and Thomistic scholasticism as well as the new humanism, befriending the future cardinal Reginald Pole. He even may have gone to Rome to assist with Contarini in the drafting of the *Consilium*. Eventually, he was elected abbot of several monasteries, chapter general of the Lateran Congregation, and prior of the basilica in Lucca, an independent republic that Rome feared would embrace the Reformation. (In fact, it was this fear that provoked the institution of the Roman Inquisition in 1542.) There Vermigli founded a college where Hebrew and Greek as well as Latin were taught and its most prestigious professors—Immanuel Tremellius, Paolo Cacizi, Celio Secundo Curione, and Girolamo Zanchi—all eventually became Reformed Protestants.

But there is something surprising about this network of Benedictine Reformers. Some, especially Vermigli and Zanchi, were influenced by Augustine and the emphasis of Bernard of Clairvaux on mystical union with Christ. However, the main source for this movement was not Augustine but the Greek fathers, especially Chrysostom. Some followed the usual monastic emphasis on the scale of perfection—a salvation of ascent, whether in a Neoplatonic-mystical vein or the more practical "imitation of Christ" detailed by Thomas à Kempis and the *devotio moderna*. Others were more impressed with the patristic (especially Greek) view of salvation by the incarnation and cross of Christ. United to Christ by faith, believers share in the "benefits of Christ." As Collett's close study of the sources demonstrates, the sharp contrast of the law and the gospel was a staple of their immensely popular writings and preaching. Repeatedly they argue that the purpose of the law is to show us that we cannot be saved by obeying it, so that we will flee to Christ. Even faith is a gift. Nevertheless, some followed Chrysostom's belief that predestination was based on foreseen faith or unbelief. Consequently, they were suspected simultaneously of semi-Pelagianism, especially by the Dominicans, and, with respect to justification, of being a seedbed of the Lutheran heresy in Italy.

Such fears, at least of defection to the Reformation, were justified. Bernardino Ochino, vicar general of the Capuchins, had embraced the Reformation and fled the approaching Inquisition for Geneva after being warned off by Cardinal Contarini as he himself lay dying from having been poisoned by enemies from Rome.[96] A few days later, Vermigli fled for Strasbourg. Later, with Martin Bucer, he accepted the call of Edward VI and Thomas Cranmer to reconstitute studies at Oxford (while Bucer did so at Cambridge) and to assist with the new Book of Common Prayer.

However, the majority of these Benedictine monks, though sympathetic to the Reformation, did not embrace its distinctive doctrines and remained loyal to the Roman church. "For them the split in Latin Christendom was the product of Latin theology, and they held the remedy—taken from the Greek Fathers—in their hands."[97]

The richest gem of the movement's evangelical wing was the *Beneficio di Christo* by Benedetto da Mantova, published in Venice in 1543. At first hailed even by some leading churchmen, the book was suspected of "Lutheran heresy," was burned in Naples, and placed on the *Index*.[98] Entire sections of Calvin's 1536 *Institutes* were incorporated into the text, perhaps as additions by humanist poet Marcantonio Flaminio, who was Calvin's friend. The content reveals the influence also of the Spanish humanist and biblical scholar Juan de Valdés, who, after holding a position at the papal court, retired to Naples where he drew a group of disciples that included Flaminio. The central emphasis was the great exchange, understood as the justification of the ungodly through faith alone. "Valdés taught that man, doubly burdened with original guilt and

---

96. Collett notes, "The year 1542 was a time of crisis for Italian evangelicals. The flight of Ochino, followed a few days later by that of Peter Martyr, was a sign of the dilemma being forced upon them. The work of reconciliation was no longer a virtue, and began to carry the smell of treachery: Contarini told Ochino that even he believed himself to be in danger because he had not opposed the Protestants strongly enough on the article of justification" (153). Ochino fled over the Alps to Geneva, then to Augsburg, on to Canterbury under the protection of Edward VI. After the accession of Mary, he fled to Zurich, where he was made a pastor of the Italian congregation and was then expelled for his controversial views on the Trinity. He lived out the rest of his life in Poland under suspicion from Protestants as a free-thinker.

97. Collett, *Italian Benedictine Scholars*, 154.

98. Collett, *Italian Benedictine Scholars*, 157.

the acquired guilt of personal sin, could not be justified through his own efforts, but only by the gratuitous gift of Christ's righteousness, which he called the 'beneficio di Christo'; man's response was to understand and accept this gift and then to manifest his salvation by good works."[99] The tract argues that only by the imputation of Christ's righteousness can we be justified: "It is necessary that we clothe ourselves with the justice of Christ through faith, and hide ourselves under the precious purity of our first-born brother if we want to be accepted as just in the presence of God. . . . One can clearly see the difference between us, and those who defend justification by faith and works. . . . We differ in that we say that faith justifies without the aid of works."[100] In any case, this impressive movement, even in its loyalist version, found no support at the Council of Trent, and Cardinal Contarini, having fallen out of favor for conceding too much to the Reformers, was murdered.[101]

In addition to the fact that nominalism found no footing in Reformation (and confessional Lutheran and Reformed) theologies, it is striking that the Catholic churchmen who were most sympathetic to the teaching of the Reformers were staunch critics of the nominalism represented by Ockham and Biel. The triumph of the latter would be realized not in the career of Luther but at the Council of Trent. By Luther's day, the *via Augustini moderna* identified especially with Gregory of Rimini had lost to the semi-Pelagian side of the *via moderna*. Contributing to the suspicion toward Augustinians by many delegates at Trent, Cardinals Contarini, Pole, and Seripando were sympathetic to the Reformers' arguments.[102] "The leading exponent of the Protestant view here, espe-

---

99. Collett, *Italian Benedictine Scholars*, 158. Collett concludes that some parts reflect a more pessimistic view of humanity than one finds in Calvin, especially where "the *Beneficio* saw fallen man as 'completely corrupted,'" to the extent that the image of God had been lost (164–65). The purpose of the law is exclusively to threaten condemnation. There is no "third use," to guide believers (167). For these and other reasons, Collett concludes that the *Beneficio* was written by two authors, "one writing in the Cassinese tradition [of the monks inspired by the Greek fathers], the other a disciple of Valdés and Calvin." Presumably, "Benedetto composed the work and Flaminio revised it" (172).

100. Benedetto da Mantova, *Il Beneficio di Christo: con le versioni del secolo xvi, documenti e testimonianze*, ed. S. Caponetto, Corpus Reformatorum Italicorum (DeKalb, IL: Northern Illinois University Press and The Newberry Library, 1972), 38 lines 281–89, and 467 lines 513–20, quoted in Collett, *Italian Benedictine Scholars*, 176.

101. As noted earlier, Contarini's covenant theology and its connections with Reformed federalism are masterfully explored in Aaron Denlinger, *Omnes in Adam ex pacto Dei: Ambrogio Catarino's Doctrine of Covenantal Solidarity and Its Influence on Post-Reformation Reformed Theology* (Göttingen: Vandenhoek & Ruprecht, 2010).

102. At the Colloquy of Regensburg (1541), Cardinal Contarini reached his famous agreement with Luther and Bucer on justification. Although the agreement affirmed imputation, it left enough confusion in Calvin's mind for him to leave the conference early in disappointment.

cially of the later view of Calvin," Schmaus notes, "is G. Seripando." "He held that the justified man could have certain hope only when he did not trust in his own righteousness but relied on that of Christ."[103] Despite wariness on the part of many delegates, Seripando was made the papal legate and president of the Council of Trent, although his own views do not seem to have made much of an impact on the final canons and decrees of the session on justification. In fact, his early draft of a potential statement for the council was rejected out of hand by the delegates after it was attacked by the Jesuit theologian Laynez.[104]

Even the Thomists at Trent were closer to Ockham's semi-Pelagian understanding of justification than they were to Aquinas.[105] The council was never attended by all of the delegates. "Representation was always rather limited" throughout the eighteen years that it met, in fact.[106] At least two-thirds were Italians. "Nor was there any real French representation until the final period," after justification had been treated.[107] In short, it was far from being an ecumenical council, just as Calvin judged: "Had it only been a provincial council, they should have been ashamed."[108]

The Council of Trent (1545–63) established for the first time Rome's official position on the doctrinal points that were at issue in the Reformation. The lengthiest of its decrees is on justification, including the following condemnations:

> Canon 9. If anyone says that the sinner is justified by faith alone . . . , let him be anathema.
>
> Canon 11. If anyone says that men are justified either by the sole imputation of the righteousness of Christ or by the sole remission of sins . . . , let him be anathema.

Wilhelm Schenk, *Reginald Pole Cardinal of England* (London: Longmans, Green, 1950), 102, reports that after the meeting, Cardinal Pole wrote to Contarini, comparing its formulation to "a partly concealed pearl, always possessed by the Church, but now accessible to everyone." I am grateful to Chris Castaldo for this reference.

103. Michael Schmaus, *Dogma*, vol. 6, *Justification and Last Things* (London: Sheed and Ward, 1977), 72.

104. John C. Olin, *Catholic Reform: From Cardinal Ximenes to the Council of Trent, 1495–1563* (New York: Fordham University Press, 1990), 28–29. Cf. N. S. Davidson, *The Counter-Reformation* (Oxford: Blackwell, 1987), 9.

105. Davidson, *The Counter-Reformation*, 10.

106. Olin, *Catholic Reform*, 27.

107. Olin, *Catholic Reform*, 27.

108. Calvin, "Antidote to Trent," in *Acts of the Council of Trent: With the Antidote*, in *Selected Works of John Calvin: Tracts and Letters*, 7 vols., ed. Henry Beveridge and Jules Bonnet, trans. Henry Beveridge (Grand Rapids: Baker, 1983), 3:57.

Canon 12. If anyone says that justifying faith is nothing else than confidence in divine mercy, which remits sins for Christ's sake, or that it is this confidence alone that justifies us, let him be anathema.

Canon 24. If anyone says that the justice [righteousness] received is not preserved and also not increased before God through good works, but that those works are merely the fruits and signs of justification obtained, but not the cause of the increase, let him be anathema.

Canon 30. If anyone says that after the reception of the grace of justification the guilt is so remitted and the debt of eternal punishment so blotted out to every repentant sinner that no debt of temporal punishment remains to be discharged either in this world or in purgatory before the gates of heaven can be opened, let him be anathema.

Canon 32. If anyone says that the good works of the one justified are in such manner the gifts of God that they are not also the good merits of him justified; or that the one justified by the good works that he performs by the grace of God and the merit of Jesus Christ, whose living member he is, does not truly merit an increase of grace, eternal life, and in case he dies in grace the attainment of eternal life itself and also an increase of glory, let him be anathema.[109]

Calvin praised the council for condemning Pelagianism, but he also concluded that the delegates were merely "more modest than Pelagius," conceding a little more grace than the heretic deemed necessary.[110] It really does not matter how much one attributes to Christ and grace if our salvation is not due *entirely* to God's grace in Jesus Christ. What sense does it make to attribute one's meritorious deeds to grace if they compete with Christ's? Commenting on this sixth session, the Italian reformer Peter Martyr Vermigli judged, "What else would Pelagius say if he were now alive? For even he certainly did not deny grace, if one takes it as admonition, calling, and stirring up."[111]

With respect to the doctrine of justification specifically, Schmaus explains, "It can be said that the council [Trent] made the state of justifi-

---

109. *The Canons and Decrees of the Council of Trent*, trans. H. J. Schroeder, OP (Rockford, IL: TAN Books, 1978), 29–46.

110. Calvin, "Antidote to Trent," 3:108.

111. Vermigli, *Locus on Justification*, 156.

cation in its entirety consist in three elements: God's declaration that he forgives the sin; the remission of guilt effected by this declaration; and the interior renewal and sanctification." Not the righteousness that God is or of Christ that he imputes, but "that by which he makes us just . . . is the single formal cause of our justification."[112] Further, "The justice found in man, created by God and mirroring the divine justice, is the formal cause, not the efficient cause, of man's justification."[113] The one position that cannot be denied, Schmaus concludes, is that justification is based on Christ *and* the intrinsic holiness of the believer.[114]

Although Trent defined intrinsic justice as essential to justification as its single formal cause, it "left open the question of the connection between the forgiveness of sin and the inner renewal, and on this subject the theological schools have proposed different views."[115] In my view, this points to the fact that in Roman Catholic theology generally, *intrinsic renewal* is the one thing about justification that is essential to its official teaching. Although remission of sin is somehow included, questions about this aspect of justification are "left open." Inherent moral transformation is not; it is the center of the whole soteriological scheme even to the present day.

It would be easy to make nominalism in general and Trent in particular the bogeyman and chalk up Luther's protest as an overreaction to an aberrant school. However, as Carlson notes, the close identification of justification with penance that was "characteristic of the Church's teaching on the eve of the Reformation was no aberration of the nominalist theologians, but had undergone a long preparation in the entire medieval theological tradition. On this point, at least, it is impossible to agree with the thesis of Joseph Lortz that the 'Occamist system' by which Luther was allegedly victimized was 'traditionally uncatholic.'"[116] Carlson observes that at Trent,

There was a prolonged debate among the council fathers as to whether or not to make some insertion of the *sola fide* in the text, but the idea was discarded as coming too close to the Lutherans.

---

112. Schmaus, *Dogma*, 6:71.
113. Schmaus, *Dogma*, 6:71.
114. Schmaus, *Dogma*, 6:72.
115. Schmaus, *Dogma*, 6:73.
116. Charles P. Carlson, Jr., *Justification in Earlier Medieval Theology* (The Hague: Martinus Nijhoff, 1975), 129, from Lortz, *Reformation in Germany*, 1:196.

Then it was proposed to deal with the Pauline *sine operibus legis* [without works of the law] (Romans 3:28 was at one point in the proposed draft) or simply *sine operibus* [without works], this was rejected because it would conflict with the James text and require explanation too lengthy to be appropriate to such a document. In effect, the council was unable to come to grips with any of the crucial Pauline texts. . . . Thus was consummated a development with its genesis among Anglo-Irish scholars of the ninth century Carolingian court.[117]

Here, Carlson adds, "the semi-Pelagian tendency was manifested by engendering a view of righteousness which, as Seeberg states 'makes its aim not a personal intercourse with God, but the making of man capable of performing good works.'"[118]

In short, the theology of Gabriel Biel—the consummate nominalist at the threshold of the Reformation—shares the closest relationship with the Council of Trent. Biel's *Defensorium* played a key role in driving the final nail into the coffin of calls for a general council to reform the church, which even the University of Paris was calling for as late as 1518.[119] In 1460, Pope Pius II, former secretary to the antipope Felix V, promulgated *Execrabilis*, declaring excommunicate anyone who dares to question a papal decree. "These words are generally regarded as sounding the death knell of conciliarism and sealing the victory of the papal monarchy."[120] Biel's lavish rationalization for such absolutism formed the basis for the extreme version of this thesis at Trent. "What the holy Church, our Mother, defines and accepts as catholic truth must be believed with the same reverence as though it were stated in Holy Scripture."[121] For his pains, Pope Pius II promised Biel any reward his heart desired.[122] Although Trent's statement of original sin is more anti-Pelagian, Biel's doctrine of the *facientibus* lurks beneath the sixth

---

117. Carlson, *Justification in Earlier Medieval Theology*, 135–36.

118. Carlson, *Justification in Earlier Medieval Theology*, 138, quoting R. Seeberg, *Text-book of the History of Doctrines*, 2 vols., trans. C. E. Hay (Philadelphia: Lutheran Publication Society, 1905), 2:121.

119. Heiko A. Oberman, Daniel E. Zerfoss, and William J. Courtenay, introduction to *Defensorium obedientiae apostolicae et Alia documenta*, by Gabriel Biel, ed. Heiko A. Oberman, Daniel E. Zerfoss, and William J. Courtenay (Cambridge, MA: Harvard University Press, 1968), 6.

120. Oberman, Zerfoss, and Courtenay, introduction to *Defensorium obedientiae apostolicae*, 3.

121. Quoted in Oberman, Zerfoss, and Courtenay, introduction to *Defensorium obedientiae apostolicae*, 50.

122. Biel, *Defensorium obedientiae apostolicae*, 67.

session on justification and is the explicit grounding of the idea of the "anonymous Christian" at the Second Vatican Council.[123]

In a very important essay, Heiko Oberman demonstrated further and more direct connections between nominalism and Trent. A key statement in the Council of Trent's canons and decrees on justification (the sixth session) affirms that "none of the acts which precede justification, whether faith or works, merits the grace of justification." This has been taken as evidence of the triumph of Augustinian Thomism and the rejection of the nominalist notion of meriting the grace of justification by works apart from grace. However, Oberman demonstrates otherwise. The verb used here is *promereri*. Long before Trent, *promereri* was used as an equivalent to the later (post-Thomas) *meritum de condigno*, that is, merit in the strict sense.[124] So, for example, a Lombardian commentary on Paul glosses that "except for Christ, no one one's merit suffices to earn (*promereri*) life eternal."[125]

After Aquinas, *promereri* was generally replaced with the term "condign merit" (*meritum de condigno*). But of course, as we have seen, Aquinas rejected sharply any possibility of merit in any sense prior to grace.

It is with the English Dominican and opponent of Thomas Bradwardine, Robert Holcot (d. 1349), that we find the first real evidence that early scholastic tendencies are reviving. In what seems to be a direct answer to Bradwardine, the nominalist Holcot states that of course no one can fully earn (*promereri*) sanctifying grace. But, he continues, this does not mean that the sinner would be unable to merit at all. He can indeed prepare himself *de congruo* for the infusion of grace.[126]

---

123. See especially Pope Paul VI, *Nostra Aetate: The Declaration on the Relation of the Church to Non-Christian Religions* (October 28, 1965), and Pope Paul VI, *Lumen Gentium: The Dogmatic Constitution on the Church* (November 21, 1964); and Pope Paul VI, *Ad Gentes: The Decree on the Church's Missionary Activity* (December 7, 1965) build even more on the *facientibus* than in any preceding magisterial declaration.

124. In the sixth century, Isidore of Seville contrasts *mereri* and *promereri*, the former "an ambiguous verb which can mean to merit punishment as well as to earn a reward," while "*promereri* can only have the positive connotation of earning a reward." Strict Augustinians insisted that only Christ could properly have merited salvation in the sense of *promereri*, and although the language of condign and congruent pushed out these verbs, they returned in the Mariological debates about Mary as Co-Redemptrix, distinguishing her work of so-called merit from Christ's outright merit. Heiko A. Oberman, "Tridentine Decree on Justification," in *Distinctive Protestant and Catholic Themes Reconsidered,* ed. R. W. Funk (New York: Harper & Row, 1967), 44–45.

125. Oberman, "Tridentine Decree on Justification," 32. Oberman notes that this thesis was condemned at the Council of Reims in 1147.

126. Oberman, "Tridentine Decree on Justification," 46: "A similar statement can be found by the Parisian Chancellor John Gerson (d. 1429), who had little sympathy for Bradwardine.

In fact, "Biel's younger friend and theological ally, the influential Strasbourg preacher John Geiler of Kaisersberg (d. 1510), emphasizes the necessity of preparation for grace and argues that it is to be believed with certain faith that God will turn to any man who turns to him. Whereas he is willing to admit this preparation as a merit *de congruo*, he denies the possibility of *promereri*."[127] Thus, in an effort to save the possibility of congruent merit prior to grace (i.e., the nominalist *facere quod in se est*) in the face of Thomism and Luther, *promereri* returned: it is only in the strict sense (*de condigno*) that one cannot merit the grace of justification.

Oberman proves decisively that the use of *promereri* in Trent's statement excludes only condign merit prior to grace: "None of the acts which precede justification, whether faith or works, merits [*promereri*—i.e., in the strict sense, or condignly] the grace of justification." He concludes,

> If this is the case, the key prooftext in the Tridentine decree cited above has to be translated as ". . . none of the acts which precede justification, whether faith or works, fully merits the grace of justification." It is usually said that the Council of Trent in its definition of the truly Catholic doctrine of justification opted for the *via media*, steering away from both the Scylla of Lutheranism and the Charybdis of nominalistic Pelagianism. If our interpretation is *e mente auctorum*, a true presentation of the mind of the fathers of Trent, the nominalistic doctrine of justification has substantially contributed to the final formulation of the decree, and the Franciscan interest in the *meritum de congruo* has been fully validated, taken into account and safeguarded.[128]

Oberman bases much of his argument on several texts produced by key leaders at Trent. First, Silvester Prierias, OP, Master of the Sacred Palace, advisor to Pope Leo X in the case against Luther, and a friend of Cardinal Cajetan, tried to "combine the *facere quod in se est* as usually understood in the late middle ages with the Tridentine emphasis on the prevenience of grace."

In his treatise on prayer Gerson denies that one who is not in a state of grace can merit *de condigno*, since *promereri* is possible only for one moved by charity."

127. Oberman, "Tridentine Decree on Justification," 47.

128. Oberman, "Tridentine Decree on Justification," 38–39.

In his often reprinted *Aurea Rosa* of 1503, he points out that without the aid of grace the sinner is able of his own free will to desire the gift of grace which God grants either instantaneously or over a period of time. Moreover, God will *never* grant his grace *unless* it is preceded by such a desire on the part of the sinner to receive it. Since humility belongs to the *facere quod in se est,* self-humiliation in the form of awareness of one's own sins can be the basis for the infusion of grace, which in turn leads to eternal glory. . . . And this is exactly what both Franciscan and nominalistic theologians intended to express when they employed the term *meritum de congruo.*[129]

Second, various *periti* or drafts of potential canons and decrees that members composed during the session include an especially important one by Andreas de Vega, who wrote a full-scale monograph on justification (*Opusculum de iustificatione, gratia et meritis*) just in time for the sixth session. "Vega is probably the co-author of the original draft for the decree on justification, dated some seven months earlier, which formed the basis for the first discussions."[130] While Vega too was eager to steer between what he saw as two extremes, his Scyla and Charybdis are not what traditional Tridentine studies imagine. Vega saw the Pelagians, the Thomists, and the followers of Biel as the three potential options. Of course, the Thomists were not willing to accept any merits preceding the grace of justification, so this option was eliminated.[131] Vega acknowledges that Biel's position is hardly new and is in fact "the common view of the schools" (*haec opinion communis in scholis*), and he even places himself in this school. So, in the view of one of the (if not the) most formative minds at Trent on justification, the via media is *nominalism.*[132]

The Dominican Dominicus de Soto sought to drive a wedge between Scotus and nominalism by insisting that the notion of earning congruently one's justification is outright Pelagianism, since it implied that one could earn his or her predestination *de congruo.*[133] But Vega is right: Biel is the real *via media,* and the Dominicans were now cast as outliers on the extreme side of the debate. "The verb *promereri* occurs three times in Trent's final decree on justification: once in connection

129. Oberman, "Tridentine Decree on Justification," 36–37.
130. Oberman, "Tridentine Decree on Justification," 39.
131. Oberman, "Tridentine Decree on Justification," 40.
132. Oberman, "Tridentine Decree on Justification," 41 (including n54).
133. Oberman, "Tridentine Decree on Justification," 44.

with the disposition of the sinner and twice in the statements dealing with man's ability in a state of grace to merit a growth of grace and eternal reward."[134] Oberman relates,

> The original proposal of July, 1546, employs the verb *promereri* in a statement cast in the form of an anathema: "Anathema on anyone saying that one can *promereri* the grace of justification with preceding works." It is immediately made clear that this applies only to *merita de condigno* and does not exclude *merita de congruo*: no such preceding works can entail a claim on God's justice. Added to this anathema we find the explanatory comment: "In this justification the merits of man have to be silent, so that the *sola gratia* of Christ may reign." It may well have been a reference to *sola gratia* which led John Calvus of Corsica, the General of the Conventual Franciscans, to ask three weeks later, on August 17, for an explicit mention of the *meritum de congruo*. The original manuscript adds the observation that the decree actually does mention this merit. Though this last clause is later deleted, it allows only for one interpretation, namely, that its author understood *promereri* to apply solely to *merita de condigno*. That same day the bishop of the Canary Islands makes a similar request. Andreas de Vega, in an effort to incorporate the suggestions made, replaces *proermeri* with the words *vere et proprie mereri*, its equivalent, as we believe, but less subject to misinterpretation.[135]

The future Cardinal Seripando, sympathetic to the Protestant view, wrote an early draft of the statement on justification on August 19, 1546, stating that "merits as such are to be excluded before justification," but "the so-called September draft significantly changes his phrasing so that only merits in the full sense of the word are excluded."[136] Just before Christmas, "Minoriensis and Bituntinus formulate the attack on the nominalist-Scotist defense of the *meritum de congruo*."

> They suggest that the verb *mereri* should be employed, which in fact means a return to Seripando's suggestion that all merits be excluded.

---

134. Oberman, "Tridentine Decree on Justification," 47–48. See Denzinger, *Enchiridion Symbolorum: Compendium of Creeds, Definitions, and Declarations on Matters of Faith and Morals?* (San Francisco: Ignatius, 2012), nos. 801 and 809.
135. Oberman, "Tridentine Decree on Justification," 48.
136. Oberman, "Tridentine Decree on Justification," 49.

This raises strong protests. Castellimaris wants at least the word *proprie* inserted, and both the General of the Conventual Franciscans and the General of the Augustinians ask explicitly for a safeguard of the merit *de congruo*. On January 8, 1547, Cervini, the presiding Cardinal-legate, asks whether it is necessary to add to *promereri* the phrase "secundum debitium iustitiae," which would make it explicit that only *merita de condigno* are rejected before justification. On that same day the weighty consensus is reached that the clause "secundum debitium iustitiae" does not need to be added, since it is sufficiently understood that *promereri* envisages only the merits *de condigno* so that the merits *de congruo* can be upheld. In the final form of the decree, this decision is then implemented.[137]

In short, "The verb *promereri* is intentionally differentiated from the verb *mereri* in such a fashion that the first is related only to *merita de condigno*, the latter to *merita de congruo*. The Franciscan party, at the beginning of the debate on the defensive, has gained sufficient power to succeed in its stand for the *meritum de congruo*."[138]

On the heels of the session, Dominicus de Soto countered that no true Catholic can affirm merit in any sense prior to grace, since it violates the decision of the Council of Orange (529): "in effect, rejecting Trent's formulation."[139] As one who guided Trent on justification, Andreas de Vega's work helps explicate the intentions of Trent.

> Vega lays the groundwork for his interpretation by pointing out that, according to the majority opinion in the theological faculties, sinners are able to earn their justification *de congruo*. It seems to him impossible to conceive how a Catholic can really doubt that all kinds of dispositions are in their own way causes of justification, regardless of whether they are prompted by prevenient grace or not. When he then turns to the crucial *promereri* clause, he points out that this is to be understood as excluding only a *debitum iustitiae* and therefore only the merits *de condigno*.[140]

---

137. Oberman, "Tridentine Decree on Justification," 50.
138. Oberman, "Tridentine Decree on Justification," 51.
139. Oberman, "Tridentine Decree on Justification," 53. Soto's *De natura et gratia libri tres* (1547) and *Commentary on Romans* (1550) attacked head-on the view that had been formulated at Trent.
140. Oberman, "Tridentine Decree on Justification," 53.

He makes the same point here as made two years earlier in his *Opusculum*: we cannot merit apart from grace only in an absolute sense (i.e., *promereri* or condignly). Vega writes, "It is therefore completely clear that there is nothing in the edict of our Council that contradicts the opinion of those who assert the merit *de congruo*. . . . And if the Holy Synod would not have thus taken the word *promereri*, it would not have rightly exegeted the word *gratis*."[141] Thus, the decree not only allows for but actually affirms the nominalist position. "Therefore," Oberman concludes, "we must point out that the fashionable presentation of the Tridentine decree on justification as the *via media* between the extreme of Pelagian nominalism and Lutheran Augustinianism stands corrected."[142]

AFTER TRENT

Two bright philosophy students at the University of Paris's Collège de Montaigu would play major roles in the Reformation and Counter-Reformation: John Calvin and Ignatius of Loyola. Calvin would one day write his own scathing review of Trent, while Loyola would become one of its leading defenders. Gathering a group of young scholars at Montaigu, Loyola formed the Society of Jesus for the purpose of advancing the papal cause against Protestantism. Loyola's *Spiritual Exercises* and Calvin's *Institutes* represent well the contrast in the two types of piety.

A remarkable intellectual and mystic, Loyola was also a masterful leader and organizer whose influence was due more to the extraordinary thinkers who were inspired by his vision. One of the chief examples was the Spanish Jesuit, Luis de Molina (1535–1600). Molina formulated the concept of "special knowledge" (*media scientia*) by which God knew infallibly what people would do given particular circumstances.[143] In opposition to the Thomists (Dominicans), the Molinists believed that God gave sufficient grace to all, but that God's effectual grace could be

---

141. Oberman, "Tridentine Decree on Justification," 54.

142. Oberman, "Tridentine Decree on Justification," 54.

143. Molina's most important defense of this view is in his four-volume *De liberi arbitriicum gratiae donis, divina praedestione et reprobation concordia* (Lisbon, 1588). He also wrote a controversial commentary on Pars Prima of Aquinas's *Summa theologiae* (6 vols., 1593–1609). This is different from knowing merely what in fact will happen in the future (simple foreknowledge); it is a certainty about counterfactuals. Thomism insisted that in knowing the future, *what* he knows is what he has decreed. Accordingly, they held with Thomas (and Augustine) that God not only gives sufficient but efficacious grace (*gratia efficax*) to the elect, guaranteeing that they would believe.

rejected; it was therefore effectual only if one accepted it. Cooperating grace produces the act conjointly with the will, which by its consent to prevenient grace, makes grace salvific. While the Thomists held that grace was God's effectual operation within us to bring us to salvation, Molina taught that grace was assistance to help us do what we could do with greater difficulty.[144] Molina also taught that "there is a permanent state of love wherein man can no longer commit serious sin."[145] Molinism regards grace as efficacious not due merely to its inner power but "as the result of the free consent of the will." "There is no need of any special impetus in order that the will informed by grace should proceed from the state of rest to that of action. The supernaturalized will provides its own motion as a result of the dynamic nature of grace itself."[146]

Schmaus interprets the main line of thinking after Trent in terms that I can only see as an entirely new doctrine of predestination.[147] The Thomists adhere more closely to the high scholastic position on predestination and effectual grace. "In accordance with his eternal decree of election, God sets sinful man in motion towards his salvation."[148] Once in motion, one may merit an increase of justification through God's cooperating grace. "Without the divine initiative no movement towards beatitude—that is, towards dialogue with God—on man's part is possible."[149]

---

144. Brian Davies, *The Thought of Thomas Aquinas* (Oxford: Oxford University Press, 1992), 226, 256, 266. Yet even the later defenders of middle knowledge differed. Molina said that God saw the heart of every individual and knew what he or she would do under particular circumstances, while Francisco Suarez said that God sees the actual act. (Not surprisingly, Bellarmine and Suárez therefore held also to unconditional election, believing that God then used middle knowledge to determine which kind of grace to grant to each person.) Following Molina, Lessius and Vasquez denied unconditional election as well as reprobation. The Thomists began with predestination and God's effectual grace and then treated human freedom, while the Molinists moved in the opposite direction.

145. Schmaus, *Dogma*, 6:119; cf. DS 2201–69.

146. Schmaus, *Dogma*, 6:40.

147. Schmaus, *Dogma*, 6:5: "The post-Tridentine theologians tried to clarify this distinction within the divine salvific will terminologically by the expressions 'total' and 'partial' predestination. If as the result of a man's flight from God the divine predestination to salvation does not reach its intended goal, it remains 'partial.' Only if it is not hindered from reaching its goal is predestination 'total.' . . . In post-Tridentine theology two schools of opinion developed, the Thomist and the Molinist. According to the Thomist view men achieve ultimate perfection because God has decided it in an unconditional decree of salvation. This decree is made by God without any anticipation of human merit (*ante praevisa merita*). . . . The Thomist thesis (whether it can be assigned to Aquinas is debatable) is clearly expressed by John Duns Scotus. It received its final form at the hands of the Dominican Banez."

148. Schmaus, *Dogma*, 6:9.

149. Schmaus, *Dogma*, 6:10.

However, Schmaus judges that the Thomist position became and remains today a minority position among Roman Catholic theologians. "The theory of the second school, Molinism, which is probably advocated by the majority of theologians today, subscribes to the idea of the total predestination of man to ultimate perfection based on his foreseen merits." "The Church has neither accepted nor condemned either theory," Schmaus adds, revealing his own preference: "It would appear that it is more difficult to bring the Thomistic theory into agreement with the overall view which Scripture presents of God."[150] Molinism may undervalue the need for grace, Schmaus concedes. "It may be said, however, that the Thomist system fails to preserve the concept of the freedom of the will."[151]

The Thomist-Molinist dispute occupied the attention of theologians for at least the next twenty years (1582–1601), pitting Dominicans like Diego Alvarez, Tomas de Lemos, and, above all, Domingo Báñez against the Jesuits who by and large adopted the Molinist idea.[152] So great was the controversy that Pope Clement VII established a special commission in 1597, but it failed to bring resolution. Finally, in 1611, Pope Paul V prohibited debates on the subject.[153] Soon the Jansenist party arose, waging a full-fledged assault on the "modern tendency" (i.e., semi-Pelagianism), targeting Molinists and Jesuits. This movement too was condemned and its members persecuted.[154] Papal prohibitions against debates on predestination, grace, and free will only seemed to privilege the Jesuits and others who continued the nominalist trajectory.

---

150. Schmaus, *Dogma*, 6:6.

151. Schmaus, *Dogma*, 6:40. For his part, Schmaus sympathizes with a conciliatory position: "What is called syncretism (advocated by Alphonsus Ligouri and the Redemptorist Order) represents an attempt to unify the favourable elements in the two systems and omit the obscure factors." Sufficient grace is *gratia fallibiliter efficax,* while effectual grace is *gratia infallibiliter efficax.* Prayer is an example of the former (41).

152. See Diego Alvarez, *De auxiliis divinae gratiae et humani arbitrii* (Coloniae Agrippinae: Apud Petrum Henningium, 1621).

153. The only full-length book on Molina is by Kirk MacGregor, *Luis de Molina: The Life and Theology of the Founder of Middle Knowledge* (Grand Rapids: Zondervan, 2015). Molinism has attracted considerable interest, ironically, through the work of evangelical philosophers, William Lane Craig and Alvin Plantinga. See William Lane Craig, *Divine Foreknowledge and Human Freedom* (New York: Brill, 1991); Craig, *The Only Wise God* (Eugene, OR: Wipf and Stock, 1999); Alvin Plantinga, *God, Freedom and Evil* (Grand Rapids: Eerdmans, 1974). Cf. Thomas Flint, *Divine Providence: The Molinist Account* (Ithaca, NY: Cornell University Press, 1989).

154. Centered at the Port Royal abbey in Paris, the circle included Antoine Arnauld, Blaise Pascal, and Jean Racine. Pope Innocent condemned their "Calvinist" views (including justification by faith) in 1653, but a new eruption provoked Pope Clement XI's anathema in *Unigenitus Dei Filius* (1713).

The thesis of pure nature (*natura pura*) also became a point of considerable debate in the Counter-Reformation era. "The belief of the Church goes further than what has thus far been said," according to Schmaus, "for it emphasizes that fallen man can by means of his natural powers, and therefore without the supernatural grace of God, come to the knowledge of God's existence and perform good actions."[155] Is not the nominalist inflation of human self-confidence, joined by the burgeoning anthropocentrism of the Renaissance, the more likely carrier of early modern secularism than a reform movement whose entire focus was the majesty of God and our complete dependence on his being, revelation and grace?

It is remarkable that views which would have been anathema to Aquinas were now the standard teaching of the Roman church. With Thomas's esteemed interpreter, the Dominican Thomas Cajetan (Luther's nemesis and prosecutor at the Diet of Augsburg), the idea of "pure nature" was proposed as nothing more than a hypothetical condition. However, we have seen the hypothesis come to actual life as a positive doctrine with Biel. Augustinians like Gregory of Rimini had rejected even of Thomas's suggestion that "works performed in a state of sin are not necessarily to be regarded as sins as favoring Pelagianism." Luther would single out Gregory as the one who stood alone against the whole scholastic tradition "in rejecting man's purely natural capacity to prepare himself for the reception of grace."[156] However, the Augustinians and Dominican Thomists had essentially lost the day.

Testing the limits to which semi-Pelagianism verges on outright Pelagianism, Michael Baius (1531–89) virtually assimilated grace to nature.[157] After the fall, he held, grace simply restores us to the primitive state of prelapsarian Adam, where we may merit salvation. The role of grace is no more than to tamp down natural concupiscence so that this meritorious obedience is easier. Even the sacraments are not means of grace, properly speaking, but means of stimulating our moral action. Although some of Baius's theses were condemned, he was made chancellor of Leuven. He was even appointed a delegate to the Council of Trent, although he arrived too late to participate.

---

155. Schmaus, *Dogma*, 6:17–18.
156. Oberman, *The Harvest of Medieval Theology*, 144.
157. On the condemnation of Baius's teaching, see DS 1980.

Despite its condemnations of Pelagianism, it is difficult to resist the impression that Trent represents the triumph of the nominalism represented by Ockham and Biel. Whatever they have to say in favor of God's sovereignty and grace, the *facere quod in se est* is an all-controlling thesis—the test for all interpretations of predestination and justification.[158] For those who use the phrase, we do not know what God might have done or might still do according to his absolute power, but we do know that he has established a covenant in which all who do what lies within them can succeed in attaining salvation. From everything that has been summarized thus far, there is absolutely no basis for seeing in Ockham and Biel any link to the Reformation doctrine of justification, except as a foil.

The full flowering of Ockhamist teaching on justification is found not in Luther (who targeted Ockham explicitly) but in the Council of Trent. Indeed, if Schmaus is correct, the majority position today is open to views that Aquinas would have viewed as at least Pelagianizing in tendency. Schmaus himself defends the merit of virtuous pagans, even judging, "With Augustine there is a change, and not a very happy one." While unbelievers perform works of civic righteousness (good works before fellow humans), Augustine argues that they do so "without love of God as the object." "They do not enter the sheepfold through the door, which is Christ. 'If they do not enter through the door, what does it avail them to boast of themselves?'" Apart from faith in Christ, all virtues are but splendid vices, Augustine says.[159] In opposition to this teaching, Schmaus insists that these noble pagans "are on the way to their final destiny, whether they know it or not."[160] Clearly, after Trent, not only was the Reformation interpretation condemned, but the Augustinian path was closed off for good.

It should be noted that the *via antiqua* held that God's unilateral grace was necessary even to desire union with God. This was established doctrine ever since the Second Council of Orange in 529, which condemned the semi-Pelagian view that one may at least pray for grace without God himself moving the sinner by grace to offer such a prayer.[161] In contrast, Schmaus says, "In both the Old and New Testaments,

---

158. Oberman, *The Harvest of Medieval Theology*, 245.

159. Schmaus, *Dogma*, 6:19.

160. Schmaus, *Dogma*, 6:20.

161. "Council of Orange (529)" in *Creeds of the Churches*, ed. John H. Leith (Louisville: Westminster John Knox, 1982), 37–44.

the preparation necessary for achieving lasting union with God—that is, for justification—is called 'repentance.'"[162] There is no mention of God's operative grace (efficient, not just sufficient) bringing about this preparatory repentance. In fact, after mischaracterizing the Reformers' view, Schmaus says that the post-Tridentine view sees grace more as a "moral influence" rather than an efficacious operation of God that liberates the sinner for the process of justification.[163]

CONCLUSION

If, as Joseph Lortz says, "the Occamistic system is radically uncatholic," and Louis Boyer regards nominalism as "the utter corruption of Christian thought," then it is not to the Reformers but the Council of Trent that the triumph of such "uncatholic" teaching is to be attributed.[164] And yet, in an era of plentiful condemnations, Ockham was dubbed *Venerabilis Inceptor.* Whatever trials he endured at the hands of Pope John XXII were provoked less by his doctrines than by his defense of Franciscan poverty. In fact, Ockham received a warm reception at the University of Paris.[165] Despite the fact that the nominalist doctrine of justification can only be "characterized as at least semi-Pelagian," notes Oberman, it became the most popular option in many theological faculties.[166] Oberman adds,

> Luther's earliest opponents, such as Johannes Eck, Bartholomaeus von Usingen, and Kaspar Schatzgeyer, are all deeply indebted to the nominalistic tradition. . . . The name of Biel and his fellow schoolmen is not only absent from the Trent Index of Forbidden Books; but in an appendix to the 1569 edition of the Index published by the diocese of Munich, Biel's name is included under the suggestive heading: "Most select list of authors from which a complete Catholic library can properly be constituted." . . . Our conclusion

---

162. Schmaus, *Dogma*, 22–23.

163. Schmaus, *Dogma*, 40.

164. Quoted in Oberman, *The Harvest of Medieval Theology*, 425, from Lortz, *Luther und Luthertum*, 1.2 (473); and Boyer, *Histoire de la Philosophie médiévale*, vol. 3, *Après le treizième siècle*, 6th ed. (Paris: Vrin 1947), 231f.

165. William J. Courtenay, "The Reception of Ockham's Thought at the University of Paris," in *Preuve et raisons à l'Université de Paris: Logique, ontologie et théologie au XIVe siècle*, ed. Zénon Kaluza and Paul Vignaux (Paris: Vrin, 1984), 43–64.

166. Oberman, *The Harvest of Medieval Theology*, 426.

that nominalism has not been able to avoid a Pelagian position should not obscure the fact that nominalism was fully involved in the ongoing medieval search for the proper *interpretation* of Augustine.[167]

Ironically, Denifle, who helped launch the thesis that Luther was the carrier of a decadent nominalism into modernity, suggested that "Rimini went too far in his rejection of the Occamist claim that man can love God above all *ex puris naturalibus*."[168] Yet as we have seen, Luther hailed Gregory as the one who stood alone in opposing this Pelagian doctrine. So if those who paint Luther a "nominalist" are more favorable to Ockham than to Gregory of Rimini, while Luther holds up the latter as a hero, then we must ask who the real nominalists are after all.

Not the Reformation but Trent represents the triumph of nominalism. The Reformers actually stand closer to Aquinas than does Trent. To the extent that they conceived election and justification as conditional and contractual, Ockham and Biel proved Aquinas's conclusion that the idea of merit could be advanced without the blemish of Pelagianism only by anchoring it in unconditional election.

The Reformation cannot be credited or blamed with being the carrier of nominalism into the modern era. We can only conclude with Oberman, "on this vital point" of justification as well as others, that "late medieval nominalism can be regarded as the forerunner of the Tridentine" formulations "and is therefore in agreement with beliefs basic and characteristic for what has come to be known as Roman Catholicism."[169]

---

167. Oberman, *The Harvest of Medieval Theology*, 427.
168. Oberman, *The Harvest of Medieval Theology*, 142, 144.
169. Oberman, *The Harvest of Medieval Theology*, 428.

CHAPTER 12

JUSTIFICATION AND THE CHRISTIAN LIFE

A purely forensic declaration as the ground for God's acceptance and God reckoning the unjust to be just—what can be more inhibiting of genuine holiness and the pursuit of union with God as well as justice in the world? Long a part of Roman Catholic polemics, Albert Schweitzer's verdict has become a staple of various Protestant critiques of Luther's construal: "Those who subsequently made his doctrine of justification by faith the center of Christian belief have had the tragic experience of finding that they were dealing with a conception of redemption from which no ethic could logically be derived."[1]

Historically, it is difficult to sustain such a conclusion. Few serious historians will hazard the thesis that the Reformation bred passivity and indifference. And few would attempt to develop an argument that the ethical condition of the church in the sixteenth century, including and even especially the curia, was in a good position to offer such a critique. However, Schweitzer's complaint is more damning: the doctrine, he says, offers a view of redemption "from which no ethic could *logically be derived.*"

Before responding directly to this charge, my final chapter explores the relationship of justification to the Christian life as the Reformers understood it. Here we return to a recurring motif in this work: the transition from penance to a life of returning to our baptism in order to die to ourselves and live to God and our neighbors. We also want to

---

1. Albert Schweitzer, *The Mysticism of Paul the Apostle* (Baltimore: Johns Hopkins University Press, 1998), 223–25.

understand how the law-gospel distinction structures the activity that is engendered by experiencing God's justification of the ungodly.

CALVIN, TRENT, AND PENANCE

The law-gospel distinction is especially important with the question of assurance. In Calvin's *Antidote to Trent*, he observes the numerous passages that promise all believers assurance. As Calvin asks, who is to deprive believers of that which Christ purchased and promised?[2]

> Why do they not remember what they learned when boys at school, that what is subordinate is not contrary? I say that it is owing to free imputation that we are considered righteous before God; I say that *from this* also another benefit proceeds, viz., that our works have the name of righteousness, though they are far from having the reality of righteousness. In short, I affirm that not by our own merit but by faith alone are both our persons and our works justified; and that the justification of works depends on the justification of the person, as the effect on the cause. . . . Hence it is a most iniquitous perversion to substitute some kind of meritorious for a gratuitous righteousness, as if God after justifying us once freely in a single moment left us to procure righteousness for ourselves by the observance of the law during the whole of life.[3]

This is no minor point. Following Jesus's teaching about the priority of the tree to its fruit, the Reformers believed that once the *person* is justified, the *works* will be as well. If merit were involved, we and our works would fall short. However, God forgives the sin clinging to even our best works so that we no longer have to be anxious about whether our actions are perfectly pure in motive and execution. It is exactly the opposite in the Roman Catholic conception: the works justify the person. If the *works* are righteous, then the *person* is or will be accepted as righteous.

Peter spoke of the law "that neither our fathers nor we have been able to bear" (Acts 15:10). Calvin comments, "It is an error to suppose

---

2. John Calvin, *Selected Works of John Calvin: Tracts and Letters*, vol. 3, *Acts and Antidote*, ed. Henry Beveridge and Jules Bonnet, trans. Henry Beveridge (Grand Rapids: Baker, 1983), 126.
3. Calvin, *Acts and Antidote*, 128–29.

that this refers only to ceremonies, for what so very arduous was there in ceremonies as to make all human strength fail under the burden of them?"[4] Circumcision and dietary laws are hardly unbearable demands. "Hence too it is that Christ's yoke is easy and his burden light because the saints feel an alacrity in their liberty while they feel themselves no longer under the law."[5] At the heart of Trent's errors lies the confusion of law and gospel, as he argues in response to canons 12 and 20. Paul "calls the gospel, rather than the law, 'the doctrine of faith.' He moreover declares that the gospel is 'the message of reconciliation.'"[6]

> For the words of Paul always hold true, that the difference between the Law and the Gospel lies in this, that the latter does not like the former promise life under the condition of works, but from faith. What can be clearer than the antithesis: "The righteousness of the law is in this wise," "The man who does these things shall live in them." But the righteousness which is of faith speaks thus, "Whoso believeth . . ." (Rom 10:5).[7]

We cannot be sure of our final justification, canon 14 asserts. Yet "Christ says, 'Son, be of good cheer, thy sins are forgiven thee.' This sentence the horned fathers abominate, whenever anyone teaches that acquittal is completed by faith alone."[8]

When it comes to assurance, Calvin agrees with Trent that we dare not speculate about our predestination:

> I acknowledge indeed, and we are careful to teach, that nothing is more pernicious than to inquire into the secret council of God with the view of thereby obtaining a knowledge of our election—that this is a whirlpool in which we shall be swallowed up and lost. But seeing that our Heavenly Father holds forth in Christ a mirror of our eternal adoption, no man truly holds what has been given us by Christ save he who feels assured that Christ himself has been given him by the Father, that he may not perish.[9]

---

4. Calvin, *Acts and Antidote*, 131.
5. Calvin, *Acts and Antidote*, 131–32.
6. Calvin, *Acts and Antidote*, 154.
7. Calvin, *Acts and Antidote*, 156.
8. Calvin, *Acts and Antidote*, 154.
9. Calvin, *Acts and Antidote*, 135.

How can the fathers at Trent withhold that assurance that Scripture freely promises to any and all who throw themselves on God's mercy in Christ? "On the whole, then, we see that what the venerable fathers call rash and damnable presumption is nothing other than that holy confidence in our adoption revealed to us by Christ, to which God everywhere encourages his people."[10]

Nor can penance be an assurance that one has regained lost grace. As for Jerome's "second plank after a shipwreck," says Calvin,

> I would ask why he calls it the second plank and not the third or fourth? For how few are there who do not during life make more than one shipwreck. Nay, what man was ever found whom the grace of God has not rescued from daily shipwrecks. But I have no business with Jerome at present. The Fathers of Trent do not treat of repentance but of the sacrament of penance, which they pretend to have been instituted by Christ.[11]

Besides, the requirement of auricular confession and penance in general was unknown "for a thousand years, until Innocent III, with a few of his horned crew, entangled the Christian people in this net, which the Fathers of Trent would now make fast," and it was never imposed as necessary in the churches of the East.[12]

> But God nevertheless still chastises believers. I admit it. But to what end? Is it that he, by inflicting punishment, may pay what is due to himself and his own justice? Not at all; but that he may humble them, by striking them with a dread of his anger, that he may produce in them an earnest feeling of repentance and render them more cautious in future. . . . To sum up the whole: Though believers ought to be constantly thinking of repentance, these Holy Fathers imagine it to be an indescribable something of rare occurrence.[13]

Calvin here reprises Luther's first of the Ninety-Five Theses: "When our Lord and Master Jesus Christ said, 'Repent,' he willed the entire life

---

10. Calvin, *Acts and Antidote*, 136.
11. Calvin, *Acts and Antidote*, 138.
12. Calvin, *Acts and Antidote*, 140. By the way, "horned" here means "mitred."
13. Calvin, *Acts and Antidote*, 142–43.

of believers to be one of repentance." We are always returning to the gospel, to our baptism, and to repentance and faith. These are not merely extraordinary occasions but the warp and woof of the Christian life.

However, with justification already given, we are free to pursue repentance and faith without making them the ground of our confidence. If God treated us according to his justice, we have no hope. After all, *all* sins are mortal.[14] It is clear enough that Calvin is concerned not merely with theological precision. His motivation is pastoral, since these are life-and-death issues. Like Paul, Calvin is asking, "Tell me, you who want to be under the law, are you not aware of what the law says?" (Gal 4:21 NIV). He asserts,

> These new lawgivers tie down forgiveness to a formula of confession, contrary to the command of God, and assert that it is redeemed by satisfaction. . . . I am desirous to be assured of my salvation. I am shown in the word of God a simple way, which will lead me straight to the entire and tranquil possession of this great boon. I will say no more. Men come and lay hands on me, and tie me down to a necessity of confession from which Christ frees me. They lay upon me the burden of satisfaction, ordering me to provide at my own hand that which Christ shows me is to be sought from his blood alone. Can I long doubt what it is expedient to do? Nay, away with all hesitation, when attempts are made to lead us away from the only author of our salvation.[15]

Like Luther and Bucer, Calvin held a deep conviction that sound doctrine is the soul of piety, not an intellectual game. He described the dogma of implicit faith (assenting to whatever the church teaches) as ignorance disguised as humility. Surely faith requires knowledge. Nevertheless, faith is supremely trust in a person—namely, Christ as he is clothed in his gospel. This Word of God captures our whole person, not just our mind or will or affections. In fact, "True faith consists more in living experience than in high-flown speculations that flit about in the brain."[16] "I have censured the curiosity of those who would agitate

---

14. Calvin, *Acts and Antidote*, 144.
15. Calvin, *Acts and Antidote*, 139.
16. *Inst.* 1.5.9.

questions which are truly nothing else than mere tortures to the intellect," Calvin said.[17] In fact, knowledge and experience are inseparable.

Calvin seems stupefied not only by their exegesis but by their expe-
riential naiveté: "It is not strange, however, that addle-pated monks
who, having never experienced any struggle of conscience . . . should
thus prate the perfection of the Law," despite their hypocrisy. "With
the same confidence do they talk of a heaven for hire, while they themselves meanwhile continue engrossed with the present hire, after which
they are always gaping." They fail to realize, he says, "that there is no
work untainted with impurity, until it be washed away by the blood of
Christ."[18] He adds, "Were regeneration perfected in this life the observance of the law would be possible. . . . But there is no wonder that they
speak so boldly of things they know not. War is pleasant to those who
have never tried it."[19] "Such boldness is not strange in men who have
never felt any serious fear of the Divine judgment," he continues.[20] They
do not know or teach others to know truly that they are "pardoned by
paternal indulgence."[21]

> We reach the haven of security only when God lays aside the char-
> acter of Judge and exhibits himself to us as a Father. . . . Therefore,
> paying no regard to the Council of Trent, let us hold that fixed faith
> which the Prophets and Apostles, by the Spirit of Christ, delivered
> to us, knowing whence we have learned it.[22]

It is similar to his passionate argument in his letter to Cardinal
Sadoleto: "Hence, I observe, Sadoleto, that you have too indolent a
theology, as is almost always the case with those who have never had
experience in serious struggles of conscience. For, otherwise, you would
never place a Christian man on ground so slippery, nay, so precipitous,
that he can scarcely stand a moment if even the slightest push is given
him."[23] Recalling his early years, he relates,

---

17. Calvin, *Selected Works of John Calvin: Tracts and Letters*, ed. Henry Beveridge and Jules
Bonnet, trans. Henry Beveridge, 7 vols. (Grand Rapids: Baker, 1983), 3:418.

18. Calvin, *Acts and Antidote*, 145.

19. Calvin, *Acts and Antidote*, 156.

20. Calvin, *Acts and Antidote*, 158.

21. Calvin, *Acts and Antidote*, 146.

22. Calvin, *Acts and Antidote*, 147.

23. Calvin, "Response to Sadoleto," 52.

I believed, as I had been taught, that I was redeemed by the death of thy Son from liability to eternal death, but the redemption I thought was one whose virtue could never reach me. I anticipated a future resurrection, but hated to think of it, as being an event most dreadful. . . . They, indeed, preached of [God's] clemency toward men, but confined it to those who should show themselves deserving of it.[24]

Then he heard "a very different doctrine," he continues, which actually "brought me back to its fountainhead. . . . Offended by the novelty, I lent an unwilling ear, and at first, I confess, strenuously and passionately resisted; for . . . it was the greatest difficulty I was induced to confess that I had all my life long been in ignorance and error. One thing in particular made me averse to those new teachers; namely, reverence for the Church."[25] Yet, Calvin says, once he opened his ears, he understood the truth from those who treasured it. "They spoke nobly of the Church and showed the greatest desire to cultivate it."[26]

DAILY DYING AND RISING WITH CHRIST: EVANGELIZING PENANCE

The imperative "Repent" (Μετανοεῖτε) means, literally, "Change your mind," but it was mistranslated in the Vulgate as "Do penance" (*poenitentiam agite*). The Reformers pointed out that according to the New Testament, repentance (μετάνοια) is a daily calling, returning to our baptism in a regular pattern of dying to sin (*mortificatio*) and coming to life (*vivificatio*). Repentance, not justification, was the first doctrine that preoccupied Luther and lay at the heart of his Ninety-Five Theses. There are two major changes effected by the Reformers to penance.

First, the Reformers "evangelized" penance. We have seen that Luther's critique of penance actually came before his mature doctrine of justification. He ultimately rejected it as a sacrament in *The Babylonian Captivity of the Church* (1520). Bucer still referred to penance as an important part of the ministry but no longer a sacrament, and he too

---

24. Calvin, "Response to Sadoleto," 61.
25. Calvin, "Response to Sadoleto," 62.
26. Calvin, "Response to Sadoleto," 63.

saw it as a means of returning offenders to their baptism.[27] Besides turning the gospel into law, penance had replaced baptism, Calvin argued against Trent.[28] Melanchthon retained it as a topic in his *Loci communes* of 1521 but placed it under baptism.[29] Notably, these Reformers also retained private confession and absolution.

Luther's *Betbüchlein* (Prayer Booklet) in 1525 treated private confession and absolution as entirely evangelical and a matter of Christian freedom. Faith is the root of confession before God, love is the root of confession to one's neighbor, and the need for gospel assurance is the motive for confessing to the pastor in private.[30] The law is not used to terrorize the conscience, as Luther experienced in earlier years. Confession to a minister is not necessary but can be a great help for those whose consciences need to be unburdened and assured.[31] Bucer and Calvin concurred on all of these points.[32] The result was a greater burden on pastors to fulfill their ministry to people beyond being mere administrators of a system of merit. Their goal, even in church discipline, was not to recover lost grace but to bring sinners to repentance and the assurance of the grace that they have already and always in Christ alone.

Second, the Reformers restored the public dimension of repentance. Not only did the Reformers "evangelize" penance; they transformed it from a private to a public practice. The focus was no longer on performing satisfactions to compensate legally for an offense. Rather, the whole church expressed its repentance, its trust in Christ, and received absolution in the public service. Private Masses (services of Communion) without the word ceased, and baptism occurred now in the public service with the whole congregation promising to contribute to the recipient's growth in Christ. Similarly, confession and absolution moved

---

27. Martin Bucer, *Concerning the True Care of Souls*, trans. Peter Beale; ed. David F. Wright (Carlisle, PA: Banner of Truth, 2009), esp. 21–68.

28. Calvin, "Antidote to Trent," in *Acts of the Council of Trent: With the Antidote*, in *Selected Works of John Calvin: Tracts and Letters*, 7 vols., ed. Henry Beveridge and Jules Bonnet, trans. Henry Beveridge (Grand Rapids: Baker, 1983), 3:178–83.

29. Timothy J. Wengert, *Law and Gospel: Philip Melanchthon's Debate with John Agricola of Eisleben over Poenitentia*, Texts and Studies in Reformation & Post-Reformation Thought (Grand Rapids: Baker, 1997), 61.

30. Wengert, *Law and Gospel*, 62.

31. Wengert, *Law and Gospel*, 61–62.

32. Calvin followed Bucer and Luther in affirming private and public confession and absolution as long as the former was not viewed with superstition (i.e., as if God could not forgive sins without private confession). See *Inst.* 3.4.12. Luther regarded public absolution a "third sacrament," while Calvin treated it as a part of the ministry of the word.

from private to public spaces, with the whole congregation confessing its sin and receiving Christ's absolution through the lips of his minister.

Church discipline also restored the corporate dimension of repentance. While private sins were handled privately, with offenders reconciling with the offended, one repented for public sins before the whole congregation. Tragically, though, evangelicals (both Lutheran and Reformed) failed to cast off the centuries-old encroachment of the secular authority in spiritual discipline.[33]

The interpersonal aspect of penance (i.e., reconciliation with offended neighbors) was included in ordinary church discipline, which had been the case in the ancient church. In fact, we saw that the precedent for the sacrament of penance was the ordinary exercise of such discipline for serious transgressions. However, in addition to turning the gospel into law in the relationship of believers to God, medieval penance had largely ignored the horizontal relation between believers. When the preoccupation is with legal bookkeeping (with roughly equivalent penalties imposed for each sin), there is little place for a deliberate process of restoring relationships.

Luther affirmed the importance of church discipline in the Smalcald Articles, which was confirmed by the Augsburg Confession.[34] Church discipline is an essential aspect of the exercise of the keys, Melanchthon argued.[35] Ironically, in fact, Luther identified it as a mark of the church in *On Councils*, while Calvin did not; yet the Reformed confessions include it as a mark (Belgic Art. 32) while the Lutheran confessions do not. Yet the magisterial Reformers agreed that the sacraments were

---

33. For centuries, the ecclesiastical authorities determined whether serious sins had been committed and then handed the offender over to the magistrate for punishment. Much more of this repentance for serious offenses took place in the church, but, tragically, Lutheran and Reformed churches capitulated to the centuries-old practice in which the church determined offenses and the state executed the punishment. In contradiction of his doctrine of the "two kingdoms," Luther allowed this practice to continue, with the Constantinian notion of the prince or city council as the "nursing father" of the church. The Swiss churches followed the Lutheran practice, except for Geneva, where Calvin's opposition to it eventually prevailed at least to some extent. Spiritual discipline must be exercised spiritually, he argued, not by the secular sword. In my view the failure of most Lutheran and Reformed churches to extricate themselves from secular interference was a large mistake with lasting consequences. In any case, it meant that church discipline was a matter of policing public order and morals.

34. The Smalcald Articles, *Book of Concord: Confessions of the Evangelical Lutheran Church*, ed. and trans. Robert Kolb and Timothy Wengert (Minneapolis: Fortress, 2000), 3.9; and the Augsburg Confession, apology 11.4 and 28.13–14.

35. Philip Melanchthon, *Treatise on the Power and Primacy of the Pope* (1537), comes after the Smalcald Articles in the Book of Concord.

the means of grace and that church discipline was the context in which genuine repentance and reconciliation occurred.

The administration of these rites offers one more example of the shift from private, introspective, and anxious piety to a public, extrospective, and assured faith. This challenges the widespread assumption that the Reformation engendered a more individualistic and introspective piety.

LOOKING UP TO GOD IN FAITH AND OUT TO THE NEIGHBOR IN LOVING WORKS

What does it say about our theology if our ethics can only be derived from some type of analytic righteousness in human beings? Or, from the other side, why do we assume a priori that a gospel of free acceptance with God in Christ alone through faith alone *cannot* yield any ethical imperatives or actions?

Critics like Schweitzer usually have the following reasons in mind for thinking that no ethic can be derived from the doctrine of justification by Christ's alien righteousness. First, we are told that it is a legal fiction that has no grounding in reality; Paul's doctrine of justification is grounded in mystical and eschatological union with Christ, over against an arbitrary declaration. In contrast, Paul proclaims a gospel of liberating and transforming power, where justification is seen as a rupture in this age of sin and death and the beginning of the new creation. Second, critics suggest that the Reformation doctrine is individualistic, obsessed with personal salvation at the expense of communal (both ecclesial and social) dimensions. Third, the overemphasis on human inability and God's unilateral grace in regeneration and justification renders passive subjects who mistake complacency for faith, presumption for assurance, and pride in being among the justified for humility in giving all the glory to God.

Before addressing the logical objections, it is important to point out that on purely historical grounds, few historians who specialize in the period would conclude that the Reformation rendered millions of Christians passive individualists. It may be said in response that this influence toward an active piety derived not from the Reformation's doctrine of justification but from its doctrine of vocation. Yet anyone familiar at all with the Reformers' writings on the latter know how inextricably related vocation is to their doctrine of justification. However, Schweitzer's sweeping assertion pertains to the *logical* impossibility of any ethic deriving from the doctrine of justification. How might one respond briefly to this charge?

First, the doctrine of justification does not say everything that is included in the good news, but apart from it there is no good news. It is a mistake, committed by friend and foe alike, to treat justification as a central dogma from which the Reformers deduced everything else. As we have seen in Luther's development, he came somewhat gradually to the doctrine of Christ's alien righteousness imputed to believers. It was questions about idolatry and hypocrisy, God's character, true penitence, genuine worship, and the life of believers in this world that provoked Luther and the other Reformers. Justification was not just a missing puzzle piece but the lid of the puzzle box that directs faith in Christ as the only way the pieces fit together. Luther, Calvin, and the others took with utmost seriousness matters of ecclesiology, liturgy, preaching, sacraments, discipline, and diaconal care. In fact, differences over these issues contributed to the tragic fractures within the evangelical movement.

Even if the doctrine of justification were as its critics describe, the magisterial Reformers were concerned with the broad sweep of Christian faith and practice. They did not speak only of this doctrine, as if all other biblical teachings could be deduced logically from it. Of course it is true that an ethical system cannot be derived from the doctrine of justification. But can any single doctrine, no matter how important, bear such a heavy burden? With justice we speak of Trinitarian ethics, but does anyone really imagine constructing an entire ethics from the dogma of the Trinity by itself? Each doctrine in the Christian faith answers a different question, exposing a different piece of the architectural framework, but only as a system of interconnecting parts does the whole constitute a building. It is not the purpose of the doctrine of justification to provide an ethic but to announce the only good news possible for sinners.

Having said this, the doctrine of justification did play a central role in the sense that the Reformers recognized its ramifications for every locus of theology and every approach to worship and life. It is not one doctrine among many. The truth of this doctrine is not determined by our experience, and its value is not measured by its ethical utility. Justification does not answer every question, nor is it the only doctrine. But it does address directly the most fundamental issue underlying our most serious problems of both an objective and subjective nature. If the guilty race has no other expectation than to be condemned on the last day, then it matters little whether Schweitzer's mystical union was better suited to a salutary ethical impact in improving our lives or our world for the time being.

Not condemnation but death is our central problem, say some. Yet Scripture declares that death is "the wages of sin" (Rom 6:23), a sentence rendered on the basis of the verdict of God's law. "The sting of death is sin, and the power of sin is the law. But thanks be to God, who gives us the victory through our Lord Jesus Christ" (1 Cor 15:56–57). Remove the *curse* and the *sentence* is lifted. For others, the alternative to justification is Christ's victory over the powers. This is no doubt a large part of Paul's gospel: "He disarmed the rulers and authorities and put them to open shame, by triumphing over them in [Christ]" (Col 2:15). Yet the previous verses read, "And you, who were dead in your trespasses and the uncircumcision of your flesh, God made alive together with him, having forgiven us all our trespasses, *by canceling the record of debt that stood against us with its legal demands.* This he set aside, nailing it to the cross" (vv. 13–14, emphasis added). Even for this central *Christus Victor* passage, Christ triumphed over the powers by cancelling the law's condemnation. Nor can peace with God—reconciliation—be set over against justification: "Therefore, since we have been justified by faith, we have peace with God through our Lord Jesus Christ" (Rom 5:1).

Second, in the Reformers' understanding, justification is not the alternative to but the basis for sanctification. In his parable recorded in Luke 18:10–14, aimed at those "who trusted in themselves that they were righteous," Jesus contrasted the Pharisee, who boasted of his piety, with the publican, who could not even raise his eyes but cried out, "God, be merciful to me, a sinner." "I tell you," Jesus concludes, "this man went down to his house justified, rather than the other." Evidently, Jesus wanted to point out that the justification of the ungodly is precisely the logic needed for an ethic of humility and for a faith in Christ that bears the fruit of genuine works. The knowledge of our justification is not only essential for reconciliation with God and for assurance but also for the pursuit of godliness. Not in spite of but because of this doctrine, the Reformers believed that the Christian is liberated to look up in faith to God and out to their neighbors in love and good works.[36]

---

36. This is the thrust of Luther's *Freedom of a Christian,* in *LW* 31:371. So too, Calvin says that since our works cannot serve God, we send them on to the brothers and sisters who need them.

Similar to Jesus's parable above, Paul points to the tragic irony that while his fellow Jews have failed to attain righteousness despite their zeal for the law, gentile outsiders have discovered it as a free gift in Christ (Rom 10:1–12). Paul moves from "no condemnation" to "new creation" in a logical sequence of sentences:

> There is therefore now no condemnation for those who are in Christ Jesus. For the law of the Spirit of life has set you free in Christ Jesus from the law of sin and death. For God has done what the law, weakened by the flesh, could not do. By sending his own Son in the likeness of sinful flesh and for sin, he condemned sin in the flesh, in order that the righteous requirement of the law might be fulfilled in us, who walk not according to the flesh but according to the Spirit. (Rom 8:1–4)

Having been freed from the curse of the law, believers can now exult, "Oh how I love your law!" (Ps 119:97). In other words, through the gospel the law becomes a friend and coconspirator in our salvation. Although it has no saving value itself, the law keeps us looking to Christ and directs our course.

Justification is not the goal but the source of love and service. In Paul's thinking, the basis for our good works is *God's* unilateral act of grace (Eph 2:1–10). Precisely because we have been freed from the law's condemnation and justified as a free gift, we are liberated for the first time to love God and our neighbors instead of using them for our own spiritual advantage. No longer employees but sons and daughters, we are being conformed to the image of the elder brother. Before sanctification can begin, there must be a cancellation of the condemnation that renders us "children of wrath" (Eph 2:3b).

Critics regard the Reformation view as a reduction of salvation to forensic imputation, but it turns out that alternative accounts are in fact reductionistic. Union with Christ—participation—is not an alternative to forensic justification.[37] The churches of the Reformation teach a

---

See Calvin, *Calvin's Commentaries*, vol. 21, *Commentaries on the Epistles of Paul to the Galatians and Ephesians*, trans. William Pringle (Grand Rapids: Baker, 1996), 278 (on Eph 4:11).

37. See J. Todd Billings, *Calvin, Participation and the Gift* (New York: Oxford University Press, 2008), and Michael Horton, "Calvin's Theology of Union with Christ and the Double Grace," in *Calvin's Theology and Its Reception: Disputes, Developments, and New Possibilities*, ed. J. Todd Billings and I. John Hesselink (Louisville: Westminster John Knox, 2012), 72–96; J. V. Fesko,

salvation that is forensic and transformative, personal and ecclesial, spiritual and sacramental, salvation-historical and apocalyptic. With union with Christ or recapitulation—the great exchange—as their broader rubric, the Reformers and their confessional heirs have no difficulty attributing salvation not only to God's grace in justification but also to election, redemption, calling, adoption, sanctification, and glorification.

The choice between imputation and participation turns out to be a false one, akin to a dichotomy between the wedding ceremony and the married life, or adoption and growing up in the family. Rather, it is in union with Christ that we receive justification and all of the blessings, including sanctification and glorification. The Reformers in fact celebrated this final installment on the great exchange. While justification remained the central gift—the basis for the others, Luther could affirm deification.[38] Calvin even named "being deified" as "the greatest of all possible blessings."[39] Continuing this emphasis, John Owen wrote, "There is no contemplation of the glory of Christ that ought more to affect the hearts of them that do believe with delight and joy than this, of the recapitulation of all things in him."[40] Yet without justification, sanctification cannot get off the ground, and it certainly cannot be complete enough in this life to present us faultless before God's throne. Apart from justification, glorification is suspended in midair—truly a "legal fiction," since it lacks the foundation in Christ's imputed righteousness. As the Puritan William Ames put the matter, glorification is "actually nothing but the carrying out of the sentence of justification. For in justification we are pronounced just and awarded the judgment of life. In glorification the life that results from the pronouncement and award is given to us: We have it in actual possession."[41] In short, while rival views reduce salvation to sanctification or deification, Reformation

---

Beyond Calvin: Union with Christ and Justification in Early Modern Reformed Theology (Göttingen: Vandenhoeck & Ruprecht, 2012).

38. See Jordan Cooper, *Christification: A Lutheran Approach to Theosis* (Eugene, OR: Wipf and Stock, 2014).

39. *Inst.* 3.25.10. See also Carl Mosser, "The Greatest Possible Blessing: Calvin and Deification," *Scottish Journal of Theology* 55, no. 1 (2002): 40. The best analysis of Calvin and "deification" is found in J. Todd Billings, "United to God through Christ: Assessing Calvin On the Question of Deification," *Harvard Theological Review* 98, no. 3 (2005): 316–35.

40. John Owen, "The Person of Christ," in *The Works of John Owen*, ed. William H. Goold (Edinburgh: Banner of Truth Trust, 1965), 1:372.

41. William Ames, *The Marrow of Theology*, trans. John Dykstra Eusden (Grand Rapids: Baker, 1968), 1.30.4 (172).

theology celebrates both the forensic and effective dimensions of the new creation in Christ.

Third, the doctrine of justification is far from rendering believers passive. As Luther said, "Faith is a busy thing." Faith "kills the old Adam and makes altogether different people, in heart and spirit and mind and powers, and it brings with it the Holy Spirit." He adds,

> Oh, it is a living, busy, active, mighty thing, this faith. And so it is impossible for it not to do good works incessantly. It does not ask whether there are good works to do, but before the question rises, it has already done them, and is always at the doing of them. He who does not these works is a faithless man. He gropes and looks about after faith and good works and knows neither what faith is nor what good works are, though he talks and talks, with many words about faith and good works. Faith is a living, daring confidence in God's grace, so sure and certain that a man would stake his life on it a thousand times.[42]

From the perspective of justification through faith, the world takes on a different hue. Not only is the Creator and Lawgiver now our Father, but our neighbors are no longer threats to our comfort, security, or happiness but are rather gifts to cherish. "This confidence in God's grace and knowledge of it," Luther exults, "makes men glad and bold and happy in dealing with God and all His creatures." "And thus," he concludes, "it is impossible to separate works from faith, quite as impossible as to separate burning and shining from fire. Beware, therefore, of your own false notions and of the idle talkers, who would be wise enough to make decisions about faith and good works, and yet are the greatest fools."[43]

But we have to recognize the proper logical order: the Spirit creates faith through the preaching of the gospel; faith unites us to Christ; united to Christ, faith expresses itself in love, and this love begins to bear the fruit of good works. Gospel—Faith—Love—Works. This is why Paul, in turning from justification to sanctification in Galatians, says that the issue now is not whether one is circumcised or uncircumcised "but only faith working through love" (Gal 5:6). The apostle is

---

42. Martin Luther, *Commentary on Romans*, trans. J. Theodore Mueller (Grand Rapids: Zondervan, 1954), xvii.

43. Luther, *Commentary on Romans*, xvii.

not describing how one is justified (thus contradicting his argument thus far) but explaining how faith *works* in relation to *neighbor*. Luther observes of Paul's agitators in Galatia,

> Oddly enough, the false apostles who were such earnest champions of good works never required the work of charity, such as Christian love and the practical charity of a helpful tongue, hand, and heart. Their only requirement was that circumcision, days, months, years, and times should be observed. They could not think of any other good works.[44]

The gospel that Paul proclaims throughout this epistle does in fact generate an ethic. But it is an ethic driven by faith in Christ rather than by the desire to justify ourselves before God and each other.

> The Apostle exhorts all Christians to practice good works after they have embraced the pure doctrine of faith, because even though they have been justified they still have the old flesh to refrain them from doing good. Therefore it becomes necessary that sincere preachers cultivate the doctrine of good works as diligently as the doctrine of faith, for Satan is a deadly enemy of both. Nevertheless faith must come first because without faith it is impossible to know what a God-pleasing deed is.[45]

Genuine holiness is the opposite of Stoic detachment from society, Luther continues. It is a perpetual warfare against the flesh in the power of the Spirit and its theater is the world with our everyday callings.

> Some of the old saints labored so hard to attain perfection that they lost the capacity to feel anything. When I was a monk I often wished I could see a saint. I pictured him as living in the wilderness, abstaining from meat and drink and living on roots and herbs and cold water. This weird conception of those awesome saints I had gained out of the books of the scholastics and church fathers. But we know now from the Scriptures who the true saints are.

---

44. Luther, *Commentary on the Epistle to the Galatians*, trans. Theodore Graebner (Grand Rapids: Zondervan, 1949), on Gal 5:14 (216).

45. Luther, *Commentary on the Epistle to the Galatians*, on Gal 5:14 (216).

Not those who live a single life, or make a fetish of days, meats, clothes, and such things. The true saints are those who believe that they are justified by the death of Christ. Whenever Paul writes to the Christians here and there he calls them the holy children and heirs of God. All who believe in Christ, whether male or female, bond or free, are saints; not in view of their own works, but in view of the merits of God which they appropriate by faith. Their holiness is a gift and not their own personal achievement.[46]

He adds,

Ministers of the Gospel, public officials, parents, children, masters, servants, etc., are true saints when they take Christ for their wisdom, righteousness, sanctification, and redemption, and when they fulfill the duties of their several vocations according to the standard of God's Word and repress the lust and desires of the flesh by the Spirit. Not everybody can resist temptations with equal facilities. Imperfections are bound to show up. But this does not prevent them from being holy. Their unintentional lapses are forgiven if they pull themselves together by faith in Christ. God forbid that we should sit in hasty judgment on those who are weak in faith and life, as long as they love the Word of God and make use of the supper of the Lord.[47]

On this basis, like Paul writing to the Corinthians, Luther can look out upon the churches and, despite their imperfections, recognize a company of saints:

I thank God that He has permitted me to see (what as a monk I so earnestly desired to see) not one but many saints, whole multitudes of true saints. Not the kind of saints the papists admire, but the kind of saints Christ wants. I am sure I am one of Christ's true saints. I am baptized. I believe that Christ my Lord has redeemed me from all my sins, and invested me with His own eternal righteousness and holiness. To hide in caves and dens, to have a bony body, to wear the hair long in the mistaken idea that such departures from normalcy will obtain some special regard in heaven is not the holy

---

46. Luther, *Commentary on the Epistle to the Galatians*, on Gal 5:19 (220).
47. Luther, *Commentary on the Epistle to the Galatians*, on Gal 5:19 (220).

life. A holy life is to be baptized and to believe in Christ, and to subdue the flesh with the Spirit.[48]

This warfare keeps us humble not only before God but before each other, he concludes.

> To feel the lusts of the flesh is not without profit to us. It prevents us from being vain and from being puffed up with the wicked opinion of our own work-righteousness. The monks were so inflated with the opinion of their own righteousness, they thought they had so much holiness that they could afford to sell some of it to others, although their own hearts convinced them of unholiness. The Christian feels the unholy condition of his heart, and it makes him feel so low that he cannot trust in his good works. He therefore goes to Christ to find perfect righteousness. This keeps a Christian humble.[49]

In *On the Freedom of a Christian* (1520), Luther famously stipulates, "A Christian is a perfectly free Lord of all, subject to none. A Christian is a perfectly dutiful servant of all, subject to all."[50] Only within the rich soil of the great exchange is this comment more than a paradoxical platitude. Luther is not offering a proto-Enlightenment dogma of liberty here, but a christologically determined interpretation of the Christian life. Only by sharing in Christ's humiliation and exaltation does the believer experience the reality of a "lordship" (as prophets, priests, and kings) that allows them to love and serve in genuine humility, regardless of how they are treated. Freed from the law as a covenantal principle of inheritance, believers are freed for God and the neighbor—precisely what the law prescribed but could not itself deliver. In Christ, the believer has a free conscience. No longer seeking to establish their own righteousness, identity, dignity, and worth, they are allowed finally to look away in gratitude to the Giver and to his gifts in the form of other creatures surrounding us.

Calvin argues similarly that when our gaze is turned in on ourselves, hoping to win God's favor and distinguish ourselves above everyone

---

48. Luther, *Commentary on the Epistle to the Galatians*, on Gal 5:19 (220).
49. Luther, *Commentary on the Epistle to the Galatians* 5:19 (220).
50. Luther, *The Freedom of a Christian*, in *LW* 31:344.

else as godly, not only the gospel but the law of love is forfeited.[51] In fact, he adds, Jesus teaches us that even our enemy is our neighbor to be loved because "he shares our humanity."[52] Thus, not only in obedience to God's command but in response to the intrinsic value and dignity of the neighbor as God's image-bearer, we offer gifts for his or her good. In fact, we gratefully receive their goods as well, which they offer for our well-being by God's common grace.[53]

Presenting our works to God as if to demand a reward, we actually subvert the intention of love. Instead of being grateful, our relationship to God is that of an employee expecting a wage. In the process, we of course are not helped but instead offend God's generosity, and our neighbor is ignored by our self-obsession—unless as a burden that we take on in order to serve ourselves by using our neighbor.[54]

There is a place for good works, but it is neither God nor we who need them; it is our neighbor. Believers are accountable to God for their neighbor. Out of gratitude, believers want to worship and honor God. "God says," according to Luther, "If you want to serve me, serve your neighbor."[55] Thus, it is far from the case that there is "nothing to do" since works do not justify. On the contrary, precisely *because* works do not merit any return from God, they are freed up to be genuine acts of thanksgiving to God and love for others. There is a circulation of gifts (*pace* Milbank's critique), but they come down from the Father of lights (Jas 1:17). God does not need anything, including our good works (Acts 17:15); indeed, we cannot give him anything that would merit his return (Rom 11:34–36). Since our good works cannot go up to God, they go out to our neighbors. In fact, they are God's works that he does to serve others through us.

John M. G. Barclay refers to Zemon Davis's monograph that "traced in Calvin an attempt to break with this ideology of reciprocity with God (and by extension reciprocity with fellow humans), contrasting Catholic 'reciprocity' with Reformed 'gratuitousness.'"[56] Barclay is exactly right in his evaluation of this interpretation:

---

51. *Inst.* 3.2.24.
52. *Inst.* 2.8.55.
53. *Inst.* 2.2.15.
54. This is Calvin's basic critique of the monastic life. See *Inst.* 3.10.6.
55. *Inst.* 2.2.16.
56. John M. G. Barclay, *Paul and the Gift* (Grand Rapids: Eerdmans, 2015), 56, citing Zemon Davis, *The Gift in Sixteenth-Century France* (Oxford: Oxford University Press, 2000), 190–203.

In one important respect, this antithesis seems incorrect. Calvin, in fact, put great emphasis on the return of gratitude to God, characteristic of a life of obedience and holiness as what is owed to God in return for the immeasurable gift of Christ. Nonetheless, it is right to say that the Protestant Reformers put great effort into figuring a return to God as always a response to the one completed and all-sufficient gift, and *not* as the means toward earning a future gift or favor from God. In that sense, human praise and obedience are never *instrumental* in Protestant theology, never part of a *repeatable* pattern of gift and return.[57]

Barclay quotes Melanchthon's comments on Colossians 1:4:

> The Colossians do not do good to the saints as if they were moneylenders, buying big profits by small favors. The world, on the other hand, is generous in the hope of getting back. All gifts are greedy, as the saying goes. . . . But the saints do good because they know this is what God wants, and because they value his will above the promised rewards. Their action is not prompted by the desire to earn something in return. For they know that all things have already been freely given, and that they cannot be won by any human merits, nor given their due value by them. . . . Thus the magnitude of the reward stirs the Colossians into doing good works, not to obtain future blessings, but because they believe themselves to have obtained so much already, that they long to show God their gratitude.[58]

If the Reformation rejected the kind of reciprocity involved in a relationship of merit, it did not adopt the sort of secularized Stoicism (pure altruism and disinterested duty, as in Kant) or pragmatism that Radical Orthodoxy attributes to nominalism. First, there is no hint of univocity. God is not an actor alongside other actors but the source of all action. By eliminating the idea of the believer's merit entirely, the Reformers left no space for debate over who does more in salvation. God does everything and gives everything, even while the believer

---

57. Barclay, *Paul and the Gift*, 56.
58. Barclay, *Paul and the Gift*, 57, quoting Philip Melanchthon, *Paul's Letter to the Colossians*, trans. D. C. Parker (Sheffield: Almond, 1989), 34.

is genuinely free and active in the process. Yet God is also a recipient in this exchange, not of anything that would obligate him (i.e., merit a return) but of the glory and joy that comes from being the Lord of love and grace circulating with growing vigor through the veins of a dying world.

Fourth, far from confining the believer's horizon to the individual and his or her inner experience, the doctrine of justification drives us outside of ourselves. Thus the familiar critique that the Reformation introduced an individualistic and introspective piety is exposed as pure caricature. On the contrary, these were the pervasive characteristics of medieval piety, particularly to the extent that it was determined by the ascent of the soul. Withdrawal from the world into introspective contemplation was not only the highest vocation reserved for the monks and mystics; with movements like the Brethren of the Common Life, it became the ideal for all believers. "In this introspective atmosphere," writes N. S. Davidson, "preoccupied with the cultivation of a personal spirituality, the nature and significance of sin and grace were popular subjects for theological discussion."

> "Grace" is God's assistance, which can help the sinner avoid sin. When an individual is brought back from sin to obedience, he or she is said to experience *justification*. At first sight these theological concepts about a private religious experience seem relatively simple, but they became the focus for almost every major doctrinal argument of the Reformation period, and they form the background to Luther's early doctrinal writings.[59]

Thus we should not be surprised that the Reformers were also concerned about personal salvation. However, their answers to these questions engendered an extrospective piety at every level: in relation to God (rather than trusting in themselves) and in relation to others (rather than being preoccupied with their own inner justification). We have explored the Reformers' shift of attention from the inner movement of the soul to the movement of God in history, outside of us, in the person and work of Christ. The key "moments" in salvation are not purgation, illumination, and union or preparation, infusion, and remission in the

---

59. N. S. Davidson, *The Counter-Reformation* (Oxford: Basil Blackwell, 1987), 6.

individual soul, but the incarnation, death, and resurrection of Christ into which we are baptized as members of his ecclesial body. There is no personal relationship with Christ apart from belonging to his body, the visible church. We become believers through the church's ministry and Christ keeps us by his Spirit through that same ministry to the end. By the proclaimed announcement of these saving acts of God in Christ, calling sinners outside of themselves to cling to Christ in faith and their neighbor in love, people found themselves in the cast of the saints cheered on by the "cloud of witnesses" who have gone before. Salvation is personal but never private.

Thus the crucial insight of the Reformation was not the movement from injustice to justice or even the recognition that all of salvation is due to God's grace alone. Rather, it was the paradigmatic shift entirely away from us—whether individuals or the church corporately—to Christ. It is there where we find the turning point, if we find it at all.

CONCLUSION

The truth or value of the doctrine of justification is not measured by its ethical utility. It answers the foremost question that lies at the heart of the cosmos and the human heart: What is to become of us? Before there is rebuilding, there must be security. Before our will can embrace God in Christ, the Father must have chosen the believer in Christ before time. Before there is the married life, there is the marriage ceremony with its forensic core, and before there is the freedom of children and heirs, there is adoption. Before there is work, there must be the rest of faith and the hope that God has intervened and will again to fulfill his promise. We cannot ask first of all how an ethic can be derived from this doctrine, as if its truth were measured by what ethical use we can make of it for our own lives. It is not a doctrine that we can use to make anything of ourselves but a crucial truth that God uses to make what he will of us. Only when we allow ourselves to be passive recipients of this word of judgment and grace are we in a position to become active in humility, love, and service.

To be a recipient before God is to be once again a creature—not just a sinner but a completely dependent work of his hands in a deeper sense than would have been true merely in a state of rectitude. In the knowledge that all has been accomplished and that the neighbor is now a gift rather than a threat, the Christian's stance in the world is one of joy. With the justification of the ungodly, the *legal* basis for the reign of the powers of death, injustice, violence, and idolatry has been established once and for all. We work not toward our justification in anxious fear but from it in confident trust that "nothing in all creation, will be able to separate us from the love of God in Christ Jesus our Lord" (Rom 8:39). One need not agree with everything that Luther, Calvin, or the other Reformers said to be able to acknowledge that the entire pith of their message was nothing more or less than that Pauline summary. And that is why the Reformation still matters to us today.

SUBJECT INDEX

SCRIPTURE INDEX

AUTHOR INDEX